Joseph B. Eastman

SERVANT OF THE PEOPLE

PORTRAIT OF JOSEPH B. EASTMAN
BY HAROLD ABBOTT GREEN
In possession of Amherst College

Joseph B. Eastman

SERVANT OF THE PEOPLE

By CLAUDE MOORE FUESS

COLUMBIA UNIVERSITY PRESS

New York, 1952

Foreword

THIS VOLUME has been prepared at the request and under the auspices of the Joseph B. Eastman Foundation, created by some of Eastman's friends after his death and now held and administered by the Trustees of Amherst College. I have, however, been left completely unrestricted, and with the understanding that undiluted eulogy is what Eastman himself would have disliked most in his biographer. I have made every effort to paint in words a faithful picture of the man's character and achievements as judged by those who knew him best.

There has certainly been no paucity of material. Ample factual information is available in his extensive correspondence, his numerous speeches, and his voluminous published opinions and reports, as well as in contemporary newspapers and magazines. Fortunately, also, Eastman's memory is still so much alive in Washington and elsewhere that it has been possible to gather impressions from a large number of people.

I cannot list here the names of the hundreds of persons who have been consulted in the preparation of this book. Among those to whom I am particularly indebted are some of his college classmates at Amherst—Ernest M. Whitcomb, W. I. Hamilton, Karl O. Thompson, and Chester A. Porter—and a few of his fraternity brothers, including Hugh H. C. Weed, Frederick S. Bale, and Eugene S. Wilson, Jr. The late Dr. Stanley King, formerly president of Amherst College, was most helpful, as have also been Albert W. Atwood, Ernest G. Draper, and other Amherst graduates, especially Paul D. Weathers, the College Treasurer, and President Charles W. Cole. Through the cooperation of Miss Elizabeth Eastman and Mr. Charles D. Mahaffie, of the Interstate Commerce Commission, the Eastman papers have been placed on deposit at

Amherst College, where they will be accessible to historical scholars. Indeed, much of my investigation and writing has been carried out in the pleasantest of surroundings in the Converse Memorial Library at Amherst, where I have had the fullest cooperation of the Librarian, Newton D. McKeon, and his very efficient staff. Earl Latham, the first Professor of Government on the Joseph B. Eastman Foundation, together with his assistant, have read most of the manuscript and given me the benefit of their professional knowledge and experience. Mr. Richard M. Clarke guided me around Katonah, New York, Eastman's birthplace, and Mr. Kenneth M. Brett was my host in Pottsville, Pennsylvania.

About Eastman's Boston period I have learned much from Mrs. Robert A. Woods, wife of the distinguished founder of South End House, and from the present officers of that institution, who placed its files and reports at my disposal. John Daniels, one of Eastman's colleagues at South End House, as well as his companion on several vacation trips, has allowed me to use his diaries and reminiscences.

Members of the Interstate Commerce Commission have been most generous with their time and have allowed me access to all the relevant documents under their control. I have also been extended gracious courtesies by the Association of American Railroads, whose library is within its field amazingly comprehensive and complete. Mr. Edward Wray and Mr. Vince D. Belnap, both of Chicago, have furnished me with excellent photographs for reproduction purposes.

I am especially under obligation to Mr. John R. Turney, the Honorable Robert B. Woolley, and Mr. Henry McCarthy, who were at one time or another intimately associated with Eastman as a public official. Others whom I am bound to mention are Mr. Justice Frankfurter, the Honorable Robert Lincoln O'Brien, Mr. Charles J. Symington, Mrs. Ernesta Drinker Barlow, Mrs. Charles J. Smith, Mr. Julian Pilgram, Mr. Merrill Bishop, Mr. Charles R. Blyth, Mr. Franklin Snow, Mr. John P. Whitman, and Mr. Harold G. Moulton.

Mrs. Edna Buchanan, Eastman's secretary in his later years, has told me much about the working habits of her former chief. The Honorable Charles D. Mahaffie, long Eastman's colleague on the

Interstate Commerce Commission, has responded to my every request for assistance and has rendered me less vulnerable in my comments on the Commission and its procedure. To Mr. Howard Hosmer, an examiner on the staff of the commission, I am deeply indebted for his continued advice and criticism. He has read carefully the entire manuscript and made many helpful suggestions. Finally I must state that the book could never have been written without the unfailing support of Mr. Fayette B. Dow, one of Eastman's friends whose name appears often in these pages, and of Miss Elizabeth Eastman, who has turned over to me all of her brother's private papers and done everything within her power to make sure that the truth was told.

I myself was an undergraduate at Amherst with Joe Eastman and looked up to him with the respect properly shown by a Freshman toward a Sophomore. Later I met him occasionally in Washington and grew to admire his unselfish devotion to the public interest. I cannot deny that I am prejudiced in his favor and believe that he deserves well of his countrymen.

CLAUDE M. FUESS

Chestnut Hill, Massachusetts
July, 1951

Contents

Illustrations

Introduction

DURING the Hoover administration, when Joseph Bartlett Eastman had been for more than a decade on the Interstate Commerce Commission, he was lunching with three friends in the grillroom of the New Willard Hotel, Washington, D.C. One of them said to Joe—everybody called him "Joe"—"I hear you've just turned down a big railroad job at a salary of more than $50,000." "It could be," he cautiously admitted. "It isn't your first offer, is it, Joe?" "Maybe not," was the modest answer, in the laconic tradition of Calvin Coolidge. Then I put in my oar—he was a year ahead of me at Amherst—and asked, "Aren't you ever tempted to accept a position with an enormous income, as compared with what you get slaving for the government, and with a lot less grief?" "Well," replied Joe, "probably it is an expensive luxury for me to stay on here, just as it would be to own a yacht—but I guess I can afford it!"

This characteristic remark reveals one pervasive element of his personality. From the day he was graduated from college until his death nearly forty years later, Joe Eastman enjoyed working for the American people, not for management or for labor, not for railroad operators or railroad employees or shippers, but for the citizens who paid his salary. He was thinking of the good of the entire population, not of one section or of any pressure group. Although he never ran for office and was even in doubt as to which party he belonged, he held one appointive job after another, in gradually widening areas. His appointment in each case was made, not through political influence, but more often in spite of it, because he was regarded as an expert who could be trusted. When Eastman died, at the age of sixty-two, worn out like an overdriven internal combustion engine, it was said of him that he had "set a pattern of intelligent devotion to the public welfare which, if extensively recognized, would greatly uplift the character of public service in the United States."

One incident will show the quality of the man. On December 19, 1918, President Wilson nominated to the Interstate Commerce Commission Joseph B. Eastman—the youngest person ever named for that office. Legally the commission had to be bipartisan, and the membership at the moment was such that the existing vacancy could be filled only by a Republican. When Eastman heard the news, eager though he was for the opportunity, he promptly wrote Senator Henry Cabot Lodge to explain that he was an independent in politics and could not permit a misleading label to be attached to himself. No one in the Senate chose to make an issue of the matter, and he was confirmed without any discussion—he never knew exactly how or why.

Again and again Eastman had to explain, to the embarrassment of his sponsors, that he had no party affiliations. As a matter of fact, he voted for Taft in 1908, for Theodore Roosevelt in 1912, for Wilson in 1916, for Cox in 1920, for La Follette in 1924, for "Al" Smith in 1928, for Franklin D. Roosevelt in 1932 and 1936, and for Willkie in 1940. Various presidents would have been glad to drop him— Harding in 1922 and Hoover in 1929, because he was considered too radical, and Franklin D. Roosevelt in 1936, because he was too conservative. But when the decision had to be made, they did not dare risk the outcry which would have arisen if they had rejected him.

During his long career Eastman became hardened to criticism and abuse. Until 1933 railroad executives felt that he was a socialistic idealist, an amateur who did not understand their difficulties. After that date he was condemned by labor leaders as a reactionary because he would not support their extreme demands. I cannot see that at either period he was prejudiced. He was true to himself and his convictions, furthering as best he could the interests of all the people.

Eastman broke down and died during the war, when he was at the height of his accomplishment and success. He had been a controversial figure for many years, denounced scathingly by both sides at different periods. But when he was gone, all factions joined in saluting him. Few men on the national stage have received such tributes as were paid to him by railroad executives and union leaders, by Republicans and Democrats.

Why is Joe Eastman worth writing about? Primarily I think because in the kind of democracy to which we seem to be committed the wise administration of governmental departments has come to be of tremendous importance. The bureau heads—cynically called "bureaucrats"—outlast most legislators and must be relied upon for advice when new laws are proposed. Many of them, ossified by the deadening consciousness of authority, settle back into routine placidity, becoming unimaginative, sterile, and obstinate. But Eastman was consistently constructive and therefore made himself almost indispensable. "My job is my life," he used to say to his friends; "I'd be lost without it." The highest praise ever bestowed upon him was that he dignified the title "bureaucrat." In the various positions which he occupied he demonstrated how an alert, resourceful, and untiring mind can function even in places where the temptation to inertia is strong.

Much of what Eastman did was unsensational and failed to make the arresting headlines reserved for presidents and their cabinet ministers. But work like his is essential for the efficient operation of our increasingly complex government. Although Eastman was not picturesque or dramatic, he set an inspiring example for others to follow—one by which they could measure themselves. His quiet independence, his lofty conception of official duty, his extensive vision, his intellectual and moral integrity, his genuine humility— traits not often found in combination in one personality—were admired by all those who came within his range. There has been no finer public servant, strictly as such, in our time.

Joseph B. Eastman

SERVANT OF THE PEOPLE

It is a common belief that the desire for financial gain is the only motive which will impel men to their best endeavors. I challenge that tenet whole-heartedly. I was brought up in a minister's family; I have enjoyed the friendship of doctors, school-teachers, and professors, and I have had an opportunity to observe men in public life as well as many engaged in private business. It is my profound conviction that the best things which have been done in the world have been impelled by higher motives than the desire for gain.

Joseph B. Eastman

I

Yankee Background

THE EASTMAN FAMILY in America has been the genealogist's delight. It started most conveniently on new soil with an immigrant ancestor who had plenty of children; it has continued in full vigor throughout several collateral lines to the present day; it has produced a sufficient number of eminent and rugged personages to justify and sustain the attention of the investigator; and its records are not difficult to run down. The Adam of the tribe on this continent was a certain Roger Eastman, from Langford, Wiltshire, England, who settled in 1638 in Salisbury, Massachusetts. The descendants of him and his Eve (who is virtually unknown) were amazingly prolific; indeed, the two fat volumes containing the biographies of discoverable Eastmans include well over two thousand names, some of them rare, like Bennajah, Bezar, Climena, Farzina, Oskella, and Ozetta, many with an obviously Biblical origin, such as Amos and Enoch and Joel and Joseph and Obadiah. Most of the annals are short and simple, but one's imagination is bound to be caught by Submit Eastman, who walked a mile on her hundredth birthday to hear a sermon in her honor, and by Hannah Eastman, who was captured in 1704 by Indians who tomahawked her infant boy, but later escaped and had eleven children and four grandsons who served in the Revolutionary War. It has been a sturdy and persistent stock. The faces of the men from generation to generation have a massive and permanent quality, and their variegated beards give them the aspect of patriarchs or prophets.

Like the Lawrence family as analyzed by the late Bishop William Lawrence, the Eastmans have been well-behaved middle-class people. So far as I have been able to ascertain, few of them have shown any creative talent in art, music, or literature, and almost none have made the *Social Register*. On the other hand, no one ever sank into dire poverty or landed in jail, and most of them enjoyed remarkably good health, the collective longevity of the group being astonishingly high. Some, of course, possessed no marked ability, but they were respectable in the sense that they did not sink into debauchery or land "on the town." An exceptionally large percentage of them chose the missionary professions—teaching and preaching—and rose to positions of leadership in their communities. The greatest of them all was Daniel Webster, who through his mother, Abigail, was sixth in a direct line from the original Roger Eastman. Joseph B. Eastman, the subject of this biography, was in the eighth, and was thus Webster's sixth cousin, twice removed. I do not find that he ever boasted of this tenuous relationship.

Several Eastmans have been thought worthy of inclusion in the *Dictionary of American Biography*. Perhaps the most versatile was Harvey Gridley Eastman (1837–78), who piled up a fortune in the 1860's out of Eastman's Business College, became the Mayor of Poughkeepsie and the Great Man of the city, and was endowed, so it is said, with "a magnetic personality and a torrential energy." Another was Charles Gamage Eastman (1816–60), who was that very rare bird a Vermont Democrat, but who also published a volume of verse which sold over two thousand copies and brought him a local Green Mountain reputation like that enjoyed by Walter Hard today. Arthur MacArthur Eastman (1810–77) was a successful manufacturer of firearms during the Crimean and American Civil wars, projected and carried through a direct ocean cable between Europe and the United States, and ended his days on a beautiful estate known as "Riverside" on the Merrimack River, near Manchester, New Hampshire. Still another New Hampshirean was Timothy Eastman (1821–93), a far-ranging cattle merchant, one of the most opulent men in the state. Occasionally one of the clan abandoned New England to venture into pioneering. Such a roamer was Enoch Worthen Eastman (1810–85), who studied law and moved to Iowa, where he joined the young Republican Party and became Lieutenant-Governor. John Robie Eastman (1836–1913) developed into an astronomer with an international reputation. William Reed Eastman (1835–1925), an engineer, clergyman, and librarian, won distinction as the foremost authority of his time on library binding and equipment.

The most celebrated member of the family in recent years has been George Eastman (1854–1932), a native of Waterville, New York, who moved in 1861 to Rochester, became the energizing spirit of the Eastman Kodak Company, and gave more than $75,-000,000 to various philanthropies. In corresponding with this distinguished cousin in 1928, Joseph B. Eastman wrote:

It is necessary to go back to the first Eastman who came over to this country about 1642, I think, before our lines converge. His name was Roger, and you descended from his sixth son, Joseph, whereas I descended from his eighth son, Samuel. There are certain coincidences, however. We are both of us in the eighth generation after Roger, although you were born twenty-eight years before I was. In both instances there were two "Joseph Eastmans" in the line, and we are both unmarried. There I imagine the coincidences or resemblances cease.

Such diversity of unusual accomplishment places the Eastman clan in the forefront of outstanding American families. But calling the roll of important Eastmans merely indicates that Joe Eastman was, to use a colloquial Yankee phrase, "well-connected." There was also good blood in his direct ancestry. Moses Eastman, his great-grandfather, born in Salisbury, New Hampshire, was graduated at Dartmouth in 1794, read law, and practiced as an attorney first in Salisbury and later in Concord, New Hampshire. By his first wife, Sukey Bartlett, he had only one child. By his second he had thirteen. On a walking trip in 1907 our Joseph B. Eastman visited Salisbury, at the foot of Mount Kearsarge, where a local antiquarian showed him the ancestral home. They were welcomed by the owner, who poured out two glasses of hard cider in quick succession and became tiresomely loquacious about the family. On this occasion Eastman was taken solemnly to the house where Dan'l Webster was married and the place where he went to school. He could have seen also the frame dwelling where "Black Dan" was born, but declared himself satisfied "simply to know that it was there."

Joseph Bartlett Eastman, Joe's grandfather, accomplished the unusual feat of practicing at different periods three professions—

medicine, teaching, and the Christian ministry. A graduate of Dartmouth in 1821, when he was only seventeen, he studied at Harvard Medical School and became a physician for some years at Waterford, Maine. Then, after turning to teaching in New Hampshire and Vermont, he spent a year at Andover Theological Seminary and was eventually ordained, in 1844, as a Presbyterian clergyman. He held various small pastorates in rural New York and finally ended his restless days by combining teaching and preaching in Windsor, a little village west of Binghamton. Meanwhile, at thirty-three he had married Mary Huse, daughter of John Huse, of Hill, New Hampshire, who bore him seven children.

When her husband died, just before the close of the Civil War, his impoverished but dauntless widow moved to Amherst, Massachusetts, with her two sons, Charles Francis Eastman (1844–99) and John Huse Eastman (1849–1917), and rented rooms next to Professor Snell's house. Why the mother did not select her husband's college, Dartmouth, is a mystery. Joe's father used to say jokingly that his mother just wandered off and did not have money enough to get beyond Amherst. At any rate, the boys, one sixteen and the other twenty-one, entered Amherst in the same year and worked their way through. They were members of both Psi Upsilon and Phi Beta Kappa.

After graduation each son became a teacher. John Huse Eastman, still too young to vote, grew a mustache to disguise his youthfulness and secured a job as instructor in Greek and Latin in the Preparatory Department of Knox College, Galesburg, Illinois. After two years he was promoted to be Acting Professor of Latin in the college itself; but the call of the Christian ministry was as compulsive for him as it had been for his father, and by 1872 he had saved enough money to enter Union Theological Seminary.

Assembling all these genealogical dry bones, we can revivify them and get an impression of Joe Eastman's biological and cultural background. He inherited physical endurance, a keen intelligence, and a pleasing personality. His father and grandfather were self-sacrificing men, unostentatious in their observance of the Golden Rule—not dreamers, but practical workers who translated their religion into terms of ordinary life. They displayed none of the intolerance and rigidity so typical of Jonathan Edwards and some of his descendants. The Eastman family traditions were those of plain living and high thinking, simplicity, conscientiousness, and devotion to duty—in short, the essence of Puritanism at its best.

II

Growing Up

IN THE SPRING OF 1875 John H. Eastman, about to be graduated from Union Theological Seminary, was so persuasive a "supply preacher" in a newly organized Presbyterian Church in the tiny village of Katonah, New York, that the congregation spontaneously decided to call him as their first pastor. At that date there were only fourteen church members, of whom five removed from the neighborhood before the year was over. Nevertheless, the youthful student accepted the challenge, began his duties in May, and was ordained and installed within a few weeks. Three years later he had built up the membership to almost a hundred. On July 11, 1879, when he was well established, he married Lucy King, daughter of Andrew L. King, of Binghamton—a slender young lady of twenty-seven, with dark eyes and hair, pleasant features, and a sensitive nature. They had two children—Elizabeth, now living in Washington, D.C., and Joseph Bartlett Eastman, born June 26, 1882, and proudly named for his versatile grandfather. During his first thirteen years young Joe was an outdoor boy among the Westchester County hills.

The Katonah of Joe Eastman's childhood was, however, a very different place from the scientifically laid out suburb which now harbors commuters to the metropolis. Old Katonah was originally a primitive hamlet called Cherry Street, on a height above the Pepeneghek River, now Cross River, about forty miles from Manhattan. In 1812 members of the Whitlock family moved down the incline to the valley, where their new settlement came to be known as Whitlocksville. A further transformation occurred in 1847, when with the coming of the New York and Harlem Railroad another business center sprang up, to be called Mechanicsville. Then the inevitable local antiquarian discovered that an Indian sachem,

Katonah, had been the traditional owner of the land thereabouts, and the village acquired a more romantic name. By the time of the Civil War, Cherry Street, alias Whitlocksville, alias Mechanicsville, had become Katonah—to the immense relief of county historians.

All this is bewildering enough, but the culminating stage was even more dramatic. In the 1890's, when engineers perfected the project for the Croton Dam and Aqueduct, they noticed on the map that Katonah was in the way. Accordingly, plans were arbitrarily made for the removal of the residents to a designated site three quarters of a mile down the road. Some of the houses, including the manse in which Joe Eastman was born, were shifted on skids to their new locations; then most of the land on which the picturesque old village had stood was submerged beneath the waters of the Muscoot Reservoir. The rolling country is still there, and the quiet, winding stream, with its border of willows and elms. But the "New Village" gives the impression of having been completed all at once—as indeed it was—on the side of a hill. What was formerly described as "a long, sandy, and desolate slope, treeless and uninhabited," has now become a model community, with two streets a hundred feet wide separated by a plot adorned with shrubs and maples.

It was the "Old Village," of course, that Joe and his sister remembered and loved. Their house, finished in 1880, just a week before Elizabeth was born, was perched on a ridge between the residences of two physicians and looked down on the Cross River, on the far bank of which rose the Presbyterian Church. As a small child Joe trudged along the woodland paths by his mother's side, while she pointed out to him the first bloodroots and hepaticas in the early spring. Later in his life, when he was walking over trails in the deep Canadian wilderness with a pack on his shoulders and his fishing rods under his arm, he would stop to pick and name the wildflowers.

Although the Eastmans had no farm, they grew their own vegetables. Mrs. Eastman ordinarily had a "hired girl," but their household was simple, and the children often ate a supper of bread and milk and apple sauce before going to bed at eight o'clock. Thomas W. Lamont, whose father was for three years a Methodist parson at Katonah and spent most of his life in neighboring pastorates, used to joke about the "Rich Presbyterians" and the "Poor Methodists." "The Presbyterians were café society," he declared, "and we Poor Methodists were the proletariat!" But the Eastmans were certainly not corrupted by luxury or in any danger of snobbery, and what social distinction existed must have been on grounds other than wealth.

When Joe Eastman, the Interstate Commerce Commissioner, made pious pilgrimages to Katonah, the Old Village had vanished. The settlements at Cross Creek and Bedford still contained people whom he had known. The ancient brick tavern was there as it had been when he was a boy. If he chose to do so, he could still ride—or even walk—to the Hudson River, flowing more or less majestically down past West Point and Stony Point to New York Harbor. With some searching he guided his companions to the Sheep Cave, which he had explored, like Tom Sawyer, in quest of romance, and to Rattlesnake Rocks, towering above the expanse of the new reservoir. The countryside was as charming as it had been in the days of Rip Van Winkle, with its small clusters of pines, its undulating meadows and its views of the peaks of the rugged Catskill Mountains. But Katonah, except for a few family friends, such as the Barretts, was not the place that he had known.

During the twenty years of his pastorate in Old Katonah, the Reverend Mr. Eastman became a foremost citizen. Although the community was fewer than five hundred souls, it included two outstanding men—"Judge" William H. Robertson and the Honorable Henry E. Pellew. With them as his backers, Mr. Eastman started many projects for helping his neighbors. He organized a Christian Endeavor Society in his church; he cooperated in founding the Village Improvement Society and was one of the first to labor for good roads and an abundance of shade trees, bringing upon himself some criticism for insisting that the Society should plant Norway maples and English royal oaks. When he departed on his honeymoon, his associates promised faithfully that they would complete a board walk to his church before he and his bride returned. On the morning of the last day a hundred feet remained to be constructed and sufficient seasoned lumber was lacking; but they resourcefully cut out timber from the forest and nailed the last board at five o'clock in the afternoon, twenty minutes before the Eastmans' train arrived.

Three significant qualities Joe inherited from his clergyman father: his public spirit (which has been mentioned), his unselfishness, and his sense of humor. One morning the Reverend Mr. Eastman met on the street "Charlie" Robinson, the local plasterer, who also sang lustily in church on Sundays, and inquired why he hadn't shown up for several weeks. Robinson explained that his shoes were worn out and displayed them to justify his absence. Taking a hasty survey to check on size, Eastman removed his own shoes and exchanged them on the spot for those of his complaining parishioner. When he returned home, he had to confess to his wife and accept the kindly scolding which invariably followed his attacks of Good Samaritanism. "But just wait and see," the husband retaliated; "Charlie will be there next Sunday."

Everybody who recalls John H. Eastman mentions his good nature. On a very stormy Sunday, when only the sexton appeared for the morning service, the clergyman said drily, "It would be a shame to waste a good sermon," and proceeded to deliver it as if the pews had been packed. When some of his more conservative parishioners objected to an oyster supper in the church, Eastman called them "kill-joys" and shamed them into silence. He was especially fond of practical jokes of a harmless type.

Although Joe Eastman in later life displayed little or no interest in formal religion, he never forgot the tradition of public service handed down by his father, who had a way of getting along with almost everybody and whose friendship with Katonah people were not abandoned until he died. John H. Eastman, like many fine men of his generation, simplified his faith and was perplexed when his son, asked to join the church and declare his love for Jesus, replied, "But I don't know Jesus!" With Joe Eastman this was not just a normal reaction against an overdose of sermons and Sunday School in his youth. It was a temperamental matter, arising out of some inner demand for proof. Transparently honest, he just

would not take anybody's "say-so." As for a possible future existence, he would have agreed with Theodore Roosevelt, who once
said, "One world at a time!"

When Joe was asked, as part of a questionnaire at the time of
entering college, which parent he more resembled, he answered,
"Half and half." The existing photographs of his father indicate
that Joe inherited many of his physical characteristics, including his
rather stocky build and short neck, his light brown hair and ruddy
complexion, his full face and high forehead. Mrs. Eastman, who
was more artistic in temperament, played the organ in the little
church, was an authority on botany, and also served on committees
and taught a class of young men. She had a positive personality,
which sometimes clashed with that of her son. The boy had convictions of his own and more than once out-argued his mother on a
question of privilege or conduct.

The parsonage was, of course, a bookish home. The family ex-
chequer permitted *Harper's* and the *Century*, as well as *St. Nicholas*
and the *Youth's Companion*, and they all kept up to date on current affairs. His sister remembers that he perused with particular
gusto Lossing's *Field Book of the American Revolution*, but it
aroused in him no military ambitions. He was fond of Scott and
Dickens, but especially of Cooper, whose *Leather Stocking Tales*
were thrilling to children who had never heard of Superman and
the Lone Ranger. I cannot discover any significant trend in his
reading except that he did early become a devourer of the Sherlock
Holmes stories and was a "Whodunit" addict all his life. In that
household the Bible, as the Word of God, was read through aloud
once a year, omitting none of the "begots" or polysyllables or
patriarchal indiscretions.

Joe Eastman had always a very strong sense of family relationship and kept in touch with his relatives by correspondence and by
frequent visits. His mother's kin were all New York State people,
who had farms near the little village of Acidalia, in Sullivan County,
up among the hills. Lucy Eastman had a brother who, like her,
died in his early forties; but his widow, with her two daughters,
continued to keep her home in Acidalia. There the Reverend John
Eastman used to go for his summer vacations, taking Elizabeth and

Joe with him. It was a period of simple pleasures, before automobiles had crowded and contaminated the countryside, and the children roamed the woods leading a healthful outdoor life. Old and young enjoyed games, including croquet, deck tennis, and badminton. One favorite evening pastime was the acting of charades, and once Joe tried to push his father into a sack to represent the word Bagdad. By nature he was buoyant and fun loving. On one of his last evenings at home before he died he played a most exciting game of Hunt-the-Thimble with some of his small relatives and seemed "as eager and gay as a child."

Even after he became Interstate Commerce Commissioner, Joe rarely let a summer go by without spending a few days at Acidalia. More than once, after a conference with President Roosevelt at Hyde Park, his cousin, Mrs. Smith, would motor him to the old home for a brief but happy reunion. Although he never owned an automobile, he liked to be driven over rutted and abandoned wood roads deep into the mountains, to places where it seemed as if they could not possibly turn around without falling over a cliff. From these minor adventures he always returned full of elation.

Joe grew up in what has been called the Age of Innocence and was undoubtedly an Age of Simplicity, before the time of Boy Scouts and supervised recreation. In the autumn of 1941 the artist Kessler published a syndicated cartoon showing a small boy with his mongrel dog, his hands deep in his pockets, strutting down the principal street of a country village with all the idlers staring at his very obvious black eye. It was captioned "Home Town Echoes" and bore the legend, "Master Joseph H. Eastman (Chairman of the Interstate Commerce Commission), son of the Reverend John H. Eastman, appeared on Main Street to-day, wearing a black eye." The atmosphere of the drawing must have given Joe nostalgic memories. To a friend who sent him the cartoon Eastman wrote that it had no foundation in fact, "because of course there was no boy in Katonah who was capable of giving me a shiner."

Life in Old Katonah was happy and healthful, with little to make it confusing. People were deliberate and unhurried, simple in their tastes, without the insecurity and apprehension which the twentieth century has endured. The so-called Gay Nineties, sentimentalized

by barber-shop quartettes, were actually in the rural districts the
Quiet Nineties. In Katonah the Eastmans lived very comfortably
on the preacher's salary of $1,000 with a parsonage. Around them
were little poverty and almost no inequality. In his fourteenth year
Joe was quickly transferred to a society of a different type.

When Old Katonah had to be abandoned, Mr. Eastman did not
wish to follow his parish to the New Village. For twenty years
he had baptized and married and buried many. Now he realized
that his two children could not be prepared for college in the local
schools; and when, in April, 1895, he received a call to Pottsville,
Pennsylvania, at a salary of $2,250 with a house, he lost no time in
accepting. By the late spring he was established with his family at
505 Garfield Square, in a three-storied Philadelphia brick mansion,
with high ceilings and white marble steps and impressive exterior.
Garfield Square was the second major street and the only really
wide avenue in the hilly town. The houses there were in good taste,
but the lots were narrow, and each building almost leaned on the
one next to it.

Pottsville then, as today, was surrounded by coal hills and coal
mines. The river winds down a valley which in colonial days must
have been very beautiful, but its charm has been obscured by piles
of waste and refuse. Because of its site in a narrow gorge, the
original settlement of Pottsville could expand only by mounting
the encircling hillsides. Thus, Mahatango Street, on which the First
Presbyterian Church is located, rises straight and steep from the
business center; and the residences on the east side are approached
by long flights of steps, which make them seem perched on a
ledge. In icy weather the slopes are very slippery, and walking is
treacherous.

Katonah had the cleanness and freshness of the unspoiled countryside. Pottsville, which was built up and has survived on coal, was
inevitably very different. In a population of more than 20,000, the
intimacy of Katonah was impossible. Everything was bigger—
their house, the church edifice, the stores, the clubs, and the congregation.

For the first time Joe found himself in an industrial community,
with all which that implies. It is true that he and his schoolmates

could wander over the trails on Sharp Mountain and pick laurel in the spring. There was for him still plenty of that woods life which healthy American youngsters love, and he had the *American Boys' Handybook* as a guide when he wished to play Robinson Crusoe. Now, however, his father's parishioners were not villagers, but mine superintendents and officers in banks and owners of stores. They were undeniably prosperous and even luxurious in their style of living; but on the borders of Pottsville the miners and their families dwelt under conditions less favorable, and even a lad could perceive the inequalities between the homes of the operators and those of the workers. He could understand that children brought up in the midst of coal piles were bound to have a harder struggle than those surrounded by green pastures. The Reverend John H. Eastman warned his family that they must make no comments or comparisons. "Wherever we live is our home," he announced, "and we must work for it." Joe described Pottsville later as "slow, Dutch, and uninteresting."

As a pupil in the local high school, Joe was not an outstanding leader, but he did play quarterback on the football eleven and is remembered as having been the star in a crucial game against Hazelton. He was also conspicuous as shortstop on the baseball nine, and when he went off to college was described by the local newspaper as "Pottsville's best athlete." The competition could not have been very keen, for in college Joe was undistinguished in any sport except tennis.

The high school principal, Professor Stephen A. Thurlow, universally known as "Buck," was an ardent chess player and transmitted his enthusiasm for the game to his students. It was a competition suited to Eastman's temperament. With plenty of time to consider what should be done, he was not forced to make decisions in a hurry. His mind even then moved surely, but slowly, and in chess he could think out problems to a conclusion. In 1896 he was photographed as a member of the school chess team—a small boy, very neatly and formally dressed, with an Ascot tie and a wing collar. By sheer persistence he eventually became the best chess player in town, his only rival being an older schoolmate, Julian Pilgram. These two and their satellites formed the Granite House, named from Jules Verne's *The Mysterious Island*, and all winter long on Saturday afternoons or snowy days they held their private tournaments and even carried on games by post card with chess enthusiasts overseas.

Although Joe was not brilliant, his marks in his studies were respectable, and he was regarded as a consistent performer. His teachers considered him aggressively argumentative, and it seems to have been taken for granted that he would be chosen class orator. His address, delivered at his Commencement, June 28, 1899, was entitled, "Wanted, a Leader!" and dealt eulogistically with Theodore Roosevelt, then at the height of his reputation as the daring Colonel of the Rough Riders. Eastman described him as the "coming American"—a prophecy which the next few years were to justify.

There had probably never been any doubt in Joe's mind that he would go to Amherst. His father and uncle were both Amherst alumni. Unfortunately the Pottsville High School did not in its regular course prepare its graduates for eastern colleges. Joe's sister had been obliged to take a post-graduate high school course in order to meet the Bryn Mawr requirements, and Joe followed the same program, reading enough Greek and Latin so that he would be ready for the Freshman Class. During this extra year he broadened his interests by becoming Editor-in-Chief not only of the Pottsville High *Monthly* but also of *The Crimson and White*, the school annual.

Julian Pilgram believes that even in his youth Eastman showed indications of exceptional talent and declares that in the 1890's he was Pottsville's Fair-Haired Boy. But on the basis of recorded performance he was no more promising than many of his contemporaries. Several of his classmates felt that while his mind was active, his body was lethargic, and they have not forgotten that he was often late for school. One of his most persistent traits showed itself early, for he cared nothing whatever about girls. During the recesses, when the other boys hunted out the girls they liked, he usually studied. He never even learned to dance, and he avoided the popular games of Post Office and Drop the Pillow. In other respects he was a normal American youngster, not averse to harmless pranks, but generally well behaved and very far from the traditional scapegrace clergyman's son. In due course he had mumps, measles, chicken pox, and whooping cough. Some of his adult characteristics were already evident—his fondness for public speaking, joined with a passion for argument and skill as a close reasoner; his interest in various forms of journalism; his admiration for "Teddy" Roosevelt; his consistency and reliability; his misogynistic tendencies; his sympathy for the underdog; and his complete independence and fearlessness as a thinker.

The Reverend John H. Eastman was a favorite with his parishioners and soon became as vital a force in Pottsville as he had been in Katonah. A committee of his fellow townsmen once called upon him to accept an appointment to fill out an unexpired term on the Borough Council. He had been preaching public service and was now told to "put up or shut up." When he consulted with the governing board of his Presbyterian Church, they agreed that he should set an example for others; and with this encouragement he accepted the appointment and was later elected to membership in his own right. It is significant that although he had served in only two parishes, and those rather small, he was awarded the degree of Doctor of Divinity by his college when he returned in 1899 for his thirtieth anniversary.

By this date his two children were without a mother. On September 27, 1897, Lucy King Eastman, only forty-four years old, died of cancer, and her husband had to care for their daughter and son during their remaining days in high school. Luckily he had many kind-hearted neighbors, and Elizabeth was old enough to keep house for him when she returned from Bryn Mawr. Indeed, she watched over him for the remainder of his life.

Joe's roots were not very deep in Pottsville, and circumstances drew him away from it after he entered Amherst. When later he took his walking trips, it was to the Catskills and the White Mountains that he went—not to Pennsylvania. When he came back as a college freshman for his Christmas vacation, he rather shocked Julian Pilgram by offering him a Rameses cigarette—a convincing evidence of depravity. Many years later, when Eastman had become Director of Defense Transportation, Pilgram, himself something of an authority on railroads, wrote to his old friend suggesting a combination of systems in the Pennsylvania area, and Joe replied that they were thinking of different ends. Pilgram was trying to put on more trains; Eastman was doing his best to take some of them off.

I cannot find that in Pottsville, where railroads were of vital importance, Joe had any great interest in them, or indeed in mines or miners. He was to spend his life working for fair play in economic and industrial affairs, but this phase of his philosophy seems to have developed later, after he had reached college. Then he remembered what he had seen in Pottsville and used it more than once to illustrate a point. His liberalism did not result from any early sensitiveness to social inequalities, but was a consequence of studies and experience in a wider area. How it was built up and made useful will be the basic theme of this story.

III

An Amherst Education

IN SEPTEMBER, 1900, as Amherst College was opening its eightieth year, a diminutive member of the incoming Class of 1904 struggled up the grassy slope leading to "Old South." Because a wagon had dumped his furniture in the road, he faced the job of carrying it to the third floor of his dormitory. Swinging a heavy mattress to his shoulders, he made his way awkwardly up the stairs. As he reached the top, almost completely smothered, he dropped his burden and looking up through the sweat pouring down his face, saw a taller young man who had just padded out of his room shoeless and stockingless and seemed to be amused at the spectacle. The small freshman took another glance and said, "You must be the first fellow to cross the Rocky Mountains in his bare feet." The other made no immediate response to this unexpected observation and seemed to be making up his mind. Then he replied in a pleasant drawling voice, "There are so many mountains," and picking up one end of the mattress, he added, "The young man who lifts up his bed and walks needs help." Together they dumped the mattress into a room.

Having performed this humanitarian act, the "barefoot boy" announced, "I'm Joe Eastman, from Pottsville, Pennsylvania." The smaller freshman was William I. Hamilton, of Elizabeth, New Jersey, who was to become one of Eastman's close college friends and has remembered the incident all these years. Eastman began his college career by helping someone else.

Fred E. Sturgis, another freshman, saw Joe first at church on the morning after the cane rush between the two lower classes. Eastman had managed to engage the college heavyweight champion in close combat, receiving as a consequence two shiny and much-inflamed black eyes, which marked him out early as a "scrapper" and brought him unsought notoriety.

Eastman already knew his way around Amherst, for he had accompanied his father to the college the preceding year, when the latter had received his honorary degree. It was then an inbred community, and most of the faculty were graduates of the college. The Pottsville freshman started his career well counseled and under favorable auspices. Early during the "rushing season" he was pledged to Psi Upsilon, his father's fraternity and one of the best on the campus.

Eastman was to pass from adolescence to maturity in a world which was orderly and hopeful. Edward Gibbon, writing during the last quarter of the eighteenth century, concluded that the happiest period in human history up to that moment was in the Age of the Antonines, when the vast Roman Empire was at peace and a benevolent despotism was functioning to keep the citizenry content. A similar claim can be made for the United States between the Spanish War and World War I, when a spirit of widespread confidence and optimism prevailed. At the Amherst Commencement in 1934 Eastman said, "I can remember the time when economic and social ideas seemed to me and to most college students comparatively well ordered and stable; but that time has certainly gone by." In the 1900's the United States, embarked rather against its better judgment on a new imperialistic policy, was beginning to realize its strength, like a child gleefully feeling his muscles. The idea of progress through evolution, popularized by Darwin and elaborated by Herbert Spencer and John Fiske, was very comforting, and few intelligent people doubted the inevitability of the millennium. Indeed, many were speaking of it in terms merely of a century or two. Although poverty, disease, and injustice obviously still existed, it was felt that their eradication was proceeding rapidly. Reformers were, of course, still uncovering corruption in politics and illegal practices in business, and men with muckrakes were finding plenty of material; but the crusading movement which "Teddy" Roosevelt was leading made the country confident that graft and vice could be eliminated. Almost any college graduate was sure of a job when he put away his cap and gown. Nobody predicted—or could have found evidence for predicting—the tragic, disillusioning years that lay ahead. So, too, the Rome of Marcus Aurelius was unaware of its impending disaster.

On a much smaller scale, Amherst College, after passing in the 1890's through a period of confusion and controversy, was entering upon an Era of Good Feeling. President George Harris, an urbane and rather easy-going man of the world, knew how—and preferred—to conciliate and avoid trouble. Under him the college settled down to a few years of *laissez-faire* and peace.

Someone has described the Harris administration as "a Golden Age in American college life," and so in many ways it was. Cynicism, neuroticism, escapism—all the insidious cankers of a later postwar generation—were not encouraged in the classrooms or in the "bull sessions" of the students, who, although they may have been childishly flippant, carefree, and even barbaric, at least did not laugh at the idea of social responsibility. Scott Fitzgerald's "sad young men" and John Held's "flappers" emerged in the wake of a war which to the collegians of the 1900's seemed impossible. These earlier undergraduates were neither blind nor stupid. They were relying on the conclusions of economists and philosophers and historians whom they trusted.

The Amherst of Eastman's period had plenty of weaknesses, some of them apparent to contemporary observers. The caustic Professor William P. Bigelow asserted that the years from 1890 to 1905 were marked by the glorification of the "All-Round Man"—the "Arrow Collar" type, with a handsome profile, skill in athletic sports, personal magnetism, and a gift for winning friends and influencing people. "Any approach to an intellectual life was impossible," and "all emphasis on scholarship was lacking," he declared, in phrasing which was clearly exaggerated, but had a basic element of truth. Several of the courses advertised in the curriculum were so easy that they required virtually no cerebration from the pupil. That there were scholars of high mentality cannot be denied, and they found in Morse and Garman and Churchill what they were seeking. But the undergraduate body—or a large Philistine section of it—rather resented efforts to make them work and think. A chorus of maledictions was shouted at John Erskine, even then a scholar and writer of distinction, when he announced that the spelling of his English classes was atrocious and that they must attend a special division until improvement was evident. "We're being treated like prep-school boys!" was the agonized wail, and Erskine became for the moment the most unpopular instructor on the campus.

In 1919, when Eastman was commenting on a proposed outline for qualifying Interstate Commerce Examiners in the higher grades, he wrote:

The requirement of a college education seems to me unnecessary and undesirable. Some of the best lawyers I know never had a college education. . . . The fact is that a very considerable proportion of our college students go to college not because they are keenly desirous of acquiring an education, but because they enjoy college life and associations. . . . On the other hand, some of the best educated men that I know never enjoyed the opportunities of college or university; but their thirst for knowledge was such that they managed to educate themselves despite their handicaps.

Whether Eastman's skepticism regarding college graduates evolved from his own experience is not easily determinable. But certainly many Amherst undergraduates of his time fell within the category that he mentioned.

On the other hand, some of them appreciated then, and later, the fact that instead of being regimented and harassed by higher authority they were permitted to choose their own interests and diversions. Of what is now called "guidance" there was practically none, except that bestowed with no lack of amateurish vigor by the upper classmen in one's fraternity. The beloved "Old Doc" Hitchcock, the majestically bearded dean, watched out for delinquencies and called daily on the victims in the infirmary to give them Bibles and remind them to keep their bowels open; but if an undergraduate secured "gentlemen's grades" in his courses and was careful not to "over-cut," he could move where he pleased when he pleased without incurring the wrath of the ruling powers. It was precisely this freedom which, without any intention on the part of the faculty or the administration, led the students to develop self-reliance. Relieved in most of their classes from the necessity of required reading, they could indulge in numerous extra-curricular activities, both legitimate and mildly illicit. A few found Rahar's Inn in Northampton a seductive excuse for not poring over their books and gathered on Saturday nights to carol "Paige's Horse is in the Snow-Drift" and other temptations to close harmony. But there were others who drifted into discussions around the fireplace and held "great argument, about it and about," and even read extensively, if indiscriminately, among the Great Books. Under such conditions education was often the consequence of casual rather than systematic living.

Furthermore, the Amherst disparaged by Professor Bigelow turned out for some reason a group of astonishingly distinguished alumni, especially in the field of public service. During those fifteen years were graduated Charles S. Whitman, '90, Governor of New York State; Harlan F. Stone, '94, Chief Justice of the Supreme Court of the United States; Bertrand H. Snell, '94, Republican Congressional leader; Calvin Coolidge, '95, President of the United States; Dwight W. Morrow, '95, Ambassador to Mexico and United States Senator; and Joseph B. Eastman, '04, Chairman of the Interstate Commerce Commission. To these bright stars could be added lesser luminaries in large numbers. These men must have derived something from Amherst College—perhaps not always from the lecture halls, but somewhere.

Amherst was then still a small college of about 400 students, and every undergraduate unless completely anti-social knew by their first names not only all the members of his class but also many of those below and above him. When Eastman entered, it had young men from twenty-four states and six foreign countries. The community had its subtle social distinctions and cliques, and the range from poverty to wealth was wide; but the life was essentially democratic, and demonstrated ability was quickly recognized and honored.

In the Greek letter fraternities, of which there were then eleven, the relations were very intimate, like those in a close-knit family, and one brother never hesitated to borrow from the others. With their literary programs they supplemented the curriculum; many an "Alpha Delt" or "Deke" can trace back to the lodge room— locally called the "goat room"—his continued interest in public speaking and dramatics. Amherst was then, as it always has been, a singing college, and at all hours of day or night passers-by could hear the constant favorites, such as "Lindy" and "Dinah" and "That Little Old Red Shawl," as well as the fraternity and college songs, of which there were many. Joe Eastman was no Caruso, but like most of us he was ready at the slightest provocation to add volume if not melody to the chorus.

Although the college ran two dining halls, most of the students preferred private eating houses, where they formed groups of ten or twelve composed of men with the same general interests. Eastman took his meals at "Mrs. Davis's," one of the more expensive and select boarding houses. He had from his father a sufficient allowance so that he could pay his way without having to do outside work. Money meant very little to Joe, either then or later, but he wore good clothes and was not noticeably restricted in his spending. He had no expensive vices. He did not gamble or take Smith girls to dances or give lavish parties. He had only one real extravagance— a fondness for a cigar called the "Bock Reciprocity," somewhat thicker than the better-known "Bock Panatela" and possibly of better tobacco. One classmate writes: "He always wanted quality, and was willing to accept the fact that it must be enjoyed less often because of the cost." Although Joe was not dissipated, he was no prig or prude. The personalities in his fraternity house were to say the least diverse, and he got along with them all.

It was a very pleasant existence for a lad fresh from Pottsville, Pennsylvania. In those remote days week-ends in the modern sense were unknown, and the students with rare exceptions found their recreations on or near the campus. Amherst is one of the most attractive villages in all New England. Trolley cars ran from it in several directions—to "Hamp" (the metropolis of the area), to Sunderland and the Bloody Brook Inn and Mount Sugar Loaf, to South Hadley and Mount Holyoke College, to Pansy Park and Belchertown. It was easy on warm spring evenings to board an open car and reach open spaces or even to find a pleasant loafing spot along the Connecticut River. In the fall the Pelham Hills and the serrated Holyoke Range are bright with yellows and crimsons blended with the green of the pines and hemlocks. On the last day of October in his Junior year, in delightful autumn weather, Joe and three classmates drove in a surrey to New Salem over rough country roads and spent three days hunting, sleeping in the open air, and cooking their own meals. Once in the following spring he took me fishing for "square tails" in the rushing brook which ran through the Orient—using worms, I must confess, and not flies.

Those four years were for Joe Eastman, as for many another Amherst man in the 1900's, very happy—years of some reading, of some not well-directed meditation, and of almost no awareness of the sinister forces gathering power for the disruption of modern civilization. Golden years they were, although we were hardly conscious of our good fortune at the time—and golden they still seem as we look back at them.

There was a presidential election in the autumn after he arrived, but Eastman was not old enough to vote and had nothing at stake. The Amherst College Republican Club was formed among the undergraduates, and it was apparent that campus sentiment was strongly behind McKinley and Roosevelt. A poll of the faculty showed that most of them were, without much enthusiasm, behind the Republican ticket, although Professor Kimball preferred Bryan, and Professor Harris declared, "I would be ashamed to vote for either candidate." Just before election a big rally was held in College Hall, and 350 students, including Joe, joined in a torchlight parade. At Amherst conservatism was still the prevailing philosophy.

Eastman was assigned a course largely prescribed and, in accordance with the Amherst tradition, laying excessive emphasis on the visual study of foreign tongues. Although the college granted the degree of Bachelor of Science to students not offering an ancient language, everybody knew that the "scientific course" as then set up was intended for the weaker brethren. Eastman's work for the first year included Greek, Latin, and German—each for four hours a week; mathematics—also for four hours; English and public speaking; and anatomy and hygiene. From the beginning Joe was a student of the "plugger" type, steady, systematic, and thorough, but never brilliant. As a freshman he received grades of "A" only in public speaking and German. In mathematics he had marks of "B," "B," and "E"—the last being the only recorded failure in his reports. In later life he was regarded as almost a wizard because of his ability to digest the financial statements of railroads.

In reflecting afterwards on his Amherst training, Joe was mildly critical of a system which placed so much stress on linguistics. He took two years of Greek, one year of Latin, three years of German, and two years of French, as contrasted with two years of mathematics and one year of physics—his only science. In spite of this, he was graduated unable to carry on a simple conversation in any language except English; and he felt that his intensive study of the classical languages had been of negligible value in his career. He had one term each of art and of music, and as a senior he took a semester of economics—an entertaining course, but one which contributed virtually nothing to his knowledge of railroads and big business.

Unfortunately Professor Garman, of the Department of Philosophy, whose influence had been so potent on Amherst men in the 1890's, was then in poor health and absent on sabbatical leave during Eastman's senior year. When Joe took his famous course in psychology as a junior, the personalities of teacher and pupil clashed sharply. It was Garman's custom to guide his students along an established route through various phases of unbelief to the goal of unquestioning Christian faith. Even then an independent in his thinking, Eastman refused to follow the conventional path and insisted on pressing Garman with searching questions, often at moments when the latter did not wish for open unrestricted discussion. Finally the ailing and impatient professor, accustomed to having his doctrines accepted without protest, sent for his too-insistent pupil and said, "Mr. Eastman, your skepticism is ruining my class. Will you kindly refrain from further disputation or else cease to attend it?" After this rebuke, Joe sat silent through lecture after lecture, but his comments in the fraternity house were pungent and very critical.

The exigencies of the humanities left Eastman little opportunity for getting even a weak foundation in science. This he always regretted. His final general average was 85, and he was elected to Phi

Beta Kappa on what was known as the "third drawing," almost on the day of his graduation.

Eastman always felt that the aspects of his Amherst education which meant the most to him in his later life were his outside activities, particularly journalism and public speaking. Following the advice of his father, he went out at once for the *Student*, the undergraduate weekly newspaper, and easily outdistanced all competitors. On March 23, 1901, it was publicly announced that he had been chosen as Associate Editor. He seems to have been indefatigable in his pursuit of news items and thorough in his coverage of assignments. Being the only freshman to make the board, he was bound, barring accident, to move on and up in accordance with established practice until he became editor-in-chief in his senior year. His election to this responsible position made him automatically one of the more prominent persons in his class.

It was primarily as a speaker, however, that Joe Eastman excelled at Amherst. The Professor in charge of debating and public speaking was George Bosworth Churchill, '89, who had returned to the college in 1898 to join the Department of English. Still under forty, he had a stalwart physique, a native dignity, and a sonorous voice that attracted attention; and he was later to move into public life as moderator of the Amherst Town Meeting and delegate to the Massachusetts Constitutional Convention, where his talent and personality won him a position of constructive leadership. He had been elected to Congress just before his untimely death, in 1925. Some undergraduates thought him arrogant and pompous, but he was warm-hearted toward those who met his stiff requirements. He found in Eastman an ideal pupil, responsive and persevering; and he was the first of several older men who had a marked influence on Joe. Eastman was always willing to follow leadership whose merit he could recognize.

Gradually Eastman was becoming interested in government and politics and the free discussion of controversial issues. To a thoroughly logical mind he added a capacity for research which provided him with the factual material for argument; his desire to develop into an eloquent speaker was supported by a crisp enunciation, a good presence, and a persuasive manner. In the freshman course in public speaking he was one of the five members of his class chosen on the basis of performance for the Kellogg contest in oratory. His "piece," carefully memorized, was Henry W. Grady's "Prohibition in Atlanta," and it was delivered with fervor. The prize, however, went to a competitor whose style was "more mature."

Again in his sophomore year Joe was selected for the Kellogg Five, but he was defeated by his classmate Fayette B. Dow. However, he was not discouraged by failure. While walking to Pelham or the Holyoke Notch he would declaim, and he often tried out his voice in the empty Johnson Chapel, with one of his friends as critic. All of us admired his ambition.

In his junior year Eastman came into his own. Under Churchill's guidance, supplemented by his own persistence, he had developed into a formidable speaker, who talked in a deliberate, reasonable, and convincing way. He had none of the rhetorical, somewhat florid style popularized by Daniel Webster, Rufus Choate, and Robert G. Ingersoll; but his simplicity, accentuated at times by a corner-of-the-mouth drawl, appealed to audiences a trifle bored by "sound and fury." When the trials for the college debating team were held in February, 1903, he was selected, the only junior, with Albert W. Atwood and Stanley King as the two senior members. Atwood has since been the chief editorial writer for the *Saturday Evening Post* and a contributor to many magazines. King was the distinguished president of Amherst from 1932 to 1946.

The debate with Bowdoin on March 6 was the first intercollegiate affair of that nature ever held in Amherst, and a crowd of more than six hundred attended it. Amherst upheld the negative of the subject "Resolved, that it is for the public interest that employers recognize trade unions in the arrangement of wage schedules." In the light of Eastman's later attitude, it seems strange that he should then have argued against organized labor, but the subject was assigned arbitrarily, and he had no choice of sides. Talcott Williams, the Philadelphia newspaper editor, sent up a vast amount of material from his files, and the members of the Amherst team were coached to meet every possible argument that their opponents could advance. Speaking second for Amherst, Eastman delivered a speech which was summarized as follows:

It would mean the greatest injustice to the non-union man if trade unions were recognized at the present time, for by far the greater number of unions make it a prime requisite of collective bargaining that the nonunionist be excluded from the right to work. Thus he would be forced either to surrender his principles and join the union, or else starve. He also said that unions were at present not fit for recognition because they are split up by the most widespread internal dissension, and also because they are absolutely irresponsible in a legal sense and finally because at the present time they show no respect for law or order or the safety of the government.

In rebuttal the Amherst team was clearly superior to Bowdoin, and the judges had no difficulty in reaching a unanimous decision in favor of the local talent. But Professor Garman invited Eastman down to his house and said to him, "I could not attend your debate, but a stenographer took your speech down for me, and I must tell you that every word you uttered was sheer anarchy."

In the autumn of his senior year Eastman was appointed one of the assistants in freshman declamation, and he learned much from coaching younger men. In his first senior debate on the subject "Resolved, that the Colombian Congress was not justified in rejecting the Panama Canal Treaty" he supported the negative—and won. Throughout that winter he discussed current topics, many of them concerned with the liberal ideas of President Theodore Roosevelt, and he talked much about "trusts" and "malefactors of great wealth." In the King Prize Debate, held in March, 1904, he upheld the negative of the question "Resolved, that aside from the matter of amending the Constitution, the best interests of the American people require federal regulation of the industrial combinations known as trusts." The prize was awarded to Joe's frequent and capable rival, "Cap" Dow, but he was chosen again for the debating team, with Dow and Frank Kane as his associates. This time something went wrong. In the debate with Bowdoin, held at Brunswick, Eastman was the first speaker on both original presentation and rebuttal, but evidently he did not distinguish himself. The verdict was unanimously against Amherst, and the *Student* reported, "Bowdoin won because of a somewhat better organized plan of attack, and because of exceedingly effective work on second appearance."

As editor-in-chief of the *Student*, Eastman did nothing revolutionary. His first editorial merely said: "With this number the *Student* passes under the control of a new board. New management, however, will not mean new aims nor new ideals. The policy of the paper will still be to print the news of the College, every week, in as complete, concise, and interesting a form as possible."

To this safe and unaudacious principle the paper adhered under Eastman's leadership. Hugh H. C. Weed, '05, wrote: "Eastman was editor of the *Student* in 1904, as I was in 1905. We spent hours together debating on what was best for the College, and it was in such associations that I learned to know him and respect his fine qualities." Whatever he may have discussed with his colleagues, the themes of his editorials were the familiar ones: comment on athletic contests, appeals to college spirit, a little mild criticism of unpopular administrative edicts, some praise of individual undergraduates for conspicuous achievements. Most of them could have been used as models for conventional collegiate journalism.

At the *Student* banquet in June, 1904, Eastman responded to the toast "The Old Board,—Though I look old, yet am I strong and lusty!" So ended his brief career as journalist. His experience had been profitable in several ways, chiefly because he had learned to write under pressure—an accomplishment which was to serve him well in the future. He went out from college accustomed to putting his thoughts down on paper for the consideration of others. He was to be doing this until he died.

Eastman's relationship to the Gamma Chapter of the Psi Upsilon fraternity, while the details cannot all be disclosed, was important in his development. Here again he was a slow starter. During his first two years other members of his delegation received more chapter honors than he, and he preferred to sit silent while they did most of the talking. He was undoubtedly restrained by his innate shyness and modesty. As he acquired confidence, however, his name appeared more frequently in the records, and it is significant that he was the first in his delegation to be elected chapter president.

For three years Joe lived in the fraternity house and enjoyed the intimacy of community life. The rooms were well-furnished, with all the facilities for comfortable existence. At any time of day or night little groups might be heard to burst into song, often with the colored janitor—one of the campus personages—leading in "Don't You Hear dem Bells," "Swing Low, Sweet Chariot," and other spirituals. Convivial alumni brethren from the outside world came back frequently to renew their youth. Tradition and sentiment combined to form a kind of religion, to which Joe was susceptible, for it was immediate and genuine. It is not for an "Alpha Delt" to interpret to outsiders the loyalty of "Psi U's"; but as I saw it from the opposite side of the street, in the old red "Gammy" house, I am ready to pay my tribute to its quality. In Joe Eastman were emotions both tender and deep, and the fraternity deposited a store of lasting memories.

According to his fraternity brothers of that period, Eastman gained steadily in poise and power. The responsibility of authority, in his case as in so many other cases, brought with it a feeling of self-reliance, resulting in an impulse to direct and lead. When a young man is accorded administrative office by the wish of his associates, his morale is strengthened, with the result that all his latent ability is likely to be brought out. Eastman's faith in himself was fostered by the trust placed in him. It is a familiar process of growth, well known to men who have attended small colleges where secret fraternities function at their best.

Although Eastman was never physically very powerful and had actually undergone a shoulder operation just before entering college, he seems to have been in the thick of every interclass fight. In one glorious battle between 1903 and 1904, all possible aid was called for, and Joe, in dressing hurriedly, put on by mistake a pair of brand-new trousers. In the melee Baker, '03, managed to get Joe down and was sitting on him heavily, when Joe exclaimed, "Damn it, let me up—my new pants are getting all mud." "Too bad," answered Baker, "but I'm staying on top." Joe soon gave up, very wisely, any ambition to be a great athlete. He was, however, fond of tennis, and his friends have declared that his type of play was indicative of his character. Never dashing or spectacular, he seldom served an ace and rarely made any startling returns, contenting himself with sending the ball back over the net with patient and irritating regularity until his opponent, nervous under the strain, was tempted to kill a lob—and missed. Joe sometimes defeated an opponent rated much better than he by pursuing these annoying tactics. His very steadiness was disconcerting to players ready to stake a point on a single ferocious drive. He did play two or three times on the college team when extra men were needed, although never with distinction.

Long before his senior year Eastman was very definitely what modern slang would call a BMOC—Big Man on the Campus—respected by the upperclassmen and "on the inside" of college affairs. To this position he had ascended by slow degrees, without intrigue or self-seeking. One classmate recalls that as freshmen nearly all the boys parted their hair in the middle. Only about eight members parted it on the side—and Joe Eastman was one. The "side-parters" were mostly wealthy and would-be sophisticated graduates of exclusive private schools; but Joe, the small-town lad, had already adopted the vogue that was to sweep masculine society. On the basis of college standards his position was with the upper social stratum.

Eastman was elected to several minor class offices, and in the spring of 1903, with about twenty others, he was picked for the recently formed Senior Club, composed of men who were supposed to have done something for Amherst. In his senior year, after a contest which had some of the aspects of ward politics, he was elected president of his class. In the final class vote he tied with "Don" Bartlett for "most representative" and ran slightly behind W. I. Hamilton and Fayette B. Dow as the member with the most promise of success. Joe, with his staying qualities, justified the early estimates of his classmates. Some of those who had shone brightly during their freshman and sophomore years faded into obscurity when they became known for what they really were. When the hour arrived for the last honest verdict, the mere athletes and the "sports" and the "show-offs" fell into the background, and the men of character were recognized.

In the Amherst of those days much excitement was caused annually by the struggle for the possession of the unclad bronze goddess, Sabrina, then held by the even-numbered classes, which had obtained possession of her as long ago as 1894 in a melodramatic coup. Each year it was the custom of the older even-numbered class to hold a secret banquet and transfer the naked lady formally to the new guardians. In the winter of 1903 every one in college was on edge awaiting the eventful evening. It was understood that some member of the Class of 1904 had the 350-pound deity stowed away and was charged with the duty of bringing her in safety to the freshman dinner. No one remembers just how it all happened, but Joe Eastman, constituted her protector because of his reliability, arranged to have the statue carried into the dining room of a hotel in Hartford, where he and the Class of 1906 solemnly caressed the goddess, kissed her cold metal lips, and chanted the famous chorus:

> All hail, Sabrina dear!
>   The widow of each passing year!
> Long may she ever be
>   The widow of posterity!

What was this young man like who was graduated from Amherst as the president of the Class of 1904? He was about five feet, nine inches tall, with a round, rather cherubic face and a faint suspicion of a double chin, brown hair and whimsical hazel eyes. His natural expression was genial, and he had a cordial way of greeting others on the street, whether he knew them well or not. By temperament he would have been rated as "sanguine," rather than "phlegmatic," and he seemed to be the embodiment of easy-going affability. He moved usually with deliberation, and some of his classmates thought him lazy. Chester A. Porter recalls that as a freshman, before getting up in the morning Joe would lie awake on his back staring up at the ceiling as if engaged in profound thought. Another classmate has described him as "physically indulgent." Edgar H. Goold wrote, "I have been surprised at his reputation for indefatigable hard work out in the world. He did not seem like that in college." But Goold admits that Eastman was a "night owl" and could often be found after midnight getting a hamburger and a cup of coffee at one of the local "dog wagons." It is significant that the *Olio,* the college yearbook, refers to him as "a good, sensible, and reliable 'old hoss.' "

Eastman always had a genuine amiable interest in other people and listened to their opinions with tolerance, if not with respect. When he disagreed, he did so without acrimony or recrimination. In all my acquaintance with him I never heard him indulge in caustic criticism or violent abuse, even under extreme provocation. He seemed always to have himself under control.

Hugh H. C. Weed, who roomed near him in the "Psi U" House and saw him intimately, maintains that all Joe's outstanding traits were evident when he was an undergraduate.

No one of my college contemporaries was nearly as consistent in later life with his college career. Then, as later, there was never anything to help the people near him that was undone. Then, as later, he had an amazingly equable disposition. When he was provoked, it was on more than just grounds, and everybody knew it. He was never too busy to stop and work out a problem for a friend or just to sit down and chat with classmates,—and that was true to the end of his life.

Joe was a slow starter. He was liked from the beginning, but it was in his Junior and Senior years that he was appreciated. He was Phi Beta Kappa, but not at the first drawing. He was a good debater, but much better towards the end of his course. He liked to play tennis, but he was forty before he was at his best. In other words, he plugged along until he was exceptionally competent at anything he set his mind to.

Like all men who succeed in their occupations, Joe moved inevitably beyond the range of his college experience. Some of his college mates outside his fraternity—men like Albert W. Atwood and Fayette B. Dow and Stanley King—kept in touch with him as he climbed up the ladder; but he was also making other friends as he entered into broader public service. His correspondence became extensive, almost overwhelming, and he traveled widely, meeting the great and the near-great. Nevertheless, his Amherst associations continued to mean much to him. He was proud when his alma mater recalled him in 1926 to make him a Doctor of Laws, and he felt that his election in 1940 as a trustee was the highest honor he had received. Even in the midst of a singularly complicated and engrossing life, he returned whenever he could to Amherst. He wrote to his classmate Ernest M. Whitcomb in the 1930's, "Every time I go back to Amherst I am impressed by its beauty. I have seen other parts of the country, but none of them is quite equal to New England, to my way of thinking, and the Connecticut Valley is one of the prize regions of New England." The same note is struck in a note to Mrs. Stanley King, under date of May 19, 1937.

I want to express my appreciation of my very pleasant, but all too brief, stay at your house. Stanley made me work for my keep, but I even enjoyed the work and hope that the boy victims got something out of it too. It is always a pleasure for me to visit Amherst, because, even without the college, it is one of the best spots on earth, but it warms the heart of an old alumnus to see the college prospering so well. Everybody tells me that Stanley is doing a splendid job, and the visible results speak for themselves.

When later, after his reputation as a public servant had been made, Eastman spoke to the undergraduates, he never failed to remind them of their responsibility as citizens. In his Commencement address at Amherst in 1904, at his thirtieth reunion, he said:

It is a common thing for men of character and education to get steamed up on the subject of good government. They work feverishly for a time, and then become discouraged and quit because they feel that they are accomplishing nothing. The fact is that no one can be at all sure that he is accomplishing nothing by his efforts, because it is quite impossible to say what the situation would have been if the efforts had not been made. Personally I have no doubt whatever that our governmental affairs would now be in much worse shape if it had not been for the activities of reformers, even though they may in their day have seemed to be mere voices crying in the wilderness. More important, however, is the fact that such efforts bring their own reward, for it is more satisfying to have made a gallant attempt than never to have tried at all.

The spring days hurried along, as they do in Amherst in the closing weeks of the college year. The Reverend John H. Eastman came back to see his son graduate and was one of the judges at the

Hyde Oratorical Contest. President Harris preached his usual urbane and witty baccalaureate sermon. As presiding officer at Class Day, Joe listened to the Ivy Poem, recited by Frank B. Morris, who was totally blind. It closed with lines declaring that he and his classmates were about

> To take our place of service in the world
> Resolved to do the work that proves us most
> And shows us loyal to Old Amherst's name.

He also heard another classmate, Sandford M. Salyer, say in his Grove Poem:

> Just watch Joe Eastman for a little while
> And see his bright expansive showman's smile,
> He's got old Barnum beaten by a mile.

He found himself voted with complete unanimity by his classmates "the greatest woman-hater,"—a label which he was never to lose. The usual "Good-byes" were said, with promises of future meetings. Then Joseph Bartlett Eastman, Bachelor of Arts, went out to make his mark in the outside world.

IV

Apprenticeship in Public Service

ALTHOUGH Eastman inherited a clerical tradition, he never considered the Christian ministry as a profession, but entered Amherst with his mind rather vaguely fixed on the law. As he grew more and more engrossed with the *Student*, he began to imagine himself as a potential Horace Greeley or Richard Henry Dana and even consulted Talcott Williams as to the best way of getting a job on a newspaper. Finally, as he engaged more and more in debating, he studied current economic and social problems and was stirred by the crusading zeal of his high school hero, Theodore Roosevelt. At this juncture, Fate—or Luck—helped him to reach a decision and determined the course of his life.

As his senior year progressed, Eastman heard of a fellowship of $500 which had been established some years before by Amherst alumni at South End House in Boston, where Robert A. Woods, Amherst, '86, was in charge. Wishing to have the position filled, Woods consulted Professor James W. Crook, of the Amherst Department of Economics, who first recommended Edgar H. Goold, one of the most outstanding scholars in Eastman's class; but he had already planned to enter a theological seminary, and Eastman was Crook's second choice. Eastman had taken economics for one term under Crook, and had been disappointed in the course. Consequently, when Woods wrote Joe formally offering him the fellowship, the latter was much surprised and rather hesitant to accept. His father, however, urged him to try it for a year, believing that the experience would be worth while. Writing Mrs. Woods in 1926, Eastman said: "Instead of my career having been deliberately planned out, it has in reality just happened. I have never looked very far into the future or attempted to reach any particular mark, and such advancement as I have had has been very largely without any design on my part."

Before he left college Eastman had definitely committed himself to Woods, and after a brief vacation in Pottsville, he returned to New England and settled in a room in South End House, at 20 Union Park, Boston. Only a few short blocks from the Ritz-Carleton and the Copley Plaza, luxurious hostelries for the opulent, lies a district of boarding houses and cheap apartments, of narrow alleys ending in cul-de-sacs, where the children on sweltering summer afternoons seek the small parks for relief and vice stalks abroad after sundown. Here are backyards designed for times when more prosperous occupants could cultivate their gardens; but they are now uncared for, and the aspect is dismal. Although on the three principal avenues—Tremont, Shawmut, and Washington—there are good stores, the side streets are much run-down-at-the-heel, and the inhabitants have either seen better days or were unfortunate from birth. In their very midst is the rambling Cathedral of the Holy Cross, the religious center of the district, with the noisy elevated trains running past its doors. It is not, strictly speaking, a slum area. It is merely drab and unprepossessing, like the disheveled and grumpy old women who in salubrious weather ornament every doorstep. Here it was that Joe Eastman, fresh from the comfort of the "Psi U" House at Amherst, began to learn how the other half lives.

Union Park, laid out in the 1860's on filled land reclaimed from the Back Bay, seemed likely at one period to become one of Boston's fashionable quarters. It is an elliptical area of considerable size lying between Tremont and Shawmut avenues, built as is Louisbourg Square around a fence-enclosed grass plot; the residences as originally constructed were of the "swell front" design then popular with the prosperous. Most of the dwellings on Union Park, including South End House, are still architecturally attractive.

South End House had been established in 1891 as the Andover House Association, sponsored by Andover Theological Seminary and especially by Professor William Jewett Tucker, later president of Dartmouth College. The object was "to establish a house where men could, as actual residents, share the life of a thickly populated part of Boston, both for the sake of learning the conditions of existence there and of developing means for their improvement." It was first located at 6 Rollins Street and called Andover House; but in 1895, in order to dispel the suspicion that the movement might be a phase of Protestant propaganda, the name was officially altered to South End House, and six years later the residence was moved to Union Park, where it has since remained.

When Eastman entered upon his duties, in the summer of 1904, Woods bore the title of "Head of the House." He was a truly remarkable soul, with a gift for drawing able young men into his orbit and inspiring them with his confident and indomitable spirit. Born in Pittsburg in 1865, he had been graduated from Amherst College, where his thinking had been profoundly affected by Professor Garman and President Julius H. Seelye. Of the latter, Woods wrote: "In one of his most solemn utterances he declared that no career could be of higher service to the nation than that of the educated man who should go among the people and in largeness of mind and heart join with them in working out the labor problem."

Under the spell of these two dynamic teachers Woods planned for himself a career of "moral adventure." He entered Andover Theological Seminary, where he saw with incredulity and disgust the most brilliant of his professors placed on trial for heresy and became an ardent supporter of Professor Tucker's liberalism. From Andover, on October 6, 1888, Woods wrote his mother: "I am trying to find out what has been done in the last five centuries to make men, especially poor men, better and happier. I look to Tucker for direction, and the more I am with him the better I like him. He is a thoroughly business-like Christian. Not too much broadcloth, not too much piety."

As his course in the Seminary was ending, Woods was approached by Tucker regarding the organization in Boston of something similar to Toynbee Hall in London, its aim to be "the identification of a group of university men with the life of people in a poor neighborhood where they would take up their residence." After an exploratory trip to Europe, Woods commenced the career of public service which was not finished until his death on February 18, 1925. Thus, from Garman and Seelye and Tucker to Woods and eventually to

Eastman and others like him the idea of practical social work was transmitted and fulfilled in different ways.

Woods became one of the foremost world authorities on settlement work, ranking with Jacob Riis, in New York, and Jane Addams, in Chicago. His book, *The City Wilderness*, published in 1898, presented a startling picture of conditions in Boston's South End, which many respectable State Streeters had never visited; and his *Americans in Progress*, which appeared in 1902, was a similar study of the North End and the West End of the same city. By 1904, when Eastman met him, he was a leader with poise and power. His mastery of details, his winning personality, his reasonableness, his freedom from starry-eyed and futile fanaticism had won him the regard and even the affection of hard-boiled ward politicians, and his influence was extending from year to year.

The South End House as Eastman knew it had three full stories, a fourth story with dormer windows, and a commodious basement, and provided space not only for sleeping quarters but also for committee meetings and other small gatherings. In it while Eastman was a resident were several other workers who made it their home. It furnished also offices for Woods and the secretary, William I. Cole, as well as for a staff of seven or eight, and it served as a convenient center for conferences of persons interested in active community philanthropy. The organization had developed in thirteen years into an extensive and complex machine, including more than forty associate workers and five professional teachers. Eastman was joining a group of people who had a passionate desire to counteract man's inhumanity to man.

To get along in a community like that around South End House requires an unusual blend of sympathy and tact. The neighborhood naturally resents being called "under-privileged" and hates condescension, especially when it is masked. Moving among these people easily, giving help without the appearance of superiority, is difficult even for persons of generous instincts. Eastman, modest, unobtrusive, and courteous, was well adapted for the service to be performed. He had not the slightest trace of snobbishness, and he also avoided sentimentality—one of the most irritating traits that a social worker can display. He did some teaching, with moderate success,

among the boys in that quarter, but soon found a new and, as he
thought, a wider interest.

It was the intention of Woods and those who made possible the
Amherst Fellowship that its incumbent should help, of course, at
South End House but should also study "not only from a theoretical standpoint, but also from close range and intimate acquaintance,
the serious problems connected with modern city life and especially
the methods by which they are being attacked." In his first year
of residence Eastman chose as his special field the subject of municipal government and state legislation, and he promptly allied himself
with the Good Government Association—locally known as the
"Goo-Goos"—in Boston. In his book *The City Wilderness* Woods
had included a chapter on "The Roots of Political Power," in
which he discussed with daring frankness "the play of personal
and social forces beneath the surface of boss rule and ward politics."
Following this trail, already blazed, Joe acquainted himself with
the practical administration of the city government, studied the
racial and other characteristics of the separate wards, their political
complexion, their party organization, and their strong personalities,
hoping to learn something of the influences, often evil, which were
brought to bear upon the average voter. After this broad and
general investigation he devoted himself to a more intensive study
of one ward in which were combined in equal proportions voters
of the floating lodging house population and of the tenement house
districts. There was much to learn, and Eastman learned it very
thoroughly.

In 1933, at a celebration of Woods's birthday, Eastman wrote a
letter stressing his own obligation to him. He said in part:

I have Mr. Woods to thank for starting me off on the line of work
which I have since followed. It was his habit to observe the boys who
came to the South End House on the college fellowships and make
up his mind what kind of work of social and political advantage they
were best equipped to pursue. He also made it a point to keep in touch,
so far as he could, with all organizations which were trying to do
something for the public good. He regarded the South End House as
much more than an association for work in the slum districts of the
South End, and liked to think of it also as an observation tower from

which all phases of community work could be watched and helped. His contacts were very far-reaching. . . . Mr. Woods was one of the few real statesmen I have known. He had an extraordinarily well-equipped and comprehensive mind and a very broad outlook on social questions. He stimulated my thought and started it in new directions. I have always been grateful for the impulse which led me to accept the Amherst Fellowship, and I am happy to pay this tribute to the memory of Robert A. Woods.

In case after case Woods was wisely content to let his helpers undertake any research agreeable to them, provided it contributed to his total program. Their investigations and publications were all part of his system. He saw that Eastman was more interested in politics than in organizing athletic contests or directing boys' clubs. It is much to Woods's credit that he perceived what was going on in Eastman's mind and encouraged him to acquire a practical knowledge of the functioning of government.

In extending his activities from the somewhat narrow locale of settlement work to the more comprehensive area of municipal affairs, Woods had deliberately joined forces with Louis D. Brandeis and his little group of very business-like reformers in their efforts to make Boston a better city. Having discovered Eastman's special talent and ambitions, Woods encouraged him to ally himself with committees formed to prevent the encroachment of private aggrandizement on public welfare. Joe's own instinct might eventually have swept him along that road without any outside propulsion; but it was fortunate for him that at that experimental stage he was assisted by Woods and Brandeis, who were reformers without being "crack-pots," upholders of evolution, not of revolution, recognizing that the sanest and safest progress is often through a series of compromises. Eastman was quick to comprehend what he was already eager to learn. All his life he preferred live dragons to windmills as opponents. Quixotism has, of course, its noble aspects, but it is often a frightful waste of time. Eastman's tendency was to set his standard high but also to accept what he could get. "All or nothing" was never his policy. His habits of mind and his disposition were both practical. This native practicality was encouraged by both Woods and Brandeis.

In the spring of 1905, while continuing his residence and some of his routine duties at South End House, Eastman became secretary of what was known as the Public Franchise League. Responding to a request from the *American Hebrew*, in 1933, he put on record his obligation to Louis D. Brandeis and also explained how he became associated with him.

The Public Franchise League was a small and informal organization of men who thought, and quite correctly, that they could do some good by studying as citizens questions of public importance which arose in regard to the local public utilities, and discussing these questions before the public bodies that had to deal with them. Mr. Woods, with entire accuracy, told me that the League was made up of able and disinterested men of public spirit and fine standing in the community. I remember that he told me, in particular, that one of the most active members was a lawyer, Louis D. Brandeis, who would, in his opinion, one day be recognized as standing at the very top of the Boston bar. He thought that I could learn a great deal by associating with Mr. Brandeis and the other members of the League, including E. A. Filene, and that I would afterwards treasure the association. He was more than right. Fortunately I accepted his advice, and the position at a salary of $1000 a year.

I was a boy of New England stock and conservative tendencies. The association with the men in the League and particularly Justice Brandeis gave me a new point of view and undoubtedly changed the current of my life. Justice Brandeis had the most powerful intellect with which I have ever had the good fortune to come in contact, and I have met a goodly number of eminent men. I do not need to say that he combines strength and nobility of character with intellect. Many of the good and respected citizens of Boston, however, did not understand him.

In the first place, he had decided that instead of going ahead with the accumulation of a fortune, which he could easily have done, he would give a large and continually increasing amount of *time* instead of *money* to what he deemed to be the public good. This was a simple idea, but a most unusual one, and hence very difficult for many to grasp. Eventually he gave at least half his time to such public work. In the second place, when he waged a battle with those who were financially powerful, he knew that he could not win unless he was able to enlist the support of a strong public opinion. For that reason he sought publicity in such contests, and he was a master hand at getting it and engaging popular interest. In the third place, he was a fighter, who asked no quarter and gave none.

For these reasons, there were those who jumped to the conclusion that he was a headline seeker, a man endeavoring to advertise himself for motives of self-interest, and generally a dangerous character not to be entirely trusted. Those against whom he was fighting did everything they could to breed and foster this idea, and he suffered at times a flood of public abuse. I remember well his saying to me in one of those periods that his enemies had tried to "get" him in every possible way. He had no fear of social or business attacks and came finally to the conclusion that the only danger lay in his caring what was said about him. "For that reason," he said, "I determined that I would not care and I would not reply to any personal attacks." And he never did.

Brandeis's influence on Eastman was so decisive and continuous over many years that it is necessary to dwell for a moment on his career. A first-rate biography entitled *Brandeis; a Free Man's Life,* was published in 1946 by Professor Alpheus T. Mason, of Princeton, on whose researches anybody dealing with the subject must largely rely. Born in 1856, in Louisville, Kentucky, of a well-to-do immigrant family, he had been educated partly in Germany and entered Harvard Law School in 1875, without any previous formal college training. Nevertheless, he completed the course in two years, making a record for distinguished scholarship which has never since been equaled. Because he was then still under twenty-one, the corporation had to suspend a fixed rule in order that he might receive his degree with his class. After a trial year in an office in St. Louis, he returned to Boston in the summer of 1879 as a partner of his classmate Samuel D. Warren, Jr., under the firm name of Warren and Brandeis. For many years after that, until his appointment to the Supreme Court of the United States, he was identified with the Boston bar, and most of his legal triumphs were won in that city.

By the 1890's Brandeis was attracting attention as a reformer, although his biographer makes it clear that "an abiding and ardent desire for reform did not make him favor drastic or revolutionary change." He was, declared a New York attorney, "the first great lawyer I ever knew who had a social conscience and a genuine desire to make a better world." Because of his advanced ideas, he was regarded as "the protector of the public interest" against the abuses of capitalism; and he was avowedly the enemy of any industrial corporation which because of its power was able and willing to crush legitimate competition or act against the welfare of labor, the consumer, or the general public.

In several ways Brandeis presented irreconcilable inconsistencies. As a corporation lawyer, he had accumulated a fortune, and he included some prominent industrialists among his intimate friends. He had been deeply disturbed, however, by the shooting down of the strikers at the time of the notorious clash at Homestead, Pennsylvania, between armed Pinkerton strikebreakers and the laborers at the plant of the Carnegie-Illinois Company. Step by step, almost without being aware of the implications of his successive acts, he espoused what seemed to him to be good causes, always refusing to accept pay for work which he was performing in the interests of the public. Like most members of his profession, he was essentially conservative, preferring whenever possible to maintain continuity with the past; and he was excited about change only when it was reasonably demonstrable that it would mean improvement. Yet again and again, as his convictions strengthened, he insisted that the truly scrupulous attorney should hold a mediating position between organized wealth and the general public, prepared to curb excesses when they became dangerous. Having grown to manhood in the age of the "Robber Barons" and watched with apprehension the rapid spread of predatory "trusts" in the last decade of the nineteenth century, he thought he saw our democracy threatened because of acts of injustice committed by certain captains of industry. As his biographer insists: "He did not hate capitalism; he deplored its abuses."

By 1904, when Eastman first met him, Brandeis was regarded by conservative interests in Boston as a gadfly whose next victim could never be predicted. His long feud with the New Haven Railroad and Charles S. Mellen did not open until a year later; but he was engaged in a grueling controversy with the Boston Elevated Railway and was also pressing the sliding-scale rate principle on the Consolidated Gas companies of Boston and vicinity. At a moment when Brandeis was planning a campaign against a powerful and resourceful group of financial manipulators, he selected Eastman as lieutenant to help plan his strategy.

Eastman did not realize, perhaps, the full significance of what he was doing. But feeling as he did a strong desire to improve the condition of individual men and women, he was naturally attracted by Brandeis's liberalism. Especially concerned with the manifest inequalities resulting from existing social systems and economic relationships, he was sure that defective legislation and corrupt politics, to say nothing of human greed, were responsible for much of the misery around him in the South End; and this fact impressed him more than theological creeds or the vagaries of metaphysics. He was much more interested in the present, where something visible could be accomplished, than in the hereafter, of which he was uncertain. He was a product, as one writer has put it, of the "new theology," which "envisaged human relations as well as divine, and saw that Christianity must be applied to those social relations and their economic and social problems." Doubtless Eastman did not reason all these matters out. Then, as during most of his career, he had little leisure for prolonged meditation. But some unerring intuition made him realize that in Woods and Brandeis he had mentors whom he could trust.

The stage was well set for the relatively minor role which Eastman was to play. The chief actor was Theodore Roosevelt, under whose direction a movement for the regulation and control of "big business" was gathering speed and force. The President himself always considered his handling of the coal strike in October, 1902, as the opening skirmish of his declared war on arrogant corporations; and his strategy was assisted by the cynical attitude of the railroad employers, represented by George F. Baer. Even before this, however, he had instructed his Attorney-General, Philander C. Knox, to bring suit against the Northern Securities Company—a so-called "holding corporation"—on the ground that it had been formed in violation of the Sherman Antitrust Act of 1890. After two years in the lower Federal courts, the Supreme Court declared for the plaintiff in a close vote of five to four, and the Northern Securities Company was declared "a trust, a combination in restraint of trade." Eastman had discussed this famous case before his fraternity in March, 1904, and had favored Roosevelt's position. The effect of the decision was sensational, and it was considered by "T.R." to be one of the supreme achievements of his administration. It was, in fact, symbolic of a change in public opinion— a change which was also shown in the appearance of young reformers like Eastman who might in an earlier generation have become ministers of the gospel, but in the 1900's heard in Roosevelt's attacks on swollen corporations something equivalent to a clarion call urging them to action. Later, Eastman was to be allied to some extent with two other reforming Presidents—Woodrow Wilson and Franklin D. Roosevelt.

Here a word of caution must be interpolated. Eastman was never disposed to condemn all big business solely because it was big. His convictions on this point followed closely those of Theodore Roosevelt, as summarized by Mark Sullivan.

Roosevelt would allow units of business to grow as large as economic conditions might permit,—but would subject them to continuous supervisions by the government. This last, that the government should have the right to regulate, and especially that the government should be recognized as above all business and above all business men, big or little,—that was the heart of Roosevelt's doctrine, the point on which he fought his great controversies.

It was the ethical aspect of the matter which aroused Eastman most in his dealings with railroads or other public utilities. If they operated efficiently and fairly for the common good, he cared little about their size.

The world is different today, after the impact of two global wars, with their disappearing aftermath. When Eastman was at South End House many wise men thought that legislation could mitigate and even eliminate selfishness, greed, and conscienceless financial manipulation. Now the cynical economists and sociologists of the mid-century look back with astonishment at the naïve optimism of their fathers. To read the newspapers and magazines of the Roosevelt-Taft era is to discover that many sensible citizens earnestly believed that if the public could only be aroused existing inequalities would vanish like the snow in spring. From our perspective we can see that these leaders were in some respects undertaking the task and meeting the failures of Sisyphus, who was condemned incessantly to push a stone up a hill only to see it roll back again; but out of the various corrective movements emerged figures like William Travers Jerome, Charles S. Whitman, Charles Evans Hughes, Henry L. Stimson, and Louis D. Brandeis—leaders who became nationally known and honored. The fact that undercover lobbyism and financial juggling still exist does not mean that these men labored in vain.

The Public Franchise League was formed in 1900, with the avowed purpose of guarding the control of Boston streets by the people. Brandeis had begun his battle against the Boston Elevated Company as early as 1897, when it had secured from the Massachusetts General Court grants of virtually permanent and unrestricted franchises in several of the important downtown thoroughfares. Among the influential citizens whose aid Brandeis secured were Edward A. Filene, head of one of the city's largest and most progressive department stores; George P. Upham and Edward R. Warren, who were concerned with preserving the historic values and the charm of the Common; Dr. Morton Prince, distinguished as a psychiatrist; Robert G. Dodge, a leading attorney; George W. Anderson, later Eastman's predecessor on the Interstate Commerce Commission and a circuit judge; and a few others who made occasional contributions, including B. F. Keith, Thornton K. Lothrop, Robert Treat Paine, John H. Fahey, Charles F. Weed, Edward A. Adler, Franklin T. Hammond, Charles H. Jones, and Robert Luce. The organization of the League was informal, there being no officers except the secretary, and it stepped into action only when there was no substantial difference of opinion among the members.

With all its informality, the League had won a decisive victory in 1901, when it persuaded Governor William Murray Crane—certainly no radical thinker—to veto a legislative act granting the Elevated a valuable monopoly in a broad public thoroughfare for a period of fifty years. When Eastman became its secretary, the League was still keeping a vigilant eye on all street legislation. What Brandeis was doing was to bring to the attention of the lethargic citizenry exactly what was going on and to make the Elevated understand that its function lay in public service on fair terms.

In May, 1905, then, Eastman was writing letters on the stationery of the Public Franchise League. He had a modest office in the Equitable Building—since razed—and his meager salary was paid largely by Filene, who also contributed to the expense of the rent and made Eastman small loans when the latter was hard up. There was no stenographer, and Joe pecked out his correspondence with two fingers on an ancient Smith-Premier typewriter. For a while he continued to live at South End House, but Woods had already made up his mind that the League was for Eastman the larger job and allowed him in the autumn of 1905 to relinquish his duties with the settlement. In his annual report sent out in 1906 Woods announced that Eastman was devoting his full working time to the affairs of the League and added: "The record of the League in its successful legislative campaigns for keeping the tracks off Tremont Street, for securing the public ownership of the Washington Street subway, and for bringing the capitalization of the gas combination down to a proper figure, decisively proves its great importance and value."

As secretary, Eastman had to appear frequently before legislative committees, especially the Committee on Railroads, and according to Robert M. Washburn, was "not fashionable in those days on Beacon Hill." Commenting on the impression which Eastman made, Washburn wrote:

There were two qualities in Mr. Eastman which struck me from the start. These were the study which he put into his work and his dogged determination in prosecuting it. He was never feazed. Whether the committee was absent or present, whether it was listening or not— which latter was often—Joe was always under constant steam. Further than this, no one ever questioned his high purpose. These qualities landed him.

Often in the State House Eastman had to speak on technical matters in opposition to well-trained, highly paid, and very clever attorneys, and at first he was timid. However, his experience in preparing briefs and presenting arguments at Amherst stood him in good stead, and he quickly mastered the fine art of legal give-and-take. He noticed early that men and women of the finest reputation and with the best of motives would frequently injure their cause by claiming too much and thus arousing antagonism. When he observed the psychological effect of such tactics, he made up his mind that he would avoid emotionalism and use the utmost care to state the facts exactly as they were. His speeches after that were marked by two characteristics—mastery of the details involved and elucidation of them with such clarity and candor that his listeners followed and believed him. He created the impression that he was a witness incapable of guile or even of exaggeration; and he was so patient, cool-headed, and unembarrassed that he readily won the confidence of neutrals. It often seemed in the committee chambers when he was pitted against William H. Coolidge, Bentley W. Warren, or Charles F. Choate—all of them counsel for the New Haven Railroad—that he was like David battling against, not only one Goliath, but many; but more than once he employed his verbal sling-shot to good effect.

At Brandeis's instigation, Eastman enrolled in the autumn of 1906 at the Boston University School of Law and completed his first year satisfactorily with courses in agency, contracts, criminal law, sales, and torts. He took two courses, also, in the following year, but was soon obliged to withdraw because of the demands of the Public Franchise League. Although he never resumed his legal studies, he did acquire a theoretical knowledge of judicial procedure which was later to be exceedingly helpful. What he really felt about the subject came out in a letter which he wrote on December 23, 1906, to his college friend, Ernest M. Whitcomb.

Law, my dear boy, is a valuable thing for the world, but it does not contribute to the general amusement and entertainment of the species. I am convinced that the worst English in the world is written by that particular brand of pre-Adamite fossils known as judges. Once in a while one breaks loose and writes in a somewhat lucid way, but as a whole they can give Henry James a lead of miles and beat him out in a walk when it comes to confusing the issue in the intricacies of the English language. Never mind, when I get to be Judge of the Supreme Court of the U.S., I am going to set some new precedents which will shake the dust on some of the old dry bones.

Eastman soon supplemented his book study by practical experience with court methods, and under Brandeis's tutelage turned from novice into professional. Later in his life he was for many years chairman of the Legislative Committee of the Interstate Commerce Commission and had to interpret the law's inherited and confusing verbiage. Once during a prolonged hearing on holding companies before the House Judiciary Committee, a distinguished constitutional lawyer pressed him hard on some matters of precedent, and Eastman showed such a facility in rebuttal that the listeners applauded. When the session was over, a visitor approached the General Counsel for the Association of American Railroads and asked, "Is that fellow Eastman a lawyer?" "No," was the quick retort, "but he's a damned good one!" Chief Justice Harlan F. Stone once said, "When our court gets a case which involves a decision and order of the Interstate Commerce Commission, we always thumb it through first to see what Joe Eastman has said in his Opinion." The Chief Justice thus indicated that his court's appreciation of Joe's ability and judgment was so great that it overshadowed what might appear in the decision as the expression of any other commissioner, or of all the other commissioners combined. Thus, with only a brief formal training, Eastman early came to think and to argue like a genuine member of the bar.

Eastman's first important job for the League brought him in touch with the Consolidated Gas Company, a combination formed in 1903 of eight gas companies in Boston and Brookline. The immediate issue in 1905 was the so-called "sliding scale" principle, providing that as the dividends paid to stockholders increased, the selling price to the consumer should drop. Brandeis contended that "the amount the Company should have should depend . . . upon what is given to the community." Thus, the price of gas to the consumer and the amount of dividends to the investor could be tied together, with advantage to both.

In the summer of 1905 several interested people went to England to study what was called the "London System"; and in the following spring, when the League, through Eastman, presented its "sliding scale" bill to the legislative Committee on Public Lighting,

Brandeis appeared in its favor. The measure, thanks to the earlier "spade work," was quickly pushed through and signed by Governor Guild. Its immediate effect was a reduction in the price of gas from 90 to 85 cents, and a year later to 80 cents. At that time Brandeis was opposed to the municipal ownership of gas production and believed that it had been blocked by the wise legislation which the Public Franchise League had promoted,—legislation which, in his judgment, supplied "the first instance in American of a reasonable alternative to municipal ownership."

Almost automatically Eastman found himself involved in the unceasing efforts of the League to check the aggressive moves of the Boston Elevated Railway. The real victory had been won before 1905, and Brandeis, defending without compensation the rights of the people, had done much to restrain the Elevated authorities. In preparing material for the later use of the League, Eastman went back into Massachusetts legislative and judicial history, reading every act and decision which had anything to do with public utilities, and he followed this with a similar intensive study of what had been done in Wisconsin. Brandeis, Anderson, Dr. Prince, and other League members who called occasionally at his office realized that they could rely implicitly on him for digests of all essential information.

One by-product of this perennial controversy was an article written by Eastman in collaboration with Woods and published in the *Outlook* for April 16, 1906, with the title, "The Boston Franchise Contest." This magazine under the trenchant editorship of Lyman Abbott was supporting President Theodore Roosevelt in his reform measures. Roosevelt only a few days before, at the laying of the cornerstone of the Office Building of the House of Representatives, had delivered his famous address, "The Man with the Muck-Rake," in which he audaciously recommended legislation aimed at "the inheritance or transmission in their entirety of those fortunes swollen beyond all healthy limits" and advocated also supervision by the National Government over corporations engaged in interstate business. He referred bitterly to "the men of wealth who to-day are trying to prevent the regulation and control of their business in the interests of the public." The *Outlook* described the speech as "the reflection of a sentiment, gradually crystallizing into an opinion, of a great body of Americans of sane mind, progressive temper, and moderate incomes."

In their article, Woods and Eastman took the same line as Roosevelt, although directing their attack specifically at the program and methods of the Boston Elevated Railway, which they condemned scathingly as "a great corporation, backed by wealth, newspapers, politicians, and powerful financial interests." The evidence indicates that Eastman did most of the actual composition, although Woods went over it carefully, making suggestions here and there and putting upon it the stamp of his full approval—which was important, for he was much better known than his younger collaborator.

The central theme was, of course, the repeated attempts of the Boston Elevated to gain control of the city's subway system. After surveying the early history of these efforts, Eastman praised the courageous stand taken by Mayor Patrick A. Collins in 1902 against the campaign of the Elevated officials to acquire a monopoly of subway transportation in Boston and called attention to the work of the Public Franchise League in arousing popular sentiment. In revealing the schemes of the Elevated, Eastman used no weasel words, but insisted that the battle was between "The People" on one side and an unscrupulous corporation on the other. The *Outlook* printed this article following an issue containing a similar essay by George C. Sikes, entitled "Chicago's Struggle for Freedom from Traction Rule," and also in conjunction with some editorial comment from week to week on the situation in Philadelphia. The Boston affair, although local in scope, attracted attention all over the nation and lent support to Roosevelt's assaults on "malefactors of great wealth." Some members of the Public Franchise Commission thought that the article surpassed the writings of Lincoln Steffens, then in his prime as a radical reformer, but this judgment was clearly biased. Eastman lacked the dramatic fervor which made Steffens's pages glow and burn.

There were moments when Joe had to assume plenty of responsibility for his organization. On December 23, 1906, he wrote Whitcomb:

The blooming Franchise League is in a pretty mess. Of a sudden the Edison Electric Company makes application for a new issue of stock, and a hearing is set before the Board for next Thursday. At the same auspicious moment a telephone war breaks out in the city. Both questions demand the careful attention of the Franchise League. The League has three mainstays and props: Louis D. Brandeis, E. A. Filene, and G. W. Anderson. No one else has the requisite ability, experience, and initiative to push any matter through, and handle it before a Commission or the Legislature or before the public. What happens at this most opportune time? Anderson accepted a commission from the telephone company to make an investigation of telephone competition in the Middle West. When the League steps into the telephone fight, Anderson steps out of the League because of his connection with the company, not through any sympathy with them, but because of a very strict kind of conscience which he has. Filene decides to go abroad this winter, and Brandeis has got so much enmeshed in his plan to reorganize industrial insurance that he has time for little else. In this juncture Little Willie is sitting on top the powder keg, and if he can keep the League from blowing up, he is doing a very keen job indeed.

The League did not "blow up." Eastman was both competent and resourceful, and his superiors were well satisfied to leave him in charge. Meanwhile he was becoming better known. In November, 1908, he attended the meeting in Pittsburgh of the National Municipal League and spoke on "The Control of Public Utilities." He opened by stating that the regulation of public service corporations by means of state commissions was a firmly established policy in Massachusetts. In his talk he traced the history of the Massachusetts Railroad Commission since its authorization in 1869, of the Gas and Electric Commission, established in 1885, and of the Highway Commission, commending them for their accomplishment. He ended:

If Massachusetts has been at all successful in regulating public service corporations by means of commissions, it is due primarily to the fact that the people of the state have not altogether failed in their duty as citizens. They have elected good governors; the governors have appointed able and courageous men; and the people have in some measure shown an active interest in the work of the commissions after they were appointed.

In this early speech, his first beyond the boundaries of New England, are apparent certain qualities of Eastman's gradually maturing talent: his easy handling of factual material; his temperate language, even when making serious allegations; his simple, often colloquial, style; and his direct method of approach. He was fully aware that improvements in the regulation of public utilities develop slowly and only in response to an educated and articulate citizenry, consequently he did not expect too much too soon.

For the next few years Eastman continued to work steadily in the office of the Public Franchise League, busy with routine assignments and seemingly unconcerned over his personal or professional future. All the while he was learning more and more about industry and labor and the relations of both to society as a whole. Some of his friends thought that he was marking time and told him so, but he was actually preparing himself in knowledge and experience for broader service.

When Joe left South End House, in 1906, he went to live with three Amherst friends: Robert J. Bottomly, '05, who had succeeded him as Amherst Fellow and was then studying law at Boston University; Wilfrid E. Rounseville, '05, who was enrolled at Harvard Medical School; and Frederick S. Bale, '06, who had followed Bottomly at South End House under Woods. All four were living on limited incomes, and they paid only two dollars a week each for one large back room on the first floor of a house on Mount Vernon Street. It had a skylight and two windows opening on a narrow area-way, and contained a fireplace, a long table, a couple of Morris chairs, a small closet, and four narrow couches for beds. How anybody studied law or medicine in such cramped quarters is difficult to explain. Bale recalls that in the winter they usually slept late on Sunday mornings and then would arrive at Young's Hotel just late enough to have breakfast "under the wire," so that their two meals would be rightly spaced. On week ends Eastman and Bale would spend Saturday night with friends at the Harvard Law School, hold a grand Amherst reunion with plenty of singing and beer, and then on Sunday take a hike into the country. When he wanted complete relaxation, he would go to

concerts by the Boston Symphony Orchestra or play bridge whist
—a game at which he was adept.

After a year Eastman moved to 73 Pinckney Street, rooming
with Bottomly, William H. Best, later a partner in a Boston law
firm, and Frank Livingstone, whose association with him was to
be close and lasting. Born in Calais, Maine, about ten years before
Eastman, Livingstone was the second of nine children. After studying law in the office of the local judge, he came to try his luck in
Boston, finally opening an office of his own in the Equitable Building. Eastman, seeking some headquarters for the Public Franchise
League, met Livingstone and hired desk space from him. As neither
was married, they were free to move as they chose, and each found
in the other an agreeable and congenial companion. Livingstone was
benevolently interested in young men, especially when they came
from his native town, and he assisted several of them to a start
in life. Indeed, he spent a large share of his modest income helping
them over rough places, enabling them to continue their education,
and even paying hospital bills or the cost of having a baby. He
attached himself to Eastman as if he had discerned from the beginning of their acquaintance the attributes which others were to discover much later.

Livingstone was a vivid, authentic personality with a keen and
penetrating mind, a sensitive social conscience, and a fearless manner
of speech. One of his friends wrote of him, "He had a peculiar
ability to understand and stimulate a young fellow's thinking, to
jar him out of his complacency, to blast him out of inherited,
easy-going prejudices, social, economic, religious. He was a Revolutionary in temperament and preference." Still another said: "He
detested stuffed shirts and was never fooled by the outer trappings
of success or wealth. He was one of the few real democrats I have
ever known, because he really thought and lived the belief that all
men are equal, and that humanity levelled down as well as upward."
He was skeptical, iconoclastic, much further to the left than Eastman, and inclined to scoff at bankers and big business; and he undoubtedly had a considerable influence on Eastman's economic and
political views. Commenting on him after his death in 1937, Eastman wrote: "Livingstone played a great part in my life,—much

greater than many realize. It was very much like the part of the wise father. He was always a great tonic when I was discouraged or blue,—and that was quite often in my early career,—and his advice filled in many of my deficiencies, for he understood human beings much better than I."

Then, as in college, Joe was unmistakably a man's man. He was still rated as a misogynist, but he was popular with the women at South End House, one of whom evidently pursued him with the predatory tactics then being publicized in Shaw's *Man and Superman*—but he successfully held her off. He was putting on a little weight, and one of the Irish women at the settlement said of him, "Ah, shure, I remember the rascal. He was fat and fair!" John R. Howard writes, "Joe looked as William H. Taft might at his age, large but well set up, with heavy ruddy features, but quick smile and laugh and level eyes." It is recalled that he had "a good-natured friendly interest in you and what you wanted to talk about." He had given up cigars because of their cost and had taken up pipe-smoking, which he was never to abandon. Indeed, he soon had a matched set of pipes, one for each day of the week.

Joe's interest in outdoor life was always an important factor in his happiness. In September, 1906, he went with a friend to Algonquin Park, in Canada, for two weeks of fishing in an unbroken forest dotted with lakes which swarmed with speckled and salmon trout. With John Daniels, a kindred spirit, he took several long tramps, one of which Daniels wrote up in detail for the Springfield *Republican*. They left Boston on August 2, 1907, spent nineteen days on the trip, and covered approximately 275 miles. They wore knickerbockers and coats of waterproof canvas material, stout shoes, soft shirts, and ancient felt hats, taking no luggage except what could be stowed away in their coats—soap, toilet articles, road maps, flashlights, and adhesive tape.

Before setting out from Concord, New Hampshire, to which they had proceeded by train, they weighed themselves, for Eastman wanted to lose several pounds. They walked from there to Salisbury, where Eastman paused to explore the homes and graves of his ancestors, stopped for the night at an inn in Franklin—where they went through "a vexatious and humiliating blister period," with their sore feet wrapped in bandages—and then when the pain was mitigated, moved on to Center Harbor and Chocorua, where they climbed that steep and fascinating peak. In Bartlett, which they reached at the end of the first week, the scales indicated that Eastman had gained twelve pounds. They ascended Mount Washington by the ten-mile bridle path, walked along the Presidential Range, and then turned west to the Profile House and Littleton. It was hard going through the Vermont Hills, and Daniels wrote: "Though your weariness tells you you've gone ten miles, your common sense forces you to admit you've gone but one. And you get thirsty and irritable, and willing to follow any road in sight, no matter in what direction it may lead." When they reached Montpelier and registered at the hotel, a quiet old gentleman, shocked by their rough and tattered appearance, exclaimd "Oh!" and drew away shuddering. They climbed Mount Hunger and Mount Mansfield—coming down in the midst of a fog—and ultimately arrived, rather ragged and weary, at Burlington, where they took the train for Boston. Eastman had gained two pounds, and Daniels had lost four.

Joe and "Bob" Bottomly, in 1908, covered the distance from Amherst to Livingston Manor, in the Catskills, making 32 miles on the last day. During most of the trip they moved steadily along, up hill and down, stopping only briefly for light lunches and often sleeping like tramps in haymows. Eastman came back, so he reported, "tanned but not even tired."

At some point during this period he acquired a competent secretary, and his correspondence after 1909 was carefully typed and decently filed. His salary continued microscopic, and he was forced occasionally to borrow from his Amherst friends small sums—which he scrupulously repaid. Meanwhile several of them had moved into more lucrative occupations. Whitcomb, after studying law for a year, had entered a bank in New York City, and Bale had followed him there a year later. Bottomly had started to practice law, and Rounseville had hung out his sign as a physician. It looked as if Eastman, with certainly no less ability, was to be stranded in the Public Franchise Commission office.

Early in January, 1912, Whitcomb, who had by then returned

to Amherst as vice-president of the local bank, had a talk with Joe and, with the best of intentions, urged him to break loose from the League and accept a position more worthy of his talents. The advice evidently got under Eastman's skin, for he replied to Whitcomb, on January 23, in one of his most self-revelatory letters.

Just a word on another subject. As I told you last night, I very much appreciate your solicitude for my welfare. I confess that, if you were another man, I should be a little irritated by your attitude; but I know you, and I value very much what I realize is the basis of the situation. But it makes me uneasy to know that my friends are worrying about me. There is no reason why they should worry. I do not want them to worry.

Let me disabuse your mind on one or two points. I am not lazy, or shiftless. I have not fallen into a rut. I think I know what I am about, and I have plenty of faith in myself. I have worked hard on some very difficult jobs, and I believe that I have now and then accomplished something. I do not look back on the last few years with any regret. I enclose copies of two letters which may throw light, perhaps, on some of these statements.

I don't want you to fall into the bad habit of measuring all men with the same yardstick. Please don't fall into the error of judging men by the amount of money they are making. That error is responsible for a great deal of unnecessary trouble in this world. Don't grow too conservative. Remember that the liberal ideas of yesterday are often the conservative ideas of to-day. That has always been so. Don't attach too much importance to any one clique, or to the opinions of a man because he happens to have power and money. Keep your eyes open, read the gospel now and then, and cultivate the widest possible sympathy with all sorts and conditions of people.

A few weeks later, dwelling again on the same subject, Joe sent Whitcomb a further letter of amplification and explanation.

When I spoke to you of your being conservative, I intended no slam. I have no objection to conservatism. In fact, I am naturally very conservative myself. All I meant was this. I am intensely interested in the question of government and its science. In my opinion we are going to see great progress in that science in the next twenty years or so. There is no question more important to the people of this country. It is the custom to sneer at reformers, but every good business man is a reformer in his own business. That is, he is always looking for improvements. Of course there is room for improvement in government, and a great deal of room, too. While I do not always agree with the so-called Progressives, I believe that they represent a very healthy movement. The man who is satisfied with himself usually doesn't amount to much, and the same rule applies to peoples. A so-called 'muck-raker,' who states facts, is a mighty useful citizen. We have got to know the facts before we can diagnose our ailments, and of course we have ailments. A 'muck-raker' who misrepresents facts, by the same token, is an undesirable citizen. The conservatism which I object to is the conservatism which hasn't an open mind, the 'stand-pat' variety, which believes that the founders of our government were omniscient, and that wisdom died with them.

This frank statement of his philosophy indicates that Eastman, not yet thirty, had been doing some very well-directed thinking and was not to be diverted from his course by criticism. As a matter of fact, events were shortly to take a turn which would relieve his friends of any anxiety about his worldly success.

V

Transition to Power

From 1905 until 1913, when Charles S. Mellen, under fire, resigned as president of the Boston & Maine and the New Haven railroads, Louis D. Brandeis was engaged in almost constant battle with him and the interests which he represented. Here, again, the story has been well told from the Brandeis viewpoint in certain chapters of Professor Mason's biography, where it may be read in full and graphic detail. When he learned of the acquisition of the Boston & Maine by the New Haven, Brandeis realized the monopolistic implications and undertook on his own accord to do some investigation into motives. After many weeks of research, he finally, in 1907, published a pamphlet revealing many inconsistencies in the New Haven's accounting and announced his startling conclusion that "if the New Haven's solvency is to be maintained a large reduction in the dividend rate is inevitable." In a locality where New Haven stock had been regarded as gilt-edge, a conservative investment for trust funds and the support of widows and orphans, this statement spread consternation and put the railroad officials immediately on the defensive.

No evidence exists that Eastman had any share in the preparation of this extraordinary pamphlet. But as Brandeis became better acquainted with Joe and watched his work, he called on him for help. By this time Brandeis had stirred up a nest of angry hornets, and the attacks made upon him by the New Haven and its defenders were unscrupulous and unceasing. Gradually Eastman became involved in the wrangle, although usually behind the scenes, and learned how to read a railroad balance sheet with an appraising eye.

Largely as a consequence of Brandeis's arguments, in 1908 the Massachusetts Supreme Court sustained a decree requiring the New Haven to dispose at once of its network of trolley lines. A few weeks later a bill was introduced in the General Court at Brandeis's instigation compelling the New Haven to sell its Boston & Maine stock. But the counter strategy of the New Haven attorneys frustrated for the moment all Brandeis's plans. A bill suggested by Governor Eben S. Draper created a holding company for the sole purpose of permitting the New Haven to acquire the stock of the Boston & Maine and was pushed rapidly through the General Court in 1909. Meanwhile, the New Haven carried on a vigorous publicity campaign through every available channel, questioning Brandeis's motives and attempting to tear his private and professional character to shreds.

Brandeis, however, proved to be an accurate prognosticator. When New Haven stock slumped badly in 1911, he persuaded Charles A. Prouty, one of the most vigorous members of the Interstate Commerce Commission, to open an investigation of the financial state of the road. He then asked Eastman to assist him in preparing a brief to be submitted to the commission. During the autumn of 1912 and until the following spring, Eastman worked in Brandeis's office and under his supervision, assembling material for his argument. He even spent three weeks in Washington examining some of the records available in the commission files, and he met three or four of the members, although, as he wrote, "They didn't pay much attention to an obscure clerk from Yankeeland!"

In its final form Eastman's brief was submitted to the commission on May 15, 1913, and was shortly published as a 126-page pamphlet under the uninspiring title "Re Investigation of New England Railroads." His name was the only one to appear on the title page, and he accepted full responsibility for the contents. Within a week after the arguments before the commission closed, the New Haven reduced its dividend rate from 8 percent to 6 percent. The Report of the Interstate Commerce Commission on July 9 recommended certain drastic changes in operation essential to a restoration of the New Haven and the Boston & Maine to prosperity. It was not long before Mellen, having lost the confidence of the stockholders and of the public, resigned both his presidencies, and Howard Elliott was elected in his place.

The aftermath vindicated Brandeis in every allegation he had made. The Massachusetts Public Service Commission revealed that New Haven officials had expended almost $350,000 in six months for lobbying purposes alone. On December 18, 1913, the directors were forced, for the first time in forty years, to pass a dividend. The final Interstate Commerce Commission *Report* presented what was described as an amazing narrative of "reckless and profligate" management; and on August 14, 1914, the monopoly was legally dismembered. To the end of his days Eastman insisted that the management of the New Haven had been stupid and even corrupt, as well as indifferent to the public welfare. The revelations about the extraordinary bookkeeping of the company were not persecution, but a sincere attempt to protect investors and promote justice.

It was a memorable and picturesque fight, which aroused tremendous animosities and led to bitter feeling. Brandeis had the tenacity of a bulldog that never lets go once his teeth are fastened. Mellen was stubborn and resourceful. But Brandeis had the facts on his side, and although defeated occasionally in minor skirmishes, he was always certain that the truth would prevail.

For Eastman, this battle was a very important stage in his education. As Brandeis's trusted aide, he carried on researches, made digests of documents, and performed the countless useful services which a conscientious and loyal subordinate can do for a stimulating master. The letters of this period, confirming the recollections of those who were in touch with his activities, indicate that he had become an expert in his knowledge of political maneuvers. He made it his business to become acquainted with every member of the General Court, and night after night he and Frank Livingstone would discuss the background, the susceptibilities, the secret ambitions, of each Senator and Representative. He was fully aware of the intrigues which take place in smoke-filled corridors and committee rooms, unreported by the press. In short, he was well known on Beacon Hill.

At thirty, Joe had reached the point when offers of various kinds were sure to come his way. Something of what was going on may be gathered from a letter which he wrote to his friend, Whitcomb, on June 17, 1912.

There was no deal with Governor Foss to appoint me on the Public Service Commission. He did offer to make me Secretary at $5000 per annum, but I told him I was not disposed to consider that. I could have got considerable backing, but I am not pulling any wires for political jobs and do not intend to. As a matter of fact, I think it very improbable that the politicians would allow me to secure such a position. Their hand is very strong in Massachusetts politics, even with Foss. As for the Public Service Commission, I never stood a chance. The Republicans had the Legislature, and they weren't going to give him the opportunity for appointments of that kind. This session has been very interesting. The Elevated outfit has been fighting Mellen. I look for his retirement before the year is out, and a proposition to put the Boston & Maine in independent hands. It is a crime the way the Legislature is pulled and hauled by private interests.

Quite apart from the solicitude of his friends, Eastman was becoming restless in his job as secretary of the Public Franchise League. His special work under Brandeis had been fascinating and important, but that was now completed, and he did not wish to be mired in a rut. In the summer of 1913, therefore, he notified the League that, while he was willing to maintain the office and be on hand to deal with any pressing matter, he wanted to complete his studies for his law degree. He went back to Pottsville for a short vacation, but on his return was approached by the Boston Carmen's Union to act as one of its counsel in connection with wage arbitration.

The union leader had gone to Brandeis and asked him to recommend a man competent to investigate the intricate financial questions involved. "I'll name a man for you if you'll let me fix his compensation," answered Brandeis. "Why do you want to do that?" "Because he doesn't know his own value well enough to fix a proper compensation for himself," returned Brandeis. The arrangement was made, and Brandeis set the fee, which was far higher than Eastman would have thought of asking. Although he was not a member of the bar, he was interested in this type of work and was complimented by the offer. Accordingly, he once more abandoned his legal aspirations—this time permanently—and spent the autumn of 1913 in preparing, with Fred Fay and John P. Feeney, a brief to be submitted to the Board of Arbitration. Because of his knowledge and experience, the other two left the actual writing of the document in his reliable hands.

The Boston Elevated Railroad, from its incorporation in 1897 until 1912, had no labor union. Early in that year the Amalgamated Association of Street and Electric Railway Employees of America succeeded in organizing the carmen, and after a strike during the summer, gained recognition of its union. By the opening of 1913 more than 7,200 employees were enrolled. It was not long before the union petitioned for a broad advance in wages and the Elevated management agreed to submit the matter to arbitration. At this stage Eastman was engaged to help.

After summarizing the early history of the company's relations with its men, Eastman made a dispassionate analysis of the different types of workers, following this with specific recommendations as to wage increases in each group. Much testimony was presented from employees as to the kind of work they did—its arduousness, its fatiguing aspects, its required skills, its duties and responsibilities —and the qualifications each must possess. The evidence indicated that a motorman had to concentrate on his task much as does a surgeon when performing a delicate operation in which a human life hangs in the balance. Eastman's basic thesis boiled down to a very simple proposition—higher pay for more difficult and dangerous work. He pointed out, for example, that motormen and conductors are the lifeblood of the company—indeed "they *are* the Company, when on duty." Although the brief contains some rather technical paragraphs, it is still good reading. No unprejudiced outsider can fail to conclude that the union had a strong case.

The arbitrators thought so too. They included three excellent men: James J. Storrow, a partner in Lee, Higginson & Company and a banker of high character, whose path was to cross Eastman's many times; James L. Richards, representing the Boston Elevated management; and James H. Vahey, for the union. It was their unanimous verdict "that the men have made out a case establishing their right to an increase in pay"; and their award, given on January 15, 1914, provided for wage increases all along the line. On one or two controversial points they were not inclined to make concessions. The union made an appeal for the abolition of piecework, on the ground that the existing policy tempted employees to overdo and thus endanger their health. The arbitrators responded, "We do not think it wise to abolish the limited amount of this class of work being carried on in the Company's shops." They also refused to grant "unlimited free transportation" to all employees when off duty, pointing out that "public opinion to-day, enforced by the legislature and the courts, demands that all elements of discrimination be eliminated by the public service corporation."

This case profoundly affected Eastman's views regarding labor unions and their policy makers. Woods and Brandeis had strengthened the liberal philosophy which he had formed in college. Now he saw the officers of the union grow in power and ability almost overnight as responsibility was placed on them. Before the discussions were over they were able to meet and deal with some of the most influential corporation lawyers in Boston on even terms, with the utmost self-reliance and dignity. To Joe labor seemed to be the "under dog" and as such aroused his sympathy. The hour was to come, however, when his sense of justice led him to emphasize with equal vigor the rights of capital—and then, to his sorrow, his union friends turned against him.

Eastman received commendation on all sides for his share in the preparation of a document which was in some respects epoch-making. James H. Vahey generously gave him credit for almost the entire financial, economic, and statistical portions of the argument, and praised him for his clear and audacious thinking. Storrow reported in State Street that Joe was "a bright young fellow." In a few months Eastman went still further in a brief which he drafted, with his previous associate Fred Fay, for Union Division 600 against the Middlesex & Boston Street Railway Company. The method was like that of the Boston Elevated argument, but Eastman was now more sure of himself and endeavored in the manner of Brandeis to establish fundamental principles in the relationship of company to employees. Moving from the immediate issue into a broader field, he made a sweeping attack on the management and practices of the Middlesex & Boston, particularly for paying unearned dividends and thus wiping out every cent of surplus which the subsidiary companies had accumulated. He maintained further that the financial condition of the company should be immaterial to the question of fixing fair compensation, but that wages, under any circumstances, should be sufficient to enable a man to support his family in health and comfort and to build up an adequate provision for his old age. He also insisted that additional compensation should be paid for work requiring more than eight hours per day or six days per week. All these policies are now commonplaces, but they were daring in 1913. The conclusion reached by Eastman and Fay was, "The wages which the Union demands are fair and reasonable and not so high, in reality, as the character of the work would justify."

Meanwhile Eastman's increasing interest in railroads had led him to write an article which appeared in the *Quarterly Journal of Economics* for August, 1913, entitled "The Massachusetts Public Service Commission." As far back as 1869, the Commonwealth of Massachusetts had led the other states in establishing a Board of Railroad Commissioners, which, under the chairmanship of Charles Francis Adams, an expert on transportation and a man of energy, probity, and persistence, became a model of its kind. After Adams's resignation, in 1879, however, the board lost much of its vigor and settled back into a routine tolerance of current railroad methods. In 1913 the so-called Washburn Bill met a popular demand by creating a new and quite different body, superseding the Board of Railroad Commissioners and called the Public Service Commission of Massachusetts. It was this commission that Eastman described in his brief article.

The establishment of this Public Service Commission was part of a comprehensive plan conceived by some thoughtful citizens, including Brandeis, for curbing the piratical tactics of the New Haven Railroad. When Governor Eugene N. Foss took office, in 1910, he sensed at once the popular indignation over the arrogant attitude of many public utilities, and decided to press for investigation and reform. During his first two terms a reactionary legislature blocked all his well-laid projects; but when he was elected for the third time, public opinion could no longer be thwarted, and the opposition dwindled. At this moment the shrewd railroad managers suddenly discovered the advisability of making concessions and accordingly approved the idea of a strengthened commission, with greater regulatory powers. They did, however, suggest a *quid pro quo*, asking in return for their consent that they be allowed to issue long term notes, unsecured by mortgage, up to twice the amount of their valuation. This demand, closely resembling blackmail, so much irritated the governor that after the measure had passed in this form, he vetoed it, explaining that he did not propose to have the Commonwealth made the victim of a "hold-up game." He asked caustically: "Is Massachusetts ready to purchase from the railroads the right to enact this law?" The bill was passed over his veto; and Eastman, who knew what was happening behind the scenes, concluded that it could not have become law without the financial sections so much desired by the railroads.

This story, in both its discouraging and its gratifying aspects, Eastman reviewed in his article. He closed by saying:

The experience of Massachusetts in the next few years will go far to determine whether or not public regulation can make private monopoly on a large scale endurable, whether such regulation is likely to become a permanent feature in the scheme of government of this country or to prove but a temporary expedient paving the way for actual public ownership of all monopolies.

This, so far as I can discover, is Eastman's earliest hint that he was dallying with the idea of the public ownership and control of railroads. He was to do plenty of thinking on the subject as his horizon broadened.

On paper at least, the new Public Service Commission had plenty of authority. It could issue positive orders on railroad rates. It could force the companies to produce books, orders, and documents. They had to file with the commission printed schedules of all their rates and charges, and could not depart from them. The commission could employ such legal, expert, and other assistance as it deemed best, provided that it did not exceed the annual appropriation of the legislature. It could also petition the Interstate Commerce Commission for relief if any common carrier was, in its opinion, violating the Interstate Commerce Act. Furthermore the commission was given jurisdiction over telephone and telegraph companies, in addition to the companies formerly under the jurisdiction of the Board of Railroad Commissioners.

Eastman's name was brought more than once to Governor Foss's attention as a desirable member of the new commission, but he was viewed with suspicion by some of the governor's intimate advisers, and when the nominations were made, he was ignored. The chairman was Frederick J. McLeod, of Cambridge, and the other four were George W. Anderson, of Boston—whose career was to be rather strangely connected with Eastman's—Everett E. Stone, of Springfield, Clinton White, of Melrose, and George W. Bishop, of Newtonville. Charles E. Mann, of Malden, was appointed to the position of Executive Secretary—the office which Eastman had refused. Quarters were assigned to the commission at 1 Beacon Street, around the corner from the State House, and it began to function on July 1, 1913, when the law became effective.

As we have seen, it would have been difficult then, and indeed at any time, to clarify Eastman's party relationship. At the moment he was, strictly speaking, a "Progressive," having voted for "T.R." in 1912, but this was an ephemeral affiliation. No information is available as to whether he voted for Foss for governor. Since leaving college he had, of course, moved somewhat to the "left," and some of his Republican acquaintances taunted him with being a "radical." The truth is that he was not much concerned with party orthodoxy, but was willing to support any platform which was clearly for the public interest.

As to his alleged "radicalism," it was largely the result of disillusionment. In an unpublished article headed "Boston and the London Sliding Scale," written about 1908, he commented bitterly on the situation as he had seen it on Beacon Hill.

For a long time now it has been the custom for public service corporations in the City of Boston to employ a small band of professional lobbyists, for the most part the same men, who loaf around the State House, act as spies, gather exact information as to what is going on, and bring influence to bear on approachable members. It has been considered that this is a necessary protection for corporations against the strong influence of popular prejudice. . . . At the present time, and for many years past, the so-called "lobby" has been the bane of politics, as in other States. The "lobby" is a red rag to the public. It breeds suspicion, distrust, and discontent; its presence is an open bid for the

introduction of "strike" bills in the Legislature, and the lobbyists themselves have been known to cooperate in their introduction; it is a direct
invitation to dishonest men to enter politics instead of practising their
crookedness in other fields; it is the one great influence which leads
corporations to meddle in the field of politics.

These are the words of an honest man, brought up in a religious
home to have a trust in human nature, who perceives to his astonishment that there are selfishness and trickery in the world. His
reaction was natural and entirely to his credit.

The newly constituted Public Service Commission gratified
Eastman by the stand which they took. In their first *Annual Report,*
they were stinging in their comments on the New England situation.

The just feeling of dissatisfaction with existing conditions of transportation in this Commonwealth, referred to in the last report of the
railroad commissioners, continues. The destructive results of the policy
of monopoly, waste, and other forms of mismanagement have become
obvious in the decreasing market value of the securities of our leading
railroads. The American people are now trying the experiment of
having their great highways, the railroads, privately owned and managed and publicly regulated.

In their *Second Report,* published in January, 1915, they commented on the agreed decree entered on October 17, 1914, in the
United States District Court, providing for the separation of the
New Haven from the Boston & Maine: "By this action the recommendations of the Commission in its last annual report have been
made effective, and the whole scheme for the monopoly of the
transportation facilities of New England, in defiance of public
morals, has come to an inglorious end."

Meanwhile, a great change had taken place in Eastman's plans for
the future. In the growth of most men are periods when they
undergo a process of acceleration—when after lying fallow for
months or years they suddenly become productive. A scientist, for
example, carries on his arduous research unnoticed and in obscurity and then presents his discoveries, after which medals and
honorary degrees descend upon him. About 1912, Eastman, forti-
fied by minor successes, acquired self-confidence and became more

sure of his ability to persuade others. He had received from his elders that commendation which means so much to the morale of a young man. People were talking about him in Boston as "a fellow who will be heard from some day." He had no thought of running for elective office, but he was ripe for any responsibility which would test his powers.

Such was Joe's mood when, in October, 1914, George W. Anderson resigned from the Public Service Commission to accept an appointment as United States District Attorney for Massachusetts. The governor was David I. Walsh, an organization Democrat, but a man of liberal tendencies, at least in those days. Anderson himself suggested Eastman to the governor as his successor, and this recommendation was supported by Louis D. Brandeis, who had Walsh's ear. When Ernest M. Whitcomb wrote Eastman, November 16, 1914, to ask whether he could help him, the latter replied:

Thank you very much for the offer of help in the Public Service Commission matter. I do not expect to get the job, nor have I made any particular effort to get it. Such support as I have received has come without any solicitation on my part, and I have been surprised and gratified that there has been as much as there has been. If you or any other of my Amherst friends want to write the Governor, it would do no harm and might do some good. If I am appointed at all, it will be a non-partisan appointment, and Republican support is as valuable to me, in a way, as Democratic. While I am a strong supporter of Wilson's, I make no pretense of being a party Democrat. I prefer to be considered an Independent in politics, and usually split my vote pretty extensively. If I am not appointed, the opposition of machine Democrats and corporation Republicans will have as much to do with it as anything.

In writing to Whitcomb again, on December 6, Eastman made an even fuller analysis of the situation as he saw it.

There seems little chance of my appointment. The Governor informed a friend yesterday that, while he considered me particularly well qualified for the job, the opposition to me was tremendous. My appointment, he said, would keep him on the defensive for six months. The charge against me is that I am destructive, unjudicial, etc., and it comes from a solid array of all the financial interests in Boston. I am quite flattered that they should think me capable of such harm as one member of a Board where I would be surrounded by four other men to whom, it seems, they have no objection. I had no idea that I possessed such persuasiveness and force. Another strange thing is that the charge against me is so general. In the past ten years I have argued a great many matters in which public service corporations were involved. So far as I know, they do not make specific indictments against me; they do not say I was unfair in this or that statement; yet my remarks on all these occasions were taken down by stenographers and are in their possession. Under the circumstances, it would be easy to become incensed and embittered, but fortunately I am not so keenly anxious for this job and have, I think, still some lingering remnants of a sense of humor. Your great financier, accustomed to dominate and have his way in every little thing, is at times an "amoozin' little cuss."

Although Joe really wanted the place more than he was willing to admit, he was not ready to stoop to get it. Fortunately, however, Brandeis was persistent in his behalf, and the governor finally yielded to what was, after all, his own private inclination. Just after Christmas he sent in Eastman's name, and found rather to his surprise that protests were very few. Whitcomb wrote Eastman on New Year's Day:

Accept my earnest and hearty congratulations on your appointment to the Public Service Commission. While I don't agree with a lot of your crazy ideas, I will do you the justice of saying that I believe you are sincerely honest and will be open to conviction, and that is why I am glad to see you appointed. There are so many darned cheap, superficial, and insincere people in the public employ to-day that I think sooner or later we are going to run up against some real problems because of them.

To this candid note of congratulation Eastman made a reply in his usual modest fashion.

Until just before Christmas I had no expectation whatever of receiving the appointment, and I was as much surprised as any one could be when the talk began to swing my way. If the appointment is confirmed, I shall try to behave with due decorum as a Commissioner and hope that my ideas will not be as "crazy" as you seem to fear. Between ourselves, my bones feel a little shaky when I think of taking my seat up there.

In commenting on the appointment, Louis D. Brandeis wrote to Norman Hapgood:

Eastman is a man of ability, a hard worker, of high character, and fine public spirit. It is particularly gratifying that a man who has in all the time I have known him never shown the slightest thought of his own interest when that of the public was concerned, should have had the success of attaining at the age of thirty-three a position of distinction, with a very good salary. It ought to prove a great encouragement to others.

Stanley King wrote from London: "What a wonderful opportunity you have. I know you will show the damned old wiseacres on Beacon Hill what a young man can do with a big job. Strength to you!"

Eastman's entire circumstances now changed within a few weeks. His first step was to resign formally as secretary of the Public Franchise League. At that time the League owed Joe $446.26 and had in its coffers only $41.09. Several members, including Eastman himself, "chipped in" to meet the deficit; and on April 22, 1915, the treasurer, Charles F. Weed, reported, "The Public Franchise League is now free from debt"—and then immediately resigned. Its work had been done, and it was never resurrected.

Although Eastman's term of office on the commission expired on July 1, 1917—for he was filling out Anderson's original term of four years—he could still make his plans for a considerable period ahead. His new salary was $8,000 a year—an amount which gave him a financial freedom which he had not felt since leaving college, where his bills had been paid by his father. In the autumn of 1915 the Reverend John H. Eastman was ordered by his physician to resign his Pottsville pastorate; and Joe, now well able to maintain his family, made arrangements for him and Elizabeth to move to Winchester, an attractive Boston suburb, and settle down in a comfortable dwelling. From then until his death Miss Eastman made a home for her brother. He had his own library, his deep, overstuffed chair, and the tranquillizing domesticity which he had not been able to enjoy in his bachelor's quarters. He now became a commuter between Winchester and Boston, walking each morning from the South Station to his office on Beacon Street, a distance of about a mile.

Eastman already knew much about railroads, at any rate in New England, but now he was obliged to become a specialist. Three systems dominated that area: the Boston & Maine, the Boston & Albany, and the New York, New Haven & Hartford. Their total mileage was rather more than two thousand miles, and the cross country subsidiary lines, of which there were many, created a complicated situation. The commission's *Report* for 1914, before Eastman became a member, fills two massive and forbidding volumes, literally packed with statistics. Eastman undertook, with characteristic diligence, to assimilate and digest these figures, with the result that before he had been on the commission six months he was its best-informed member, as Charles Francis Adams had been on the previous Board of Railroad Commissioners. Most of Joe's time during the sweltering summer of 1915 was spent in acquainting himself with his duties. Besides the trunk lines, he had the various trolley and elevated systems to consider. Writing years later to Senator Norris, Eastman said: "When I was on the Massachusetts Commission, for the first three years more than half, I think, of our time was taken up with the trial of vexatious cases involving the service of the Boston Elevated Railroad System, which operates all the rapid transit and surface lines of Boston and vicinity."

Before he had been very long in office, Eastman became involved in the most complicated case of its kind that any Massachusetts commission had ever been called upon to settle. The Bay State Railway Company was the successor of 65 separate street railway companies which by gradual steps had been consolidated into a single corporation operating in all 951 miles of single track. In September, 1917, this company, as it had a legal right to do, notified the commission of a proposed increase in passenger fares, together with certain modifications of existing fare limits and transfer privileges, to take effect on November 1. It was estimated that these changes would yield an increase in passenger revenue of nearly $1,250,000, or about 14½ percent. On October 21 the commission, using its authority, suspended the application of the new schedule until May 1, 1916, pending hearings for the remonstrants.

Public hearings started on November 8, 1915, and closed on July 25, 1916, occupying sixty days in all. Eastman did not miss one of them. The Bay State Company operated in 85 cities and towns of the commonwealth, each of which was represented by counsel. Lawyers appeared from Abingdon and Andover, from Wilmington and Woburn, from Beverly and Haverhill and Lowell, protesting eloquently against any raise in rates. Again and again the company was described as a heartless and mercenary corporation, adding one more to the many burdens of the poor. The attorneys for the Bay State, on the other hand, asserted that it could not provide adequate service without additional revenue.

The *Report and Order* of the commission, issued under date of August 31, 1916, was drafted mainly by Eastman, and some of the broad principles laid down anticipate his later opinions on the Interstate Commerce Commission. Very early appeared a paragraph stating the philosophy which the Public Service Commission had agreed upon as its guide.

A public service corporation is, in a sense, an agent of the State, for it is performing a function which the State might well perform for itself. The duty of a supervising commission, broadly speaking, is to see that the corporation furnishes reasonable service and that it does not exact an unreasonable compensation. There are no mathematical formulas for determining what is reasonable; it is, in the main, a theoretical question. So long as the field is left to private enterprise, rates should be high enough to attract, under normal conditions, the capital necessary to assure the service for which there is a public need. The public should pay what is reasonably necessary to have the work well done, and it ought not to pay more.

The commission had for once to face squarely a question which Eastman was to meet again and again in his later career. The general rule laid down by court decisions had been that a public service corporation is entitled to a reasonable return upon the "fair value" of the property—but what is a "fair value"? Some had argued that the "reproduction cost" should be the determining factor. Others had urged the "original cost" as the only just criterion. At Eastman's insistence, the commission promptly adopted a rule already laid down in the Middlesex & Boston Case of the previous year—

"that under Massachusetts law capital honestly and prudently invested must, under normal conditions, be taken as the controlling factor in fixing the basis for computing fair and reasonable rates." Thus, Eastman committed himself to the "prudent investment" theory, of which we shall hear much more later.

The underlying weakness of the Bay State Company is not difficult to understand. The original error lay in the too hasty combination, on an equal basis, of all sorts and conditions of branch lines, without any adequate consideration of the fact that some of the older properties had suffered in capitalization and physical condition from the operations of plundering syndicates and that many of the newer ones were manifestly speculative in their nature and constructed in territory from which the hope of an early return was exceedingly small. The president of the Bay State admitted that the equipment had never been in a "normal" condition and that it had been allowed to deteriorate in a manner which was indefensible. Furthermore the company's counsel failed to satisfy the commission that costs could not be lowered through more efficient management. The conclusion reached by Eastman and his colleagues was that the company must expect temporarily to suspend dividends on its common stock and plow back its earnings into the property. This was a drastic prescription, but necessary if the future earning power of the system was to be placed upon a stable, long-term basis. To implement their recommendations, the commission ordered, "that the Bay State Street Railway Company be and is herewith notified and required to cancel the rates and charges of fare limits and transfer privileges stated in the schedule specified in said orders of suspension."

In March, 1916, the commission published its *Report* on the capital expenditures, investments, and existing contingent liabilities of the New York, New Haven & Hartford Railroad Company. It was actually a careful analysis, under Eastman's direction and encouragement, of the financial situation of that much embarrassed railroad. Here, again, the situation was not pleasant, for, as the commission stated, "The capital transactions of the New Haven Company . . . have been numerous, intricate, and confusing." The *Report*, with its various appendices, was printed in a volume of more than 300 pages and is a fine example of searching investigation and mastery of figures. The conclusions reached were summarized in three propositions: any great interstate railroad company ought to be confined, in general, to the railroad business; its corporate power ought to be carefully limited, with no gaps in the program of public regulation; and its corporate structure ought to be simple and easily understood. Finally the commission submitted to the General Court a plan for putting the New Haven on a stricter business basis and, to use their own phraseology, for "adjusting the relations between the Commonwealth and the New Haven Company." All this was old stuff to Eastman, who had threshed it out while working for Brandeis; but now he was in a position where he could speak with more authority.

It would not be altogether accurate to say that Eastman determined the policies of the commission, for his fellow members were competent, and their working creed had been determined before he took his seat with them. They did welcome him, however, because of his knowledge, his prestige, and his almost limitless capacity for what most people would have called sheer drudgery. From his college mathematical accomplishment it could never have been predicted that he would develop a passion for columns of figures; but in his study of railroads he had become a statistical fiend, able to detect with unerring eye any noteworthy discrepancy in accounts. His complete devotion to his job gave him an advantage over his colleagues and even over the astute attorneys for corporations, who discovered, usually too late, that he knew more about their affairs than they did.

The year 1917 was a war year, and most Americans forgot domestic perplexities in their desire to build up our production and send an army as soon as possible overseas. In the spring, as Eastman's term on the Public Service Commission was running out, Governor Samuel W. McCall, a Republican, had to face the question of his reappointment. This time, however, no opposition from Eastman's earlier critics was audible, and his ability was conceded. McCall did have some doubt as to Joe's devotion to Republican principles—which he may well have had, considering that Eastman had been originally placed in office by a Democratic governor.

But Calvin Coolidge, then lieutenant-governor, testified as to Joe's competence and assured McCall that he was no violent partisan in the other camp. So it was that without any excitement in the press or anywhere else Eastman was appointed and confirmed for a second term, beginning on July 1, 1917.

State commissioners are as gregarious as other public officials, and Eastman soon took an active part in their national conventions. At one of the first meetings of this kind, in 1916, in Chicago, he came to know such men as Clifford Thorne, Milo Maltbie, and Charles Elmquist, and was chiefly responsible for arranging to have the state commissions represented by a solicitor in Washington. The person selected was Clyde B. Aitchison, then chairman of the Public Service Commission of Oregon, who courageously accepted the formidable title of General Solicitor of the National Association of Railway and Utilities Commissioners. Within a year, by President Wilson's appointment, Aitchison became an Interstate Commerce Commissioner.

As he became better known, Eastman served on several committees of national scope, including the Special Reconstruction Committee and the Valuation Committee. One of his significant projects was his effort to secure fuller cooperation between the state commissions and the United States Railroad Administration, mainly with the aim of protecting their authority. He participated in 1918 in the first joint hearing of the state commissions with the Interstate Commerce Commission, sitting on the New England Rate Case with other members of the New England state commissions in the jury box in the old federal courtroom in Boston, with George W. Anderson, now Interstate Commerce Commissioner, on the bench.

Eastman now had an opportunity to measure himself against transportation experts from other sections, and the danger that he might lapse into provincialism was passing. On his excursions to Washington he learned much about the Interstate Commerce Commission, its personnel, and its powers. He found that he was under no disadvantage in arguing with leaders outside of New England. It was an important moment in his development when he realized that others were seeking his advice as often as he sought theirs. Actually he was getting more recognition than he, in his modesty, was aware of. After all, he had been well trained under Woods and Brandeis.

Eastman was troubled, as the war went on, by the fact that he was having no share in military activities. In September, 1918, through the intervention of a friend, Max Thelen, he received from General Goethals notification that he had been named as one of three members of the Board of Contract Adjustment, with the rank of lieutenant-colonel. He promptly declined, stating that he had just been placed by his local draft board, in Winchester, in Class I-A and that when he was mustered into the army he would go where he was assigned. He added that in his opinion there were many older men, not eligible for military service, who could fill the offered position as well as he. Thelen got busy very quickly, and soon Eastman was informed by the local board that orders had been received to induct him into service in the Purchase, Storage, and Traffic Division. Again, as he was entitled to do, he indicated his declination, but added that if the Government still thought that he could help best in this capacity, he would prefer to do it as a civilian. Thelen, somewhat annoyed, replied that the members of the board had to be commissioned, and there the matter rested when Armistice Day arrived. It would appear that in this perplexing situation Eastman was letting his conscience be his guide. He was anxious to do his duty where he could be of the most value. Even in a private's uniform he would have been a good public servant.

Throughout these years Eastman's acquaintance and outlook were broadening. With his increased income he was able to join social clubs, and he once more resumed tennis as a recreation. Conservative bankers and industrialists who met him at dinners discovered to their astonishment that he did not really have horns and a tail and that he was a convivial addition to any company. In short he was on his way to becoming one of the Solid Men of Boston, lauded by Daniel Webster. Then, quite unexpectedly, just as the war was closing, came a chance to widen his circle even further.

VI

From State to Nation

THE STORY of Joseph B. Eastman's appointment to the Interstate Commerce Commission shows how an older person's sponsorship can at a doubtful moment determine the course of a promising younger man's career. Mr. Justice Holmes had a genius for selecting as his secretaries ambitious law school graduates who turned out to be sound jurists and administrators. Louis D. Brandeis was also a good picker. Perceiving early the outstanding qualities and potentialities of Felix Frankfurter, Joseph B. Eastman, and several others, he did his best to place them where they would be most effective. In Eastman's case he was behind the scenes, saying just the right word at just the right time to make it decisive.

Brandeis was the more sympathetic with his juniors because of his own painful experience. On January 28, 1916, President Wilson appointed him Associate Justice of the Supreme Court to succeed Justice Joseph L. Lamar, who had died a few weeks earlier. The reaction against this nomination was spontaneous, nation-wide, and violent. Protests were voiced from many quarters, including a group of fifty-five Proper Bostonians, headed by Charles Francis Adams and A. Lawrence Lowell. Naturally, all the railroad men and financiers whom Brandeis had assailed were among those who raised objections. There was an under-cover campaign because of his race, but openly his critics declared that he was temperamentally unfit for a high judicial position, and it was asserted that his reputation as a lawyer was such that he did not enjoy "the confidence of the people." Even a number of former presidents of the American Bar Association, including William H. Taft, Elihu Root, Joseph H. Choate, Moorfield Storey, and others of hardly less distinction, expressed the opinion that "taking into view the reputation, character, and professional career of Mr. Louis D. Brandeis, he is not a fit per-

JOSEPH B. EASTMAN AT THE AGE OF
THREE YEARS AND EIGHT MONTHS

THE FIRST PRESBYTERIAN CHURCH IN KATONAH, NEW YORK
WHERE EASTMAN'S FATHER WAS MINISTER

son to be a member of the Supreme Court of the United States." Eastman, of course, was on the other side, but found himself, not for the first time, butting his head against the rigid wall of Boston conservatism.

A Senate subcommittee sat during the spring listening to the evidence, which was obviously prejudiced and frequently acrimonious. Finally the President took the unusual step of writing a letter defending his choice. After confirmation had been held up for five months, the Senate Judiciary Committee voted, ten to eight, in Brandeis's favor, and his nomination was shortly confirmed in the Senate by 47 votes to 22.

When Brandeis took his oath of office, on June 5, 1916, he moved from his New England environment to a broader field, but his potent influence continued to operate in Massachusetts. He still kept in touch with Boston, following with approval what Eastman was doing on the Public Service Commission. In 1914, when Fayette B. Dow came to Washington as Attorney-Examiner for the Interstate Commerce Commission, he had a talk with Brandeis—who was then acting as special counsel in the famous *Five per cent Case*—about their mutual friend, Eastman. It was at that time that Brandeis made the statement, often since quoted, "Joe Eastman has more interest in the public service and less in his own career than any man I have ever known."

In November, 1918, George W. Anderson, whose place Eastman had taken on the Massachusetts Public Service Commission, resigned from the Interstate Commerce Commission to accept an appointment on the United States Court of Appeals, and it was natural for Brandeis to think at once of Eastman, another New Englander, and to recommend him to Wilson as a suitable candidate. The President's confidence in Brandeis had been strengthened by the dignified manner in which the latter had conducted himself while he was being unfairly denounced; and at a period when most of Wilson's attention had to be devoted to international issues, he was glad to have this domestic problem so easily solved. Some powerful labor groups, headed by the Brotherhood of Railroad Trainmen, promptly added their approval, and several of Eastman's friends on the state commissions rushed to his support with letters to the White House.

In 1918 Eastman was far from unknown in Washington. In the spring he had been one of a party of thirty state commissioners who had gone to White Sulphur Springs to confer with Director-General McAdoo. To his cousin, Margaret I. King, he wrote:

Washington I am sure I shall like. It isn't a strange country, you know, for I have been down there a dozen times in the last year, and once I stayed there three weeks. . . . What I like most about Washington is that there is such a mixture of all sorts of people,—most of them interesting. I have greatly enjoyed serving on committees of the National Association of Railroad Commissioners and meeting men from all over the country.

Nevertheless, although Eastman was certainly not obscure, Brandeis was taking no chances. Accordingly, with the idea of gaining the backing of the commission itself, he asked Robert W. Woolley, one of the more liberal members, to call on Eastman in Boston and look him over to see whether, as he expressed it, the latter was the type of man "who might be appointed to some administrative post in the capital." Woolley, a Kentucky Democrat, went to Massachusetts for a conference with Eastman, with only a vague suspicion of Brandeis's beneficent conspiracy. Nor did Eastman himself attach much importance to the incident. Although Woolley was eleven years older and a loyal Southerner, the two men took to one another at once; and in making his report, Woolley offered a glowing description of Eastman's personality and ability. Indeed, he announced to Brandeis and also to his fellow commissioners: "That Eastman up in Boston is one of the most remarkable men I ever met!" This, of course, was no news to Brandeis.

The story of how Eastman explained to Senator Lodge that he was not affiliated with any political party has already been recounted. Lodge was at first rather disconcerted at Eastman's independence, but after some investigation he found that the latter had the support of some cautious Massachusetts business leaders whose wishes he could not disregard. He could doubtless have blocked the appointment, but did not choose to do so; accordingly, Wilson sent in Eastman's name to the Senate on December 19, 1918, and he was confirmed on January 24, 1919, in routine fashion and without open discussion. Eastman had himself some doubt as to whether he would be acceptable. As late as January 15, 1919, he wrote his cousin: "As you see, I am still hanging around Boston, waiting for the Senate to act. It wouldn't surprise me if complications arose, but so far as my information goes, no opposition has shown up yet."

It was slightly astonishing that a man who had been so widely denounced in Massachusetts as a "radical" should have been regarded in the national capital as innocuous, and especially in view of the squabble over Brandeis and Eastman's well-known relationship to him. It is true that a position on the Interstate Commerce Commission was not regarded as so important as one on the Supreme Bench. Furthermore, the mind of the country was in early 1919 focused on the Armistice and the events following it. It could have been pointed out, however, that Brandeis and Eastman were substantially in agreement on most public questions and that one was just as dangerous as the other, seen through conservative glasses.

On March 22, 1919, nearly two months after he had been approved and taken his seat, Eastman wrote a letter to the President in longhand, as follows:

I want you to know my deep appreciation of the confidence you reposed in me by appointing me a member of this Commission. You may be sure that I shall do my best to be worthy of it and to administer the office in the public interest.

This letter will, I fear, seem somewhat belated, but I refrained from writing before because of your absence abroad and the feeling that even a note like this would be an additional and unnecessary burden. One who knows better than I, however, assures me to the contrary.

I have, I think, some faint realization of the load you are carrying. Permit me to say, also, that I believe you are struggling bravely and wisely to serve the best interests of mankind, that this is now appreciated by the mass of the people, and that it will be even more generally appreciated when history is written.

To this note President Wilson replied from Paris, a few weeks later:

Thank you very much indeed for your letter. You may be sure that I welcomed an opportunity to give you an evidence of my confidence in you. Although I have not personally come into contact with your work, I have repeatedly learned of it and am sure that you will repeat in your present position the successes of the position which you have just held.

Joseph B. Eastman was now on the national stage, where he was to remain until his death, a quarter of a century later, a member of what has been called by Robert V. Fletcher "the most powerful body in the world, administrative or otherwise." No doubt this is an exaggerated estimate; but the Interstate Commerce Commission has often been described as almost a model instrument for its purposes. Its history has been written *in extenso* up to 1937 by Professor I. L. Sharfman, and any examination of its origins, evolution, and accomplishment must necessarily be based on his five scholarly and comprehensive volumes. Of all its personnel, Eastman has been the one most frequently quoted, and by common consent he is regarded as having been its ablest member.

The Interstate Commerce Commission, created by a Congressional Act of February 4, 1887, during the Democratic administration of President Grover Cleveland, was the consequence of a widespread revolt against a situation which had become intolerable, and was the first effective attempt to assert Congressional control over unscrupulous methods in private transportation. For half a century, as pioneers steered their way across the continent, carriers had been encouraged by extensive land grants and even by cash subsidies from a sympathetic government, and had then been left free to do as they pleased without interference. The story of the resulting iniquities has often been told, sometimes sensationally and seldom without picturesque embellishment. Senseless and destructive competition, irresponsible speculation, and financial manipulation of the type censured by Charles Francis Adams in his book *Some Chapters of Erie*, gross abuses in the fixing of rates—all these had by the 1880's aroused resentment, first shown in state legislatures in the Middle West and eventually stirred to the boiling point by the report of the Cullom Committee, which in 1886 brought under more intensive scrutiny the sinister aspects of uncontrolled railroad competition. The Interstate Commerce Act, although frankly experimental and obviously tentative, was designed to extend Federal authority in a field over which it had hitherto claimed little domination. The authors of the measure builded better than they knew, even though parts of their philosophy did not stand the test of later experience. It was ironic, for example, that the monopoly regarded as sinful in the 1890's was to seem unobjectionable, even desirable, to the generation following World War I.

The powers invested in the commission, although they had appeared sufficient to its proponents, soon proved to be inadequate, mainly because its orders and decisions had to be finally adjudicated by the Supreme Court, which was then in a conservative groove and whose thinking was not yet adjusted to the expanding interpretation of the Commerce Clause of the Constitution and to regulation under it. Furthermore, the open hostility of the railroads led them to take advantage of legal technicalities in order to thwart the considered will of the commission. Thus it lost—or rather never acquired—prestige in those early days; its authority, because of unsympathetic judicial interpretation, was radically curtailed. Whatever teeth its edicts possessed were quickly extracted, and by the turn of the century it was impotent and ignored.

One of the most discouraging developments came almost a decade after its establishment, when two Supreme Court decisions—in the *Social Circle Case* (1896) and the *Maximum Freight Case* (1897) —with only Justice Harlan dissenting, asserted that "the power to prescribe rates or to fix any tariff for the future is not among the powers granted to the Commission." Thus, as Sharfman says, the commission found itself emasculated, "without any real power to fix rates," and its status was "critically impaired." What was the use of having a commission which was unable to enforce its own decisions? The administration of President McKinley was hardly the period when the Federal Government was likely to initiate or encourage attacks of any kind upon combinations of capital. The influence of Mark Hanna and his satellites was too strong. With the accidental accession of Theodore Roosevelt to the Presidency in 1901, however, a new spirit came into the White House and spread into the corridors of the Capitol. The Elkins Act of 1903, making general rebating unlawful, was sponsored by the railroads themselves, and turned out to be, in the words of the commission, "a wise and salutary measure." But it did not do enough to correct the serious weaknesses of the Act of 1887.

Meanwhile, President Roosevelt's dynamic personality and conceptions of justice were modifying public opinion. Eastman had been only one of many college undergraduates of that generation who were excited by the "Square Deal" slogan. I well recall debating for Amherst against Bowdoin in the spring of 1905 on the subject, then very timely, "Resolved, that the recommendation of President Roosevelt that the Interstate Commerce Commission be given the power to fix railroad rates, subject to judicial review, be adopted." Unfortunately, our Amherst team had to uphold the negative of the question, and we lost. Time was on the side of our opponents—and the arguments also. The agitation of that period was aimed chiefly at implementing a theory which the advocates of the Act of 1887 had believed in, but which the courts had consistently nullified.

Roosevelt seldom delayed long in turning his words into deeds, and he began to bring pressure upon Congress to get things done. The Hepburn Bill in 1906 somewhat rectified conditions by giving the Interstate Commerce Commission the power which it needed and thus "bolstered up the system of federal regulation in various directions." This measure was passed at a moment when the average voter's distrust of large corporate activities made him favor any bill for the more vigorous control of transportation. At last, in explicit terms which no court could misunderstand or evade, the rate-making authority was embodied in the commission, which quickly took on a positive character, supported as it was by the machinery for enforcing its decisions. The commission still encountered obstacles and equivocations; but the Congressional legislation, backed by unmistakable popular approval, laid the foundation for consistent administrative supervision. That the hour had arrived for such support is now admitted by every unbiased student of transportation problems.

The Mann-Elkins Act of 1910 continued the good work by giving the rejuvenated commission even more vitality. Slowly, but with impressive certainty, its dominance was being declared, guaranteed, and recognized. But a new group of difficulties now appeared. The situation during the years preceding World War I was complicated by a peculiar inconsistency—the fact that the railroads, although inherently a monopoly, were prevented legally under the judicial interpretation of the Sherman Anti-Trust Act, from adopting a policy of voluntary cooperation. With "pooling" prohibited, it was impossible for even the best intentioned lines to achieve any form of unity. It has been well said that "enforced competition was imposed upon an industry assumed to be naturally monopolistic." Furthermore, because of the difficulty of establishing concepts of "fair value" and "fair return," the rate policy of the commission tended, in the opinion of experts, to become too rigid, with the result that while operating expenses and taxes were going up, operating revenue was shrinking year by year. Finally a very heavy burden was imposed upon railroads by the issue of conflicting and confusing directives from the Federal Government and by the lack of any wage control whatever by the commission or any other agency. All these problems Eastman saw when he was still in Massachusetts, in close touch with the railroads of that area.

Even before the entrance of the United States into the war in 1917, the carriers, and especially the trunk lines, found themselves unable to meet the country's rapidly expanding commercial and industrial needs; and when large bodies of troops and a vast amount of material had to be moved in a hurry, the schedules and rolling stock proved inadequate. The hard-pressed Interstate Commerce Commission, seeking relief, was permitted to function by divisions of its members, and at the same time the membership was enlarged from seven to nine. At once the nine commissioners organized into three divisions of three members each, and each division was charged to perform certain functions. Each division was authorized to decide specified minor issues, but the action of any group was to be subject to appeal to the entire commission. Through this plan the work of the commission was expedited, and the burden on each commissioner was lessened.

During the early months of the war, the Federal Government, relying upon a voluntary association called the Railroads' War Board, interfered scarcely at all with private enterprise. Toward the end of 1917, however, conditions became much worse, and the growing congestion on the Atlantic seaboard, gradually spreading across the continent, threatened complete paralysis of the transportation structure. Things sank from bad to very bad, and from very bad to terrible. Everybody was complaining, but nobody was doing anything about it—including the railroad executives.

At last, on December 5, 1917, the Interstate Commerce Commission, which had been watching the collapse with grave apprehension, sent a special report to Congress, declaring in substance that unification of operations under some central authority was necessary for the duration of the war. This could be done in one of two ways: the management of the roads as a unit by the carriers themselves, with all the jealousy and rivalry which that entailed; or the combination of the roads under the direction of the President. Commissioner Charles C. McChord came out in an even more vigorous statement of his own, asserting that "the strong arm of governmental authority is essential if the transportation problem is to be radically improved."

Day by day the confusion was spreading, and it looked as if the failures in railroad operation might seriously impair the war effort. None too soon, in a proclamation issued on the day after Christmas, the President took over control of all the rail and combined rail and water systems in the United States and appointed William G. McAdoo, Secretary of the Treasury, to the important post of Director-General of Railroads, with power to operate them as "a national system of transportation." As Professor Sharfman puts it, "the method of compulsory unification displaced the policy of voluntary cooperation." The railroad executives had not been able to meet the crisis, and even the Interstate Commerce Commission had missed its opportunity.

During the crucial period which ensued and continued until after the Armistice, the prestige of the commission deteriorated. The Railway Administration used its rate-making authority in many important cases, generally with wisdom. Federal control accomplished much that had been expected of it and did prevent a complete breakdown at a moment when that would have been an irretrievable disaster. It was not perfect, and the "die-hards" made the most of its mistakes; but it was "at least as successful

as private management would have been under the circumstances."
Eastman had watched all these developments with keen interest.
He joined the commission at a time when it and the public were
able to appraise the success of government control and operation
and to profit by the lessons learned under the stress of war. His
own views on the subject were fully formed before he settled in
Washington.

On the date when Eastman's appointment to the commission was
confirmed, his sister was overseas with the Young Women's Christian Association. His father had died in Winchester on November
9, 1917, so that Joe was free to move in a hurry. After several
farewell dinners and "presentations" in Boston, he and his loyal
friend Frank Livingstone went to Washington and settled down in
bachelor quarters until Elizabeth's return, living first at the Cosmos
Club and later, after June 1, at the Wyoming apartment hotel.
Eastman's salary was to be $10,000 a year,—more than enough for
even his extraordinary needs, for his tastes were simple. Livingstone's status was for the moment uncertain. He could not expect
much in the way of compensation, and the prospect of advancement
was, to say the least, remote. But apparently he cared nothing about
money or personal distinction and was determined to follow Eastman and assist him, regardless of tangible reward. He was content
with being made Confidential Clerk, which meant that he could be
on hand if or when he was needed. Eastman was glad to have somebody around him who knew his ways and whom he could trust.

Of Eastman's colleagues on the commission, the first one with
whom he had become acquainted was Balthasar H. Meyer, whom
he had met in 1909, at a conference in Pittsburgh. Meyer, who had
been a professor at the University of Wisconsin and had published
in 1905 his authoritative book *Railway Legislation in the United
States,* was fifty-six years old. At the date of his retirement, in
1939, he had held office for almost thirty years—a record at that
time and one which has been surpassed since only by commissioner
Aitchison. Even older in point of service in 1919 was Edgar Erastus
Clark, a former railroad brakeman and conductor who had been the
Grand Chief of the Order of Railroad Conductors when he was
named to the commission in 1906. In 1919 he was sixty-three—

the oldest member. The chairmanship of the commission—then a rotating position—was held when Eastman arrived by Winthrop M. Daniels, a Princeton graduate who had held a professorship of political economy at that institution for twenty years—a sound scholar, a conservative by temperament, and an author of distinction, then only fifty-two. Henry C. Hall, an Amherst graduate who had been an attorney in Colorado Springs specializing in mining and transportation and later president of the Colorado Bar Association, was fifty-nine. Charles C. McChord, a lawyer who had been chairman of the Kentucky Railroad Commission, had just turned sixty. The two men just senior to Eastman in both age and service were Robert W. Woolley, who had been for some years in charge of Democratic national publicity, and Clyde B. Aitchison. These two had been appointed by President Wilson in 1917. Woolley was forty-eight in 1919 and Aitchison was only forty-four. Eastman himself was in his thirty-eighth year.

So far as age was concerned, then, Eastman, when he joined his new associates in the Old Interstate Commerce Building at 18th Street and Pennsylvania Avenue, may have felt at some disadvantage. But although he was relatively young in years, he was by comparison with them no novice. Among the assets which they were not slow to recognize were a considerable familiarity with transportation facts and figures and an extensive knowledge of railroads and their intricacies; an intimate acquaintance with the problems of employees, gained while he had been counsel for railroad unions; a theory, already well formulated, regarding the proper relationship of transportation, in all its phases, to the areas which it serves; an orderly economic philosophy, the product of both practical experience and some meditation; and a devotion, deep-seated and unselfish, to the public interest. He was genuinely humble, tolerant, and eager to learn. But he was also, when he thought he was right, courageous and not easily put down. No member of the commission has ever been better prepared to meet its demands.

When Eastman joined the commission there was one vacancy, due to the expiration on December 13, 1918, of the term of James S. Harlan. Three of the members—Hall, McChord, and Aitchison

—had been practicing lawyers; two—Meyer and Daniels—had been
college professors; one—Woolley—had been a writer and politician; and only one—Clark—had been a practical railroad man.
To his cousin Margaret King, Eastman wrote: "Your two Kentucky men, McChord and Woolley, are the most human and
personally attractive of all the Commissioners." This was the group
with whom Joe was to be thrown into a very intimate relationship,
which was to reveal their idiosyncrasies, their weaknesses, and their
often astonishing strength.

Eastman's private file in the office of the commission started
on February 18, 1919, with a letter to his friend and former associate
on the Massachusetts Public Service Commission, Fred J. McLeod:

Just a line to inform you that I arrived safely in Washington last
Sunday evening, with my new travelling bag, which was much admired
by everybody who saw it. Early Monday morning I was duly sworn
in before the Secretary of the Commission, and entered upon the duties
of this office, or at least made an attempt to enter upon them. Most
of the time so far I have spent in the process of listening. The organization is rather complicated and there is a great deal, of course, to learn,
but I think that I shall become acquainted with the ropes with a fair
amount of rapidity, and also feel that I shall, on the whole, like the
work.

On the morning of his official arrival in the building, Eastman
reported to Chairman Daniels, who escorted him ceremoniously
from room to room, introducing him to the other commissioners
and to the staff, some of them already known to him. His own power
of appointment was limited to a private secretary—Frank Livingstone—all the other assistants being subject to Civil Service regulations. His first recorded request was for an examiner to be assigned
to his office. The examiners are for the most part lawyers employed
to conduct hearings and write reports for the commission. They
are on the permanent staff and have a full knowledge of the commission's practices and routine and a mastery of the multitudinous
complexities, terminological and technical, which are so difficult for
the average layman to understand. They qualify for appointment
by examinations set by the commission and function under Civil

Service rules. More than one examiner has later been appointed to the commission, and many of them have held other important positions.

As a matter of procedure, Eastman quickly discovered, the large majority of cases were handled by the chief examiner and his assistants up to the point where the issues were ripe for disposition by a division or by the full commission. Sometimes, indeed, a matter of considerable importance was assigned to an examiner for entire handling from the beginning, and he supervised it at all stages up to its consideration by the entire body. The role of the examiners, then, was of the highest significance, and Eastman soon learned, like his brethren, to depend on their expert judgment. He never learned to refrain, however, from checking details himself, and often went back to the very sources for his facts.

His colleagues were impressed at once by his vigilance, thoroughness, and persistence. He was still asking "Why?" and "How?" as he had done in Massachusetts; and he set a strenuous example for those in his vicinity. Items which would have bored most men seemed to him fraught with fascination and romance. The examiners, most of them shrewd observers, respected his inquisitiveness and passion for getting to the bottom of every question under debate. A quarter of a century later J. Carter Fort, speaking for the practitioners before the commission, said reminiscently:

At this time, believe it or not, we belonged to the younger group. We were very proud of the Commission and of our association with it. And we subjected each new Commissioner to that scrutinizing appraisal which a superior officer so often receives at the hands of his subordinates. We examined Mr. Eastman under the microscope of daily contact, and knew that another jewel had been added to the crown of the Commission. We were much pleased, I think, to find that one more or less in our own age bracket could sit so firmly in the seat of the mighty and breathe the rarefied atmosphere in such a seemly fashion.

A later commissioner, Thomas F. Woodlock, a former member of the New York Stock Exchange who was appointed by President Coolidge in 1925 and served until August, 1930, when he resigned to become editor of the *Wall Street Journal*, wrote after his retirement a series of articles for *Barron's Weekly*, commenting wittily and delightfully on his own experiences. He pointed out that to any untutored outsider the reports of the commission seem to be written in a "maze of jargon." What is a "combination rate" which "makes on" the Ohio River? What is a "joint through rate?" What, in the name of Heaven, is "fourth section relief?" What is Rule 77? What is the "intermediate rule?" What is "open routing?" I must confess that when I began to peruse the files of the commission, I found myself learning what amounted to a new dialect, if not an actual foreign tongue—although to those ensconced within the sacred precincts, the idea that they dwell in a realm of mystery seems absurd. Eastman was not, of course, to be daunted by a trifling matter of vocabulary, and some of these technical terms were already familiar to him. Nevertheless, he had a good deal to learn.

Each newcomer soon discovers, as Mr. Woodlock suggested, that every human being in the Interstate Commerce Commission Building is there to help him and that he can procure all the assistance he requires by merely asking for it. Moreover, the older members are tolerant of a tyro's ignorance and blundering efforts to feel his way. A new commissioner is urged not to be too hasty and is seldom given any important assignment until he declares himself ready. The examiners, as I can testify, are extraordinarily patient with the uninformed and bewildered.

As he became better acquainted with the strange and often seemingly archaic procedures of the commission, Eastman noticed how vital to its effective functioning was the trained and permanent personnel. On December 21, 1936, he wrote a very illuminating five-page letter to President Conant, of Harvard, regarding the plans for the proposed Harvard School of Public Administration. Referring to his own experience, he said:

One of the things which have disturbed me in my work on this Commission is that it is so difficult for the members to give proper attention to the staff and to the development of the best possible administrative methods and policies. So much time is required by our quasi-judicial functions in hearing arguments and deciding cases that we tend to lose the close contact with the staff and their problems which is essential to the best administration. That is why, in my plan for a reorganization of the Commission, I provided for a permanent Chairman who would be divorced from much of the quasi-judicial work and could devote much of his time to administrative matters.

In my 23 years in the public service, I have never been disappointed in the quality and quantity of the work which can be secured from the rank and file of the personnel when conditions are somewhere near right. I have always found them willing to work hard and faithfully, as well as honestly, provided:

(1) They feel that they are engaged in useful and important work.
(2) They have confidence in the ability and purposes of the man at the top.
(3) Their immediate superiors handle them with sympathy and understanding, and *justly*.

Much of Eastman's daily routine was already as fixed as the calendar, and he merely carried with him to Washington the techniques which he had acquired in Boston. William James once wrote, "The human individual . . . lives usually far within his limits; he possesses powers of various sorts which he habitually fails to use. He energizes below his *minimum*, and he behaves below his *optimum*." Eastman was exceptional in that he regularly toiled his hardest and performed his best. To his cousin he said, "Already I find myself at the office nights and Sundays, and while I have done that sort of thing for a long time (several years in fact), I don't believe in it. Human beings weren't made to work all the time, and they ought to have their play." His reputation as a model of punctuality and animation was soon widespread, for he arrived at the main door promptly at eight twenty-five each morning, left at exactly twelve-thirty and remained out at luncheon until two, and then resumed his labors until five, when he departed to play handball or squash at one of his clubs. Before leaving to enjoy his exercise, he often napped for a few minutes on the sofa in his office. He had the priceless gift of being able to go to sleep when he wished and of waking up at any hour he had set for himself in advance. He customarily returned in the evening to sink into a giant chair in his office, and there, with a board on his knee, he scribbled notes in a peculiar style of shorthand which he had devised in his early days with the Public Franchise League. His disposition was rated by his subordinates as calm and amiable, and his secretary for many years can recall seeing him angry only twice—and in both cases he was amply justified.

Seated in Eastman's outer office behind a flat-topped desk was Frank Livingstone, shaggy-haired, with penetrating eyes, sizing up and classifying visitors and soon knowing the history of everybody in the building. Within a few weeks he was as much of a fixture as the commissioner himself, whose protector he conceived himself to be. But he was much more than a watchdog. With him after hours Eastman discussed his perplexities, and Livingstone's obstinate radicalism jarred beneficially his chief's more equable temperament. Joe tried his ideas out on the critical Livingstone, who, as an economic and social philosopher, often modified Eastman's thinking. In public he never presumed on their relationship, but in private the two were equals, not employer and employee. Livingstone was too honestly independent to be subservient to anybody. Those who knew Eastman best in those days stress the influence of Livingstone's blunt and uninhibited personality on his younger and far from static friend.

The impression which Eastman created during his novitiate was decidedly favorable, even with those who did not agree with him. He seemed to be tactful and thoughtful, with no disagreeable traits, such as pomposity, garrulity, or irritability, which sometimes make the "Boss" unbearable. He was soon, however, to take an official stand which proved that he had not by any means discarded the liberal ideas for which he had been conspicuous in Massachusetts.

VII

The Independent Commissioner

SOMEONE in Washington said to me recently, "Joe Eastman set the ICC in a turmoil as soon as he arrived and kept it boiling until he died." Although it really wasn't quite as bad as that, Joe was unaccustomed to being a mere "Yes man" and did have a vigorous mind of his own. He had not long been a commissioner before official Washington was to learn precisely where he stood.

During the war, while transportation was being operated under the Director-General of Railroads, the powers and opportunities of the Interstate Commerce Commission were necessarily much curtailed; and as Professor Sharfman has stated, "some of the normal functions and processes of the Commission were pushed into the background." The Director-General not only resorted to every legitimate device to speed up traffic, as he was expected to do, but also ordered both horizontal rate increases and large wage advances; and the commission, while viewing some of these innovations with alarm, lost its traditional leadership in the field of regulation. It was Eastman who, more than any other member, won for the commission confidence and prestige.

Everything considered, Federal control did accomplish satisfactorily its primary aim of moving the vast flow of war traffic. After the Armistice, however, it was clear that some permanent policy would have to be adopted. The Federal Control Act of March 21, 1918, which had supplied legislative sanction to Wilson's taking over of the railroads, had been expressly declared to be an emergency measure for correcting evils arising out of the war. Eastman reached the capital at a moment when everybody concerned with transportation was wondering what would, or could, happen next; and although he had no desire for publicity, he soon attracted attention by taking a position opposed to all but one of his new

JOSEPH B. EASTMAN AND STANLEY KING
AT A SPRINGFIELD BANQUET IN 1939

EASTMAN AND HIS FRIEND FRANK B. LIVINGSTONE

associates and coming out boldly for a continuation of Federal control. Immediately he was branded as a "radical," as he had been in Massachusetts, and the Old Guard denounced him bitterly as "another Brandeis."

What Eastman said and did seemed dramatic, but it was in accord with the texture of his thinking. Within a few weeks after the signing of the Armistice, Director-General McAdoo formally recommended that Federal control of railroads should be extended for a period of five years, until January 1, 1924, mainly in order to test the possibilities of unified operation under normal peace conditions. The proposal evoked wails of protest from the various managements, accompanied by the presentation of their own plans from many individuals and organizations. Hearings began on January 5, 1919, before the Senate Committee on Interstate Commerce, and were continued, with some recesses, until October 25. Similar hearings before the House Committee on Interstate and Foreign Commerce opened on July 15. Never had such widespread interest been shown in railroad legislation. Never had so many conflicting views on transportation been expressed. Before Eastman was sworn in, the Interstate Commerce Commission, with only Commissioner Woolley dissenting, had defined its position as follows: "We are led to the conviction that with the adoption of appropriate provisions and safeguards for regulation under private ownership, it would not be wise or best at this time to assume Government ownership or operation of the railroads of this country."

Commissioner Woolley filed with the Senate committee his separate statement favoring the extension of Federal control as recommended by McAdoo, adding that so far as he could determine no concrete plan for the restoration of private management had been proposed which would be likely to work satisfactorily.

It was not Eastman's custom to form opinions hastily, especially in a strange environment, and for some weeks he was busy mastering his new duties and getting acquainted with the personalities around him. The fact that the commission had already put itself on record naturally served as a brake on any impetuous action. His correspondence shows that he discussed the matter with both Woolley and Brandeis, but the first mention of it in his files occurs in a letter of April 19, 1919, to Governor Calvin Coolidge, recommending first B. Loring Young and then Charles F. Dutch for the vacancy on the Massachusetts Public Service Commission. After praising these two men, Eastman continued in another strain:

In addition to the extremely perplexing and troublesome street railway situation, Massachusetts ought to be devoting all the thought at its command to the future of the New England roads. Rates have been greatly advanced, yet the roads are now barely earning operating expenses, if they are doing that. Only government credit has made it possible to reorganize the Boston & Maine; and only government credit has procured the funds which have kept additions and improvements in prices during the past year. A return to private ownership would leave the roads practically without credit, unless I am very wrong in sizing up the situation. Nor am I able to reach the conclusion that it is public operation which has brought about this situation.

Eastman knew very well that he was being studied by his fellow commissioners. He was also aware that his decision on this crucial issue would label him with the public for many years to come. Finally, after much heart searching and several consultations with Livingstone, he sent direct to the Committee on Interstate Commerce of the United States Senate a comprehensive letter, which was printed in the 33d *Annual Report* of the Interstate Commerce Commission. Prepared with scrupulous care, it sums up his philosophy at this period and therefore must be quoted at some length. The letter opened:

At the time last winter when the Interstate Commerce Commission appeared before your Committee, I was not a member of the Commission and therefore had no opportunity to concur in or dissent from what was then said in regard to the general railroad situation. Under the circumstances, I take the liberty of submitting this statement, wishing in a matter of such importance to let my views be known for what they are worth.

Stating these views concisely, I believe that the roads should continue in the possession and control of the nation, for the following principal reasons:

(1) To ensure necessary capital, at low cost.

(2) To avoid unduly high rates.

(3) To solve the problem of the "weak" roads.

(4) To obtain the operating advantages which come from unification.

(5) To promote right relations with labor.

I further believe that while unfavorable criticism may be made of "Federal control" as it has been administered, the record is not discouraging, and the defects may be remedied. Better results can, I feel, be obtained by maintaining and improving national operation than by returning to old methods in whatever guise.

These opening paragraphs summarize Eastman's thesis, and the remainder is explanation and amplification. In commenting on the success of government control, he said:

Probably the sentiment in favor of a return to private operation springs chiefly from a feeling that national operation has been a failure. Such discouragement is not justified. . . . In spite of many handicaps the Railroad Administration succeeded in relieving congestion and handled both troops and all manner of war freight with credit to itself.

Characteristically, Eastman moved from the specific instance to the broader theme and anticipated a certain type of criticism by clarifying his economic creed.

I attach little weight to the distrust of "socialistic" experiments. "Socialistic" is a catchword loosely used as a means of discredit in default of argument. It has long been recognized that transportation by rail is a public business which the Government might properly carry on, and it is no more "socialistic" to do so than to provide and care for schools, highways, and water activities now publicly administered. The question is one of practical expediency rather than of political theory.

His argument also offered him an opportunity to express his confidence in government management as compared with private enterprise. It was to be a favorite topic of his in Washington.

From experience in both state and federal service, I am confident that no greater opportunity for useful and genuinely creative work anywhere exists than in the public service; that the great body of employees are faithful, loyal, and willing to work; that inefficiency in the service springs from the top rather than from the bottom; and that all the efficiency that is wholesome and desirable can be developed, without the incentive of excessive financial rewards, if constructive thought and criticism are substituted in sufficient measure for mere cynicism.

After commenting briefly on some aspects of Federal control as he had observed it during the war, he concluded:

The suggestion which I respectfully offer for your consideration is that the present form of national operation, with the modifications proposed in the so-called Cummins Bill, be continued for an appropriate period of time in order that uncertainty as to the immediate future may be ended and sufficient time gained for the deliberate and constructive consideration of the entire problem.

It took no small amount of courage for the youngest member of the commission in both age and service to disagree with his colleagues on such a fundamental matter. Some of them were openly annoyed, but Joe's frankness was disarming, and they did not indulge in feuds even when they learned that an independent thinker had been deposited in their midst, one who cared more for truth, however disturbing, than for precedent or placidity. Not unaware of the implications of his letter, Eastman sent copies not only to Anderson and Brandeis, his old and understanding friends, but also to Governor Coolidge, Director-General Hines, and President Wilson. He afterwards allowed it to be printed, with some revisions—which did not alter its basic argument—in the *Annals of the American Academy of Political Science*, under the title "The Advantages of National Operation." When he had had a chance to consider some of the many hostile comments, he wrote to Frank B. Kellogg: "It is still my belief that national operation of the railroads should be adopted as a permanent policy. . . . The choice seems to be between bankers and the government, and the latter is to be preferred."

As soon as this "Credo" had been completed and despatched to the Senate committee, Eastman left for the Far West, where he held hearings for the commission in San Francisco, Portland, and Seattle, and even stopped for a few hours in Los Angeles. It was his first journey beyond the Mississippi, and he was tremendously impressed by what he saw along the way. He took the trip at just the right moment, when he was moving from his somewhat insular post in New England to a position in which he had to consider the nation as a continental whole. In his progress from city to city he learned that his advocacy of government operation of railroads stirred no responsive enthusiasm. He also discovered that the great cross-country routes were different from the Boston & Maine and the New York, New Haven & Hartford.

On August 16 the *Nation* published a symposium of articles by persons supposedly competent to speak on the railroad question. Director-General Hines himself, at the request of the editors, presented his personal and official views, advocating a return of the railroads to private management, but under conditions providing for "proper government regulation." The solution offered by Labor was explained by Glenn E. Plumb, a Chicago lawyer and author of the "Plumb Plan," which involved the purchase by the Government of all private interests in the railroads and their operation under a board of fifteen members—five to be appointed by the President, five to be elected by the operating officials, and five to be chosen by the employees. Included in this much discussed plan was a division of profits—if any—among the workers. There were several other contributors, and to Joseph B. Eastman and his opinions one whole page was devoted, stressing his desire for a fair hearing of the case for government ownership and control. Nobody else agreed with him; or perhaps it would be fairer to say that he agreed with nobody else.

Meanwhile, his devoted sister Elizabeth had returned from Europe, and Livingstone had secured for her and her brother a house at 2325 20th Street, where they shortly settled down to a comfortable, domestic life. Most ironically, the car loaded at Winchester with the family furniture was lost *en route*, and the new commissioner with jurisdiction over freight transportation had difficulty in locating his possessions and getting them to the capital. Although Eastman had now become a Washingtonian, he kept himself on the voting list at Winchester, and when the town officials notified him that they were erasing his name, he replied with some irritation: "It is my present intention to return to Winchester when my duties here are over." He was never to go back, except for casual visits.

Throughout the autumn of 1919 the railroad controversy continued, not only in the press but also in the discussions of the commission and in Eastman's correspondence. Replying to certain questions of detail, he explained more fully his views in a letter to Senator Frank B. Kellogg.

I should agree with you that the present "federal control," under which the Government simply pays for the use of the properties, probably could not be continued indefinitely; but I should suppose that the period now provided for could be extended somewhat, pending further action by Congress, and I understand this is the view of the Director-General's legal advisers.

The advantage of such an extension would be the additional opportunity for working out the details of the permanent plan of national operation. Perhaps this could be done in a comparatively short time. I am not suggesting delay, but merely the lengthening of the *maximum* period provided for the present arrangement, so that neither Congress nor the nation need feel driven to hasty action. The extension would in no way conflict or be inconsistent with the policy finally to be pursued. . . .

You ask how I propose that the Government shall acquire the roads. It has not seemed to me that the question of compensation finally to be paid to the owners could be dealt with satisfactorily until greater progress had been made in the valuation now under way, and possibly not until the basic principles had been enunciated by the court of last resort. It seems desirable that the flotation in the open market of a large issue of government bonds should be avoided, and that the properties should chiefly be acquired through negotiation and by an exchange, gradual if possible, of such bonds in proper proportions for the railroad securities now outstanding. I doubt, however, whether this can be done until the owners have a clearer idea of what they might expect to receive by forcing the exercise of the power of eminent domain.

You further ask me what I should consider an "appropriate period of time" for the continuance of the present form of national operation. I should consider the five-year period proposed by the Director-General as the maximum which might be desirable. It would not, of course, be necessary to postpone final action until the end of such a period, if the details of a permanent plan could be satisfactorily determined in a shorter time.

During the autumn of 1919 Eastman made at least two hurried trips to Winchester, but his first public appearance in Massachusetts after his appointment to the Interstate Commerce Commission came on November 12, at a dinner of the well-known Twentieth Century Club, in Boston. He was greeted warmly, although one of his banker acquaintances said to him, "Joe, you can raise more Hell in a few months than anybody I ever knew." The address was not printed in its entirety, but the Boston *Evening Transcript* published the following brief abstract, without comment.

Speaking before the Twentieth Century Club last evening as its guest, Joseph B. Eastman of the Interstate Commerce Commission advocated the retention of the railroads under federal control. He argued that if they are returned to their private owners, they will have to raise rates, and rate increases will be felt in the cost of living; but the government can operate them without raising rates even if earnings fall below expenses. Furthermore Mr. Eastman argued that the advantages of unionized control have been recognized, and that every one of the bills providing for the return of the railroads to private ownership provides means for keeping the advantages of unionized control. Mr. Eastman declared that the impression that government ownership results in inefficiency and political graft is wrong, because the roads have been well operated by the government, and there has been no politics in it. In conclusion, he maintained that the roads should be kept by the government until the present unrest is over.

It will not have escaped notice that Eastman cleverly presented arguments which would weigh heavily with railroad management as well as with the general public. When the Government took over the roads, the New Haven was again in dire straits, and if the Director-General had not loaned it a large sum to fund its floating debt, it might have sunk into the hands of a receiver. In addition, the Government had spent almost $20,000,000 on improvements for the New Haven, $15,000,000 for the Boston & Maine, and over $2,000,000 for the Boston & Albany. The aggregate for New England was more than $60,000,000—a very respectable amount, as Eastman liked to point out.

But cogent though his logic may have seemed to him as he sat at his desk, Eastman sensed that his ideas did not meet with widespread approval. The majority members of the commission were not pleased, and when, at Judge Anderson's suggestion, he circulated among them a memorandum on "The Essentials of a Sound and Progressive Railroad Policy," they behaved very much like teachers on a high school faculty being lectured by a pupil. Professor Sharfman concludes that "there was an unmistakable popular mandate for the restoration of private management under corporate ownership," and the editorial comment of leading newspapers substantiates this opinion. Writing to Anderson on December 10, Eastman declared, "I am still as confident as ever that the results will be bad for all concerned if the roads go back in the near future, but apparently very few in power agree with me. Perhaps they will later on."

A week later President Wilson announced that the railroads would be turned back to their owners, in accordance with the original plan, on March 1, 1920, and Congress was thus obliged to take legislative action, for it was now evident, after the long discussion of the summer and fall, that the existing machinery of control was inadequate. Eastman wrote Anderson on December 26:

I suppose you have read the President's proclamation in regard to the return of the railroads. I am myself disappointed in what he has done and fear he has placed himself in a position where he is morally bound to approve any legislation which Congress may enact. However the final outcome seems to me still problematical, and even at this date I should be willing to bet even money that the roads do not go back on March 1.

On January 2, 1920, Eastman wrote to Lawrence B. Finn in a slightly different tone, but still with a rather defiant note of prophecy:

Down here everything seems slated for the return of the railroads to their private owners on the first of March, but I still have the feeling that obstacles to this program will develop; but even if it is carried out, I am confident that sooner or later they will become permanently the property of the government. The other day in writing to one of my friends who objects to my views in regard to government ownership of railroads, I told him that I was merely establishing a claim to charter membership in the "I told you so" club.

In this case Joe was a poor prognosticator, but he had been goaded by criticism into a position more positive than he usually took. His relations with one or two of the commissioners were actually strained, and several examiners recall that in some rooms in the Interstate Commerce Building he was regarded as a menace, potentially if not actively dangerous. One examiner who was transferred to Eastman's office was agreeably astonished to find his new "Boss" rather benign than savage. Eastman was not himself the man to let a difference of opinion cause a break in friendly relations. Like a lawyer in court, he could dispute with a rival attorney in the heat of debate and then walk out with his arm around the other's shoulder. Unfortunately, there were those who were less equable and tolerant.

The Congressional committees, faced with their responsibility, had a busy winter considering the numerous suggestions which had been proposed and attempting to frame a measure which would furnish the needed effective control. Commissioner Clark, delegated by his associates, assembled and presented the data required from the commission. The only other commissioner to give testimony was Woolley. Eastman was not called upon officially, but did informally advise several members of Congress. There was much confusion, much discussion, and plenty of disagreement. Finally, just under the wire, Congress passed on February 28, 1920, the Esch-Cummins Bill, better known as the Transportation Act of 1920. It has been rightly described as "highly eclectic in spirit, drawing its principles and expedients from diverse sources." It was, indeed, a complicated measure, the result of rather hurried compromises and concessions, but for the moment it satisfied the majority of the commission. Under it and some later amendments the Interstate Commerce Commission functioned while Eastman was a member.

In the preceding acts constituting and affecting the commission it had been regarded largely as a punitive body, charged with enforcing certain regulations. The Transportation Act took a broader view, assuming that the commission's duties were constructive and that it had a positive responsibility toward everybody concerned—the railroads and shippers, of course, the different geographical sections, and even the hypothetical man in the street who occasionally took a train trip. Explicit recognition was given to the needs of the carriers for sufficient revenue. In commenting on the underlying philosophy of the act, Mr. Justice Brandeis said in 1923:

Theretofore the effort of Congress had been directed mainly to the prevention of abuses, particularly those arising from excessive or discriminatory rates. The 1920 Act sought to ensure, also, adequate transportation service. That such was its purpose, Congress did not leave to inference. The new purpose was expressed in unequivocal language.

Furthermore the Act—at least by implication—discarded the theory of the 1890's that anything resembling a railroad monopoly was pernicious. Instead, formal combinations and pooling agreements were expressly authorized, even encouraged; and the commission was instructed to prepare a comprehensive plan for consolidating American railroad properties into a limited number of systems. This extraordinary reversal of economic trends seemed at first to be of far-reaching significance. As events turned out, however, the consolidation plan proved to be impracticable; but the fact that it was even thought to be desirable shows how much sentiment had shifted since 1887.

On paper, the power of the commission was vastly augmented. It was entrusted with control over the issuance of railroad securities and could impose restrictions on the qualifications and duties of railroad directors. It was also for the first time authorized to fix minimum as well as maximum rates. One peculiar provision, which later proved to be ineffective and was eventually nullified, was the notorious "Recapture Clause," providing that a carrier receiving in any one year a net operating income in excess of 6 percent should be obliged to divide this additional revenue between its own reserve fund and another fund established by the commission to be used for making loans to weaker carriers in need of assistance. The legal questions involved ultimately became insuperable, and the plan had to be abandoned, but not until a great deal of vexatious litigation had sprung up.

On the question of cooperation between the commission and the various state bodies concerned with railroads—a matter which had much disturbed Eastman during his last year on the Massachusetts

Public Service Commission—the act confirmed the dominance of the commission's rate-making authority, while stressing the necessity of their working with the state bodies. What happened as a direct consequence of the act was that the powers of rate regulation were centralized far more than ever before. The commission was granted more comprehensive control over railroad service, and the Transportation Act included a large number of beneficial service provisions. It certainly looked as if the Interstate Commerce Commission, with ampler and better-defined jurisdiction, could now work out a permanent solution of the baffling transportation problem. That it did not—indeed, could not—was due to many interwoven factors, but especially to the difficulties involved in dealing with "a declining industry in a period of marked economic instability." At the time, however, even Eastman thought that some major reforms had been effected.

To bring relief to the overworked commission its membership was raised from nine to eleven, and its prestige and desirability were improved by increasing the salaries of the commissioners from $10,000 to $12,000. President Wilson, who had been incapacitated by a paralytic stroke, was thereafter in no condition to pay much attention to the affairs of the commission. Furthermore he had difficulty in filling the panel, for the Republican Senators, remembering how Democratic Senators in 1913 had held up nominations made by President Taft so as to allow vacancies to be filled by the incoming Chief Executive, now improved their opportunity for revenge. On May 4, 1920, Wilson nominated Henry Jones Ford, Commissioner of Banking and Insurance in New Jersey and a friend of long standing, to succeed Commissioner Harlan, and James Duncan, of Massachusetts, a labor official, to fill one of the two new vacancies; two days later he appointed Mark Winslow Potter, a New York lawyer and railroad president, for the other newly created position. Although he was never confirmed by the Senate, he was given a recess appointment and served until Harding's inauguration. The Senate refused also to pass on Duncan's name and, even though he was offered a recess appointment, he never took the oath of office. Potter, who went through the same embarrassing ordeal as Ford, was eventually nominated by President Harding and quickly confirmed. He shortly became one of Eastman's warmest friends and admirers, and even after his retirement in 1925 the two men maintained a regular correspondence.

Woolley, whose term expired on December 31, 1920, was an ardent Democrat not to Harding's liking, and the latter therefore named to succeed him John Jacob Esch, one of the two authors of the Esch-Cummins Act. He was a Congressional "lame duck" who, after serving twenty-two years as Representative from Wisconsin, had been defeated in 1920; but he knew railroads in all their aspects as well as any man in the United States. The commission was filled by the appointment of Johnston Byron Campbell, a Spokane attorney who had been active in commission litigation relating to the Intermountain Territory.

This is not, however, the story of the Interstate Commerce Commission, but of Joseph B. Eastman, who observed these changes in personnel with the keen interest of one who would have to work with these new men. He was promptly assigned, with Commissioners Clark and Hall, to Division III, having jurisdiction over Board of Review cases not orally argued; and on February 26, when he had been at his desk only seven days, he joined in pronouncing decisions in 15 cases, all of a routine nature. This was partly the polite docility of a man not fully acquainted with a new environment.

However, at the end of a report in a case of minor importance decided by Division III, March 21, 1919, appear the words, "Eastman, Commissioner, dissents." He did not feel it necessary here to explain the reasons for differing with his colleagues. Two months later he was less hesitant. In *Tanner & Co.* v. *Chicago, B. & Q.R.R. Co.*, 53 I.C.C. 401, decided June 9, 1919, the commission struck down a rule followed by the defendant railroad governing the distribution of cars to grain shippers—a rule which had originally been formulated by the Nebraska Railway Commission. Having so recently come himself from a state commission, Eastman was reluctant to agree with the majority. In justifying his attitude, he said:

I am not unmindful that we possess the power in the present instance to do this; but a principle of somewhat basic importance is involved.

It is highly desirable, if undue centralization and concentration of governmental powers in Washington are to be avoided, that every question should be left to the disposition of the state authorities which can reasonably and with a proper regard for the general public interest be dealt with in that way. Nothing is more objectionable than to require the people of this country continually to resort to Washington for the decision of questions which are only or chiefly of local concern. . . . I am unable to believe that any important useful purpose will be served by overruling the views of the local tribunal in a case of this sort.

This defense of the rights of states as opposed to Federal domination is one expression of a principle which in Eastman's thinking was fundamental and to which he was to revert frequently in some of his future decisions. The common-sense approach was also an early indication of a quality which was to add weight to all his opinions.

It does not appear that Eastman's later reputation as a nonconformist was foreshadowed in the first twelve months of his service on the commission. In this period his dissents numbered only five —few in comparison with the total decisions in which he participated. He soon displayed his competence to carry his full share of the load. In the summer of 1919 he was the author of a report in a case of major importance involving reconsignment rules relating to grain, hay, and seeds. Later in the year the commission adopted his conclusions in a proceeding of extraordinary significance—the perishable freight investigation, relating to charges for refrigeration service. He heard much of the testimony himself, gaining knowledge which gave him an expert's understanding of this technical subject—knowledge which was frequently utilized by the commission in later years.

Before very long his power as a writer of forceful dissenting opinions was more fully revealed. It was a widespread practice at that time for companies having large manufacturing plants requiring an extensive layout of railroad switching tracks and sidings on their properties to form subsidiary railroad corporations to perform transportation on these tracks as theoretical common carriers. These industrial railways, as they were then called, would then claim to be performing services for which they were entitled to compensation from the line-haul or trunk railroads either in the form of allowances or of divisions of joint rates. Early in its history the commission had frowned upon such enterprises, but by 1919 the pendulum had swung in the other direction. In *National Tube Co.* v. *Lake Terminal R.R. Co.*, 55 I.C.C. 469, the commission bestowed its approval upon such an arrangement, but Woolley and Eastman, the two liberals, were unable to go along. Eastman voiced their objections in a carefully worded dissent, concluding with a prophetic paragraph.

The questions involved in this case are of large public consequence. As I view it, a great and prosperous industry is here seeking to fasten upon the trunk lines,—and through them indirectly upon the public,—the expense of a service which it has undertaken to perform for its own benefit and which it would continue to perform for the same reason if it were obliged to bear the entire cost itself and although the trunk lines were willing to undertake the service. The result of the majority decision will, I fear, be to impose a further and serious drain upon railroad revenues at a particularly inopportune time and with advantage only to industries who need and are justly entitled to no such advantage. The possibilities of the situation may be indicated by the fact that evidence was herein offered to show that there are now 400 industries located on the trunk lines performing the spotting service with their own power, or with the power of their industrial railroad, and without compensation from the trunk lines.

In the course of time it became apparent that these industrial lines were indeed a serious cause of revenue losses to the trunk lines. The commission investigated the situation and under Eastman's leadership in 1935 abandoned the policy which had prevailed sixteen years before.

Gossip spreads quickly in a closeknit organization like the Interstate Commerce Commission, and it was soon being whispered about that the new member was worth watching. Although he was assigned some very experienced and reliable examiners, he took nothing for granted, but scrutinized their reports with microscopic eye. Furthermore, his dissenting opinions brought him the same distinction—or notoriety—enjoyed by Mr. Justice Holmes on the

Supreme Bench, and the two Massachusetts liberals, so different in other respects, were often compared because of their independence. As we have seen, Eastman's conclusions in the Chicago, Burlington & Quincy Case attracted the attention of the practitioners, who watched with increasing interest the repeated appearance of such expressions as "I find it difficult to go along with my colleagues"; "I am in doubt in regard to this case"; "I cannot accept this view as convincing." In *Ex Parte, No. 76, Express Contract, 1920*, he announced: "I am unable to bring myself to the conclusion that Article V of the proposed contract between the American Express Company and individual railroads will be 'in the interest of better service to the public economy of operation' or that it is otherwise in the public interest."

Lawyers and railroad men were really aroused when he printed dissenting opinions in the Burlington and Lackawanna Stock Dividend Case and the Northern Pacific–Great Northern Bond Issue Case, for these were to set far-reaching precedents. People were beginning to ask, "Who is this fellow Eastman, and why is he so often out of step with the others?"

Although far from tractable, Eastman was not disputatious or arrogant; consequently his insurgence, although not welcomed, seldom stirred his colleagues into active animosity. His honesty was transparent, and he never bore any malice. Even in his disapproval he was invariably good-natured and was ready to present convincing reasons—or reasons which seemed to him convincing —for voting as he did. Occasionally he did wonder why he could so often be in the minority, but he assumed no "holier-than-thou" attitude. Writing to Judge Anderson on April 19, 1921, he said: "It is my impression that all the members of the Commission are striving very hard to do their duty as they see it. Their views do not always coincide with yours or mine, but I have come to regard that as normal." Although he must have been sensitive, he seemed undisturbed or discouraged by hostile criticism. I recall his saying at luncheon in Washington in 1921, "They've been calling me a 'crack-pot,' but I guess I can take it. I'd rather be right, even if I am a little 'cracked.'"

Dissenting opinions on the Interstate Commerce Commission accomplish almost nothing except to give the Lone Wolf the satisfaction of howling. The decision of the majority, whether in a division or in the full commission, even when close, is final; and Eastman's vigorous expression of divergent conclusions had no effect on the fortunes of the litigants. But the other members did in some degree look askance at Woolley and Eastman; and when Woolley, in accordance with the swing of the rotation system, was elected chairman, to take office on March 17, 1920, he declined, feeling that since he was not in accord with his colleagues on the paramount question of Federal control, he ought not to accept a position entailing leadership. Eastman, the next in chronological order, also refused. Professor Holcombe, of Harvard, wrote him:

I have just read a despatch in the *Herald* stating that you declined the presidency of the Interstate Commerce Commission because of your lack of sympathy with the Esch-Cummins Act and the abandonment of full federal control, believing that the head of the Commission should be able to give it his unqualified support. This action on your part is very creditable, both to your sense of honor and your judgment. I am convinced that the Act is unsound and that its failure will be apparent in a very few years. You and Woolley will then be available for further usefulness in the working out of the railroad problem.

After Woolley and Eastman had both declined, Commissioner Edgar E. Clark was duly elected chairman and served in that capacity until August 31, 1921. Eastman's decision not to accept election was, under the circumstances, both tactful and wise.

The culmination of the various differences in political philosophy between Eastman and the older members of the board came with the so-called *Increased Rates Case* (*ex parte* 74, 58 I.C.C. 220), submitted July 6, 1920, and decided on July 29. It will be recalled that Eastman had then been in office only a little over a year. This particular case was one initiated by the commission with the intent of determining whether there should be a general increase of rates following the termination of hostilities. The commission itself had suggested that the carriers apply for authority to increase their freight revenues to an extent that would enable them to earn an annual net railway operating income equal, as nearly as possible, to 6 percent upon the aggregate value of the railway property of such carriers held for and used in the service of transportation. The commission was unanimous in its finding that the increases should be allowed without delay.

Eastman, however, insisted on "sticking his neck out" in a Concurring Opinion, which was signed also by Woolley. There was no necessity for them to make this important Opinion the occasion for the presentation of their views on Federal control of railroads; but Eastman, sensitive and on the defensive, was anxious to make his position clear. He said in part:

I was one of those who opposed the early termination of federal control of railroads. The truth in regard to federal control was then obscured, in part by natural misunderstanding of circumstances arising out of war conditions and in part by propaganda which was often deliberately mendacious. It was my hope that federal control might be continued, because it was evident that the transition back to private operation would create additional disturbance in a time of unsettlement and unrest.

The situation, however, received the careful attention of Congress, and after long deliberation other conclusions were reached which were embodied in the *Transportation Act, 1920.* It is our plain duty to do everything possible to make the plan of operation adopted by Congress a success. . . . It is my best judgment that the railroads cannot function successfully without materially increasing rates, and I am also persuaded that it is in the best interest of the country that the present plan of operation should receive without delay the best test that can be given it.

This would seem to be a temperate statement, considering Eastman's well-known attitude and beliefs; but the Elder Statesmen on the commission, persuaded that Eastman and Woolley were young "radicals" and merited rebuke, selected Commissioner McChord to apply the rod. Following Eastman's Concurring Opinion, McChord said, in language which no one could misconstrue:

The concurring report of Commissioners Woolley and Eastman injects into this case large political questions of governmental policy which are nowhere in issue here. . . . For more than thirty years this Commission has stood four-square to every wind that blows, confining its activities within the four corners of the law, and it is unwise in this critical period to complicate the real questions involved with extraneous issues. This is neither the time nor the place. The Congress is the forum, and should Congress fail to meet the views of a dissatisfied public, if indeed it is dissatisfied, then the final remedy is to be found in that still greater forum, the august tribunal of the people, which is continually sitting, and over whose judgments on the conduct of public functionaries the courts exercise no control.

Thus, with solemn rhetoric, were the two "immature" members notified that they would better attend to the matter at hand and avoid such broad issues as Federal control and that it was neither the duty nor the privilege of the commission "to pass beyond its appropriate sphere of action." For a few months feeling ran strong on the commission, and Woolley and Eastman were made to feel the disapproval of their seniors. Woolley was not reappointed and caused no further trouble; Eastman, however, was in some quarters always under suspicion, even though his colleagues came to respect his ability.

The question has often been asked, "How did Joe Eastman become so ardent a supporter of government ownership?" or, to put it more strongly, "How did he develop into so 'rabid' a 'socialist'?" He was really neither socialistic nor rabid, but a practical economist facing very practical problems. But the answer to the query lies partly in his disheartening experience with the New England railroads. While working with Brandeis during the latter's prolonged duel with the New Haven, Eastman thought he found indisputable evidence that it was badly managed, arrogant, indifferent to the legitimate demands of both the public and its stockholders, and even downright dishonest. Thus, he arrived in Washington with a deep-rooted feeling that railroad executives and the financial interests behind them should be carefully watched and kept within bounds. He was so scrupulous himself that he detested wastefulness and irresponsibility in others.

Then, too, what he had seen of government management during the war convinced him that its evils had been deliberately exaggerated for selfish reasons. It had dealt well with labor, and labor, as Eastman wrote Kellogg, was "the most serious problem of all and will grow in importance as time goes on." However misled he may have been in other respects, he was indubitably right in this. He had not yet been disillusioned with regard to labor as he had been with management. But on the broad issue of Federal control, Eastman had no ingrained prejudices. His approach was realistic and free from any personal motives. He had weighed the evidence, as he had been taught to do in college, and had tried to reach a just conclusion.

Although Eastman continued for some years to be a theoretical believer in government ownership of railroads, he was too well-informed to be optimistic and too wise to make himself a nuisance. On November 2, 1927, he wrote Senator George W. Norris:

You may be right in believing that government ownership and operation are more imminent than I think they are. It happens that in my work on the Commission I encounter very few who are friendly to such a policy and many who are strongly opposed to it. The latter seems to be quite a general attitude upon the part of shippers. They have in mind various experiences during the war when the railroads were under federal control, and they also set great store upon competition.

By that date Eastman was himself less ardent on the subject than he had been in 1920; and, as we shall see, the hour was to come when he was prepared to repudiate some of his earlier views. On this, as on some other subjects, he enjoyed the privilege of changing his mind.

Although Eastman was now no longer a resident of Massachusetts, his relations with New England railroads, especially the New York, New Haven & Hartford, were by no means over. The Transportation Act of 1920 had provided for a revolving fund of $300,-000,000 to be lent to needy railroads, and the Boston & Maine, taking advantage of the opportunity, applied at once for a loan of $8,843,-000. When the New Haven also requested a large loan, Eastman hinted that it might be well for the road to do its own financing; but E. G. Buckland, vice-president and general counsel, stated that this would be impossible. In reply, Eastman wrote much more sharply than was usually his custom.

Your letter of June 23, 1920, with respect to the practicability of obtaining capital from New England banks and shippers is disappointing, although your talk with me a few days ago had prepared me for it. To speak frankly, it seems to me that you are approaching the matter from the standpoint of an attorney making the best possible case for his client and more anxious to show why cooperation is impossible than to do any cooperating. . . . So far this is the first case we have met where there has been no apparent appreciation of the necessity of co-operation.

As the weeks went by, Eastman's distrust of the policies of the New Haven executives found vigorous expression. On August 13 he wrote F. A. Howard: "Ever since I became a member of this Commission, and while I was on the Public Service Commission of Massachusetts, I have continually heard criticism of the way opera-tion was being conducted by the New Haven, and the fault has been laid at the door of certain operating officials." "I don't want to seem like a persecutor," he wrote to another friend, "but there are some evasions which, as a Commissioner, I just don't like."

Eastman's own judgment was shortly to be corroborated by the New England Joint Railroad Committee, headed by James J. Stor-row, whom he had known and liked back in his Boston days. After months of investigation Storrow, who was certainly no radical, pre-sented a report condemning harshly some of the practices of the New England railroads. The operators, not relishing being put in the wrong, argued that "long-continued government regulation, capped by actual government operation for two years, were well calculated to dim the enthusiasm of the most optimistic men," and therefore took refuge in an attitude of fatalism. Bentley W. Warren, who had followed the dispute since its beginning, wrote, "in a de-bate on this question it must be obvious that neither side could con-vince the other." Eastman, on his part, felt that the inefficiency, the lack of initiative and resourcefulness, dated back to before the war and that the executives had done little to correct it.

A series of cumulative irritations arising out of the inertia of the New Haven finally induced Eastman to write to James L. Richards, a member of the Executive Committee of the New Haven Directors and a friend of his since his struggles with the Consolidated Gas companies, asking him to make a personal investigation of the rail-road. "The reports which have come in from time to time," he said, "both as to service and as to financial results, have, as you know, been most discouraging." In this informal and unofficial letter Eastman made a comprehensive and fearless indictment of New Haven policies, in the crisp style which he had learned from Brandeis. Naturally much disturbed, Buckland called on Eastman in September, having heard that the latter felt "dissatisfied and apprehensive in regard to the management of the road." Things had certainly changed since the old days when Charles S. Mellen defied Louis D. Brandeis and girded himself for a fight to the finish. Now the New Haven executives, having learned a salutary lesson, were in a chastened mood and eager to forestall trouble. Richards soon named a special committee of the New Haven directors, with himself as chairman, to investigate the quality of the management, and their report did largely whitewash Buckland and his associates. There was nothing Eastman could do for the moment but accept their conclusions. Although he wrote Anderson that the report struck him as "at least a somewhat unenthusiastic defense," he was willing to give the management a further trial and wrote Richards: "The conclusion is, I think, sound that the present organization is fairly entitled to a better opportunity than it has yet had to prove its worth." The incident shows three things: that Eastman could now speak with more authority and command more compliance than ever before; that railroad officials were at last disposed to be conciliatory; and that Eastman was willing to modify his verdict when it proved to be too severe. He was not, however, yet done with the New Haven.

There were other indications that Eastman was not slumbering at his post. On August 24, 1920, he wrote Harris, of the New York Central, warning him that advertisements of a proposed issue of securities had been sent out with a statement that the commission would shortly give formal approval, when as a matter of fact even informal sanction had not yet been agreed upon. He bluntly criticized Carl M. Gage, president of the Huntingdon & Broad Top Mountain and Coal Company, for the confused condition of his accounts. He reminded Boston & Maine officials that the financiers of New England should be able to take care of its refunding bonds, "leaving the government fund for more constructive purposes."

During the summer of 1920 New England went through another of its perennial fuel crises. A runaway market in the tidewater ports had enabled speculators to pile up fortunes almost over-night, with the result that the Northeast was in grave danger of being unheated during the coming winter. Governor Calvin Coolidge came to Washington, interviewed Division V of the Interstate Commerce Commission—made up of Clark, Aitchison, and Potter—and returned feeling that they were prejudiced against New England. Eastman felt rather helpless during this dispute, for friction still existed between him and his associates. He did, however, persuade them to adopt a service order giving preference and priority to coal moving to Atlantic ports. Fortunately New England struggled somehow through her dark hour, as she had done so many times and will probably do again.

One problem which Eastman had very much on his mind, then and later, was the consolidation of railroads into a limited number of systems. The Transportation Act of 1920, as we have seen, required the commission to prepare and adopt such a plan of consolidation; and Professor William Z. Ripley, of Harvard, an acknowledged expert, was employed to lay out a tentative grouping of the different railroads. Writing to him on November 17, 1920, Eastman said:

I have some doubt whether, under present conditions at least, any important results would be accomplished by consolidating the New Haven, Boston & Maine, Maine Central, and Bangor & Aroostook. Owing to their present financial condition, and particularly the financial condition of the New Haven Railroad, such a combination would apparently be no easier to finance than the present separate companies, and perhaps not so easy.

Eastman's own tentative view at the time was that it might be feasible to join the New Haven with the Pennsylvania, and the Boston & Maine with the Delaware & Hudson, the Erie, and the Lackawanna, or with the Canadian roads. The Boston & Albany was, of course, already merged with the New York Central. Eastman's opinion, however, did not prevail, and when the report of the commission appeared in August, 1921, it suggested alternative methods of dealing with the New England situation: a so-called "trunk line consolidation," linking the Boston & Maine with the New York Central and the New Haven with the Baltimore & Ohio, and a strictly New England plan, bringing together all the railroads in that section with the exception of the New York Central.

Each scheme had from the beginning its stanch supporters, but sentiment in New England was slow to center on either one. The matter was obviously of so much importance that the New England governors, headed by Channing Cox, of Massachusetts, appointed a joint committee to study the situation. This committee, organized on August 15, 1922, with James J. Storrow as chairman of its Executive Committee, carried on an enormous amount of research and finally produced an exhaustive report, described by Bentley W. Warren as "frank, open, and uncompromising," in which it argued that New England should "wear its own breeches." What was needed first of all, it declared, was not consolidation, but "the rehabilitation of the two major systems so that they can be lifted out of their present acute difficulties and give to New England industry and to the New England public the grade of transportation service that is vital if New England is to hold its place against the keen competition of other districts." Storrow knew as well as Eastman that the New Haven was in a "water-logged condition," and therefore he called upon all Yankees to help: "Putting in a stream of alibis why we are not what we want to be here in New England is dull stuff. It isn't half as interesting as getting all together as our fathers did at the opening of the railroad era and being what we would like to be."

The Joint Committee put the power of its prestige directly behind the plan which provided for the consolidation of the important New England railroads. Its report was widely distributed, and not only Storrow but also several New England governors appeared at the hearings before the Interstate Commerce Commission in the autumn of 1923. Eastman, who had not originally favored the proposal of the Joint Committee, was won over by Storrow's persuasive arguments. Unfortunately nothing came of it. The record of the hearings held before the commission, completed December 4, 1923, included fifty-four volumes comprising 11,713 pages of testimony and 711 exhibits. But as it turned out, the commission was divided in its views on the question and only half-hearted in its attempt to carry out the mandate of the Transportation Act. The discussion over New England lingered along through the prosperous Coolidge era, when nobody wished to disturb the existing situation. Not until December 9, 1929—and then only to relieve uncertainty—did the commission recommend a consolidation plan for the entire country. By that date the Depression hung over all industry like a pall, and mere survival seemed much more important than reorganization.

As New England's only representative on the Interstate Commerce Commission, Eastman was frequently consulted by members of the Joint Committee, including Storrow, who was its driving force and inspiration. Eastman and Storrow were alike in their sincerity of purpose, their tireless energy, and their dependable character, and they were both working for the best interests of the northeastern states. On October 28, 1920, Joe spoke in Boston before the members of the Associated Industries of Massachusetts, and two days later he addressed the Chamber of Commerce. Asked by the chamber president whom he would like to have at the head table, he named the following as his most intimate friends in that area: Judge George W. Anderson, Charles F. Weed, George S. Macfarland, John H. Fahey, March G. Bennett, Bernard J. Rothwell, F. J. McLeod, Alonzo R. Weed, Charles R. Jones, James H. Vahey, and Stanley King. The title of his address was "The Railroad Transportation Situation and the Way Out"; and he still had the courage, in spite of what had happened in the commission, to call attention to the advantages of government ownership and operation. He was not so self-deluded as to expect to make conversions, and he wrote his friend Elmquist, "My talk was very attentively received by the audience, and they threw no bricks at me, but I doubt whether many of them agreed with me. I shall have to wait for the future for agreement, I guess."

More and more Eastman was becoming known as an acceptable public speaker—not of the soul-stirring or rabble-rousing type, but straight forward, with a sense of humor which was seldom apparent in his printed addresses, but was revealed to his audiences through interpolated amusing anecdotes and homely phrases. He faced them with a genial, conciliatory smile, with no bitterness in his heart, and though he met with resistance to his ideas, he made no enemies. Most of his talks had to be prepared under pressure, for the Transportation Act had much increased the routine business of the commission. As the year 1920 closed, Joe wrote Max Thelen:

We are plugging away, endeavoring to do our little duty under the Transportation Act without too much delay. I feel like a man who never has time to get a good solid meal, but has to snatch a bite here and there on the run. This almost applies to real meals, but what I am talking about is metaphorical meals. We dabble in the questions in the cases, and seldom have a chance to make a good solid study of any of them.

Eastman was already regarded as the most industrious member of the commission, and the lights in his office often shone far into the night. On January 20, 1921, he wrote Thelen:

I find it very difficult to keep up with all we have to do. . . . It has seemed to me sometimes that the Commission was in danger of giving, or at least appearing to give, too little attention to the public, or shippers' side of questions, and that such an impression, however ill-founded, might be cause for concern a little later.

Occasionally, when annoyed or fatigued, he "blew off steam," as in a letter on February 1, 1921, to Professor Edward W. Bemis:

The great trouble in the discussion of railroad and public utility questions is that both sides have so little regard for the truth. They continually indulge in overstatements or positive misrepresentations, and it has seemed to me that people in general are becoming tired and perhaps disgusted with this sort of thing, to which they give the appropriate name of "bunk."

To those whom he could trust he spoke out with disingenuous frankness, disclosing the apprehensions which were on his mind. On April 13, 1921, he wrote Anderson:

There is little new in the railroad game except that I seem to notice on the part of newspapers, statesmen (or politicians), and financiers a somewhat gentler attitude towards labor. From his Message to Congress I take it that President Harding will have nothing to do for the present at least with public ownership, and that he wishes to have both wages and rates increased. This will not be altogether pleasing to the railroads. I assume that if the present administration is finally obliged to accept something in the nature of public ownership, they will call it by a different name, just as, if they are finally obliged to accept the principle of the League of Nations, they will call that by a different name.

In 1922 he was fortunate to have assigned to him as examiner a lawyer named Howard Hosmer, who was to become his trusted adviser and who quickly learned to study facts and in general to write reports in the same way that Eastman did. Hosmer was a man of scholarly temperament and discriminating judgment who profited, as did Eastman, by widening experience. One of Joe's weaknesses in the opinion of those who were close to him was his unwillingness to delegate authority or to rely on others for even routine research. He loved to marshall figures himself on coarse yellow paper and ponder on their significance. Even though he came to have confidence in Hosmer's accuracy and common sense, he never ceased to scrutinize even his opinions with critical care before placing upon them his official "O.K." Eastman was aware that he had much to learn. In 1919 he wrote to Dr. Clyde L. King, "My acquaintance with railroad *operating* problems is very limited." So, too, on the legal side Eastman felt often that he needed the advice of a competent lawyer, and here Hosmer was able to assist him greatly.

As Eastman adjusted himself more completely to his official status, he broadened his social contacts and sought relaxation from the tension of his commission schedule. In the summer of 1922 he permitted himself a long-delayed vacation and went on a canoe trip with his friend Charles E. Elmquist, during which he lost sixteen pounds. Writing to Elmquist later, he confessed: "I get tired of living in Pullmans and getting too much food and too little exercise. Pretty soon I shall have back all the weight I lost last summer." He joined several clubs, including not only the Cosmos but also the Racquet, Chevy Chase, and the Columbia Country Club, and started to play tennis again, particularly with his college classmate Fayette B. ("Cap") Dow. This marked the resumption of an intimate relationship which was to mean more and more to Joe as the years passed.

For the first time in his life, also, Eastman had the money he needed to provide all the necessary comforts as well as the few luxuries that he desired. He declined to act as chairman of the Washington District for the Amherst Centennial Fund in 1921, pleading his crowded days as an excuse, but he did contribute a $1,000 Liberty Bond to the cause; and he also sent $100 to help pay off the mortgage on the "Psi U" House in Amherst. When he was asked to subscribe to the Amherst *Student*, he sent $10 instead of $1.50, explaining, "This is to pay up for all the years when I meant to subscribe and didn't. My work on the paper was one of the most enjoyable features of my college days."

Almost for the first time since he had graduated from Amherst, Eastman could snatch a few precious hours for general reading. I find that in 1919 he drew from the Library of Congress Beaumarchais's *Memoirs*, Charnwood's *Lincoln*, Bertrand Russell's *Proposed Roads to Freedom*, Barvin's *The Economic Foundations of Peace*, and many others, especially in history and biography. He was an ardent supporter of Wilson's League of Nations and followed current discussions on that controversial issue. He kept up also his subscriptions to Boston newspapers, including the *Herald*, the *Post*, and the famous *Evening Transcript*. He was traveling much more than he had ever done and constantly meeting able people with fresh points of view. If he had had any tendency to provincialism, it was disappearing in his cosmopolitan surroundings. Even in Washington, with the great of the nation close at hand, he was a personage; but though he did figuratively, if not literally, walk with kings, he never lost the common touch.

As 1922 drew to a close and Eastman's term was about to end, there was some speculation as to whether the conservative President Harding would reappoint a commissioner whose conduct had been so liberal. Commenting on the subject to W. L. McMenimen, Eastman wrote:

I have made no campaign and have been content to let matters take their course, but I understand that quite a number of representations have been made to the President in my behalf. Such gossip as has reached me leads to the conclusion that my chances are pretty good, but it may be that I hear the good news, not the bad news.

Eastman did have warm backing from men of all political affiliations. Colonel Charles R. Gow, of the Associated Industries of Massachusetts, sent the President a letter praising Eastman highly and saying that his appointment would be acceptable to all New England. Frank W. Stearns told me that once after a cabinet meeting Vice-President Coolidge said to Harding, "Eastman's a good man— for a Democrat!" But Harding, in one of his more impulsive moments, had half promised the place to a friend of Senator George H. Moses, of New Hampshire, who had much influence with the ruling clique of the Republican party. One morning in late November Judge Anderson and Commissioner Winthrop M. Daniels called on James L. Richards, in Boston, to ask him what could be done about the President. Richards thought that it might be too late, but he did ring up several persons on the telephone, including Senator Henry Cabot Lodge and finally Senator Moses, who was persuaded to withdraw his candidate. The result of the negotiations was that no obstacle was left to the naming of Eastman. The President in any case could hardly have disregarded the fine record which Eastman had made as a public servant. Harding sent in Eastman's nomination on December 20, 1922, for the term ending December 31, 1929; and on the following afternoon the Senate, without discussion or opposition, confirmed the recommendation.

Eastman spent most of Christmas day answering the letters and telegrams of congratulation which had piled up on his desk. To John F. Meany he said, with obvious satisfaction, "Hitherto I have for the most part been filling out George Anderson's unexpired term, and I am glad to have one now on my own account." He struck a similar note in replying to George N. Brown, "I am afraid your reference to it as a 'sentence of seven years hard labor' is about right. However they say hard work never killed a man, and on the whole I enjoy it." To Judge Anderson, his stanch friend, he confessed modestly:

I am inclined to think that some of the support which has come to me has been caused by the reputation for hard work created by the fact that, owing to the small size of my home, I have been obliged to do night work at the office instead of working at home as so many of the Commissioners do. The result is that counsel appearing before the Commission see the lights in my office at night and gather the impression that I must be working harder than the rest of the Commission, which is not at all true. I think that some of the support may be due to the inheritance of a non-friction disposition.

Eastman minimized in this letter the amount of time which he devoted to his job. But as the year closed and his second term was about to begin, he confided to Anderson some of his "gripes":

One thing that I meant to say when writing you in regard to my reappointment was that I am constantly impressed by the difficulty down here of any constructive thinking along broad lines. It is appalling how much work there is to be done which cannot be delegated to subordinates. At the present moment I have several important cases which demand attention, which I cannot neglect, and which will consume a large quantity of time. I should much prefer to devote this time to a study of the New England situation, or to a study of valuation, or to a study of the plan for the concentration of our railroad systems under national guidance. But I find it almost impossible to give thought to these important questions except at random moments.

Although Eastman was not the first public servant to describe himself as enslaved by routine, the servitude in his case was the direct corollary of his character, and he would have resented pity. Like Wordsworth's Happy Warrior, he was one

> Who comprehends his trust, and to the same
> Keeps faithful with a singleness of aim;
> And therefore does not stoop, nor lie in wait
> For wealth, or honours, or for worldly state.

The conscientiousness which was one of his dominating traits would not allow him to neglect the undramatic day-to-day jobs for something more sensational. In this respect he resembled Grover Cleveland and Herbert Hoover—men who have never been mentioned as "clever" or "astute," but rather "painstaking," "scrupulous," and "reliable." On a body like the Interstate Commerce Commission these qualities are of supreme importance. The commissioner who neglects the small routine duties and seeks the center of the stage or uses his position for personal ends is always a drag and may become a menace. Eastman was not a man of this self-seeking type. By 1923, when his second term began, he had made a reputation for integrity, intelligence, and industry and was regarded as one of the most useful persons in Washington.

VIII

The Prosperity Era

THROUGHOUT the Harding administration, when the capital was packed with professional lobbyists and "fixers," Eastman was dissatisfied with what was going on and kept aloof from political intrigues. I cannot find that he was invited to the White House, and he knew none of the members of the Ohio Gang, Harry S. Daugherty and Jess Smith and their satellites, who used their previous acquaintance with the good-natured President for their own sinister purposes. They wouldn't have liked him or have understood him. At heart a philosophic liberal of the Woodrow Wilson type, he was unimpressed by party tradition and rather distrustful of conservatives. Orthodoxy was to him no virtue unless it had a logical justification. The threads of his experience had woven themselves into an altruistic pattern by which he measured all novel problems. His choices at election time were consistent, for he was adhering to his own deep-seated principles, which were more stable than Republican or Democratic platforms, composed to attract votes. Some of his letters of this period indicate clearly where his sympathies lay. When he was allowed to read certain statements by vindictive industrialists, he wrote on April 14, 1923, to Wilbur LaRoe:

I thank you for letting me see the file of letters, chiefly the "hard-boiled" type. . . . The letters which you have received would convey the impression that all the authors of these letters were earnest workers for the unadulterated truth. As a matter of fact, most of them have minds which, quite unconsciously, are full of preconceived notions and are not open to the truth. Overstatements or misleading statements by a radical they can perceive at once, but overstatements or misleading statements by a conservative they cannot perceive at all. As you know, more deliberate lies were told in regard to what happened during federal control than there have been upon almost any subject that I am acquainted with; yet I doubt whether these gentlemen who write to you in their search for truth have ever stumbled or are likely to stumble across that particular fact. . . . I am merely putting on paper some stray thoughts that come to my mind as I read the expressions of joy which flow from the pens of men of conservative tendencies when they read a criticism of something which a man reputed to be a radical, although not in fact a radical, has written.

A further quotation, this time from a letter on March 31, 1924, shows how quick he was to resent and denounce intolerance.

I note in your letter and in the enclosed file of correspondence rather derogatory references to the "Brookharts and LaFollettes" and also to "Bert Jewell" of the Railroad Shopmen's Union. Has it ever occurred to you that these men, although they may be mistaken in some of their views, have perhaps more sincerity than you give them credit for and are trying to do their duty as they see it? I have never met Senator Brookhart, but I do know Senator LaFollette and Mr. Jewell and I have a high regard for both of them, although I do not always agree with them and I presume they do not always agree with me. I am inclined to think that in this country we damn men too readily without undertaking to understand what they are trying to accomplish and by this very process we drive them to extreme views. I have been damned myself now and then and therefore know something about the reaction.

In both these letters can be detected an undertone of sensitiveness probably related to the criticism which his advocacy of Federal control of railroads had brought upon him. His friends who visited him in Washington noticed that although outwardly his usual imperturbable self, he seemed to have his defenses up against a possible attack. In Eastman's outer office, Frank Livingstone spent a considerable part of his time ridiculing the three Republican presidents —Harding, Coolidge, and Hoover. Joe was not, of course, so indiscreet. He voted rather lukewarmly for Cox in 1920, not because he thought him a superior candidate but because he preferred him to the reactionary Harding. Although Calvin Coolidge was a fellow Amherst graduate whom Eastman had known slightly in Massachusetts, the two men were temperamentally imcompatible. Writing on December 15, 1923, to Albert H. Mellen, Eastman said: "As for the President's Message, I liked his simplicity and the directness of his statements but can find nothing very inspiring in it. A message which Judge Gary and the *Wall Street Journal* regard as a masterpiece is not one which arouses enthusiasm on my part."

When a third party was projected in 1924, Eastman wrote Mellen: "Not being a member of either of the present major parties, I find it easy to think of a new one." As a matter of fact, he was one of the 4,822,856 American citizens who voted that autumn for LaFollette, but he was not excited over the election and had no illusions as to the prospects of his candidate. He wrote to Anderson, "I think that John W. Davis is an able and polished gentleman who would in many ways adorn the White House. I should not mourn greatly if he were elected, although there are other men whom I should prefer. . . . I feel certain that LaFollette will have a larger vote than many anticipate."

The fullest expression of Eastman's philosophy at this stage in his development was elicited by a nonpolitical matter. Alexander Meiklejohn, president of Amherst College since 1912, had gradually lost the confidence of a majority of his faculty, of the entire Board of Trustees, and of many influential alumni; and the board, after a careful study of the situation, concluded that the best interests of the college required his withdrawal. Finally, at the insistence of the trustees, he submitted his resignation in June, 1923. Although the president of the board, George A. Plimpton, stated publicly that the dispute was "not one involving questions of educational policy," some well-meaning persons not fully informed about the real issues chose to bestow martyrdom upon Meiklejohn; and a small group of Amherst reactionaries helped the battle along by denouncing the president's "radicalism." Among these were two of Eastman's classmates, who published an open letter calling Meiklejohn a "confirmed Marxist." Now fully aroused, Eastman consulted his trusted friend Stanley King, who gave him a confidential version of what had happened behind the scenes. Joe answered, July 3, 1923, in his judicial manner.

I have never had the opportunity to go into the Meiklejohn affair carefully, but I am quite ready to believe that the Board of Trustees had sound reason for its action. It is a matter of great regret, however, that it should be necessary to lose a man who has gained the good-will of the students in so marked a degree and who had brought so many good men to the faculty at Amherst.

Eastman accepted without question King's frank disclosure of the motives of the trustees, but he was not entirely satisfied, and on July 5, 1923, he wrote his friend Charles J. Symington: "I thought the remarks made in the public prints by my classmates, Harry Taylor and Frank Kane, were very foolish, and I think they injured the college." The incident still lingered in his mind during the hot Washington summer, and a few weeks later he unburdened himself to Taylor in a letter which he carefully prepared and which reveals a great deal about himself and his opinions.

The mere labelling of a man as a "Marxist" does not impress me, for I have frequently been called "socialistic" or "bolshevistic" by those who are accustomed to resort to that style of argument. Some men might regard a professor as "socialistic" who advocated that the town of Amherst own its lighting plants or that the estates of deceased persons should be appropriated by the State; yet both of these things could be accomplished without trespassing upon our present Constitution.

Furthermore, it seems to me that socialism is a question of practical wisdom rather than a moral question. It is probably true,—at least many of those who have thought most deeply about the matter have been of this view,—that a socialistic form of government would be nearer the ideal than the form we now have. The difficulty with it is the practical one that we have not reached the stage of human development and altruism which permits such an organization of society to be carried on successfully. The mere fact that a professor believed in socialism would not prove to me that he was a dangerous teacher. If college teaching is to err at all, it may well err on the side of the ideal, for there will be plenty of experience with the practical when college days are over.

To take actual illustrations: Bernard Shaw and H. G. Wells are both socialists, yet I think it would be an excellent thing for college boys to come in contact with their minds. The same might be said of the English socialist, Sidney Webb, or Ramsay MacDonald, and with even more emphasis of such an economist as J. A. Hobson, whom many in this country would regard as having socialistic leanings. On the other hand, if I were to consult my own mental preferences, the first college president whom I would fire would be Nicholas Murray Butler, whose mental operations fill me with loathing. Yet I presume he fills a useful purpose, and that the boys are not permanently injured by coming into contact with his mind. . . . I do not believe that college boys are so easily influenced in their opinions if once they are taught to think and are separated from the notion that they must continue to hold the opinions that their fathers happened to hold.

Eastman's liberalism—which at times disturbed some of his most devoted friends—was never fanatical and was always tempered by Yankee common sense. In August, 1923, replying to a correspondent who had urged him to take a stand against the "Jim Crow" car in the South, he remarked that he had noticed during his recent trips through that area that the cars assigned for the use of colored people were of the same type and design as those set aside for the whites. He then continued:

It occurs to me that little is to be gained by discussing the Jim Crow car question unless the rest of the country is prepared to *impose* a change in policy upon the South. I cannot imagine that views in the South with respect to this question are likely to be modified by discussion or that any change in policy is likely to be made voluntarily; nor can I imagine that the rest of the country is prepared to impose an involuntary change.

Even on a more crucial contemporary issue he did not permit his impulses to sway his judgment. Writing to Judge Anderson, September 6, 1927, he said, "I was profoundly shocked at the Sacco-Vanzetti affair, and not well impressed by the statements of the Governor and his advisory council, but perhaps I do not understand the situation as well as those who are on the immediate ground."

To round out this analysis of Eastman's economic and social philosophy during the 1920's it is necessary to quote at some length from a letter written on January 17, 1923, to his fellow commissioner Mark W. Potter. For him the transmission of his thoughts to paper was a means of clarifying and integrating the ideas which were passing through his mind. As if talking from an easy chair near the fireside, he said:

This notion of "regulating" an industry by superimposing upon its activities a public inquisitorial body functioning by means of public hearings conducted in the manner of a court is wholly unsound. When an industry becomes of so much public consequence that it cannot be safely permitted to conduct its affairs in the ordinary way, I think the situation should be met frankly and that the industry should become openly and directly a public industry. The system of public regulation of a so-called "private industry" duplicates effort, is grossly wasteful of time and energy, and is inconsistent with any sound theories of administration.

I agree with Mr. County that railroad officials cannot be expected to give proper attention to their real duties when their time is constantly consumed by investigations and public hearings. The only class in the community to which the present system is of benefit is the legal fraternity. . . .

A further reason for turning from a wholly unscientific plan of private management subject to public "regulation" is that a frank recognition that transportation is a public industry will make it possible at once to get rid of the complications and confusion which came about through the fact that our railroads are owned by a large number of separate companies, each one of which is seeking to favor its own particular ends without regard for the interests of the transportation system as a whole. I am wholly convinced that the reason why our rate structure is so illogical, chaotic, and so complicated that even experts are not always able to determine the applicable rate is because of the existence of these separate companies. Each one is trying to secure some traffic "velvet" which does not really belong to it, and the result is circuitous routes and depressed rates which create havoc in the rate structure. The existence of separate companies is also a reason why it has been impossible to deal at all effectively with the terminal problem, and is one reason why we have so many labor troubles.

I hope very much that you can turn your thoughts in this direction. The problem of government ownership and operation, to my mind, is simply a problem of devising a scheme for management which will avoid undue centralization and undue political influence. The avoiding of political influence, I believe, is not at all difficult. I am absolutely confident that the people of this country are heartily opposed to the injection of politics into government management of railroads and that any administration which would attempt to keep politics outside with an iron hand would meet with immediate approval. This is true in Massachusetts, and apparently is true in Canada. I do not recall that anybody sought the appointment of politicians as public trustees of the Boston Elevated, and Governor McCall met with some criticism because he made his private secretary one of the trustees. The latter, however, was a well-informed and capable man. As a matter of fact, the chief danger would come from Congress, and it is my personal opinion that the people of this country are becoming weary of the insincerity and bunk that characterize our Congressional activities to so great an extent.

If the railroads should be taken over by the Government, the way to do so is by the acquisition of the stock of the present railroad companies. The stockholders could be offered a good trade in government bonds, and if they will not accept, their stock should be taken by process of government domain. I see no need for the condemnation of the physical property of the railroads; and on the contrary I think it would be better to have the roads continue under the ownership of one or more corporations wholly controlled by the Government. . . .

I may say, also, that I do not agree at all with the idea that we should have a Secretary of Transportation so long as the roads are privately managed and publicly "regulated." That would merely introduce another disturbing factor and make confusion worse confounded.

Please give these thoughts your prayerful consideration!

Here, as lucidly and as completely as Eastman ever phrased it, is Eastman's conception in the 1920's of the future of American transportation. He was later, during the Great Depression, to modify his views in certain respects; and the increase first in motor cars and afterwards in airplanes introduced new factors which compelled him to revise his theories still further. But in the record of his evolution as a thinker this is a most significant document. After pondering on every aspect of a very intricate problem, he had reached a logical and definite conclusion. On this ground he stood firm, and no fleeting gust of popular sentiment or demagogic denunciation could sway him.

What he could express without restraint in private correspondence was not, however, what he was saying publicly in his speeches. On October 22, 1924, addressing a large audience at the dinner of the Associated Industries, in Boston, he was naturally somewhat more cautious.

My own views in regard to public ownership and operation have been a matter of slow development. I hope they will continue to develop. I think I am familiar with all the arguments against such ownership and operation, and for a time I found them convincing. So far as my views have changed, it is as a result of close observation of the operation of railroads and public utilities over a period of twenty years. . . .

On the other hand, while I believe that we shall eventually have public ownership and operation of railroads in this country, I doubt whether there is any immediate prospect of such a change. But I should have said the same thing ten years ago of prohibition. . . . Public ownership and operation are not likely to be achieved except in the event of either intense dissatisfaction on the part of the public or intense dissatisfaction on the part of investors with the conditions prevailing under private ownership and operation. Probably they are not likely to be achieved unless these two states of dissatisfaction coincide. . . .

One final word on public ownership and operation, and I am done. It is an issue which at the present time has little more than academic importance, but whatever else may be said of it, this may be said with truth,—that the fear of government ownership is the best incentive to efficiency and zeal in the handling of the privately owned railroads that has yet been discovered.

With Eastman's candid admission that government ownership and operation constituted for the moment an issue of little more than "academic importance," we can leave the subject, although it will recur later in this narrative. The talk in Boston was only one of several which he made that autumn. A good speaker as a college undergraduate, he had with practice become a distinguished one. At first wth resignation and then with pleasure he had faced the fact that he was in demand by transportation organizations and chambers of commerce. "Making an address," he wrote in 1922, "is no easy task for me, and I find it consumes a good deal of energy in addition to the time necessary for the trip." He composed his own speeches, writing them out in longhand; and he preferred to read the more important paragraphs, for he dealt frequently with statistics which could not be retained accurately in the memory. He did, however, adopt the technique of opening with an appropriate story or two and then deviating now and then from the text in order to make a jocular comment or drive home a point. His unpretentious style had none of the sonorous rumble of Winston Churchill or the crisp and vivid phrasing of Franklin D. Roosevelt; but his subject matter did not lend itself to Ciceronian oratory. He seldom indulged in sarcasm or irony, preferring less subtle methods of attack or defense. Although his voice lacked carrying power and was not exceptionally melodious, it was well adapted to gatherings where substance was more highly regarded than sound. Often he spoke with his left hand in his trousers pocket, gesturing occasionally with his right arm for emphasis. He had a politician's faculty of remembering names and faces, and he dealt without embarrassment with all kinds of people, both management and labor, with ease, even when hard pressed by questioners. In short, he had become the mature and seasoned speaker, accustomed to sitting on platforms and at speakers' tables and aware that he must always be prepared to make a "few remarks."

Among the many invitations which he received, he accepted those which suited his convenience and seemed likely to be interesting. On May 12, 1920, representing the commission, he spoke at Atlantic City before the Railway Accounting Officers Association, confiding to them humorously some of his perplexities as a new member; on April 1, 1921, he addressed the New Haven Railroad Club, telling them that although the immediate future of transportation in this country seemed dark, very dark, and nowhere more so than in New England, extraordinary changes might be expected during the next twenty years; on October 12, 1921, he talked to the National Association of Railway and Utility Commissioners, at Atlanta, Georgia, on the broad problem of public utilities, reminding them frankly that railroad discussion had recently been "on a painfully low level." There were many others, but I have named these three because they illustrate so perfectly his themes. These were not routine utterances, but carefully thought out papers going to the very heart of current issues. Again and again he told his hearers that "railroading is not an old and senile, but a young and growing industry with immense possibilities before it," and in the 1920's he believed this. He warned the members of the New Haven Railroad Club of the dangers inherent in the promiscuous use of such words as "Americanism," "red-blooded," and "two-fisted"—"too much red blood stirs up bad blood, and two fists can be worse than useless if they are not guided by sound sense"—

and "propaganda." On the subject of labor problems he was bold enough to say:

The day of mere driving has gone, but new incentives will come. Some one will eventually make the discovery that labor leaders and executives,—and I have seen fair samples of both,— are all Americans with the interests of their country at heart, and for the most part reasonable human beings able to pull together in double harness.

Although Eastman looked outwardly very calm, even phlegmatic, he could be easily aroused over what he thought to be injustice. During the Christmas holidays in 1924 he went to Eagle Bay, on Fourth Lake, in the Adirondacks, with "Cap" Dow, as the guest of Henry R. Howard. They camped out in the cold, plodded on snowshoes through the surrounding forest, and fished successfully through the ice. Their Indian guide had applied some months before for a license to carry a pistol and had sent in the necessary $1.50. A few weeks later state troopers entered his cabin and confiscated his automatic pistol and holster. Meanwhile the guide had procured a license from another county, but had been unable to get back the $1.50 or his revolver. Eastman became so angry over the incident that he wrote Judge Timothy D. Sullivan, of Hamilton County, some scathing letters, but received no satisfaction. Finally he sent a note so corrosive that it brought about the return of the money and the weapon to the astonished guide. The occurrence in itself is trivial, except for the fact that Joe spent as much time on it as he would have given to an event of national importance.

For his associate Mark W. Potter, Eastman had a genuine regard, and he took the trouble in November, 1925, to write President Coolidge recommending his reappointment, saying, "We frequently disagree, but he abounds in energy, works and thinks hard, has a creative mind, and is of the utmost value to the Commission because of his wide experience, enthusiasm, and ideas." Potter did receive his reappointment. Within a few weeks, Eastman sent to the other commissioners an office memorandum as follows:

Permit me to register a heartfelt protest against Brother Potter's indictment of Mr. List in the memorandum which he has circulated to-day. In his restrained judicial way Brother Potter accuses List of being insubordinate, disloyal, incompetent, and unfit. His reason is that List, after hearing certain rumors reflecting on the integrity of certain of our employees, endeavored to secure some corroboration of these rumors before reporting them to Division I. This may have been poor judgment, although I would not concede that, but how on earth could it show insubordination or disloyalty or even incompetence or unfitness? Were there any orders or instructions outstanding which governed the behavior of an employee in such a contingency? Was List trying to help or hurt the Commission? Must a man run to his department head with every rumor that he hears and is he debarred from obtaining evidence of crime until he has received orders to obtain it?

I was outraged yesterday that a man who has been trying to protect the Commission and the Government should be subjected to inquiries which took the form of sneers. I am outraged by Brother Potter's memorandum of to-day. The situation seems to me to demand a wholly different attitude of mind.

These two unrelated episodes and others demonstrate that Eastman, although ordinarily even tempered and amiable, could react angrily when his sense of fairness was challenged.

Some things had happened to make him more sure of himself. In 1922 an uncle left his sister and him an unexpected legacy of $8,000 apiece. He wrote "Al" Mellen characteristically, "Owing to my duties as a member of the Commission, I do not wish to invest either my money or hers in any company over which we have jurisdiction." He had, as it turned out, his own plans for the bequest, and in 1924 purchased the house on Cathedral Avenue where he lived with his sister up to the time of his death twenty years later. It was a small, but very well-arranged residence, not far from Rock Creek Park, away from the business section and with as much cool air in hot weather as Washington affords. Eastman soon formed the habit of walking even in inclement weather the two miles or more to the Interstate Commerce Building, following a route mostly downhill and not very exacting. Although many of his evenings were spent in his office, he could always find refuge in the atmosphere of domesticity which his sister provided. He had, as he said, "all the comforts of married life without its inconveniences." He was growing a little portly now, and his cheeks were chubbier and redder than they were when he arrived in the capital. No matter how hard he worked or played, he had lost forever his slender boyish figure. This was one of the penalties of middle age.

In accordance with the rotation principle, in 1926 Eastman was elected Chairman of the Interstate Commerce Commission, and this time did not decline the honor. The additional responsibility was not onerous, and his routine program remained little altered.

He was even more gratified by a letter from President George D. Olds, of Amherst College, who had been his professor of mathematics, telling him that the trustees had voted him the honorary degree of Doctor of Laws. In citing Eastman for this distinction at the 1926 Commencement, the president said:

Joseph Bartlett Eastman, of the Class of 1904; fellow at the South End House, Boston, for two years; secretary of the Public Franchise League; member of the Massachusetts Public Service Commission; member of the Interstate Commerce Commission since 1919 and now its Chairman; enjoying the full confidence of Presidents of opposite political faiths; administering a great trust with the knowledge of an expert, and the fidelity and wisdom of single-hearted devotion to the best interests of the nation.

In a speech delivered in 1924 Eastman lamented the fact that the commission seemed "to be travelling at so snail-like a pace towards any ultimate goal with respect to railroad rates." At that period the numbers in its formal case docket were running close to 16,000, and the bound volumes of its decisions stacked up into a pile more than fourteen feet high. Obviously it would be impossible here to consider any but a few of the most typical and significant; furthermore, most of the cases are so highly technical that to a layman they seem cryptic. As I have pondered this mass of commission literature, I have been reminded repeatedly of what Eastman wrote on July 3, 1928, to Professor William Z. Ripley, who had asked him for some recent documents: "I have your letter and am very glad to know that your condition is improving. Your letter is eloquent evidence to that effect, because any man who can take an interest in reading the reports of this Commission must be in fairly good health."

What Eastman and his fellow members confronted during the decade following the passage of the Transportation Act, 1920, can best be brought out in a brief discussion of one important piece of research. A fine specimen of rate structure in its most complicated aspect is the Southern Class Rate Investigation (No. 13494), which rested like an Old Man of the Sea on Eastman's shoulders during many months in the 1920's. In 1921, following a conference in Atlanta, representatives of the southeastern railroads and of the Southern Traffic League jointly petitioned the commission to institute an investigation into the class rates to, from, and within Southern territory. In accordance with their customary practice in response to such appeals, the commission delegated one of their number to make definite recommendations outlining the scope of such an investigation. Eastman was the one selected—possibly because some of his more friendly colleagues, knowing that his term of office would expire at the close of 1922, wished to make his preoccupation with such a tangled investigation seem to be a convincing reason for his reappointment. However that may be, Eastman was far from displeased with his tough assignment, and undertook its duties with what resembled enthusiasm. He called a preliminary conference in November, 1921, with a committee of shippers and carriers, to consider the methods of procedure and finally submitted to the commission the draft of the necessary order.

The investigation formally authorized in February, 1922, was initiated upon the commission's own motion and with a full perception of the difficulties which had to be faced; indeed, it was described by Eastman as a proceeding "unique in its scope and in the opportunity which it affords for fundamental consideration of railroad rates." Something of the kind had already been done in an experimental and limited way. In the *C.F.A. Class Scale Case*, 45 I.C.C., 254, the commission had fixed the rates of what was called "Central Territory"; in *Proposed Increases in New England*, 49 I.C.C., 421, a similar survey had been made of the northeastern area; and in *Memphis-Southwestern Investigation*, 55 I.C.C., 515, the situation in a large portion of the Southwest had been explored and to some extent adjusted and rectified. But these had been, so to speak, pioneering cases, and no one of them had covered the entire area of one of the great classification territories; no one had dealt with interterritorial as well as intraterritorial rates; and not one had been so intricate and confusing.

The first memorandum on "Proposed Investigation of Class Rates to, and from, and within Southern Territory" was followed by a long series of hearings, beginning May 22, 1922, and not concluded until March 14, 1923, at strategic points, such as Atlanta, Asheville, New Orleans, Cincinnati, and New York. In one discouraged mood Joe declared that he was "weary to death" of Pullman berths and early morning arrivals, of a shifting panorama of human faces and the familiar voices reiterating the ancient arguments. The mere transcript of testimony contained over 15,000 pages, and more than 2,000 exhibits were introduced. Eastman would sometimes take along his tennis racquet and play a set or two on Sunday mornings in the South; but he complained that most of the witnesses were too old for this form of outdoor recreation.

During the early stages of the hearings Eastman was assisted by two veteran examiners, who it was anticipated would later prepare the proposed, or tentative, report. Before that point was reached, however, both men resigned from the commission's staff, and rather than impose a complicated and arduous task upon an examiner unfamiliar with the record, Eastman undertook the job himself. The burden was heavy, often monotonous and disagreeable, but Eastman considered that he thus gained valuable experience in doing the "spade-work" on a commission report.

Just before the hearings were completed, Eastman undertook to address to his associates a few thoughts on rate-making in general.

It is best to be frank, and I start with the thought which to me is the most important of all, namely, that any study that we may make of rates should be made in a scientific spirit. What are needed are the real facts and the sound principles, regardless of how they may cut and of the political exigencies of the moment. Day by day in every way I become more disgusted with political "bunk". . . .

In the Southern Class Rate Investigation which I have been conducting I have learned far more about railroad rates than I ever knew before. I fear that the hearings have been prolonged by my insatiable curiosity. I am thoroughly convinced that such a proceeding is by far the best foundation for the public regulation of railroad rates. At the same time

I do not underestimate the difficulties of such an immense proceeding, and my confidence in my own ability to deal with the great issues presented often wanes. But given time and capacity, I am confident that the results will measure up to the magnitude of the undertaking, and that it is only through proceedings of such wide scope that we can ever bring rate structures into some degree of harmony and consistency. . . .

There is much more that I should like to say, but I have no time for more, so I shall reserve further discussion for another occasion. Possibly Brother Lewis and Brother Campbell will join me in the thought that what we need above everything else is a unified national system of railroads. If eventually, why not now?

I approve Brother Potter's idea that we should employ a man for the purpose of general research with respect to railroad rates of the country. . . . There are certain facts of great significance which I believe such a department could develop.

Before he had been involved in it very long, Eastman wrote a friend describing the investigation as "one of the most far-reaching matters which have yet come before the Commission for decision." He early set up for himself a chart of fundamental principles to serve as a guide: every reasonable effort should be made for simplification; attention should be paid to the national need for a properly coordinated railroad service; certain public interests which are seldom equipped for self-protection, like small towns and small consumers, should be safeguarded; everything possible should be done to promote harmony between intrastate and interstate rates; and finally the new rate structure should be as coherent and consistent as it can possibly be made, and any inconsistencies should be susceptible of intelligent defense. This was a broad, far-sighted, and intelligent policy, establishing very high standards for rate-making—higher, in fact, than had ever been set before. If the investigation had produced only this body of doctrine, it would have justified itself.

Fortunately the carriers agreed on the premise that they would not ask for authority to "patch a wornout structure" or permission to establish any "temporary storage" for their problems. Instead, they expressed the profound hope that the fixing of charges by the commission would be permanent. It was not actually too difficult for Eastman and the carriers to agree on a scale of distance rates; and he reached the conclusion, after even a superficial reading, that the schedule proposed by them was a vast improvement over that which existed.

But the shippers also had to be considered. One aggressive group felt that the hour had arrived for breaking with the past and fixing uniform rates on class traffic. On the other hand—and this illustrates the obstacles which Eastman frequently had to confront— the Virginia Shippers' Association and Virginia Traffic League were emphatically opposed to any scheme of uniform distance rates, and consequently objected vigorously to the suggestions of the carriers. The various interests involved had no inhibitions in voicing their needs, and pressure groups were skilled in the gentle art of making themselves felt. Virginia shippers wanted this; St. Louis shippers wanted something quite different. Charleston wished one concession; Nashville pressed hard for another. Meat packers had their own problems, often quite different from those of cotton growers. Among the early decisions was the establishment of a "single scale of distance rates." In applying this scale, however, distances in Kentucky, Tennessee, North Carolina, and Virginia were to be computed at 90 percent of actual mileage; while distances on standard lines in Florida, other than the Florida East Coast, south of the line of the Seaboard from Jacksonville to River Junction, were to be computed at 110 percent of actual mileage. All this seems like something from *Alice in Wonderland*—and this finding, it may be added, was simple as compared with others that might be quoted. Selfishness, inertia, even stupidity, to say nothing of provincialism and sectionalism, all unhappily had a chance for display. In the midst of all the confusion, Eastman wrote:

A discouraging feature of our work has been the fact that rate complaints tend to increase rather than diminish in number. Once a controversy is apparently set to rest, new and unexpected complaints often crop out in other quarters. It is possible that the broader consideration which an investigation like this permits may result in a rate structure that will have more elements of permanence.

In the summer of 1923 Eastman was so completely absorbed in the Southern Class Rate Investigation that he abandoned his vacation plans, although sorely tempted by invitations to go to Maine and Canada on fishing trips. In September he wrote Edward G. Niles, "I have amused myself in between long hours of reading the record in the Southern Class Rate Investigation Case by tennis and swimming, and am now becoming quite an aquatic sport." To another friend he declared his hope that his report might "beat the ice harvesters on the Hudson." To R. Hudson Burr, in late November, he said:

I am very anxious to put out a tentative report in the Southern Class Rate Investigation at the earliest possible moment, for many adjustments of rates are being held up awaiting our decision in that proceeding. I am very glad to say that I have been able to make substantial progress, but it is a long tedious undertaking, owing to the great number of issues and the tremendous volumes of the record. What I hope to do is to have a report out before the end of the year, although I am beginning to be afraid that even that will be impossible.

The preliminary report of 168 pages was written by Eastman in his scrawlly handwriting, some of it on trains when he could steal a few peaceful and unmolested moments. This was sent out early in March, 1924, in mimeographed form to all interested persons. In forwarding a copy to his friend Elmquist, Joe said:

I am sending you herewith a copy of my *magnum opus*, the proposed report in the Southern Class Rate Investigation. I am sending it to you to look at, but not to read. No one ought to be compelled to read it unless it is part of the work for which he has been paid a considerable fee. It does represent considerable hard work on my part, but whether or not it will stand up on final argument remains to be seen.

This was, indeed, Eastman's *magnum opus*—comparable, for him, with what *Paradise Lost* meant to Milton or the *Forsyte Saga* to Galsworthy. He was alluding to this when he wrote Walker D. Hines, on March 18, 1923: "The case is more comprehensive than any of similar character which we have ever decided." To a layman, as Eastman suggested, the report reads as if it were in a foreign tongue. In commenting on this fact, he said: "The subject is not a simple one, and we become accustomed in dealing with the traffic men representing the carriers and the shippers, to the use of certain more or less technical terms, and at times fail to realize that these terms are not so readily understood by those who are not in so intimate contact with these matters." Plenty of people were genuinely interested, however, and the original edition of 800 copies was soon exhausted. So, it may be added, was Eastman!

He had watched the Willard-Firpo prize fight in July, 1923, and must often have wished that the Southern Class Rate Investigation could have been settled as expeditiously and decisively. But that was not to be. When Eastman's preliminary report had been distributed, exceptions were taken by those who regarded themselves as aggrieved, and new hearings were held, attended by many of the old witnesses. Actual traffic tests were tried out in 1924 to see how the suggested schedule would work. The definitive report was submitted by Eastman to the commission on January 17, 1925, and its approving decision was announced on July 7 of that year, duly labeled 100 I.C.C., 513 (1925). To an outsider unacquainted with the commission routine it would seem that Dickens's "Circumlocution Office" had been outprocrastinated. Yet I have been convinced, after consulting persons familiar with the job of taking and appraising this kind of testimony, that Eastman proceeded as rapidly as could have been expected under the circumstances. It was far better to be slow than sorry, and he was establishing precedents for nobody knew how many future investigators.

Even now it was not over. On October 5, 1925, the carriers filed a voluminous statement of reasons why they were unwilling and unable to accept the findings of the report. Although the commission in its review found no cause for reopening the case for further hearings, it did concede that some of its judgments should be modified. With an impressive attempt at complete justice, Eastman, still the representative of the commission, undertook to explain decisions and justify each debatable conclusion. At his recommendation the commission set aside its earlier order and issued a new one, known officially as 109 I.C.C., 300 (1926), allowing a few alterations. On July 19 Eastman submitted a second supplementary report on reconsideration, and additional modifications were made. Even after that date further petitions were filed—most of which were denied —and Eastman prepared still another supplementary report, resulting on July 19, 1927, in another modified decision. On this date the commission said:

The consideration and disposal of these petitions will, we believe, mark the last stage in this proceeding prior to the publication of the rates. Since it was first instituted, a long period of time has elapsed. Under the circumstances the interested shippers have shown remarkable patience. They have doubtless appreciated the fact that a rate decision involving changes in the class rates between every point in Southern Territory and every other point east of the Mississippi River and Lake Michigan cannot be accomplished in short order.

The shippers were doubtless very patient, but their endurance was more than equaled by that of Joseph B. Eastman. Without any visible irritation and with an obvious desire to be fair to everybody, he went again and again into explanations of his decisions. His motives were impugned; his logic was attacked; but still he remained unperturbed. His reputation for personal integrity survived a severe test. When it was all over and the attorneys, having done their best for their clients, sat down to discuss frankly the treatment they had received, they agreed that he had given them a square deal.

Some Southern spokesmen, mostly politicians, took a recalcitrant position and perpetuated the myth that Eastman and the commission had discriminated against their area. In 1932 Eastman wrote to Bolling H. Jones, of Atlanta: "The idea . . . that the members of the Commission are prejudiced against the South because of party affiliations or the fact that they hail from other sections of the country is in my opinion utter nonsense. I have been thirteen years on the Commission and have seen no indication whatever of any such feeling towards the South." As late as 1943 an article appeared in the *Saturday Evening Post* by Governor Jones, of Louisiana, resurrecting the ancient libel that somebody had done the South wrong on the matter of railroad freight rates. When the Honorable Josephus Daniels sent Eastman a letter of inquiry regarding the facts, the latter replied in an eight-page document, charging that Jones was reviving a political agitation which had no foundation whatever and regretting that there should be such an obvious attempt to throw the whole matter into the turmoil of politics. He summed up his own views as follows:

I would have you understand that I am not unaware of a considerable amount of dissatisfaction on the part of many people in the South over the class rates, particularly those between the North and the South. More than twenty years ago, when these class rates were in much worse shape than they are now, the Commission entered into an investigation of them on request of the Southern railroads and business interests. I was in charge of it, and it proved to be a very interesting but difficult task. Some of the leaders among the Southern industrial traffic men at that time were inclined to favor a rather high level of class rates between the North and the South as a sort of protective tariff for Northern business. This is because most of the Southern products moved north on commodity rates, whereas class rates were more generally charged on the northern products moving south. The rates which we prescribed were protested by the Southern railroads, on the ground that they were too low, but there was comparatively little protest from Southern shippers. They certainly were a great improvement over those previously in effect.

Although these rates, which went into effect in 1928, were to a large extent the result of my labors, I fully realized that they might need modification with the unfolding of time. I was, therefore, not unsympathetic with the criticism of the class rates which began about eight or ten years ago. In 1937, we were asked by the Southern state commissions and some of the shipping interests to enter upon another investigation of the class rates *within* the South. We did so, and on our own initiative broadened it to include the class rates between the South and the North, which we knew were intimately connected with the intraterritorial rates and of even greater importance. For reasons which have never been clear to me the Southern people were opposed to that broadening and, preferring no investigation to one of the scope which we believed to be necessary, they asked us to discontinue the proceeding. We did so. Had that investigation gone ahead, it would no doubt have been out of the way by this time. If Governor Jones had known of that circumstance, he might not have said anything about getting that "skilful brush-off" in Washington. In any event, the important thing to keep in mind is that the whole question is now actively before the Commission and is not one which can be dealt with advantageously by political means.

The most illuminating aspect of this incident is the confirmation which it offers of the fact that the work of the commission is never done. Twenty years or more had gone by since Eastman had commenced his researches, and few of the participants were really satisfied. The same situation exists at the time this biography is being written.

In the Southern Class Rate Investigation, Eastman was from the start the dominant figure, and the technical questions were automatically referred to him as the authority. He also had an important, although far from exclusive, share in the *New England Divisions Case*, settled in 1922. After the general rate advances allowed in 1920, the New England railroads, still in dire straits, instituted proceedings to secure a larger share of what were known as "joint rates"—that is, rates paid by a shipper to cover the cost of transportation over two or more lines. Much testimony was taken, and Eastman had a vigorous correspondence with New England executives about their needs. The commission finally tried to pacify complainants by suggesting that the carriers involved modify if possible their rate divisions and then submit their readjustments for consideration. Human nature being what it is, this compromise plan pleased nobody. After further hearings, the commission directed that the shares of New England railroads in these "joint rates" be increased by 15 percent, mainly in order to relieve their urgent financial needs. This decision of the commission was later upheld by the Supreme Court of the United States.

Eastman was under normal conditions a calm, dispassionate man, but in his dealings with the New England railroads, especially the New York, New Haven & Hartford, he was often highly critical. To his former adversary E. G. Buckland, he wrote on May 5, 1923:

As for the credit of the railroad companies, I am surprised that they are able to persuade anybody to invest in their securities. For many years now their representatives have indulged either in constant snarling or chronic pessimism. To paraphrase something that Mr. Hines said not long ago,—they have applied the reverse of Coue's formula, and when they get up in the morning repeat publicly, "Every day in every way the railroads are getting worse and worse!" It is a wonder that they have any credit at all.

He told James J. Storrow, whom he very much respected, that the two great weaknesses of New England railroads were lack of financial strength and inferiority of management.

New England officials function in a depressing atmosphere. I anticipate no great vigor or enterprise in management so long as so much attention must be given to the wolf at the door. The various ways in which inferiority in management manifests itself I need not undertake to explain. You have better information on the subject than I have. One way, which has some importance for present purposes, is lack of cooperation between the various New England railroads.

In the same candid and friendly spirit, Eastman wrote Storrow on May 24, 1923:

At the close of the two-day argument which we have just heard in the New England Port Differential Case, you may be interested in certain impressions which it left on me, aside from the merits of the case. I cannot help feeling that Boston, like the railroads, makes a mistake in overdrawing its evil state and indulging in an overdose of pessimism. . . . There was constant reference to the decline of the commerce of Boston, as if it were on its last legs and about to stumble into the grave.

The Railroad Strike of 1922, a manifestation of postwar unrest, offered Eastman another opportunity to voice his opinion of the policy pursued by New England management. On March 26, 1923, he wrote to James L. Richards, strongly condemning the New Haven for its unwillingness to settle the dispute. He added:

With respect to labor, if the policy of New England industries is to be controlled by short-sighted, narrow-minded reactionaries, interested primarily in keeping labor in what they call its "proper place," the day of reckoning for these industries will not be far removed. . . . My best judgment is that the shopmen's strike could and should have been settled without sacrifice of any principle at the time when the President intervened last summer, and that the managements of the New Haven and the Boston & Maine were unwise when they placed obstacles in the way of such settlement at that time.

Eastman's broad attitude toward the whole New England situation was probably best summed up in a letter to his intimate correspondent Judge Anderson, on September 5, 1923.

My belief is that the federal government has done about all that it can be expected to do in behalf of the New England railroads. It has permitted all the increases in rates that were asked for; it has loaned them over $100,000,000 in cash; it has given them an immediate increase in divisions and it had held the door open for a further increase, provided they are able to prove it. My belief is that the problem has now become one primarily for the New England people, and that it affords a test of their present vigor, courage, and constructive ability.

This series of quotations may well be rounded out by a passage from a letter written on November 6, 1924, to Buckland, who had apparently sent him a propaganda pamphlet.

I have your letter of November 3, and thank you for sending me the address of Martin W. Littleton to the American Defense Society, delivered October 2. I have glanced through this address and am not inclined to take much stock in it. It resembles so many of the unwarranted charges that have become current in the past few years to the effect that various reputable citizens are "Reds," in the pay of Soviet Russia, etc. I know of instances where such charges have been directed against persons with whom I am personally acquainted and for whom I am able to vouch. As ordinarily employed, it is merely a nasty method by which ideas which for quite different reasons are objectionable to men of wealth are attacked under false premises and false colors. The use of such tactics arouses my indignation and contempt.

This was an instinctive outburst of plain speaking which reveals where Eastman's sympathies lay. His liberalism led him to see all sides of a controversial question, but he always was ready to defend the "under dog." In this case he was convinced, with much justification, that the New Haven management, symbolized by Buckland, was reactionary. James J. Storrow reached independently the same conclusion. Later, when Eastman found a similar indifference to the public good in labor "bosses," he did not hesitate to denounce them with equal impartiality. This was a period when he was reading William Graham Sumner and Veblen and even Henry George, and greatly enjoying Robinson's *The Mind in the Making*, sent to him by E. A. Filene. Unlike some of his contemporaries, he was not lulled into intellectual somnolence by the material prosperity around him. He was thinking very hard, and he had the courage to speak out what he thought.

What Eastman did almost unaided in the *Southern Class Rate Investigation* was pioneer work in the course of which he devised methods and set precedents which were to guide others. As the commission's foremost authority on rates, he inevitably took a conspicuous part in the *Eastern Class Rate Investigation*, which had been initiated before the Great Panic of 1929 had made such inquiries seem a little absurd. In undertaking this task, he declared that his chief purpose would be "to adopt a class-rate structure as simple as it can be made, with due regard for the public interest, and free from undue prejudice. . . . This does not mean, necessarily, that proposed rates will be rejected upon the ground that they increase or decrease aggregate revenue." Eastman resorted again to the procedures which he had originated and followed in the *Southern Class Rate Investigation*, and once more succeeded to some degree in simplifying the rate structure and freeing it of improper relationships.

Definitive though these earlier projects seemed at the time, they were obscured by the general inquiry known as the *Rate Structure Investigation*, necessitated because of the so-called Hoch-Smith Resolution, approved by Congress on January 30, 1925. This measure, jammed through Congress by the "farm bloc" during a period of agricultural depression, authorized and directed the commission to make a thorough study of the rate structure of all common carriers subject to the Interstate Congress Act, in order to determine in what manner and to what extent existing rates and charges were unjust and discriminatory and then to make such alterations as would promote the free movement by common carriers of the products of agriculture. The act was described by Eastman privately as "a sordid demonstration of the selfish maneuvers of pressure groups." Nevertheless, the commission had no alternative but to perform its legal duty by ordering a comprehensive investigation of rate structures. Soon it was embarked upon what Professor Sharfman has called "without question the most important and most extensive proceeding ever undertaken by the Commission." Commissioner Aitchison has gone even further by declaring that the investigation was "the most far-reaching and important one ever entered upon by the Interstate Commerce Commission or by any other human tribunal among civilized peoples." This is strong language, but it is used by a man who was at the center of the inquiry and had every reason to know how much labor was entailed.

Without any appropriation, the commission was obliged to make an effort to reconsider the rate structure of the entire country and reapportion the burden under it. It went at its stupendous task sincerely and vigorously, well aware, as Commissioner Meyer said, that literal and complete execution of all the provisions of the resolution was "probably beyond the power of any body of men." First of all, it created a new division of its membership, known as Division VI, to direct the proceeding, and then divided the country into sixteen subdivisions. Examiners were then assigned to conduct or participate in hearings in all parts of the nation. A group of cooperating committees of state commissioners and rate experts was established. According to Professor Sharfman, the *Rate Structure Investigation* for a considerable period "unquestionably made abnormal demands upon the time and thought of the Commission"; and he added that "it confused rather than clarified its standards of decision, and served to complicate its pending efforts to rationalize the rate structure through sweeping readjustments in freight charges."

A decision of the Supreme Court in 1930, in the appealed case of *Ann Arbor Railroad* v. *United States*, described the Hoch-Smith Resolution as "more in the nature of a hopeful characterization of an object decreed desirable if, and in so far as, it may be attainable, than of a rule intended to control rate making." For all practical purposes this nullified the resolution, and a good part of the commission's conscientious efforts to meet the wishes of Congress proved to be futile and even meaningless. Naturally the members of the commission, with Eastman among the leaders, had become sick of the whole business. In its *Report* for 1932, the commission said frankly:

Generally speaking, the Docket 17000 cases have developed into unwieldy proportions. Our experience with them has shown that the country is too big to make it practicable to deal with it as a whole or even with the major classification territories, except in proceedings especially adapted to large territorial treatment, such as the classifications themselves.

By this date the railroads were in such straits that public sympathy was even more strongly with them than with the farmers. The commission dutifully reported to Congress that the investigation had been "largely completed" and ordered that it be discontinued. In 1934 Eastman, who had become Federal Coordinator of Transportation, told Congress: "As matters now stand, the Hoch-Smith Resolution has ceased to have any important legal effect, in view of the interpretation placed upon it by the Supreme Court. . . . It serves no useful purpose and may well be repealed, although its appeal is not a matter of large importance."

One cannot help feeling that much of Eastman's labor throughout this period was without constructive results and that he himself, much as he enjoyed strenuous work, felt like a mule in a treadmill. He did not like the "special privilege" implications of the Hoch-Smith Resolution; he knew that the commission, against its will, was undertaking an almost hopeless task; and at moments even he, with all his native cheerfulness, became discouraged. Furthermore, he was out of sympathy with the objectives, so far as they could be ascertained, of the Coolidge administration. He could even be jocular about it, as when he wrote Elmquist, January 26, 1924:

You must be having sort of an Arctic time at St. Paul right now, judging from your account of the temperature. This reminds me of a story which I heard yesterday in regard to Senator Dill. In objecting to the proposed trip of the Shenandoah over the polar regions, he suggested that any land discovered in those regions might well be called Coolidge Land, because of the silence and cold. He also suggested that any oil discovered might be placed in charge of Albert B. Fall.

During the 1920's the activities of the commission expanded amazingly. The informal complaints increased from 4,450 in 1919 to 8,211 in 1928, and in the same period the formal complaints rose from 838 to 1,693. The number of hearings held in 1919 was 839. This had grown by 1928 to 1,415. These figures are cold in print, but they indicate a widening of the influence of the Interstate Commerce Commission and a disposition to rely on its justice.

New problems, like those introduced by the spectacular advance in motor truck transportation, were becoming more insistent. The Lindbergh flight across the Atlantic opened up a far horizon to the imaginative mind. The prospect was one of immediate and progressive advancement toward a goal of economic happiness for every citizen of our incredible land.

IX

"Valuation Is Vexation"

IN ONE of his notable dissenting opinions, Eastman wrote: "If anything can be called fundamental in the public regulation of privately owned and operated railroads, it is this valuation question." The average citizen, however, after reading a succession of discussions on this subject, is likely to feel like Omar Khayyam, who confessed:

> Myself when young did eagerly frequent
> Doctor and saint, and heard great argument
> About it and about, but evermore
> Returned by that same door in which I went.

Professor Sharfman devotes his entire Chapter XII, of 222 pages —virtually a monograph in itself—to a discussion of "The Valuation Problem." Clearly this biographer would be swamped if he attempted to do more than suggest in a few pages what were the vital issues. In some moods I have found myself wandering in a world of fantasy, where the language seemed like the "matter" in *Hamlet*—"Words, words, words!" It has been comforting to remember what a very practical Yankee, Commissioner Charles A. Prouty, after serving four years as Director of Valuation, said of the original Valuation Act of 1913, "I would rather undertake to recite the Chinese alphabet backwards than read the thing anyway, because it does not mean anything after you have read it."

Valuation is in itself a research undertaking, dealing with figures and expressed in dollars and cents. By an amendment to the Act to Regulate Commerce, passed in 1913, Congress directed the Interstate Commerce Commission to prepare an official Federal valuation of all railroad property in the country. The next and inevitable question was how to do it. Many important elements were involved, including taxation, depreciation, and capitalization; but the essential aim was to find a sound basis for allowing the carriers a fair return on the investment value of their holdings—with no measure of such value available, except what each road chose to fix for itself. It was argued very sensibly that no tribunal could pass a satisfactory judgment upon the reasonableness of railway rates without taking into account the value of railroad property. The higher it was valued, the more the carriers could legitimately demand; hence they were, as businessmen, in favor of any procedure which would raise their valuation. This is undoubtedly oversimplification, but it does bring out one cause of continued disputes. The commission had long recognized what it called "the inadequacy of private valuations" made by railroads in a quite natural but clearly selfish attempt to make their investment seem as large as possible. They contended from the beginning that they were entitled to a decent return from their property, just as a stockholder in an industrial plant expects large dividends as only his due as an investor.

In estimating valuation, the commission was required by law to consider various factors, such as "original cost to date," "cost of reproduction new," "cost of reproduction less depreciation," and "other values and elements of value, if any"; but Congress said nothing as to how these various items could be combined into a final usable figure. This was left to the judgment and discretion of the commission; and here is where the trouble began. Always in the background was the decision of the Supreme Court in 1898 that the railroads are entitled "to a fair return upon the fair value of what they employ for the public convenience." What this should be had to be determined at a later date in case after case, many of them highly controversial.

By the close of World War I, the commission, employing all its research facilities, had completed most of its field work on valuation and had spent almost $19,000,000 in the process. As might have been expected, however, nearly half the railroads, when their valuation was announced by the commission, made "an intensive effort to upset that finding and to increase the total amount of the valuation." As one authority has put it, "When the final value became an issue, the Commission was confronted with a persistent attack on its methods, its policies, and its decisions." Some indication of the burden which descended upon the commission may be gathered from the hearings on the Great Northern's protest against the tentative valuation of its properties, which covered 137 days, with a record covering 12,518 pages of testimony and 462 exhibits. And this was only one of many. In executing its overwhelming task, the commission tried to stress practical considerations; but cost figures were not always in existence, or were so confused that they could seldom be accurately separated, and the investigators had to rely on expert guesswork, never satisfactory to all the parties concerned.

It is obvious that in a period of rapidly rising prices, such as that following the Armistice of 1918, a railroad would get a higher valuation by adhering to the "cost of reproduction" theory, which established the valuation as what would have to be spent to replace the property if it should be destroyed. Eastman, who thought that the railroads were too grasping, held consistently to a policy which would bring the valuation closer to actuality. Thus, he became the open advocate of the "prudent investment" doctrine which he had upheld as a member of the Massachusetts Public Service Commission. It was his conviction that "value for rate-making purposes should be based on the amount invested honestly and with a reasonable degree of providence in the property." In a letter to Wylie, March 24, 1924, he explained more in detail what he meant.

I think that you are under some misapprehension with regard to the manner in which "prudent investment" cost is determined. Such cost is ascertained, in the absence of accurate records of original cost, by inventorying the property and determining the dates when the various items came into existence and applying then in the case of each piece of property the price prevailing at the time when it came into existence. In other words, it is an attempt to ascertain what the property should reasonably have cost.

This is probably Eastman's most lucid statement of the "prudent investment" theory of which he became the sponsor and in some degree the symbol. It is evident that when costs are rising, valuation under this principle is certain to be lower than it would be under the application of the doctrine of "cost of reproduction."

This makes it clear why railroad executives and their attorneys fought it as hard as they could.

The first important test of the Valuation Act was the so-called Texas Midland Case—*Texas Midland Railroad*, 75 I.C.C., 1 (1918) —decided before Eastman came on the commission. This presented a very complex problem, especially because so much of the property had been acquired at various times from other carriers. In this case the commission adopted the "cost of reproduction" method, less depreciation of the carrier's property. This has been officially defined as "the cost of duplicating the existing plant at the current level of prices, under either present or original conditions." In reaching their conclusions under this test case the commission assumed that the road under consideration had been obliterated and had to be rebuilt under current conditions and prices. The commission admitted that the "cost of reproduction new" was at best an estimate, but maintained also that "the estimates regarding different properties are comparable in all cases." In other words, all the railroads were to be treated exactly alike. It must be remembered that at this time building costs had not really commenced to rise.

The celebrated "recapture clause" in the Transportation Act of 1920 provided that one half of the annual net railway operating income realized by any carrier in excess of 6 percent on the value of its property was to be segregated in a reserve fund, to be drawn upon only for the purpose of paying interest, rentals, and dividends when its normal income fell short of meeting these commitments. The other one half of the excess earnings was to be held in trust for the United States as a "railroad contingent fund," to be used either for making loans to less prosperous carriers or for leasing facilities to them.

It was inevitable that this Recapture Clause, with all its implications, should focus the attention of carriers even more closely on the ticklish matter of Valuation, which had now become for some of them a critical matter. It took no Solomon to perceive that while a return of $100,000 annually on a valuation of $1,000,000 may seem too large, it becomes only normal if the valuation is fixed at $2,000,-000. It was thus of paramount importance to the railroads that their valuation should be made as high as possible; and they were not slow to espouse, with all their weight of legal counsel to support them, the "cost of reproduction" theory.

The first significant decision rendered by the commission under the Recapture Clause was in the famous San Pedro Case—*San Pedro, Los Angeles & Salt Lake R.R. Co.*, 75 I.C.C., 463 (1923)—in which, following the method pursued in the Texas Midland Case, it used the "cost of reproduction" method, less depreciation of the carrier's property, and reported a final "single-sum value" of $45,-000,000 for the railroad for rate-making purposes. In announcing its conclusions, the commission said, "Every contention and consideration which the carrier has brought to our attention in this connection was before us in the Texas Midland Case."

In his dissenting opinion Eastman devoted more than forty pages to a carefully reasoned discussion of the entire theory of valuation. He opened by saying: "This case deals with an issue of greater moment to the country than any that we have ever determined. . . . This fact will, I hope, be deemed a sufficient apology for the length of this separate expression." In commenting on the "cost of reproduction" theory, he declared that its application led "into the realm of unreality, speculation, and conjecture" and added that the Supreme Court itself had recognized "the absurdities into which the reproduction theory may lead when pressed to its logical conclusion." He asked pointedly how the "cost of reproduction" theory would operate in a period of falling prices and wages, asserting that under such circumstances its application would be "wholly destructive not only of the interest which the stockholders have in the railroad properties but of much of the interest of the bondholders and other creditors." He concluded:

Is it not "just and right" to urge, under modern conditions, with the wealth of statistical information now available, that services taken as a whole are "reasonably worth" their reasonable *cost*, including in that figure such cost of capital as is involved in securing the funds necessary for both the establishment and continuance of the business?

Although this final *Report* was presented by the majority of the commission, the members differed among themselves on various minor details. Commissioners Hall, Potter, and Cox all concurred in part. The chairman, Balthasar H. Meyer, in his separate concurring

opinion, ventured the observation that "the valuation of great properties and small cannot be made an exact mathematical process"—
a remark which is a masterpiece of understatement. He went on to
say, "Substantial accuracy is the zenith of success in this work, and
such a result will, I believe, appeal to the conscience of the American
people as just and right." In commenting on his colleague's argument, Meyer said:

Commissioner Eastman's dissent is a dissent only in a figurative sense.
I agree with most of what he says, and I believe that if the majority had
had the greater part of what is contained in his "dissent" incorporated
in the report before adoption, it would have commanded approval.
However, as Commissioner Eastman points out, much of his discussion
relates to matters not directly connected with the case. It is difficult
enough to find language to which even seven Commissioners will agree
without going afield to cover matters not required in the disposition
of the question immediately before us.

Commissioner Daniels was the only member to side unreservedly
with Eastman, and the latter was thus overwhelmingly outvoted.
Newspaper comment, however, was inclined to favor the two dissenters. In a letter to Professor Frank H. Dixon, of Princeton University, on November 21, 1923, Eastman referred to the background
of his opinion.

As you say, valuation is an extremely perplexing problem. It is one
to which I have had occasion to give some thought for a good many
years, and I endeavored to put these thoughts on paper in the San
Pedro Case to the best of my ability. I am glad that you liked them.
They represent the point of view which has prevailed in Massachusetts
for a long time and which has been applied in the actual regulation of
the public utilities of that state. Justice Brandeis and I used to work
together on these matters in Boston, and that is perhaps the reason
why we have arrived at so nearly the same conclusion. The question is
one which it is very difficult for judges, unless they have had the
experience which Justice Brandeis has had, to fully understand and
determine. I am hopeful, however, that out of the mass of discussion
on the subject, something like sound doctrine will emerge.

No doubt there was a link between this particular issue and Eastman's belief in public ownership of railroads. At this time he still

felt that government ownership might not be far off, and he was convinced that some operators were trying deliberately to raise their valuation as high as possible in order to secure a larger reimbursement from Washington. This was part of a general distrust of railroad management which influenced all Eastman's thinking on the subject. When he was accused of being prejudiced, he retaliated by saying that he was only facing the truth.

The Recapture Clause, which had so much aroused railroad executives, was declared constitutional in the *Dayton–Goose Creek Railroad Case* (1924); indeed, the Supreme Court went somewhat out of its way to declare it the "key provision" to the Transportation Act. The next step in this "strange eventful history" was the picturesque O'Fallon Case, legally known as *Excess Income of St. Louis & O'Fallon Ry. Co.*, 134 I.C.C. 3 (1927) involving the question of valuation in all its aspects. It grew directly out of the Recapture Clause and eventually, through a peculiar chain of events, was selected by the commission as an opportunity for a declaration of policy. A tiny railroad only nine miles long, worth less than a million dollars, thus became the focal center of a far-reaching controversy; but the issue, in essence, as Eastman pointed out, was "presented as clearly as it could be in the case of a railroad involving hundreds of millions of investment."

Omitting various technical and irrelevant details, the O'Fallon Case concerned the attempt of the Interstate Commerce Commission, obeying its mandate, to fix a single-sum value for a small and comparatively insignificant Missouri railroad. The commission employed its own valuation engineers, probed into every aspect of the little road's accounting, and uncovered some evidence that the officials had diverted to "operating expenses" funds which should legally have been subject to recapture. The important fact for this narrative is that the commission not only laid no emphasis upon "cost of reproduction" as a fair means of determining value but also actually argued that it was unimportant. This somewhat startling shift in sentiment was partly due to Eastman's unceasing stress on "prudent investment" as he discussed the matter with his associates.

The *Order* and the *Report* of the commission, drafted by Commissioner Meyer, were based, he claimed, "on a consideration of all relevant facts." Since 1923, however, the Supreme Court had laid down certain decisions which seemed to emphasize the "cost of reproduction" theory to the subordination of other factors. Thus it was at once evident to those "on the inside" that the commission and the court might disagree and come nobly to the grapple. To anticipate this dilemma, Eastman produced a "concurring opinion," replying in advance to the possible charge that the commission's *Report* and the assumptions therein disregarded the law of the land as laid down by the highest judicial tribunal. In this document Eastman made his famous statement that in railroad matters the commission "occupies a daily front seat upon the stage, while the Supreme Court of necessity is only an occasional visitor in the balcony." To validate his position, Eastman continued:

I cannot avoid the conclusion that the Commission would be derelict in its duty in this case if it should confine its attention, as far as the fundamental law is concerned, to past utterances of the Court in more or less analogous cases and should neglect the illumination which is thrown upon the law by its own intimate knowledge of transportation affairs and problems. . . . After the Court has heard what we have to say, it may decide that our conclusions as to the fundamental law are erroneous, and that will end the matter; but certainly we ought not to deprive the Court of the help which it may gain from the special knowledge which it is our duty under the law to acquire. The Report in this case seems to impart this knowledge, so far as it seems pertinent, respectfully but candidly.

This was a frank and courageous declaration, quite characteristic of Eastman; but it was also a direct challenge to the Supreme Court, and some of the justices unquestionably accepted it as such. Having thus made himself understood as to his conception of the relationship between the commission and the Supreme Court, he reiterated some of the arguments for his favorite "prudent investment" theory, even going so far as to maintain that "acceptance of the current cost of reproduction doctrine would in its ultimate results be disastrous to private operation of railroads and public utilities, not only in periods of low prices but in high-price periods as well." This was further than the argument for "cost of reproduction" had ever been carried, and it was generally regarded as a personal triumph for Eastman that a majority of the commission were ready to side with him.

Four commissioners—Hall, Aitchison, Woodlock, and Taylor—had a narrower conception of the functions of the commission and held that it was not authorized to "act as an arbiter in economics." They contended that in *Smyth* v. *Ames* (1898) the Supreme Court had stated unequivocally that, in the process of valuation, consideration should be given to "present as compared with the original cost of construction" and that in the *Minnesota Rate Cases* (1913) these principles of valuation had been reaffirmed. They asserted also that in a long series of decisions the Supreme Court had emphasized "the present as compared with the original cost of construction," continuously and consistently, as among the relevant facts to be included. These conservatives took a limited view of the authority of the Interstate Commerce Commission "under the law." Aitchison, in a separate dissenting opinion, said categorically: "This is not the appropriate place to discuss the economic and political results of a rule laid down by the Supreme Court. Our present duty is to ascertain the rule of law and to enforce it." The split in opinion was perfectly honest on both sides and represented a basic divergence in temperament and philosophy, with Eastman defending a free interpretation of the responsibilities of the commission.

Eastman wrote Professor Ripley on April 2, 1927, describing the O'Fallon report as "without doubt one of the most important that the commission has ever handed down"—one which "goes to the very foundation upon which all public regulation of railroads and utilities rests." But, as everybody knew, the question still had to be submitted to the Supreme Court, where Brandeis and Pierce Butler were in opposite camps, one liberal, the other regarded as reactionary. Eastman, whose intimacy with Brandeis was common talk in Washington, was regarded with distrust by Butler and those who agreed with him.

Professor Sharfman has pointed out that this was "the first proceeding in which the use of the Commission's valuations as part of its regulatory process, on a national basis, was challenged in the courts." The Supreme Court gave the case its usual careful con-

sideration and finally, on May 20, 1929, after more than two years
had passed, overruled the commission's Order in the O'Fallon Case
by a vote of six to three, with Justices Holmes, Brandeis, and Stone
the dissenters. Mr. Justice Stone let the cat out of the bag by frankly
admitting that if the commission in its *Report* had not turned aside
to point out the economic fallacies of the "cost of reproduction"
theory, nobody on the Supreme Bench would have questioned the
soundness of its Order. The majority of the Supreme Court unquestionably felt that the liberal group on the commission, headed by
Eastman, had exceeded their powers under the statute; consequently
they administered what was, in effect, an official reprimand. The
Supreme Court opinion, written by Mr. Justice McReynolds, generally regarded as a conservative, said in part:

The Report of the Commission is long and argumentative. Much of
it is devoted to general observations relative to the method and purpose
of making valuations; many objections are urged to doctrine approved
by us; and the superiority of another view is stoutly asserted. It carefully refrains from stating that any consideration whatever was given
to present or reproduction costs in estimating the value of the carrier's
property.

In several places the decision of the Supreme Court betrayed irritation over the attitude taken by the commission. Professor Sharfman feels that their adverse ruling was largely because of the commission's open attack on the "cost of reproduction" theory; and he
lends the weight of his scholarly authority to the conclusion that
the commission's Order in the O'Fallon Case "unquestionably constituted the high-water mark of its valuation project, despite the
subsequent reversal by the Supreme Court." Eastman felt that the
Interstate Commerce Commission had its own dignity to maintain
and that it should hew to the line, even though chips annoyed the
Supreme Court. The layman who studies the arguments is likely
to decide that the reasoning of the commission, as expressed by both
Meyer and Eastman, is difficult to refute. The consensus of opinion
today is that they were right and that the majority of the Supreme
Court judges were too sensitive about their prerogatives.

One highly intelligent lawyer, Professor Felix Frankfurter, wrote
to praise Eastman's argument. Writing on June 3, 1929, he said:

I hope that you did not for a moment think that I belong to those who "criticise the Commission because in its decision in the O'Fallon Case it did not sugar-coat the pill in a way that might have made it more palatable to the majority of the Supreme Court." Not only do I not belong to these critics, but I wholly admired your refusal to make yourself a party to such a hokum game. . . . When I think of the ferment which you have been on the Commission and the influence which you have exerted, even when your views have not prevailed with the majority, I realize anew how profoundly important may be the influence of a few men upon the development and application of social and economic ideas.

Eastman's own personal feeling was that the Supreme Court had left the valuation situation in such confusion that the outcome and effect would be difficult to predict. He did feel that conditions were such that the "prudent investment" theory might soon seem to be of advantage to certain classes of utilities. As a matter of fact, and rather ironically, the exponents of the "cost of reproduction" theory found themselves embarrassed after the autumn of 1929, when prices sharply declined. Acting as usual from selfish motives, they quickly reversed their position. Sponsors of the "original cost" doctrine, to their amazement, found themselves being described, not as "advocates of confiscation," but as "forces working for the protection of legitimate investment." The whole controversy had been basically between the defenders of property rights and the advocates of justice to all, between vested interests and the public welfare. On the policies as presented, it is not strange to find Holmes, Brandeis, and Eastman standing shoulder to shoulder. Eastman was much flattered when the magazine *Plain Talk* called him the "Judge Brandeis of the ICC."

Other cases, meanwhile, continued to be brought to the attention of the commission, and Eastman took occasion to express more than once his unaltered confidence in the "prudent investment" doctrine. But as a matter of fact, after the decision of the Supreme Court in the O'Fallon Case the carriers either simply refused to pay up under the Recapture Clause or paid under formal protest. Writing in 1929, in answer to a query by F. Lauriston Bullard, of the Boston *Herald*, Eastman said:

It seems to me that this decision leaves the valuation question very much up in the air. Practically all that the Supreme Court decided was that we had not given consideration to the cost of reproduction of the property at current prices. The Court did not in any way indicate what weight should be given to this element when it is considered. . . . Summing the situation up, it seems to me that the decision in the O'Fallon Case left a great many questions still to be answered, and probably also created certain new questions of importance.

Another factor, already mentioned, operated to change the situation. On October 18, 1929, Eastman wrote to Anderson, "I agree in general with what you have to say in regard to the speculative stock market at the present time, and am much afraid that it will cause trouble later." A few days afterward, and less than six months after the O'Fallon decision, the price of common stocks tumbled. Values fell so rapidly that not even experts could prognosticate what the end would be. Inevitably, as severe economic depression ensued, railroad revenues fell off. The business of "recapturing" excess profits from the railroads was shortly to become a subject for jest. There were no excess profits to recapture.

The commission, which had never been overenthusiastic about the Recapture Clause, said in its *Annual Report* for 1930, after outlining some of its problems: "We are inclined to the opinion that these practical objections outweigh the theoretical advantages of recapture, and that the wiser course is to repeal the recapture provisions in their entirety, rather than attempt to improve them by amendment." Up to December 17, 1931, less than $11,000,000 had been paid in under the Recapture Clause, as contrasted with the commission's estimate of $300,000,000; and much of the small amount received was subject to litigation. Finally, by the Emergency Transportation Act of 1933 the Recapture Clause was retroactively repealed. What the commission once described as "a great national problem affecting public policy and welfare in a most profound way" is now as dead as the Fugitive Slave Law.

Eastman was himself often amused by the very specific valuations, even down to fractions of a dollar, assigned to railroad properties, and by the wide divergencies resulting from the employment of different systems. The gap between the amount reached by using the "cost of reproduction" theory as compared with that of original cost was, in a year like 1920, nothing short of astounding. One gets the impression that much of the attempted valuation was not absolute science, but well-intentioned surmising, based on quick judgments, the advice of professional accountants, the interpretation of profit and loss, and a mass of miscellaneous evidence. As an experiment, it was doubtless a waste of time, energy, money, and temper, but it did reveal Joseph B. Eastman as a public servant who under any and all conditions recognized his obligation to the American people.

X

Problems and Policies

THE INTERSTATE COMMERCE ACT of 1887 had been, as we have seen, an expression of the popular agitation against monopoly which culminated in 1890 in the Sherman Antitrust Act. By forbidding "pooling" it attempted to enforce competition—always a difficult matter, human nature being what it is. But although public sentiment frowned on railroad mergers, clever financial manipulators and corporation lawyers had little trouble in bringing them about; indeed, they developed throughout the "tolerant 1890's" until by 1906 almost one third of the country's railroad mileage was dominated by the Harriman interests. It will be recalled that in 1893 the New Haven entered into an arrangement for dividing the New England region with the Boston & Maine, and that Eastman later assisted Louis D. Brandeis in his long fight for the dissolution of the New Haven's holding company, when in a campaign of expansion it had acquired a virtual monopoly of New England transportation. Mention has already been made of the Supreme Court's dramatic 5–4 decision in 1904 ordering the breaking up of the Northern Securities Company, which aimed at the consolidation of two of the largest transcontinental systems. The experience of World War II, however, led earlier critics of railroad monopoly, like Eastman, to perceive the advantages of eliminating cut-throat competition and encouraging friendly cooperation. If government ownership and control were not possible, he was willing to accept voluntary legal consolidations, provided they were sufficiently well regulated. He could never be stirred to ardent enthusiasm on this subject, however, and it was to some extent owing to him that the commission did not move decisively toward a nation-wide organization.

It has been pointed out in an earlier chapter that the Transportation Act of 1920, reflecting a shift in popular sentiment, reversed the policy of the Interstate Commerce Act and required the commission to prepare as soon as practicable a plan for dividing the railroads of the country into a limited number of independent systems, with three stipulations laid down—that competition among them be preserved, that existing routes be maintained, and that earning capacity be equalized. Professor William Z. Ripley, an outstanding authority on transportation, was employed by the commission to advise how the roads could best be grouped in accordance with the statutory requirements; on August 3, 1921, with commendable speed, the commission published its tentative plan for the consolidation of the railroads into nineteen separate systems, basing its proposals largely upon Professor Ripley's recommendations. He had himself previously rejected the idea that systems of continental scope should be created, and had supported the formation of groups which would naturally compete within certain well-defined territories.

As could have been predicted, opposition and complaint started at once and mounted rapidly. Extensive hearings were held, running from April 24, 1922, to December 4, 1923, at which a wide diversity of opinion found excited expression. Defects in the suggested groupings were indicated. Skeptics questioned the advisability of any experimentation at a moment when the railroads were enjoying one of their rare spurts of prosperity. The contented Republicans, under the leadership of Calvin Coolidge, were adhering to a policy of "hands off" toward business. Laissez faire was having a last mad fling before the debacle of 1929. Some timid souls were afraid that the imposition of such a plan would introduce an element of rigidity into what should be a flexible situation. Several commissioners, including Eastman, feared that the remedy might be worse than the alleged disease. No one in high authority was willing to bring pressure to have the plan adopted.

The truth is that a majority of the members of the Interstate Commerce Commission really preferred to do nothing. Therefore nothing was done. Although the presentation of a consolidation plan had been required by Congress and officially favored by Harding and Coolidge and Secretary of Commerce Hoover, the commission, after its first gesture, kept stalling, and up to 1929 no progress had been made. In his book *Main Street and Wall Street*, Professor Ripley wrote in 1927, "Six years and no plan yet!" By that date, he had reached the reluctant conclusion that it would be expedient to take up the problems one by one, making or permitting such consolidations as the immediate need might justify. From time to time the commission approved some voluntary mergers, and others had been independently consummated by the railroads themselves through ingenious devices for circumventing the intent of the law. To some of these obvious evasions Eastman referred scathingly in his private correspondence. Finally, weary of continued inaction, the commission asked the Senate Committee on Interstate Commerce to introduce legislation relieving it of the duty of submitting a comprehensive consolidation plan, and an amendment was introduced in Congress to repeal the objectionable obligation. No action was taken, however; meanwhile the commission's long delay had virtually nullified one of the purposes of the Transportation Act.

While the commission thus vacillated, the intense competition among the major railroad systems did not slacken; the formation of noncarrier holding companies to elude its regulations continued. Some of the more powerful lines, acting on the advice of alert and none-too-scrupulous counsel, succeeded in effecting consolidations which to Eastman seemed dangerous. He was especially disturbed by the growing influence of the Van Sweringens' Allegheny Corporation and the Pennsylvania's Pennroad Company, and he was the author of a resolution forbidding further approval of railroad mergers until legislation to protect the public interest had been enacted. Unfortunately, the authority of the commission did not extend to cases where noncarrier holding companies were being used as instruments to unify carrier properties. Consequently Eastman could do little but growl about it with Frank Livingstone and write futile protests to his colleagues. In 1928, in his partial dissent to the attempted control of the Erie & Pere Marquette by the Chesapeake & Ohio, he mentioned especially "the shoe-string financial operations of the Van Sweringens." He added, so that he might not be misunderstood: "The policies and practices of the Van

Sweringens in the railroad field have in many important respects been inconsistent with the public interest. We have had occasion to criticise these policies and practices extensively in the *Nickel Plate Unification Case*, and not all was there said that might have been said."

Speaking on October 10, 1932, to the American Bar Association, with several well-known corporation lawyers in the audience, Eastman said in measured words: "In my humble judgment, the holding company, working with its ally, the dummy convenience corporation, has been one of the most effective instruments of exploitation which this country has known." In the *Cleveland Passenger Terminal Case*, 70 I.C.C., 659, Eastman expressed his opinion freely as to the notorious Cleveland Station project and "the wholly unnecessary opportunity for great private profit which the carriers thus bestowed upon the Van Sweringens."

Eastman's attitude toward the methods of railroad executives is bluntly stated in a letter to C. M. Rand, under date of October 6, 1932.

If the railroads of the country had been run and managed from the start on sound, conservative business principles and had been content with liberal dividends, sufficient to attract needed capital, using surplus earnings to retire indebtedness or render unnecessary the creation of additional debt, they would not now be in any serious financial trouble. Of course this is all water over the dam, and in a rapidly growing, pioneer country, such as ours until comparatively recently, it is not surprising that we fall short of the ideal, although I cannot help feeling that we missed it by more miles than was at all necessary. . . . It seems impossible in private business to resist successfully the urge of those who are not content with a reasonable and stable return on investment but wish to exploit and draw out huge and undeserved gains by various devious methods.

This was a period when Eastman was frankly lined up with the liberals in opposition to what he regarded as privileged and selfish vested interests. In a dissent in the case of the *Michigan-Kansas-Texas Reorganization*, he remarked:

Certainly the affairs of sick or dying corporations have become a most profitable field of exploitation for bankers and lawyers. Such a situation challenges attention, particularly where the corporations are engaged in the public service. . . . Taking all the facts into consideration, I am not persuaded that the bankers and lawyers in question are entitled to more than half of the compensation which they ask.

In connection with the receivership of the Chicago & Alton in 1931, he reiterated this opinion, saying: "Railroad receiverships as they are now handled prove a juicy feast for lawyers, bankers, and the like. They fatten on the corpse. I believe it possible to handle these bankruptcies in a more rational and economical way."

Eastman also felt strongly that railroad securities should be marketed by open bidding instead of being assigned, as was usually the custom, to single brokerage houses like J. P. Morgan & Co. or Kuhn, Loeb, & Co. He was especially irritated over the practice of feeling out the market on competitive bids and then making a sale to a noncompetitive banker. He had some doubt as to the commission's power to enforce competitive bidding, but was willing, like his colleagues Meyer and Porter, to take the risk. In a Concurring Opinion on September 12, 1925, in the case of the Chicago, Milwaukee & St. Paul Equipment Trust, he said:

I have had occasion in other cases to remark upon the fact that two large banking houses in New York City have a virtual monopoly on the purchase from carriers of most railroad securities for distribution to investors. In my judgment this is an unhealthy state of affairs from more than one important point of view, and I have expressed the opinion that the time has come to break away from these monopolistic conditions.

With complete consistency Eastman was also opposed both to the device of "no-par stock" and to what he called "the arrogant assumption of control over the issue of securities by the management without the sanction of the stock-holders." On many counts he was out of sympathy with the economic philosophy which dominated American business in the 1920's. At this period a little group of "liberals" organized a club called The Penguins and rented an old house not far from the Interstate Commerce Building. For a few months Eastman took an active part in the proceedings and enjoyed the associations which it brought with Washington "intellectuals." There he heard ideas which stimulated him and confirmed his distrust of the current Republican way of thought. But eventually the members became themselves so discordant that the club fell apart, and Eastman, who was at heart a "middle-of-the-roader," found radical socialism as little to his taste as the reactionary conservatism of the White House. When he was described as the "most socialistic" commissioner ever appointed, he simply smiled and asked: "What's your definition of socialism?"

On October 18, 1929, Eastman wrote to Anderson, "I expect that we shall get out a consolidation plan before the end of the year, although I regret the necessity for doing such an unwise thing. It will undoubtedly have the effect of stimulating the speculative market for certain railroad securities." As a matter of fact, the long-delayed plan for consolidation was published at a most unpropitious moment, on December 9, 1929, just after the bottom had dropped out of the stock market and holders of railroad securities, like all other investors, were shrouded in gloom. In its final form, it named twenty-one separate systems, Number 1 being the Boston & Maine and Number 2 the New Haven, and so forth across the continent, Number 21 returning to the Canadian Pacific lines in New England. In an attempt at conciliation, it left undisturbed most of the new alliances which had been created since 1920; furthermore, it admitted that its decrees were not sacrosanct, but could well be modified from year to year as conditions changed. Nevertheless, this long-delayed plan failed to arouse any enthusiasm, either within the commission or outside. The feeling could not be eradicated among the members that Congress should have withdrawn its mandate as unsound and let events take their course. Professor Ripley promptly called the plan "decidedly startling and disconcerting because it does not seem to be worked out either on a basis of operating efficiency or financial equality in strength." Nearly every expert poked an accusing finger at some weakness, and nobody seemed willing to defend the project *in toto*.

Certainly Eastman was not. His separate Opinion, although labeled as "concurring," closely resembled a dissent. Although he was willing to go along with the suggested plan in default of a better, he favored a considerable increase in the number of systems proposed. In justifying his position, he said:

Although I do not approve of it in important respects, I concur in the adoption of the consolidation plan. . . . because it has many good features, because it is necessary under the law to adopt some plan, and because it is not very important, after all, whether it is the best plan that could be devised. We may modify it at any time hereafter, and no consolidation for which it provides can be accomplished until we have found, after full hearing, that the public interest will be promoted thereby. There is, I think, much misunderstanding on this point. The plan is very little more than a procedural step. There is nothing compulsory about it, nor even assurance that authority will be sought to carry out the consolidations which it proposes.

Eastman's mild approval was almost negated by another paragraph in his separate Opinion.

Such sentiment as appears to exist in favor of the consolidation of the railroads into a few great systems is, I believe, largely artificial. According to my observation, there is very little sentiment of this kind among either shippers or railroad officers. For the most part I think it emanates from financial circles which are likely to reap large profits from the mere process of putting the roads together. Furthermore, there is reason to believe that the country is becoming considerably alarmed by the progress of consolidations and unifications among industries in general. It is feared that control of industry is rapidly passing into a few hands, with the danger that we shall become predominantly a nation of clerks and subordinates. . . . There are strong grounds for belief that the best results in operating efficiency and service are secured when a railroad system is small enough so that the executive can maintain something like personal contact with the employees all down the line and also with the shippers in the territory served.

As Eastman predicted, no actual consolidations were sought or effected under this plan. The financial confusion of the next few years was not favorable to a rearrangement of railroad systems. Four trunk-line groups—the Pennsylvania, the Baltimore & Ohio, the New York Central, and the Van Sweringens—did in 1931, at Professor Ripley's instigation, meet in a series of conferences, and their efforts received the public endorsement of President Hoover. Their so-called "four-party plan," with some modifications, was approved by the commission on July 13, 1932, but Eastman, supported by Commissioner McManamy, expressed a vigorous dissent. In his sometimes satirical and often bitter comment, Eastman said:

Events suggest that it would have been simpler to have asked a few of the larger roads to agree upon a plan for the distribution of the lesser railroads among them. The virtue most persistently urged in support of this 4-system plan is that it is a "practical" plan which can be accomplished because the four leading railroad executives of eastern territory have, after many conferences, agreed to it. In fact, this plan has already in large part been accomplished. This has been done at great cost and mostly without our approval. We have found that to a very considerable extent it was done illegally, and we could with propriety have spread this finding over much more ground. The fact remains that many important and strategic parts of the plan have been accomplished. With these trump cards in hand the four executives went into conference. Their agreement was shaped accordingly, and upon it is now fixed the stamp of Commission approval.

Professor Sharfman, after surveying the evidence, concludes that the commission's approval of the "four-party plan" was justified. But Eastman had cogent reasons for his stand. He thought that the interested railroads had cynically disregarded the plan sponsored by the commission, and when he learned that the Pennsylvania was aiming to swallow up the Lehigh Valley, he wrote: "In its arrogance the Pennsylvania consulted neither the Commission, nor the law, nor public opinion, and it set at naught the consolidation plan without even a suggestion that it be changed." He emphasized particularly the fact that the carriers lacked the funds for carrying out the proposed consolidation—unless, of course, they could borrow from the Government. His irritation was accentuated by the knowledge that the proponents of these vast mergers had secured the preliminary backing of Herbert Hoover. Indeed, according to his correspondence it would appear that his objection to this four-system consolidation resulted more from his resentment of executive interference than from weakness in the plan itself. Then, as always, Eastman was jealous of the prerogatives and prestige of the commission and wished to have its independence preserved. Dictation from the White House was never to his liking.

By this time it was obvious that planned consolidation on a nation-wide scale, as contemplated in the Transportation Act of 1920, had very little chance for success. Dr. William N. Leonard, in his excellent volume *Railroad Consolidation under the Transportation Act of 1920*, says rightly: "Not a single consolidated system proposed in the complete plan of 1929, or in the modified plan of 1932, was ever brought into being; and neither at the time of its birth nor at the time of its extinction did the consolidation plan correspond to the actualities of railroad control."

Leonard also points out that the membership of the commission in the 1920's, strongly affected by a series of five appointments in one year by the conservative President Harding, was not of the type to take resolute action against the abuses of the various combination movements initiated by aggressive railroad executives. But this is not the whole story. Even liberals like Eastman were at that period unenthusiastic regarding comprehensive consolidation. Maneuvers of "big business" toward that end he profoundly distrusted, and he was suspicious of what he called "the merry-go-round of finance associated with combinations then being manufactured." Not until after his experience as Federal Coordinator, beginning in 1933, did he become an open advocate of consolidation by government order. Thus, in the 1920's, when prosperity was widespread and few people wished to rock the industrial boat, the commission delayed, fumbled, and never met the problem squarely.

Although Joe voted in 1928 for "Al" Smith, he was not at first critical of President Hoover. Writing to Elmquist on March 19, 1929, shortly after the inauguration, he said:

I must say that I have been agreeably surprised by what Hoover has done to date as President. He has acted with very considerable expedition and wisdom, it seems to me, in a number of important matters, including the attitude of the country towards the Mexican revolution, the matter of oil leases, and the matter of publicity for income tax refunds. I also like the steps he has taken to permit direct quotation by the press in place of the use of an "official spokesman," and also what he has done in the way of curtailing indiscriminate hand-shaking, photographs, and perfunctory public addresses. This is all to the good, for it seemed to me that the office of President was in danger of being cheapened by undue and inappropriate newspaper publicity. For a time it seemed as though it was part of the duty of the President to have his picture taken with every delegation of citizens that might happen to visit the White House. The appointment of Walter Newton as one of the secretaries also pleased me, and I think it is a good idea to have three secretaries, for that will help the President to keep in touch with the executive departments and Congress. I think it will be a mistake, however, if he attempts to keep too closely in touch with the affairs of independent commissions like this. So far there has been nothing to indicate that he has this in mind.

Eastman saw very little of the President, officially or unofficially, during the next few months; but this was not strange, for no problem arose on which Joe's counsel was needed. In the late autumn, however, when the financial world was in despair, his term of office as commissioner was about to end, and as early as November his friends, especially James L. Richards, began to send telegrams and letters to the White House urging his reappointment. While Eastman himself kept scrupulously aloof, he did not try to restrain his backers and was pleased with the notes which he received. In commenting on the situation, he wrote his classmate Donald L. Bartlett: "One of the distasteful things about public life is the fact that periodically one is likely to become the center of such controversies. . . . So far as I can learn, the prospects that I shall be reappointed are good, but of course I have very little definite information on the subject."

There was more doubt than Eastman supposed. Washington gossip whispered that the President was not much impressed by Joe's record. Mr. Hoover may have learned that Eastman voted for "Al" Smith in the election of 1928; he may have been displeased because Eastman had criticized his plan for putting the Interstate Commerce Commission under a cabinet officer; he certainly had listened to executives of holding companies who had expressed their disapproval of Eastman's attitude toward them. The rumor spread that Hoover was waiting to see how much resentment would be aroused if he followed his inclination and failed to reappoint Eastman.

He soon found out. The support which Eastman received from

all sorts and conditions of citizens was spontaneous, and a little overwhelming. The National Sugar Refining Company, the Swift Packing interests, the Cadillac Motor Car Company, the Associated Industries of Massachusetts, the National Association of Railroad and Public Utility Commissioners, as well as all the Railroad Brotherhoods, volunteered their endorsements. His sponsors included men of diverse political affiliations: Senators George H. Moses and Hiram Bingham, not generally regarded as radicals; Senators Carl Hayden and Kenneth McKellar, Progressive Democrats; Senators Arthur Capper and James Couzens, Progressive Republicans. The Boston *Herald* came out on November 20 with a ringing editorial, written by F. Lauriston Bullard; and other prominent newspapers including the liberal New York *World*, followed suit.

James L. Richards was approached during the late summer of 1929 by a group of conspirators from New York who wished to ascertain whether Eastman would be satisfied to withdraw his name and accept instead a seat on the Court of Claims. Richards did consult Eastman, who declared emphatically that he knew nothing whatever about the Court of Claims, but, when pressed, admitted modestly that he did think himself to be moderately well acquainted with the Interstate Commerce Commission job. When Eastman was unreceptive to this lure, the plot fell through. In December, however, one of Richards's friends called him from Washington to say that Eastman's nomination was about to be "pigeon-holed" and a mysterious unknown to be appointed in his place. This time Richards really went into action. He immediately telephoned Charles L. Underhill asking him to obtain the written endorsement of the entire Massachusetts Congressional delegation for Eastman. This Underhill accomplished miraculously within twenty-four hours; and for good measure he secured the signature of every Senator and Congressman from the New England area, both Republican and Democratic. The White House shortly distributed to the press a list of Eastman's sponsors covering six long single-spaced pages—a most impressive aggregation of names. Finally, on December 17, President Hoover reluctantly sent Eastman's nomination to the Senate.

When Senator Couzens, of Michigan, who although a Republican

EASTMAN AT HIS DESK AS INTERSTATE COMMERCE COMMISSIONER
From the files of the Office of War Information

EASTMAN AND FAYETTE B. DOW
ON A FISHING TRIP IN CANADA

was one of Joe's strong supporters, expressed his confidence in Eastman, he also declared that the latter was a Democrat. This labeling Eastman quickly disclaimed by writing:

I do not consider myself a Democrat. . . . I have not, for example, participated in any party primaries since 1912, although I have been and am a registered voter in Massachusetts. . . . In the case of presidential candidates, the fact is that I have voted for the Democratic nominees since Mr. Wilson, and including Mr. Wilson. In 1924 I voted for Senator LaFollette.

Nobody seems to have been much concerned, any more than they had been in 1919 or 1922, about his party affiliations or delinquencies, for he was promptly and unanimously confirmed. While the issue was pending, he said and did nothing in his own behalf. He was conducting a hearing in Chicago when the telegraph announced the President's decision; and when he was told, he merely said, "Well, I guess I can't get out of it!" On December 19, he sent a note to Richards.

I want to take this occasion to thank you again for all that you did in connection with my reappointment. I do not believe that any one did more, and I doubt very much whether the reappointment would have come without your help. Apparently there was a rather strong and bitter fight against me, on the inside, although it was not exposed to public view to any great extent.

The comment in *Barron's Weekly* for December 30, 1929, sums up the situation from the viewpoint of business.

Eastman's renomination to the job by President Hoover is the most humorous current incident in Washington affairs and is the direct result of his working so much and so hard that not even his so-called "radical" opinions could debar him from the right to remain in public life. Commissioner Eastman is a believer in the principle of public ownership and operation of public utilities such as railroads, and says so. President Hoover is a firm believer in avoiding just as much public ownership and operation as possible. The "radicals" in legislative circles waited to see Mr. Eastman thrown out of the Interstate Commerce Commission into the street by the President. . . . The President, however, was impressed by Mr. Eastman's industriousness and learning and efficiency as a railroad regulator, and determined to appoint him.

Regardless of Mr. Hoover's method of reaching his decision, Eastman accepted the appointment graciously and wrote to W. H. Day, on December 20: "It is all over now, and I am happy to say that I entertain no grudges." The Chicago *Journal of Commerce*, in an unfortunate manifestation of disgruntled reactionaryism, published an editorial headed, "A Socialist Appointed," in which it styled Eastman "the clever socialist member of the Interstate Commerce Commission"; but this was an isolated judgment. David Lawrence, of the Consolidated Press, represented public opinion much more accurately when he said: "The Eastman appointment . . . will be particularly well received in the West, and will have a moral effect on members of various government commissions, so many of whom have become more or less intimidated by political considerations or at least a fear of Senate punishment when they come up for reappointment.

So, too, the Boston *Evening Transcript* spoke of the importance of keeping the Washington bureaus independent.

The opposition to Mr. Eastman is understood to have been inspired by railroad interests that do not like his attitude in cases in which they have been concerned. It is well to have it understood that what appears to be a grudge is not to be a factor in determining whether or not a man of marked ability and experience shall be continued in the public service.

In the Eastman files is a stack of letters more than a foot thick, from all parts of the nation, congratulating him on his reappointment. The writers included dozens of members of Congress, college classmates, employees of the commission, cabinet members, Federal judges, union leaders, corporation executives, and even people whom he had never seen—a cross section of American life. It took him several weeks to reply to the complimentary messages with which he was greeted.

So it was that the only member of the commission who ever confessed to being an "Independent" found himself in for still another "seven years of hard labor." The situation was indeed paradoxical. Nearly every one on the commission disagreed with him on one or more important matters. Yet dozens of those who had been his critics came to his rescue when there were rumors that he was to be shelved. Some thought that he was too strongly slanted toward government ownership and operation; others felt that his views on valuation were not tenable; and many were convinced that his condemnation of holding companies had been prejudiced and severe. Yet all, or nearly all, recognized that they could depend on him for fair play. The pressure for his reappointment was a tribute to his honesty and his sense of justice as well as to his ability.

The period of the 1920's was the time when Eastman was laying the foundation for his later reputation as the foremost transportation statesman in America. These years were also probably the happiest of his life. He was working hard, but his health was as yet unimpaired. He had the leisure and the vigor for tennis and his summer vacation trips to Canada. He enjoyed the theater, especially musical comedies, which Frank Livingstone would persuade him to attend for refreshment when he was fatigued. He instituted a policy of afternoon teas in his office, where he could meet with his subordinates in friendly, informal fashion. He had work which tested all his powers, but did not wear him down.

When Eastman was Chairman for the first time, in 1926, he once at a department gathering told a story to illustrate the fact that even after seven years in the building, he was still inconspicuous. He was walking along Sixteenth Street one morning and happened to catch up with a young woman, a stranger, but not averse to a casual conversation. When they reached the Interstate Commerce Building, the girl turned in and was about to say "Good-Bye," when she saw that her companion was coming along also. A trifle embarrassed, she asked, "Oh! Do you belong here too?" He had to confess that he was her Chief Boss.

In the 1920's Eastman was the wholesome safety-valve of the opposition, and the fact that he was often in the minority gave him no concern. When the *Railway Age* named him, in 1932, as "the most powerful man in the country, but, unfortunately, also the most dangerous man in public life," Eastman could afford to laugh. "I fall very short of dominating the Commission," he commented. "The necessity which I find for frequent dissents is a sufficient indication of that fact." His real power, such as it was, lay, not in his economic views or any irrefutable logic or any mysterious dramatic quality, but in the respect that his character inspired.

XI

Federal Coordinator of
Transportation

IN 1930 Eastman became chairman of the commission's Legislative Committee, and at once, without seeking publicity, he found himself one of the key figures in the unpredictable realm of politics, facing squarely some of the complicated problems tormenting the Hoover Administration. From time to time he had diagnosed the maladies which afflicted the railroads, and he was now called upon to prescribe the remedies. No act affecting transportation was considered without seeking his advice, and he was present as witness or adviser at every Congressional hearing on the subject. He came to know important Senators and Congressmen on Capitol Hill; he walked, undeceived and incorruptible, in the midst of intrigues, jealousies, and chicanery, wondering at what he saw and heard; he was consulted because of his knowledge and approached because of his supposed power. Naturally, his experience made him wiser, and he wrote in 1931: "There aren't many of the tricks that I don't know!" His passion and aptitude for research, his independent views and convincing manner of expounding them, pleased Congressional leaders weary of bombast and ulterior motives. This quiet, unobtrusive gentleman, uncorroded by personal ambition, had made himself master of a field described in 1933 by Harold G. Moulton as "the most important single element in our social and economic life."

The Legislative Committee, created by the commission in 1916, was furthermore charged with preparing all the numerous written reports requested from time to time by the Congress. Eastman had never been precisely an idler, but now, as chairman of this important committee, he had even heavier responsibilities, especially because in his position he was virtually the mouthpiece of the commission in the opinion of Capitol Hill. Although his three associates were able, experienced men, the burden fell largely on him.

In 1933, moreover, on the basis of his record and because of his outstanding qualifications, Eastman was named by President Franklin D. Roosevelt as Federal Coordinator of Transportation, to meet an urgent national need. He was drafted to test and exemplify a new principle—that of coordination among competing units in the vast railroad empire of more than three million souls, which, as Professor Lloyd K. Garrison once remarked, has "its own customs and its own vocabulary, and lives according to rules of its own making." For a period altogether too brief, Eastman was the leader and observable symbol of a novel experiment in governmental guidance and regulation.

Ten years earlier, Will H. Hays had been chosen by the Motion Picture Producers and Distributors of America to be their salaried president; but the railroads, habituated to "cut-throat" tactics, had not been able in a similar way to reconcile their conflicting interests. Now, at a new President's instigation, the Congress attempted to bring them together. That is what the title "Coordinator" was intended to connote. The act which thus encouraged the harmonious adjustment of disagreements has been called "diminutive," and it is true that it created only a small-scale administrative agency. But its ramifications were far-reaching, and its consequences significant. To understand how it came about, it is necessary to take another short excursion into economic history.

Profiting by increased rates, followed naturally by larger earnings, railway credit had improved gradually from 1920 to 1929, and what had been a shaky structure in its physical or pecuniary aspect had been transformed, in the words of the commission, into a "well maintained, financially strong transportation system." Equipment had been modernized; old and obsolete items, such as locomotives and rails, had been replaced; morale among the workmen was good. Indeed, the railroads of the 1920's were prosperous, although it was clear to some prescient persons—of whom Eastman was one—that the automobile and the airplane and the pipelines were offering each year more vigorous competition.

The Great Depression had no effect on Eastman's bank account, for he possessed almost no securities. But when recovery, far from being "just around the corner," was indefinitely postponed, he was gravely and justifiably concerned over the fate of the railroads. They did not immediately feel the repercussions of the Wall Street panic, but early in 1930 traffic suffered an ominous decline. Fortunately, most of the stronger companies had enough accumulated reserves to continue their interest and dividend payments for a few months, while they anxiously awaited developments. By 1931, however, the full impact of the disaster was evident, and railroad management, undertaking to counteract the decline in earnings, brought about some economies, chiefly through a 10 percent reduction in wages arrived at through negotiation with the unions and effective in 1932.

This, as everybody acquainted with the situation knew, was only a feeble and temporary shot in the arm. On June 17, 1931, the carriers in desperation filed an application for a sweeping 15 percent advance in freight rates. Nobody in his right mind could doubt that they had endured a shrinkage of income and an impairment of credit, but it was questionable whether this particular relief would arrest their progress toward disaster. Throughout the humid summer the commission held hearings at various strategic points, more than 560 witnesses appearing to give evidence. Eastman and Examiner Hosmer went to Atlanta, Dallas, and Kansas City for this purpose and received a very disturbing impression of the prevailing slump in business. On October 16, 1931, the commission announced its decision, denying the application on the ground that the proposed increase would assist revenues only temporarily, if at all, and that it would raise the charges on many kinds of traffic above a "just and reasonable rate."

The commission then, on its own accord, offered a substitute plan of relief, involving small advances on specific articles and commodities, the proceeds to be earmarked for distribution to needy carriers and the authorization to be conditioned upon the establishment of a working pooling arrangement among the stronger roads.

The operators responded with the blueprint of a Railroad Credit Corporation, which would receive the additional revenue from increased rates and with it make loans to companies unable to meet their fixed charges. The point at issue was whether the railroads should be *forced to give* or *allowed to lend*. A majority of the commission were willing to make the desired concession; but Eastman, supported by McManamy, Porter, and Mahaffie, wrote a blunt dissenting opinion, emphasizing the fact that the Railroad Credit Corporation would be under no legal obligation to distribute the improved earnings and might conceivably not choose to do so.

Despite Eastman's opposition, the Railroad Credit Corporation project, controlled by the carriers themselves, went into operation in 1931 and was continued, with moderate success, until the date of the expiration of the original order on March 31, 1933. No doubt Eastman had grounds for questioning the good faith of the transportation executives, but in this instance, and in view of the crisis, he seems to have been oversuspicious. Professor Sharfman feels that the determinations of the commission, viewed in their entirety, were "liberal as well as far-sighted."

The chief source of emergency aid, however, came through the Reconstruction Finance Corporation Act of January 22, 1932, as amended, which permitted loans to be made on adequate security to railroads which could not secure the needed funds on reasonable terms through banking channels or from the general public. Writing to Professor Frankfurter on February 27, 1932, Eastman confessed that he had not been able to give these loans as much attention as he wished to give, largely because his time had been so much taken up with legislative hearings. He did say, however:

At the outset we decided to give full publicity to our action upon every request for a loan. In each case a report is prepared giving the pertinent facts, as we are able to develop them, and our conclusions based upon these facts. . . . We also give full publicity to all applications for loans filed with us. For your information, I may say that this policy was adopted not without opposition from the Reconstruction Finance Corporation, whose tendency has been towards secrecy.

As soon as the RFC went into action, a veritable flood of applications for loans poured in, some of them requiring quick action.

Thus, in the early stages decisions had to be reached in a hurry, often without complete investigations and upon "hearsay" evidence. But the commission was soon stabilized, and Eastman reported to Senator Couzens, "In nearly every case so far decided, I think, we have approved a loan much smaller than the amount asked, and have also been instrumental in securing very material increases in the collateral offered as security." As the months passed, Eastman felt that the RFC was well conceived and administered, although he insisted that it was of necessity only an emergency measure.

In March, 1932, when the Missouri Pacific was in grave trouble, Eastman attended a White House Conference on the matter, together with representatives of the RFC, the Railroad Credit Corporation, the railroads, and the commission. The President, anxious to avoid any further receiverships of Class I railroads, was critical of the two New York banking companies which had refused to make a small loan to the Missouri Pacific. When Professor Frankfurter wrote Eastman suggesting that Hoover had "again mischievously exerted his pressure in a field outside his authority," Joe came to the President's defense and declared that his attitude was in every respect correct.

In its decision in the *Fifteen per cent Case*, the commission, seeking to dispel the current pessimism, said:

The railroads now furnish the backbone and most of the other vital bones of the transportation system of this country, and we believe this will be the situation for a long time to come. We are not impressed with the thought that they are doomed, in anything like the near future, to go the way of the stage coach and the canal.

These were cheering words, but the commissioners knew in their hearts that the situation was frightening. Business was bad and getting worse. Bank after bank closed its doors. England went off the gold standard. As the number of unemployed rose to more than fifteen million, bread lines formed in the larger cities. New York Central dropped from 256 in September, 1929, to 9 in 1932. It has recently been said that Herbert Hoover's misfortune was "that of a bewildered technician adrift on strange forces he could only in part identify." Although he was a man of deep humanitarian feelings, he did not know what course to take, and his constructive measures were too few and often too feeble. His most intimate advisers, trusters in traditional American individualism and initiative, waited disconsolately for the law of supply and demand to rectify conditions. Meanwhile the administration was making little headway in its attempt to restore public confidence.

Pondering sadly their monthly reports, railroad executives saw that the decline in the volume of traffic and in revenue had become alarming. In 1926, for example, the total number of passengers carried throughout the country was 874,000,000; in 1933 it was 434,848,000. The aggregate operating revenue dropped during the same period from $5,955,000 to $2,858,784—a little less than half. It was estimated that during this "hard times" era more than 750,000 employees had to be released from the payrolls of the railroads. The slump was not mitigated by the vigorous competition from other transportation agencies, especially the motor truck and the motor bus, which had no hesitation in engaging in "cut-rate" warfare. Among other factors, as Eastman saw clearly, was the conventional thinking, the unyielding conservatism, which cursed most of the industry. If people have less money, they take fewer vacations and send less goods by freight. The trouble was that the railroad executives displayed little imagination in trying to stimulate rail travel on the one hand and to bring down its cost on the other. According to one shrewd commentator, the railroads had given out on every one—"the consumer of their services, the investor, the worker, and the public generally." This was a comprehensive indictment, perhaps a little exaggerated, but it contained many elements of truth. Whatever the cause, things were indeed deplorable when one sixth of the railroad mileage of the country was passing into the hands of receivers or trustees.

Even when the disastrous consequences of the depression had become unescapable, the railroad leaders did not admit the need for voluntary cooperation. If they had been willing to drop their jealousies and suspicions and work together for reform, they could have done much to reassure their stockholders and encourage one another. Instead, they procrastinated, and for months took no action. In one of his finest speeches, delivered on May 20, 1931, before the New York Traffic Club, Eastman told his audience the truth.

If cooperation cannot be brought about by voluntary act of the railroads themselves, the alternative is action by the Federal Government. The study and research into the facts which I have suggested to be necessary could be carried on by a federal agency. It might be done by the Commission, or a new department of government could be organized for the purpose.

What the railroads would not do was finally undertaken patriotically by a large group of insurance companies, together with four colleges—Harvard, Yale, Columbia, and Chicago—which agreed to subsidize a committee to survey the railroad problem and, if possible, recommend a solution. Those requested to serve were former President Calvin Coolidge; Bernard M. Baruch; Clark Howell (editor of the Atlanta *Constitution*); Alexander Legge (president of the International Harvester Company); and Alfred E. Smith. These five universally respected citizens, functioning as the National Transportation Committee, met for organization on October 7, 1932, and engaged Dr. Harold G. Moulton, of the recently endowed Brookings Institution, in Washington, to assemble a research staff. The conclusions of Dr. Moulton and his associates, published in February, 1933, in a volume entitled *The American Transportation Problem*, formed the basis of the final report of the committee and constituted the most thorough survey up to that time of the transportation situation in the United States. No one could have accused them of having any axe to grind.

Perhaps for this reason the committee, with brutal frankness, dared to condemn "the almost baronial spirit sometimes disclosed by railroad spokesmen" and urged them to bring themselves up to date in a democratic society. It was recommended that the railroad executives cooperate voluntarily to reduce competitive expense; that metropolitan terminals be consolidated in such cities as Boston and Chicago and unnecessary items scrapped; that financial management be improved and securities scaled down; that transport methods and equipment be modernized; and that regulatory jurisdiction be extended to the entire national transportation system. Hardly a proposal in the report had not been made repeatedly by Joseph B. Eastman in public addresses and statements.

To meet the obvious emergency, the committee advised that a new regulatory body be created, with more power than the Interstate Commerce Commission, headed by "either one man or at most an executive committee of three." Calvin Coolidge, who took an active part in the early deliberations, died on January 6, 1933, before the final report had been presented. Baruch, Legge, and Howell signed it *in toto*, and Smith with a few minor reservations. He personally favored the abolition of the Interstate Commerce Commission and the substitution of a new Department of Transportation headed by one man, or of a one-man bureau in the Department of Commerce.

The committee members were certainly no dreamers but practical men of affairs, and their conclusions undeniably shocked some railroad presidents who had regarded Eastman as a visionary. No one could misinterpret the motives of the committee when it said, "The railroads should do much that they have not done to improve their condition without any government help at all." This was language which sustained all that Eastman had been pressing on the executives for many months.

In asserting that he saw "little in recent history to justify the continuance of the Interstate Commerce Commission as now organized," Smith was merely voicing what a number of intelligent observers were beginning to think. James M. Beck, whose hostility to it was undisguised, regretted that it seemed to be a species of treason to question the beneficence of the commission. But plenty of responsible persons rushed to its defense, including Chief Justice Hughes, Justice Roberts, and ex-President Coolidge. The real difficulty, as Eastman knew, was that its members had too little time for planning and administration. On December 2, 1932, as a means of clarifying his own thought, he submitted to his colleagues two possible schemes for reorganization: Plan I, which delegated much of the routine work then devolving on the commission as a whole to individual commissioners or to its staff of employees; and Plan

II, which he regarded as less desirable, dividing the commission into two groups, one of seven members and one of five, each with different duties.

In January, 1933, while the report of the National Transportation Committee was going through the press, Eastman testified before the House Committee on Interstate and Foreign Commerce in favor of a bill authorizing the commission to delegate some of its powers. Without complaining, he mentioned that during the previous year he had written, as chairman of the Legislative Committee, sixty-five reports to committees of Congress in addition to spending many days in appearances and in the presentation of testimony before such committees. Eastman pointed out that it was exceedingly difficult for commissioners to steal the time for studying the essential statistics of railroad operations, for grasping the trend of events, and especially for pondering quietly over the really big national questions of policy and principle. No method was suggested in 1933, however, whereby the commissioners could be freed in any considerable degree from their overwhelming burdens. Eastman could, of course, have liberated himself largely at any moment by turning over some of his responsibilities to competent examiners, but he could never rid himself of the conscientious habit of checking personally on even trifling items. Nothing came of all this, for the majority of the commissioners did not desire any change.

Gratified though he was by the conclusions of the National Transportation Committee, Eastman was dubious about achieving reform under an administration with so little imagination. In its perplexity, the Association of Railroad Executives had presented a somewhat cynical statement outlining two contradictory proposals —either complete government regulation or the open unleashing of competition. To these suggestions Eastman replied: "Clearly of these alternatives the first is much to be preferred, if utter demoralization is to be avoided." Within a month before the close of the Republican regime, he wrote to George Foster Peabody, the banker:

I am glad to know that you are endeavoring to show Mr. Roosevelt the importance of giving consideration to possible radical steps in connection with the railroad situation. If conditions do not improve materially and rapidly in the near future, I feel sure that some plan for their unified operation under government auspices will be necessary.

Following his nomination for the Presidency in June, 1932, Franklin D. Roosevelt had toured the country preaching the gospel of the "New Deal." He touched on many topics; and on September 17, at Salt Lake City, he dealt primarily with railroads, advocating a comprehensive reorganization of our transportation structure to the end of coordinating all carrier service, eliminating waste, and serving the public reasonably, safely, and well. A mimeographed copy of this speech annotated by Roosevelt's official stenographer is in the Franklin D. Roosevelt Library at Hyde Park, showing his interpolations and "ad libbing," but there is no clue as to who, if anybody, contributed ideas and phrasing. It was hinted at the time that some paragraphs were composed by John J. Pelley, president of the New York, New Haven & Hartford Railroad, but he denied having been consulted. The later report that Roosevelt had been advised by Eastman was also erroneous, for the two men had not yet met. It seems clear that both Raymond Moley and Adolf A. Berle had a share in the preliminary preparation of this address, but nobody remembers just how much. During a later discussion of origins, Bernard M. Baruch is quoted as saying: "After all, nobody writes the old man's speeches, although he often uses the substance of what is drafted for him." At any rate, Eastman read the Salt Lake City speech in the newspapers the following morning and was delighted with its tone and temper. After the ordeal through which he had been passing, he looked forward eagerly to the accession of a dynamic leader, with a fresh approach to the familiar problems. He would have voted Democratic in November on general principles, but he was very glad to learn that his candidate had a transportation program of which he could approve.

As soon as the election had been decided, Roosevelt's Brain Trust swung into action, aiming to formulate a series of measures which would meet the current exigency. Hoover, although he had exerted the power of the Federal Government, lacked both vision and daring, and had failed to convince the American people that he had any real understanding of their needs. It is true that the RFC had paid out over two million dollars in loans up to March, 1933, but the gloom had not been lifted. Roosevelt had the gift of making the disaster seem personal. With his buoyant optimism, he was thinking in terms of quick relief from a situation which was tragically intolerable.

In late December, 1932, Robert W. Woolley, formerly a member of the Interstate Commerce Commission and later a politically minded attorney in Washington, saw Roosevelt and suggested that a meeting be arranged for the purpose of discussing railroad problems. On January 5, 1933, Felix Frankfurter, who had become one of Roosevelt's trusted advisers, wrote Eastman: "Roosevelt told me last night that he is going to send for you and Mahaffie shortly. I assume it will be in New York and before he goes South." To this advance information Eastman replied by telegraph: "Do not anticipate visiting New York unless summoned." He did not tell Frankfurter that two days earlier he had sent his colleague Mahaffie a memorandum outlining a series of recommendations on which he hoped they might agree if they were invited to confer with the President-elect. Charles D. Mahaffie, a lawyer who had been made Director of the Bureau of Finance of the Interstate Commerce Commission in 1922, had been appointed commissioner in 1930 and was very close to Eastman. Indeed, the latter had written Frankfurter regarding Mahaffie: "It is fortunate, I think, that we now have a man who possesses the confidence of the financiers and who at the same time is absolutely honest and inclined towards liberalism in his views."

Eastman's carefully drafted memorandum was divided into two sections, one dealing with "Suggested Emergency Measures," the other with "Suggested Normal Measures." As he was well aware, the basic railroad problem was the huge debt piled up through overcapitalization. More than 60 percent of the financial obligations of the railroads was in bonds, on which the fixed charges were naturally heavy. What was needed most was ruthless refinancing— the squeezing out of watered stock. Naturally this situation could not be remedied in a few weeks, and meanwhile the RFC was being harassed for loans. Under the legislation which created the RFC, loans could be made only by a pledge of adequate collateral—

and this at a moment when most of the companies appealing for succor had exhausted their available resources.

Eastman believed that the policy of using government loans to save railroads from insolvency was sound only when a temporary and brief stringency had to be allayed; and, as he pointed out in his memorandum, the financial depression had by 1933 already been prolonged and its end was not in sight. He still did not feel, moreover, that it would be wise to institute a policy of making completely unsecured loans. Thus, and by a familiar course of logic, he fell back on the policy of the assumption in some measure of direct financial responsibility by the Federal Government. This would, he argued, not only cure the credit stringency but would also "make possible at once the realization of economies which can be obtained through the elimination of competition between the railroads themselves." With stubborn persistence he urged that the possibility of government ownership should be examined thoroughly "if only as a necessary precaution for the future," and he went so far as to suggest that it might be practicable to take the railroad systems over "by voluntary transfer without exercise of the power of eminent domain." Perhaps the railroads were so desperate that they would accept with relief an alternative to which they had long been hostile.

In Section II of his memorandum Eastman mentioned certain "normal measures" which ought not to be omitted from any long-range program. Among them were the complete regulation by some national authority of motor and water transportation, comprehensive police rules governing the use of highways by motor vehicles, repeal of the obnoxious recapture provisions of the Transportation Act of 1920, and some reorganization of the Interstate Commerce Commission to make it more effective.

Into these two significant documents Eastman compressed much of what he had learned through rich experience and long meditation. Despite the objections, he still had faith in government ownership and operation as a solution which, although drastic, was for him the simplest and surest road to order out of chaos.

The conference with the President-elect finally took place on

January 11, at the Roosevelt home in New York City. Among those present besides Mr. Roosevelt were Raymond Moley, Rex Tugwell, Eastman, and Mahaffie. William H. Woodin, president of the American Car & Foundry Company, who was slated to become Secretary of the Treasury, was detained, but participated actively in some of the later meetings. Although Felix Frankfurter was kept away at the last moment, he took part in the proceedings rather extensively by telephone.

At Roosevelt's request, Eastman took the lead in the conversation, although since a good deal had to be said about the financial plight of the railroads, Mahaffie, who was an expert in that field, was called upon to express his opinions. FDR, in his familiar debonair mood, set everybody at ease, listened attentively to Eastman's arguments for Federal operation, and asked a few searching questions. He admitted that he knew very little about transportation, except shipping, where he regarded himself as an authority. Eastman regretted, as he wrote Felix Frankfurter, that he had no opportunity to discuss with the President-elect many of the matters taken up in his memorandum, but Roosevelt seemed especially concerned over the financial status of the railroads. Joe, who saw Roosevelt here for the first time, went away favorably impressed, but observed later that little of importance was accomplished. It seems evident that the President-elect, following out his habitual practice, was sizing up the man whom he was later to appoint as Coordinator.

After all, at that moment Mr. Roosevelt had many other things to think about. He did, however, designate a group to consider and, if possible, to develop a program for aiding railroads in financial distress. This was headed by Woodin and included, among others, Henry Bruere, of the Bowery Savings Bank; Earle Bailey, of Seligman & Company; Alfred P. Thom, General Counsel of the Association of American Railroads; E. G. Buckland, of the New Haven and the Railroad Credit Corporation; and Mahaffie and Eastman, of the Interstate Commerce Commission. Their work proceeded rapidly, and on January 18 Mahaffie addressed to Woodin a memorandum in which Eastman concurred, suggesting a possible amendment to the Reconstruction Finance Corporation Act, allowing

Acme Photo

A GROUP OF RAILROAD EXPERTS IN 1938

WENDELL WILLKIE, FRANK KNOX, AND JOSEPH B. EASTMAN
AT DARTMOUTH COLLEGE

loans to be made, speaking generally, for the purposes for which receivers' certificates properly could be issued if the property were in receivership. The views of the railroad interests, however, differed very widely from those of Eastman and Mahaffie, and that difference could not be adjusted, with the result that nothing was done until the new administration took over.

Plenty of intelligent thought was being given at this stage to the situation. Shortly after the New York conference, Frankfurter sent Eastman a memorandum in which, after dwelling briefly on some of the more serious current problems, he outlined certain bills which, he thought, should be introduced on the floor of Congress to give more real power to the Interstate Commerce Commission. He wanted it to have the authority to pass upon all purchases of rail securities by holding or operating companies; to prevent uneconomical management, whether because of competition or in the absence of competition; to control receiverships and reorganizations; to eliminate competitive waste; and to compel roads to set up substantial reserves—although how that could be done out of nothing he did not explain. "The point is," continued Frankfurter, "that such legislation should be put through when it can be; and if there is any time for doing it, now is the time."

To this sage counsel Eastman made a reply which he very carefully drafted and then revised more thoroughly than was his custom. It is too long to print here in full, but one section will show his state of mind.

For a long time I wavered in my views upon competition. There are impressive evidences that competition is a stimulus to alert, aggressive management, while monopoly may lead to an indifferent and unprogressive management. However, I am convinced that the evils and wastes of competition can be saved from dry rot. This points to the conclusion that competition among railroads should be eliminated and that they should be operated as a unit. But I do not believe that the country will stand for that without government ownership, and it is also clear that this is the simplest road to unification. . . .

I fear this will be a discouraging letter. Frankly, I think that we have got about as far with regulation as can be got, and that if better results are desired, direct governmental responsibility for transportation is the path to follow.

Professor Frankfurter was not, of course, the only other person who was trying to pull the railroads out of the slough. A group of powerful western railroad executives had set up on December 15, 1932, a coordinating committee of their own under a "Commissioner of Western Railroads" and were planning to assert themselves with vigor when the new administration came in. A Railroad Bankruptcy Act, toward the improvement and passage of which Eastman made an important contribution, was signed by President Hoover on March 3, 1933. Several energetic Congressional leaders were merely biding their time, waiting for the next President to take charge in order to transmute his ideas into legislation. The enemies of the Interstate Commerce Commission were plotting to abolish it; its friends were conspiring to increase its power. The railroads were afraid of any further governmental control; the union representatives wanted to prevent any increase in unemployment; the holders of railroad securities panted for their postponed dividends. Ideas were being tossed about; little self-constituted committees were meeting behind closed doors; eager promoters of wild theories dictated long memorandums. Lobbyists and politicians disputed bitterly. But no unanimity was discernible. Everybody was waiting for the Republicans to go out and the Democrats to come in.

To Eastman, who knew as much as anybody about causes and cures, much of the discussion seemed fantastic. Answering a request from William G. McAdoo, he said:

I have prepared no memorandum on government ownership of railroads to which any publicity has been given. However I have felt very strongly that the remedies which have been and are being applied to the situation are merely temporary palliatives, and I doubt very much whether it is going to be possible for the railroads to operate successfully through the medium of private enterprise and private credit unless economic conditions improve very materially and rapidly. It is quite possible, therefore, that the government will have to assume direct responsibility in some form for the railroads and perhaps for the transportation system in general.

With his letter the persistent Eastman enclosed "a skeleton plan for the voluntary transfer of the railroads to the government." "Mahaffie thinks much less well of it than I do," he admitted. "I am by no means committed to it and realize that it is probably full of defects. I drew it up principally as something to shoot at."

While Eastman tenaciously renewed his devotion to government operation, trains still continued to run, although the transportation leaders seemed to be discouraged and helpless, wondering what more shattering blow would fall next. Roosevelt had declared that he wanted "a reappraisal of values." What did that imply—or forebode?

Then, with the industrial fabric of the nation in danger of falling apart, came that historic first Saturday in March, 1933, when Franklin Delano Roosevelt took the oath of office. Eastman had invited several commissioners to his room to watch the inaugural parade from its windows and listen to the new President's address. There they heard the voice of the Chief Executive, calm and confident, reaching millions of Americans over the radio. "This great nation," it said, "will endure as it has endured, will revive and will prosper. So, first of all, let me assert my firm belief that the only thing we have to fear is fear itself,—nameless, unreasonable, unjustified terror which paralyzes needed efforts to convert retreat into advance." When in ringing tones he called for "broad executive power to wage war against the emergency," he offered a frightened people a new hope. The amazing period of the Hundred Days had opened, when Republicans as well as Democrats, manufacturers and bankers as well as laborers, were ready to welcome vigorous leadership. Among Eastman and his friends at that moment any legitimate gamble for prosperity seemed well worth taking. Inertia and half measures had both been tried, with meager results. The hour had come for action which would be courageous and drastic.

Although Eastman had occupied a position which Washington regarded with much respect, he had hitherto seen very little of the White House, either socially or officially. With FDR, however, he soon found himself on fairly intimate terms. The President promptly hailed him as "Joe" and invited him to conferences in his office. With much satisfaction Eastman observed that the "Boss" was acting with directness and decision. Because he was in sympathy with the "bold persistent experimentation" which Roosevelt was advocating and illustrating, he was at first identified with the New

Deal. Indeed, one newspaper spoke of him as "one of the magic symbols of the national recovery formula." John Gunther, in his book *Roosevelt in Retrospect*, mentions Eastman as one of those on the fringes of the so-called Brain Trust.

But although warmly welcomed, Eastman was never admitted to the exclusive inner circle around the President. On April 6 he wrote: "I fear that my efforts to solve the transportation problem have been much exaggerated in newspaper accounts. My association with the President in this matter has been quite limited." He was probably too outspoken, too far from being a "Yes-Man," to be long close to the throne. On April 15, for example, he sent a very interesting letter of protest to his Chief.

At our conference at the White House last Tuesday evening you mentioned the fact that a reorganization of the transportation activities of the government was in contemplation which would be made effective by executive order. Last night the *Star* contained an outline of such a proposed reorganization. Whether or not this outline is correct I do not, of course, know. However, I thought that you ought to know that this Commission has in no way been consulted with respect to any proposed plan and has had no opportunity to express any views upon it. If the plan outlined in the *Star* is approximately correct, I fear there is grave danger that a serious mistake will be made which will result in no economy but will impair the efficiency and effectiveness of this Commission, and in addition place certain highly controversial matters of great public importance within the control of an executive department, although they are matters which most decidedly ought to be dealt with in a judicial or quasi-judicial way. I hope, therefore, that the Commission may have an opportunity to express views to you upon any proposed plan before it is made effective by executive order.

This frank statement had one immediate consequence. The President invited Eastman to the White House, explained that no slight had been intended, and in his gracious manner promised to consult the commission on whatever steps were taken toward transportation reform. For the moment a possible breach had been avoided. But as spring turned into summer and Eastman perceived that the administration was not only trumpeting a crusade but also playing partisan politics, his initial enthusiasm slightly waned, and, as did his friend Justice Brandeis, he became more critical. He did not really enjoy the easy-going jocularity which pervaded the White House discussions. Furthermore, although he was no stiff-necked prig, he was disturbed by the intrigues and bargains which went on around him, and in his private correspondence he compared Wilson with Roosevelt, to the latter's disadvantage. "Expediency" and "opportunism" were two words which did not appeal to Eastman very much. The President early asked him to recommend candidates for the Interstate Commerce Commission, and then later wrote him:

I shall be delighted to have you submit the names of some men of the type that you and I have in mind. I agree with you as to the type, but it is also important to remember that we must have men who are honestly and sincerely in favor of the general policies of the administration,—men whose loyalty we can count on.

In matters of this nature Eastman was concerned mainly with finding the men most likely to work unselfishly for the public interest, and he cared little whether they were willing to commit themselves in advance to the administration program. Two fundamental and in some degree irreconcilable conceptions of duty were involved. Eastman may have been slightly naïve, but his responses were refreshing. One of Eastman's close friends writes: "At first he was a believer in FDR, for his judgment of motives was generous, but after a while he regretfully came to the conclusion that Roosevelt was an opportunist, insincere and primarily interested in FDR's place in the public eye." This is probably an exaggeration, for Eastman never lost his admiration for Roosevelt's dynamic and persuasive qualities and thought him to be an inspiring and supremely capable war leader. But his disagreements with him on domestic subjects were numerous, and his lack of subserviency often irritated the President.

There was no need for Eastman to have any sense of inferiority, even when he sat with the Brain Trusters. During the spring of 1933 the *Railway Age* had answered its own question, "Who is the most powerful man in the United States?" by asserting that Joseph B. Eastman was not only the "most powerful" but also the most dangerous, because he had suggested that the Government "take over the public functions, such as railroads, and assume complete and undivided responsibility for their management." It is interesting that this magazine suggested still another candidate for the position of "most powerful"—John Nance Garner, the Vice-President, "because of his almost limitless power in expediting or preventing legislation." The article continued: "We have gone a long way when responsible men look upon two government servants, one in appointive and the other in elective place, as more powerful than any of the great money kings who used to control the nation's destinies." When a conservative publication could employ such extravagant language about a mere Interstate Commerce Commissioner, it is easy to understand why he was welcomed gladly to White House conferences along with Tugwell, Moley, Berle, and the others.

Under the stimulus of the President's "fireside chats," with their calculated optimism, the Congress had proceeded with rapidity and almost unprecedented unanimity to pass one emergency bill after another. For a few weeks the administration was concerned with such basic matters as the devaluation of the dollar, the alleviation of unemployment, and the restoration of bank stability. In April several conferences were held in the office of Daniel C. Roper, the new Secretary of Commerce, to whom the President, without thinking things out very carefully, had entrusted the problem of transportation relief. To the first meeting Roper invited three members of the Interstate Commerce Commission and a few of his own departmental staff, with the aim of considering some proposals from the western railroads. Roper then appointed a special committee of three to continue the hearings and discussions and report their conclusions. The trio consisted of Eastman, who was still chairman of the Commission's Legislative Committee, Walter M. W. Splawn, who was then special counsel to the Committee on Interstate and Foreign Commerce of the House of Representatives, and A. Lane Cricher, chief of the Transportation Division in the Bureau of Foreign and Domestic Commerce.

From the beginning Eastman felt that Roper, who had been Assistant Postmaster General, was an astute politician, seeking principally the aggrandizement of his office and trying through various devices to bring the commission under his control. On this point Eastman had written in 1932: "A transfer of the Commission to any executive department, where its policies would be subject to the changing influence of a cabinet officer, would be disastrous. It ought not to be considered for a minute." Once, after a stormy session, Eastman said to FDR: "Mr. President, the Secretary and I just don't speak the same language. I can't learn his, and he doesn't want to understand mine!"

But although Eastman and Roper were not congenial spirits, the newly constituted committee labored diligently, listening to various groups who had their own ideas about legislation. Most of these could be summarily rejected, for they were selfish in their motives, and finally Eastman, Splawn, and Cricher drafted their own measure. This was communicated to the President, who gave his approval in principle and indicated his desire for haste. There followed a further series of conferences in the office of the Secretary of Commerce, attended by representatives of all the interested parties —shippers, railroad employees, security owners, the United States Chamber of Commerce, union leaders, and railroad executives. With more information at their disposal, the committee met again with the President, who now named a special group to get the bill ready for Congress. The members of this Committee of Six—each one selected for a particular purpose—were Eastman and Splawn, Senator Clarence E. Dill (from Washington), Representative Sam Rayburn (from Texas), Secretary of the Treasury Woodin, and Secretary of Commerce Roper. They held several more meetings, examining carefully new suggestions for improving the plan and phrasing of the measure. The results of what were rightly described as "extended deliberations" were submitted to the Congress by President Roosevelt through a special message under date of May 3, 1933, less than two months after the inauguration. Very few bills have been so relentlessly scrutinized by experts who knew their business.

Eastman followed the act through every stage of its evolution and was responsible for much of its phraseology. His private feeling about it was expressed in a letter to Paul V. Anderson, in which he said:

The Coordinator idea did not originate with me (nor do I think it originated with the railroads) and I have never regarded the bill as more than a useful interim measure which might pave the way for a more radical and thorough-going treatment of the transportation situation. That was the substance of my advice to the President. . . . Probably it is unnecessary for me to tell you that I have no overwhelming personal desire for the job of Coordinator, and from that point of view am indifferent as to the fate of the bill. I would not accept any increase in income from the job; the chances that I would gain more credit than discredit would not be better than even; and the chances of sapping health from overwork and strain would be very good indeed. There would be a momentarily flattering increase in notoriety, but the only real attraction would be the new work.

Eastman added, as his considered opinion: "My own judgment, in brief, is that while the Coordinator Bill is far from a final answer to the transportation problem, it will serve a very useful purpose and help to find that answer, if properly administered."

Adopting Eastman's advice, the President in his special message told Congress that he was not yet ready to submit a "comprehensive plan for permanent legislation." He did, however, recommend a repeal of the annoying and now anachronistic Recapture Clause of the Transportation Act of 1920. He strongly advocated a bill, long favored by Eastman, placing holding companies under the jurisdiction of the Interstate Commerce Commission. More important still, he proposed the creation of a Federal Coordinator of Transportation, who, working with groups of railroads, would be able "to encourage, promote, or require action on the part of carriers, in order to avoid duplication of service, prevent waste, and encourage financial reorganization." He concluded: "The experience gained during the balance of this year will greatly assist the Government and the carriers in preparation for a more permanent and a more comprehensive national transportation policy at the regular session of the Congress in 1934."

Secretary Roper, in testifying before the House Committee on Interstate and Foreign Commerce, said that the bill "was really an answer to the plea of railroad management to be permitted to work out their own salvation, or at least to be granted a reasonable time within which to do so, under governmental guidance." He added: "The results will depend not so much upon the Coordinator as upon the railway executives themselves. If the results are good, the executives will deserve the credit." Eastman would probably not have expressed it precisely that way.

Eastman was naturally a prominent figure at the Congressional hearings on what became known as Emergency Railroad Transportation Act, 1933. On May 9 he appeared before the Senate Committee, following Secretary Roper, and on the next morning he was one of the first witnesses before the House Committee. His statement had been drafted with exceptional care, and he was allowed to read it in its entirety, with occasional interruptions from committee members. On the stand Eastman was always at his best, coolheaded, even-tempered, tactful, and yet fearless, and his knowledge and grasp of details did not escape the notice of attentive legislators. He did not weaken under heckling, even when the irrepressible Senator Huey Long indulged in his "wise-cracks" or the truculent Montana Democrat Senator Burton K. Wheeler charged him with being anti-labor. After all, he was dealing with a subject to which he had devoted his life, and his opinions were not "snap-judgments." He was interested, he said, in the specific provisions of the bill, but he regarded as crucial the section providing for further observation and analysis of railroad troubles. In this connection he remarked:

The transportation of this country is in a period of grave unsettlement pending important changes. New transportation agencies have appeared on the scene in great force. It is a period of strife, confusion, and instability. The proper place for each of these agencies must be found, and in some way they must be coordinated and welded into a well-knit whole, into a transportation system operating more nearly as a unit, without cross purposes and all manner of lost motion.

The provisions in the measure for the reduction of costs had never appealed to union leaders. According to statistics, 800,000 employees were already out of work and most of those still on the job had been obliged to accept wage cuts. In his testimony, Eastman had said without evasion: "To a very considerable extent the elimination or reduction of wastes will involve loss of employment to railroad labor; indeed economies in operation and service mean reduction in labor, and there is no escape from it." But for him it seemed an unsound conclusion that "employment should be preserved by retaining waste and inefficiency." Personally he hoped that the Government would move in the direction of the elimination of unemployment "along a wide front." The solution for the roads, however, did not lie in a resort to "feather-bedding."

At the Senate hearing Donald R. Richberg, whom Eastman had come to know well and respected highly, appeared in behalf of the twenty-one standard railway labor organizations affiliated in the Railway Labor Executives Association. He announced that his clients opposed the bill principally because it provided a mechanism of false economy which would seriously reduce transportation service for the public, render from 50,000 to 500,000 employees idle, retard business recovery, and work "infinite harm" to the public interest. At Richberg's insistence Section 7 was so amended as to specify that the number of employees in the service of a carrier should not be reduced below the number on the pay rolls in May, 1933, after deducting up to 5 percent for deaths, normal retirements, or resignations. Since no far-reaching economies could be accomplished without cutting down the personnel, this amended Section 7 emasculated the original plan. Eastman did what he could to show that this amendment nullified the whole philosophy underlying the act. It is questionable, however, whether the bill as introduced could have been passed against the opposition of organized labor; furthermore, the President would doubtless have interposed his veto if the concession had not been made. Labor would have been as much aroused as it was later over the Taft-Hartley Act—which, it will be recalled, was vetoed by Mr. Roosevelt's successor.

Aside from this major change, the Emergency Railroad Transportation Act, 1933, went through Congress without too much difficulty. The trifling differences between the Senate bill and the House bill were readily adjusted, and the measure as amended passed the Senate, in charge of Senator Dill, after two days of perfunctory debate. Representatives Rayburn and Parker put it through the House in nine days, and the bill became effective on June 16, 1933.

When the Act was in its formative stages, Eastman wrote:

The Secretary of Commerce, Senator Dill, and Congressman Rayburn have grave doubts in regard to the wisdom of pressing this proposed bill at the present time. This question is outside my field. It is true,

I think, that the bill will be vigorously opposed by railroad labor and that railroad shippers will, at best, not be enthusiastic. It should be well received by railroad security holders and, in general, by the railroads.

As late as April 18 Eastman confessed to a friend: "There is still some doubt as to whether even this measure will be pushed through." But the popular response to the various phases of the New Deal had made it seem expedient and wise for all parties to go along with the program. Eastman was correct when he wrote: "The choice is probably between some such bill and no bill at all." In neither chamber was the discussion very vigorous, and there was, except for Section 7, no organized or consistent opposition. Senator Wheeler declared that the measure was backed by a small group of heavy investors in railroads who wished to safeguard their property, but no one took him seriously. Senator Borah and Representative Beck raised the familiar cry of unconstitutionality, but did not press the matter. Although the labor amendment evoked some hostile comment, only a few Congressional veterans realized its full import.

Eastman, however, was not deceived, and he finished the battle both hurt and disillusioned. Concerned as he was in creating workable legislation for the benefit of all the people, he was irritated by the tricky maneuvers of pressure groups. Up to this time he had been generally sympathetic with organized labor and had been greeted warmly by union leaders at their gatherings. Now he discovered that labor officials could be just as aggressive, just as ruthless and indifferent to the welfare of others, as the employers had ever been. It was at this period and because of this episode that Eastman remarked to a friend: "Labor executives are drunk with power!" In commenting on the situation in a letter to Paul Y. Anderson, under date of May 23, 1933, when the full intent of the labor leaders had been made clear, Eastman said:

If I understand the theory on which the Administration is now proceeding, it is that all waste and nonessential expense should be eliminated in Government service and elsewhere, and that along with this policy should go companion measures which will stimulate business activity and provide for increase in employment in useful, needed work. In other words, the relief from retrenchment for purposes of sound economy is to be provided by expansion in other sound directions. Whether or not this is the best plan for beating the depression I am not wise enough to know, but I see no reason why railroads should be excepted from that plan.

Long before the Emergency Act became law, it had been understood that Eastman would be the Coordinator. Early in May the President had sounded him out on the subject; and on May 31 Joe made overtures to some of the men whom he wanted as his associates, saying: "It is possible that I shall have a job as so-called Coordinator of Railroads." He wrote Judge Anderson on June 9: "I shall take the Coordinator job if it is offered, notwithstanding the labor amendments, because I think it will still be possible to do some concrete things and to accumulate much worthwhile information for future use." Although his appointment as Coordinator actually dated from June 16, he did not receive the formal "go ahead" from the President until July.

Even the crotchety *Railway Age* was forced to admit that probably no railroad executive would have been acceptable to his competitors—or would have been willing to take the position. George Creel, writing in *Colliers* for August 12, 1933, bestowed upon Eastman very high praise, describing him as "a prize nuisance to gentlemen accustomed to having things their own way." He declared, however, that in spite of this reputation the "magnates" were virtually a unit in approving the appointment, believing that Eastman was "the last word in absolute fairness"; and he added: "Joe Eastman may fight tooth and nail to keep the railroads from getting the best of it, but he is just as insistent that they shall not get the worst of it." As a matter of fact Eastman was the only one ever mentioned seriously for the job, and his nomination was taken for granted. Things were still moving fast in Washington. Legislation was still being rushed at the White House and carried out on Capitol Hill with a minimum of obstructive delay. To most of the conservatives, now very silent, Joe Eastman was just another "New Dealer," to be accepted as a necessary evil.

Representative James S. Parker, of New York, described the Emergency Railroad Transportation Act, 1933, as "probably as complicated and complex a bill as ever came before the Congress of the United States." It was not really quite so bad as that. Title II of the bill, in accordance with the expressed wishes of the President and the desire of a majority of the Interstate Commerce Commission, brought about some permanent modifications in the Transportation Act of 1920. It included provisions for bringing holding companies within the jurisdiction of the commission. It eliminated the almost unenforceable Recapture Clause, which had provoked so much litigation; and it promulgated a new rule of rate making by instructing the commission to consider, among other factors, the effect of rates on the movement of traffic, the need of adequate railway transportation service at the lowest possible cost, and the desirability of revenues sufficient to enable the carriers, under honest, economical, and efficient management, to provide such service. These were reforms which were badly needed and warmly applauded.

Title I, which created the office of Coordinator and defined his functions and powers, was the controversial section of the Emergency Act. To the Congressional committees Eastman, in a sense on exhibition, had expressed frankly his views regarding the position which seemed likely to be his. The Coordinator, in his conception, was to be in no sense a "czar of railroads" or an irresponsible autocrat, but an administrative officer of the Government whose principal duty was "to aid and promote and, if necessary, require the co-operation on the part of the carriers which it is believed the emergency demands and which it is difficult, if not impossible, for those companies with their jealousies and intense rivalries and individual interests and present legal inhibitions to accomplish without outside, disinterested help and the aid of government." The sting of this sentence lay, of course, in the words "and, if necessary, require," which carried with them the hint of a threat. Eastman was later, after his appointment, to describe himself as a "catalyst"—a substance which accelerates a chemical reaction. Possibly Joe did not look up the dictionary definition, which states that the original substance "may be recovered practically unchanged at the end of the experiment." He was to find himself very much altered by the time his ordeal as Coordinator was over.

All through May and June Eastman was hounded by applicants

for jobs, by letters from Congressmen urging consideration for needy constituents, by pitiful pleas from old friends or from employees of the Interstate Commerce Commission who had been furloughed in the interests of economy. At first he could reply that he did not know who would be designated as Coordinator and therefore was hardly in a position to make commitments. Later, when his status was clear, he was obliged to say that only a few places would be open and those only to exceptionally well-qualified specialists.

Eastman at once transferred some key members of his clerical staff to his new organization so that he might be able to start without delay on his duties. He borrowed other help from the commission; indeed, he had no hesitation, under an arrangement made with his colleagues, about asking for aid whenever he needed it. The expenses of the Coordinator's office, according to the terms of the Emergency Act, were to be met by the railroads, each company paying each year $1.50 for every mile of road which it operated. This unique method of meeting costs, although agreed upon by the roads, did not escape comment from the executives. "Damn it," said one of them, "it's almost like paying for our own executioners." As a matter of fact, Eastman's staff was never very large, and for awhile he actually had no available funds. As late as July 6, he wrote: "We are marking time here awaiting action from the White House to get going." On that very afternoon, however, he saw the President and explained to him that while for most of his assistants he did not expect to pay in excess of $8,500 a year, he would require four bureau heads at the rate of $15,000. This, it will be noted, was much more than Eastman himself was receiving, or had ever received, but that made no difference to him. In justifying this apparent extravagance, Eastman reminded the Chief Executive that the appointments were temporary and might last for only one year; that he was not seeking the services of top industrialists with huge incomes, able to accept heavy sacrifices because of past accumulations, but rather of promising junior executives; and that the cash in any case would come from the railroads, which would certainly raise no objections, knowing that judged by their standards $15,000 was very small remuneration for such an important position. Fortunately Eastman did not need to consider civil service regulations, but he did have to secure the approval of the President, who was quite willing under the circumstances to ignore political considerations.

Joe had to struggle through the tropical early July days in Washington with the problem of building up with great celerity a staff of experts in research and administration to whom he could guarantee little in the shape of salary or tenure. Even on the July 4 holiday he spent the entire day in his office. Fortunately his acquaintance was wide, and he knew personally many of the top men in their respective fields. He sought the advice of many railroad presidents and tried to lure their ablest assistants into his organization. Some of those whom he selected, such as William H. Day, of Boston, declined. But he kept the telephone and telegraph busy, and was actually able on July 10 to issue a memorandum giving a skeleton chart of his organization, with brief biographical sketches of department heads.

Eastman's Executive Assistant, upon whom he was to rely with justified confidence, was John L. Rogers, who had served his apprenticeship as a boiler-maker, had become a mechanical engineer and a lawyer, had entered the commission's Bureau of Locomotive Inspection in 1917, and had finally been named in 1925 as Special Examiner in the Bureau of Service, where he had handled capably some complicated cases. Rogers was versatile, indefatigable, and loyal, as well as highly popular with his commission associates. Still another wise choice was John R. Turney, a St. Louis railroad attorney, who accepted the post of director of the Section of Freight Service. Long connected with the St. Louis Southwestern Railroad, he ultimately became its vice-president and acquired an extensive knowledge of practical railroad operation. Turney, who was a robust personality, at times argumentative and never docile, was an excellent foil for his undemonstrative chief, and became one of Eastman's most trusted advisers. Another rare find was Leslie Craven, an Oregon lawyer who had been since 1932 a professor in Duke University Law School. He had represented the western railroads in the O'Fallon Case and was an authority in the field of valuation. In the Coordinator's office he was first a member of the

research staff and later counsel. Otto S. Beyer, another member of
the research staff, had been a consulting engineer who had devoted
much time to the furtherance of good relations between operators
and employees and was soon to be chosen by Eastman as director
of the Section of Labor Relations. R. L. Lockwood, director of
the Section of Purchases, was an engineer with long and varied experience whom Eastman took from the Department of Commerce.
James W. Carmalt, a member of the bar who had formerly been a
commission examiner and was in 1933 in private legal practice in
Washington, became the Coordinator's Executive and Legal Assistant.

In accordance with the set-up it was necessary to have three
regional directors: H. J. German, of Pittsburgh, president of the
Montour Railroad, for the East; Victor V. Boatner, another former
railroad president, for the West; and Clarence E. Weaver, of Savan-
nah, general manager of the Central of Georgia, for the South.
These three and Turney were paid $15,000 apiece; the others re-
ceived either $8,000 or $8,500. The assembling of such a competent
body of specialists on such short notice was a remarkable achievement.

According to the terms of the Emergency Act, when Eastman
assumed the position of Federal Coordinator of Transportation,
he still remained as Interstate Commerce Commissioner, although
not allowed to sit on proceedings for the review or suspension of
any orders issued by him in his new capacity. Furthermore, he was
to receive no increase in compensation beyond and above his salary
as commissioner, which had been reduced in 1932, under the terms
of the Economy Act, first to $10,000 and then to $8,500. Against
such sharp reductions Eastman had protested to the Director of
the Budget, not because the cut made much difference to him, for
he was a bachelor, but because it caused much hardship to some of
his associates with large families.

Naturally, the relationship between the Coordinator and the
commission were bound to be intimate, for the two were interde-
pendent. For a time he continued to occupy his familiar office on
the tenth floor of the building at Eighteenth Street and Pennsylvania
Avenue. His room had a green plush carpet—which he never really

liked—and was usually littered with papers and commission documents. In 1934, however, the new Interstate Commerce Building —one of the most beautiful and imposing in the capital—was opened at the corner of Twelfth Street and Constitution Avenue. This had been authorized in the Hoover administration as part of a comprehensive plan for the development of the city. When it was ready for occupancy, he found that his commodious quarters in Room 1536, overlooking the Mall and the Smithsonian Institution, were ornamented with four elaborate gilt chandeliers, and he insisted that they should be removed. When the Federal Government had to accept the building, however, it was discovered that the valuable decorations were missing, and they had to be restored before the acceptance could be formalized. As soon as that ceremony was over, Joe gave orders to have them and some rather rich colored draperies taken out. "Too showy for this kind of office," he said —and that was that!

In general, newspaper comment was favorable to Eastman's appointment. The conservative press did do a little grumbling and questioned whether "an advocate of government ownership" was qualified to administer the Emergency Act fairly and constructively. But Eastman had somewhat disarmed his critics by confessing at the Senate committee hearing that he had been unable to draft a plan for government ownership which satisfied him. Goaded by Senator Huey Long, Eastman had amplified his first statement, as follows:

I think that there are disadvantages in Government ownership. I would not expect any system to be perfect and certainly not a system of Government ownership, but when it comes to the question of whether the Government should take over the railroads at the present time, I see many difficulties in the way because of the uncertainty as to the future of the railroads and the question of what price shall be paid for these properties, and also the fact that the roads are becoming much more than they have been in the past a part of the entire transportation system.

Never did Eastman retract his belief that government ownership and operation would some time be inevitable, but like many an idealist he had to abandon his theories in order to adjust to a current situation. It would have been a grave blunder, even a catastrophe, to press the matter in 1933.

Almost at once Eastman had to confront and settle a question of jurisdiction with the Department of Commerce. On June 16, the day when the Emergency Act was signed, the President wrote to Secretary Roper asking him to organize a committee for the purpose of making a comprehensive survey of the transportation situation—"this committee to include, among others, a representative of the office of the Railroad Coordinator." When Roper sent Eastman a copy of this communication, the latter "blew up." He replied formally and politely, saying that unfortunately he had another engagement on the date suggested for the first meeting of the proposed committee. He then quoted the section of the Emergency Act making it the duty of the Coordinator "to investigate and consider means . . . of improving transportation conditions throughout the country." He continued:

The Act also equips me with the means for conducting such an investigation. This is, as I understand it, a duty imposed by law upon the Coordinator, and which he must perform. Nor do I see how he can lawfully share the responsibility for the performance of this duty with any one else. I have always regarded it as, perhaps, the most important duty to be performed by the Coordinator, and so expressed myself in testimony before both committees of Congress.

While, therefore, I desire to cooperate with you in your work to the fullest extent feasible and practicable, it must be with the reservation that such cooperation cannot conflict with any duty which the law has imposed upon me, while I occupy the position of Coordinator.

Thus early did the mild-mannered Joe Eastman make it clear that he did not intend to tolerate the interference of the Executive Branch of the government with a department created by Congress. It was a declaration of independence which did not ingratiate him with the Administration, and he and the President later had a few caustic words on the subject. But it did clarify the atmosphere. The issue was to be presented again from a higher governmental level before many months had passed.

XII

The Coordinator's Task
and Achievements

ALTHOUGH the Coordinator had an impressive title and some prestige, together with broad power to issue orders—a power which was later to be declared constitutional by the Supreme Court —he was hampered from the beginning by lack of support from the operators. Felix Frankfurter had written him in May: "Who would have thought that you would end up as one of the country's czars?" But Eastman was temperamentally no despot, and he also realized that he could not gain his desired ends by force. Unfortunately for his theory, however, the operators responded to suggestions by declaring either that everything possible had been tried or that changes were unnecessary or too costly. When he pointed out specific wastes in time and money, the executives told him coolly that attempts were being made to eliminate them—and he did not wish then to declare open war. Counseled by their attorneys, railroad presidents stubbornly assumed that they need not accept advice unless it was to their liking. The truth was that they did not want any government official prying into their business affairs. The *Traffic World* complained that there was no consistent or constructive leadership among railroad executives. Consequently Eastman was like a preacher outlining a code of ethics to a congregation of delinquents or a schoolmaster anxious to secure obedience, but unwilling to use the birch, even though it was hanging near at hand. Speaking on March 7, 1934, before the New York Chamber of Commerce, Eastman, out of bitter experience, said: "To me the railroads have seemed more zealous to prove that my staff was wrong in its conclusions and recommendations than to find, with the help of our reports, ways and means of improvement. Their attitude, in short, has been one of defense."

As month followed month and subjects for controversy became more frequent, Eastman found little reason to alter his views on this matter. In his fourth and last report, published in 1936, Eastman again declared that the railroad leaders had given the Federal Coordinator scanty cooperation. In one paragraph he said:

Their habit of mind is intensely individualistic and suspicious of collective action. When such action is proposed, notwithstanding that it may be good for the industry as a whole, the normal executive will at once seek to determine how it may affect his railroad in comparison with others. It is easy for him to fear that it may have an adverse effect from that point of view, and if he does, he is against the proposition. He is particularly wary of any collective proposal which has a nation-wide aspect, for he sees in it what he regards as a tendency towards "nationalization" of the railroads, and, at all events, a decrease in the importance of the local managements.

This indictment was written under strain and was undoubtedly too comprehensive. Eastman was not unaware that men are largely motivated by self-interest, but his own reactions were so different that he could not understand why they so constantly asked, "What is there in this for me or my company?" In his position as Federal Coordinator, his instinctive faith in human nature suffered many shocks, but he persisted in his conviction that people, once shown the gleam, are bound to follow it. This confidence, though often shattered, sustained him through many trials and tribulations.

Before the passage of the Emergency Act the railroads in several areas had established what were known as "economy committees"; and by the terms of that measure the systems were officially divided into three groups—eastern, western, and southern—with the carriers in each section directed to choose the members of their own regional coordinating committees. On June 29, 1933, Eastman was notified of the election of the five regular members of the Eastern Regional Committee—a strong group, comprised of Atterbury, of the Pennsylvania, Pelley, of the New Haven, Willard, of the Baltimore & Ohio, Bernet, of the Chesapeake & Ohio, and Williamson, of the New York Central. The representatives from the other two sections were equally outstanding, including Gray, of the Union Pacific, Bledsoe, of the Santa Fé, and Downs, of the Illinois Central. Eastman, who knew their motives and sensed their opposition, politely welcomed their help in carrying out the purposes of the new act.

The first real "show-down" was not long delayed. As early as June 21, 1932, Eastman, as commissioner, had sent to Senator Couzens at the latter's request a list of all railroad salaries of $10,000 a year or more, as of December, 1929, and of March, 1932, his object being to find out what had been done toward economy on that level. The information thus presented was complete, disclosing salaries as high as $135,000. The median salary of eighty-three presidents (or receivers) was $30,000. During the period mentioned many roads had reduced salaries of all employees by 10 percent or more. A bill had actually been proposed allowing no railroad to pay any officer a salary of more than $15,000.

On July 14 Eastman invited the fifteen members of the three regional committees to meet with him in Washington on the tenth floor of the Transportation Building. He was very definitely "on the spot." The operators, as we have seen, did not wish to be coordinated; and knowing Eastman's avowed leanings toward government control, they were fearful of what might lie ahead of them. In his carefully phrased statement, Eastman left them in no obscurity as to his progressive philosophy:

I shall have at my command an organization which will supplement some of my own technical deficiencies, and in choosing that organization my aim has been to select men who think that improvement is possible. Some of them are proponents of plans or have ideas which it may be that some of you do not accept. They have been chosen, not because I am committed to any particular plan or ideas, but because we shall never get anywhere in our search if we do not have with us those who think there is something to find.

What followed was also, to those familiar with his career and his thinking, consistent with the pattern of his economic creed. He pictured the situation as he would like to see it—each transportation agency playing its part with a minimum of duplication and destructive competition and everybody, including shippers and employees, satisfied. It was, of course, a dream, but one which the average American could understand. He then reached the crux of the matter by telling the executives quite fearlessly that their salaries, considering the existing depression and the sacrifices which others had been forced to make, were regarded as "excessive and unjustified" and appealed to them to take some action voluntarily at a moment when millions were out of work and millions more living on a pittance, and when thousands of investors in railroad securities were receiving no dividends.

It will be easy for you to get your backs up on this matter [he admitted], but I ask you not to let that happen. . . . I am putting the question up to you, as I must do in the first instance under the law, because I believe very sincerely that there must be an adjustment of this matter of salaries before the railroads will stand right with the shippers, investors, and labor under the conditions which now exist.

After reading this formal statement—which had previously been distributed to the press—Eastman told the group off the record that in his judgment no one of them should be receiving more than $60,000 a year. He said this to men who were accustomed to having their own way and who resented anything resembling dictation; but he was strategically in a strong position to advance his argument. They all knew not only that his own modest compensation had been cut to $8,500 but also that he had declined more than one business offer which would have paid him several times that amount. Oswald G. Villard said: "When I contrast the character and talents of Mr. Eastman with those of some of the men who have been paid a million dollars a year by banks and steel companies, it is to laugh." The executives, however, were in no altruistic mood. They were photographed, looking none too genial, with Eastman in their midst, but this was conventional courtesy, and in their hearts they repelled the Coordinator's suggestion.

At this point, according to the story remembered in the Transportation Building, a new element was introduced into the situation. Jesse Jones, from Texas, chairman of the Reconstruction Finance Corporation, had been making loans to several of the railroads represented and charging them substantial interest. He now approached a few of the leaders privately to drive a bargain—he would reduce the interest rate to 4 percent if they, on their part, would voluntarily lower their salaries. It was difficult for an executive with any sense of responsibility to resist a practical argument of that nature, although the roads which had not been obliged to call on the RFC were less sensitive to the proposal than those who had. Whatever their motives—and they were undoubtedly mixed—most of the railroad chiefs complied with reasonable promptness to the Coordinator's request. As an economy measure it was, as Eastman admitted, insignificant, but its effect on public opinion was salutary.

Of the many letters which Eastman received on this occasion, the one which he valued most highly came from Felix Frankfurter. In part it read as follows:

Let me thank you very warmly for your address to the railroad executives. It was admirable, if I may say so, both as to matter and manner. The newspapers, of course, featured your insistence on reduced salary scales, and rightly so. That item, to be sure, is, as you pointed out, monetarily a small one in the total railway bill. But as you also indicated, its psychological significance far transcends its financial. Generalities will not settle the complicated and technical railroad problem,—not even the generalities on which agreement can be reached. But equally clear is it that the technical solutions based on technical knowledge are dependent upon the right atmosphere in which alone they can be achieved. And indispensable to the creation of that atmosphere is a drastic cut in the salaries of the executives for the reasons that you indicated. That demonstration of good faith in all this talk about economy and that surrender in many instances of greed will have tonical persuasiveness for all the other concessions to which the different elements in our society must yield. I hope only that the executives will respond to you quickly and handsomely. In good feeling and in more practical ways it will be repaid them a thousandfold.

In any event, the country is your debtor for arresting its attention in a striking and persuasive way to the problem that perhaps transcends all others,—the irrelevant and excessive use of the money standard as the measure of reward and achievement.

Efficiency experts and even the Coolidge Committee had perceived that the railroads were "delinquent in the matter of scientific research and inquiry" and had recommended that they emulate far-sighted corporations such as General Electric and the American Telephone and Telegraph Company. When Eastman, in his first report as Coordinator, renewed this suggestion, some of the leading carriers formed in October, 1934, the Association of American Railroads—commonly known as the AAR—a merger of several previously existing organizations, with national headquarters in the Transportation Building in Washington. Representing a large proportion of the mileage, not only in the United States but also in North America, it had plenty of funds at its disposal and powerful interests to serve, and it soon spread abroad the idea that the Coordinator's work was superfluous. On the surface the relations between Eastman and the AAR were amicable, but the tension was never relaxed while he held the position of Federal Coordinator.

Months before the AAR was organized Eastman had important research projects under way. He carried into his new office the methodology which he had learned first under Louis D. Brandeis, and had later perfected in investigations of his own. The members of his staff were peculiarly well qualified for work of this kind, and during his first two years as Coordinator they devoted themselves largely to preparing reports which would later be useful. Much of the material was gathered through elaborate questionnaires, which finally became so numerous that their inspirer became known as "Questionnaire Joe."

The data were usually collated and analyzed by a specialist and then submitted to the Director in Charge, who put together a tentative report. After the Coordinator had given this his customary careful scrutiny, it was transmitted to the regional coordinating committees for their consideration and approval. The final step was a series of informal conferences in Eastman's office, where the report in its revised form was discussed paragraph by paragraph. Eastman had always been a "night owl," but during this strenuous period he stayed up often until early morning, reading and checking the page proof of the documents going out from his office.

Three of the major reports were prepared under the personal supervision of John R. Turney, director of the Section of Transportation Service. The so-called *Merchandise Traffic Report*, dealing with all less-than-carload freight, was submitted on March 17,

1934. Questionnaires dealing with eleven topics were sent out to approximately 100,000 shippers, and 40,000 replies were received, of which about 5,000 were incomplete. The number actually available for study was 35,468. The entire report, including exhibits, covered 422 pages, packed with column after column of figures. In his own conclusions Eastman pointed out that this form of traffic had been declining for some years "long before the present depression"; that it had been wastefully handled, at a loss; that motor trucks in most cases were furnishing better service; and that the rate structure was extraordinarily complex and unsuited to the competition from motor carriers. Eastman's somewhat novel recommendation was that merchandise should be handled by two nation-wide competing companies, "resembling the Express Agency and controlled by rival groups of roads." He forwarded the complete report to the regional coordinating committees on March 22, 1934, telling them that they should be able to reply not later than June 1 and adding, with a firmness which he did not always display, "I shall expect such a report within that time." While the committees conceded that the Coordinator had stated accurately the defects and deficiencies of the existing practice, they did not like the "pooling principle" and felt that the report was too radical for voluntary adoption. They therefore referred it to the newly formed AAR, where it was put in cold storage, in accordance with the policy of that unprogressive organization.

Perhaps the most interesting document from the layman's point of view sent out from Eastman's office was the *Passenger Traffic Report*, also prepared under Turney's supervision, covering 272 pages, with two appendices of exhibits, filling 520 pages. Turney admitted at the beginning that a study which had as its objective constructive criticism could hardly avoid at times being hypercritical, but its general tone was friendly, and its motives needed no defense. It discussed a variety of topics relating to the operation of passenger traffic, starting with the assumption that trains should be run first for safety and secondarily for comfort. It commented, for example, on the absence "of personal helpfulness and courtesy" among the employees and described the stations as resembling mausoleums or "echoing vaults." Turney made nineteen specific recommendations—eight to modernize the service, eight to eliminate the waste, two to promote travel, and one to coordinate transportation.

One basic idea was to make the service "as easy to procure as a daily newspaper and as accessible as one's own car." The report recommended that tipping be abolished and that the porter cost be included in the fare. Thus, a single ticket would cover several special services, as it does in airplane transportation today. It was advised that stations be less dingy and be furnished with comfortable chairs instead of "rows of pews"; that upper berths have windows; that restaurant service be installed on all through trains; that railroads issue catalogues; and that quantity discounts be allowed for families, parties, and habitual travelers. It made a caustic attack on the abuses of free transportation through the issuing of passes, maintaining that at least 16 percent and probably twice that proportion of the total number of passengers carried were "dead heads." It had sensible ideas about unifying depots and terminals, consolidating duplicate train services, and eliminating complex, multifarious, and unnecessary tariffs. In forwarding this comprehensive report to the regional coordinating committees, Eastman urged them not to allow "minor and controversial matters (such as tipping and passes), nor the feasibility of the particular remedies suggested, to play too large a part in its consideration."

This "Section Report," as it was usually called, pulled no punches, and the railroad executives did not like it. When they were told that their passenger service was lacking in popular appeal and had ineffective sales promotion, some of them cursed, and others just laughed. One of them declared that Turney's conclusions reflected "the feeling of a writer who was more inclined to be interested in things as they should be than in things as it is practical to make them." Eastman retaliated that this was one of the unmistakable merits of the report. "It is astonishing," he commented, "how often the impractical can be converted into the practical, given the will to do it." An outsider, while recognizing that some of the proposed reforms were difficult to achieve, is likely to conclude that the report showed imagination and a recognition of what the public wanted. It is interesting to recall, however, that an attempt fifteen years later by the Chesapeake & Ohio to abolish tipping proved unsuccessful, although President Robert R. Young did his utmost by advertising to make it popular and workable.

The regional committees referred this report to the Association of American Railroads, which received it as if it were a general indictment of its passenger officials and at once pleaded "Not guilty!" The AAR committee announced that there was "nothing in the passenger report of value to the carriers for general application nationally," and in their ensuing "Railroad Report" said substantially, "Things are not really so bad, and we see no occasion for raising a fuss." The one point of serious conflict was that the "Section Report" stubbornly maintained that there was a large amount of potential traffic which could be secured by vigorous salesmanship, while the "Railroad Report" contended that the opportunities for the recovery or the creation of traffic by the railroads were negligible. Fortunately a group of the saner and more cooperative railroad leaders, after blowing off steam, did do something more than just "stand pat." Indeed, on June 12, 1936, just before the office of Coordinator was abolished, Eastman went out of his way to congratulate the railroads on "the fundamentally important steps they have taken and are taking towards a profitable passenger service" and declared that "the whole railroad attitude towards the passenger service seems to have changed, and this was necessary." It is only fair to conclude that the much criticized "Section Report" did bring sharply to the attention of the public, and also to railroad executives, some badly needed reforms.

Still another stupendous accomplishment was the *Freight Traffic Report*, submitted by Turney and his associates on May 1, 1935, covering 115 pages in addition to a "Factual Summary of Underlying Data" and a volume of "Statistical Analysis," filling 287 pages. In transmitting these massive and somber-looking tomes to the railroads, Eastman declared: "In my judgment, the Section has done an extraordinary piece of work in gathering and analyzing these data, and it has involved constant, unremitting labor in which regular hours of service have been completely disregarded." This report boldly suggested the need for "far-reaching changes in service, rates, equipment, and methods of operation." "Some of these conclusions and suggestions," Eastman confessed, "will be regarded as radical or revolutionary, and I anticipate they will be received with skepticism. This is a normal attitude and an entirely appropriate one, so long as the skepticism is open-minded." It was especially significant that this report paid particular attention to the opportunities for substituting truck for rail service, not only in terminals but also on the line itself, wherever it seemed likely that the truck would be able to operate more conveniently and cheaply.

The three major reports just discussed represented only a part of the contribution made by the Federal Coordinator to the education of the railroad industry. Among the subjects which he investigated during his three years in office were the possibility of car pooling; the handling and disposition of scrap; the leasing of grain elevators; the preservative treatment of railroad ties; the use of transportation by traveling salesmen; the annual earnings of employees from 1924 to 1933; the cost of railroad equipment; the improvement of purchasing methods; and the broad question of economical accounting. Professor Earnshaw has pointed out that "the great bulk of the studies dealt with national problems as national problems, which meant that a new perspective was gained which had never been realized before." This vast amount of research could have been accomplished only by a body of men with scholarly instincts and devoted to their chief. Eastman was not content to watch, command, and take the credit. He often worked with his associates, inspiring them with his own dynamic drive and following them critically from one stage to another.

The Coordinator besieged the railroads and the shippers for exact information; and in all fairness to them, it must be admitted that they did very little grumbling. It was only when Eastman published his conclusions that they were distressed. To the executives he was an amateur interfering with professionals. Like every man in a position of high authority, Eastman found himself dealing with human nature in some of its less attractive aspects. Although he did his best to reconcile differences and bring conflicting interests together, heavy demands were made upon his tact and tolerance, and the hour came when he gravely doubted whether the railroads were even trying to help. On February 5, before the Traffic and

Transportation Association, in Pittsburgh, he let himself go even more frankly than usual.

At bottom, the trouble is that the managements think narrowly in terms of their own particular roads, rather than in broader terms. Quite naturally, and quite properly, they put the welfare of their own particular road first and foremost. What they do not appreciate, as I think they should, is the extent to which their individual welfare will be promoted by action which is for joint benefit or common good.

It was Eastman's considered opinion as he digested the vast amount of statistical material in his office that the railroads were not "an obsolescent form of transportation," but that "a comparatively sudden but great change in conditions had outmoded many of their ways of doing business and accelerated obsolescence in their equipment and other property." His survey led him to the unpalatable conclusion that most of the troubles of the railroads were due to inefficient managerial policies and that they "could be rectified primarily, not by government regulation, but by the persons concerned, in the offices and shops and laboratories."

It was in this period of disillusionment that Eastman apparently began to lose confidence in government ownership and operation as a magic formula for eradicating greed, obstinacy, inertia, and waste. In his first "Report on Legislation," under date of January 20, 1934, he did reiterate his conviction that "theoretically and logically public ownership and operation meets the known ills of the present situation better than any other remedy"; but in his discussion he enumerated six disadvantages which kept him from recommending it at that moment. One of them was, of course, the immense cost at a time of acute financial stringency. Another was the fact that nationalized railroads "would start off as a subsidized institution, and steps along that path are hard to retrace." Some of Eastman's more radical advisers, especially Frank Livingstone, felt that he was "going reactionary" and chided him for not improving the opportunity, while he was Coordinator, of putting his philosophy into immediate operation. But Eastman, who had become almost of necessity a thoroughgoing pragmatist, could see the practical objections better than bay window doctrinaires. Furthermore, his experience on the Interstate Commerce Commission had taught him caution. In this connection, Professor Carl B. Swisher tells an illuminating story:

George Creel once told Eastman's sister that her brother had made a big mistake in not using his position as Coordinator to bring about public ownership of railroads. When told that Eastman felt this was not the time for bringing about such a change, Creel remarked that Eastman's mode of procedure reminded him of an elephant crossing a bridge. With supercaution that animal was wont to put down each foot carefully and to test the strength of the bridge at the taking of each step. When Miss Eastman told her brother about the conversation, he smiled and replied, "Well, the elephant got to the other side, didn't he?"

Whether or not this somewhat cryptic remark indicates that Eastman still hoped sometime to get the railroads under government control, the fact remains that he never again openly advocated government ownership and operation. At Senator Wheeler's request, he drafted in 1935 a bill providing for the acquisition by the Federal Government of the railroad properties, the payment for such properties and for their operation thereafter to be made by a government-controlled corporation. But Eastman himself was not prepared to recommend the passage of this measure, and it never reached the floor of Congress.

For many years Eastman had been regarded as the friend of organized labor; and union leaders, feeling that he was their champion, had favored his reappointment to the commission in 1922 and 1929. Here too, however, his attitude underwent a change, largely because of what he believed to be the selfish and inordinate demands of the employees. When the Railway Labor Executives' Association clamored for a six-hour day, Eastman opposed the demand, pointing out that this would put on the railroads an extra burden of some $400,000,000, which they could not stand unless an equivalent handicap were put upon their competitors and, indeed, on all other industries. He showed conclusively that the unions would really be widening the gap between methods of transportation and would thus be jeopardizing their own bread and butter. Eastman also came out strongly against larger train crews, more numerous bridge inspections, and other projects of the "feather-bedding" type. He was consistent in opposing special privileges of any kind, and when labor became unduly aggressive, he defended the interests of the public. Naturally he made enemies by so doing.

During the acute depression following the Wall Street crash of 1929, a temporary cut of 10 percent in wages had been reluctantly accepted by the railroad workers, on the theory that in a period of falling prices they, as well as the executives and the stockholders, should take their loss. On June 14, 1933, President Roosevelt wrote Eastman regarding the compensation of railroad employees, asking him to use his influence "to see that the question of a general revision of rates be postponed." Considering this rightly as a command, Eastman at once talked over the telephone with representatives of both operators and employees and invited representatives of the two groups to meet with him in his Washington office. The Association of Railroad Executives came united and argumentative in support of their plan for a further reduction of 12½ percent in the prevailing rate of pay to workmen, but after hearing the President's wishes, they soon calmed down. As a result Eastman was able to secure an agreement between the parties under which the earlier 10 percent reduction was extended from October 31, 1933, to June 30, 1934. As Federal Coordinator, Eastman had actually no jurisdiction over wage controversies and could do nothing in this instance but express unofficially the views of the President. The conservative *Traffic World* condemned both Roosevelt and Eastman for bringing pressure on railroad managers to abandon their attempts at a reduction in wages. "This whole transportation situation," said the magazine, "has been bungled from the start of the present administration." But the New Deal was still in its honeymoon period, and nobody had any desire to embarrass the administration in its efforts to revive prosperity.

When the issue arose again, however, in March, 1934, neither group was so tractable. Management still wanted the additional cut of 12½ percent; labor insisted that the wage level of the 1920's should be restored. The Coordinator found himself assailed by both sides and was blamed for the failure to reach an agreement. The President obviously wished him to repeat his success of the previous year and settle a disagreeable dispute to the satisfaction of all concerned. The labor leaders in this instance were so stubborn that Eastman finally had to take a resolute stand against their proposals. Thereupon the operators, playing some very unsavory politics in an attempt to discredit the Coordinator, made some concessions on their own. The incident did not improve the relations between Eastman and the aggressive labor leaders.

It has been noted that Eastman did not like the modification of the Emergency Act providing that any proposed economies should not involve a reduction in the number of employees. On the other hand, he did not think that the operators should offer this as an excuse for inaction. He said more than once that the labor provisions of the act had made him a "prober of possibilities" instead of a doer of deeds—but he continued to function as well as he could under the circumstances. On June 22, 1933, he wrote to H. T. Newcomb: "Like you, I was disappointed by the restrictions of Section 7, but I feel very confident that much work which will be worth while can be done nevertheless." When railroad executives maintained that this section absolutely prevented consolidation projects, Eastman, in his fair-minded way, pointed out that they had shown no disposition or ability to put through any such plans before the Emergency Act had been introduced. Furthermore, when the executives sought to evade the labor provision by claiming that it did not apply to a coordinated project unless that was handled by either the Coordinator or the coordinating committees, Eastman invoked the spirit and true intent of the law and notified the railroad men in writing that the labor article must be construed as covering any coordinated plan.

Eastman unquestionably did his best to formulate a policy which would protect employees against sudden discharge, but yet open the door to badly needed economies. His Section of Labor Relations, headed by Otto S. Beyer, lost no time in surveying the situation, with the assistance of an advisory committee which included such outstanding economists as Isaiah L. Sharfman, of Michigan, Sumner H. Slichter, of Harvard, and others. Although pension plans had been in existence in the railroad industry for at least half a century, most of them were outmoded, and their liabilities were heavy, and there were practically no reserve funds to meet them. Early in 1934 an aggressive labor lobby introduced into Congress a bill providing for a pension plan which would compel the railroads to contribute about $60,000,000 the first year and after that $200,000,000 annually. Called upon to testify before a House committee, the Coordinator, although conceding that the measure was a well-intentioned effort to meet an acute need, said that the information then available did not permit of "wise and well-considered legislation on the subject of pensions" and asked for delay until the analysis which his section had undertaken could be completed. The labor interests, however, were not in any mood for postponement. It was not good politics to put off action of some kind. In the end the bill had the unanimous approval of Congress and was signed by the President in June. It was declared unconstitutional by the Supreme Court in the case of *Alton Ry. Co.* v. *Railroad Retirement Board, 295, U.S. 330.*

Although his advice had not been taken, Eastman had the matter of pensions very much on his mind. In his report for 1934 he said that "employees who have given the best years of their life to an industry are entitled to reasonable protection, so far as practicable," and he added, "it is not just, under such circumstances, to throw an employee on the street without relief, especially if, as is often the case, the years which he spent in the industry have unsuited him to other employment." He then drafted and recommended his own bill for dismissal compensation which, he contended, would serve three purposes: to provide a just reward for long service; to compensate for the loss of skill and experience; and to assist the displaced employee during the interval before a new position could be found. This was in accord with one of the more commendable New Deal objectives—to relieve unemployment or at least to care for those who through no fault of their own were unemployed. Eastman felt that the cost of dismissal compensation might well be the responsibility of the employing industry, on the ground that displacement due to labor-saving improvements might result in savings and therefore in increased earnings. In his discussion of the proposed measure he carefully differentiated between employees removed from the pay roll because of labor-saving improvements and those who leave because of permanent recession in traffic, resignation, or disciplinary reasons.

Although Eastman was sure that his Dismissal Compensation Bill was "sound in plan and principle," he believed that the best possible method of solving the problem was by negotiations between the management and the labor organizations. With the backing of President Roosevelt, he volunteered to confer with the railroads or their employees—or both—in an effort at compromise. National representatives of both employers and employees met in the spring of 1936, and finally, on May 21, they reached an agreement setting up a scale of dismissal compensation for union members under three wide age distributions. Undoubtedly the persistent threat of legislative action by Congress was used as pressure on the reluctant railroad managements. Both sides recognized that it would be far better for them to agree on their own initiative than to be subjected to a Congressional directive. What Roosevelt felt about it is apparent in his remark to Eastman: "Legislation has its place. But it is a remedy to be taken with great caution or it may prove worse than the disease." At any rate, Eastman, although many of his ideas were rejected, did secure the approval of some details of his plan, and through a method which he had advocated. One result of the meeting, however, was that both employers and employees, although at odds on many matters, were united in opposition to the Emergency Act and to the Coordinator. He suffered the traditional fate of the outsider who undertakes to adjust a family quarrel. With his patience almost exhausted, he was ready to cry, "A plague on both your houses!"

During his three years as Federal Coordinator, Eastman delivered fifty-two prepared addresses, in various sections of the country and before many types of organizations. His first public official speech, on September 23, 1933, at Springfield, Massachusetts, before the Traffic Club and Shippers' Advisory Board, was certainly one of his happiest efforts. He was frank, conciliatory, occasionally humorous, and modest in his claims for everybody except his staff, whom he described as "creative, practical, faithful, and ready to work all hours of the day and night." He spoke especially of the studies being made in the standardization and reduction of the number of varieties of equipment; of the attempts to pool equipment and thus make the best possible utilization of cars; of the improvement in merchandizing and passenger service; and of economies planned through unification of terminal operation, joint use of facilities, abandonment of lines which had outlived their usefulness, restrictions on circuitous routing, and the employment of improved motive power. He went on:

Perhaps this recital of the studies which are under way will give you the impression that so much is being attempted that the work is likely to end up in confusion. My experience has been, however, that in such work the time comes when the issues resolve themselves and are found to be less complex than they at first seemed, if proper watch is kept for the forest instead of the trees. I believe that will be so in this case.

While the ensuing speeches were by no means repetitions of the first, Eastman never forgot to emphasize his primary function as Coordinator. It was his business to coordinate, and to this end he did his best to reconcile the conflicting views of the various interested parties—the carriers, the shippers, and the general public. Naturally he did not stress the same point with every group. When he talked to the Railway Labor Representatives in Chicago he had a different approach than he had with the Institute of Public Affairs at the University of Virginia. The American Association of Port Authorities was not like the National Association of Motor Bus Operators or the Birmingham Traffic and Transportation Club. The National Petroleum Association scarcely had the same objectives as the Society of Automotive Engineers. But Eastman had learned the value of tact, propriety, and even judicious silence, and adjusted himself without much difficulty to the people whom he had to face. After all, he did have the same mission, whether he was at Sioux City or Atlantic City, at Atlanta or White Sulphur Springs or Houston.

To those around him he seemed tireless, whether in the long conferences in his office or on the tedious trips which he could not avoid. Without seeming to get weary, he journeyed from one city to another, until they were blurred in his memory, pausing long enough to consult with the representatives of local organizations and often scribbling away at speeches as he sat in lounge cars or compartments. Throughout it all he appeared even-tempered, outwardly placid, listening to criticism with the patience created by long exposure to attack. His mildness of manner disarmed impending denunciators, and he won the grudging respect of railroad tycoons who had condemned his theories without ever meeting him personally. The leaders in the American Association of Railroads gave him no quarter, in public or in private, but he had mastered the soft answer which turneth away wrath. On the whole, he stood up under the strain without weakening or wincing. The full effects of the ordeal were not apparent until it was all over.

Speaking before the Interstate Bus and Truck Conference on October 20, 1933, at Harrisburg, Pennsylvania, Eastman reminded the delegates that the President and Congress had instructed him to study the ailing transportation systems, make a diagnosis, and submit prescriptions which could be considered when Congress, the supreme economic physician, convened again. He added that he was trying to develop a pleasing bedside manner which would establish confidence in his patients and promote good cheer. In this, his first speech before the motor truck industry, he had much to explain. The invention and rapid spread of the automobile as a means of passenger and freight transportation had had, of course, an immediate effect on the railroads. For short hauls the motor truck proved usually more economical for the shipper; consequently the railroads were shortly deprived of a considerable amount of lucrative business. Furthermore, the motor transport industry had grown from infancy to maturity without any Federal control and, until the 1930's, without even any effective state control. It was easy for anybody to enter the trucking business with only a small initial capital expenditure, and the highways were accessible to all-comers. What resulted was a dangerous form of unrestricted and uncontrolled competition, made worse by the abundance of cheap labor which, during the depression, had lowered standards throughout the areas where this type of transportation was becoming popular. Even on hauls of considerable length the motor truck had some manifest advantages, although in 1934 the full extent of truck competition with rail service had not been investigated and was difficult to determine. It was indisputable, however, that the highways throughout the nation were being traversed more and more by giant trucks, which were wearing out the road surfaces and taking business away from the railroads.

Eastman warned his audience at Harrisburg and other listeners that same autumn at Cleveland and Chicago that regulation of the motor trucking industry must come—and soon. But he bided his time until his assistants had marshaled the evidence. All that winter his research department was busy collecting and collating material, and in March, 1934, he transmitted to Congress—as usual through the Interstate Commerce Commission—a report covering nearly 400 pages on the regulation of transportation agencies other than railroads, in which he included not only motor transportation but also water transportation, air transport, and pipe lines. In the preparation of this comprehensive treatment of the subject, Eastman's research staff leaned heavily on certain chapters in *The American Transportation Problem* (1933), but the economist of the commission, Dr. C. S. Morgan, had a large share in the preliminary drafting. The chairman of the commission, William E. Lee, in addressing the President of the Senate on the subject, said: "While we are required to comment only on the recommendations of the Coordinator, we cannot refrain from commending to your careful consideration his excellent discussion of the many situations associated with his recommendations. His analysis of the contemporary situation is illuminating."

Chairman Lee was not exaggerating, for the material in the report was extensive, and the argument was irrefutable. In pondering on contemporary problems, Eastman early reached the conclusion that "unregulated competition may be quite as much of a public evil as unregulated monopoly." He perceived also that the American transportation system everywhere interlocking in its diverse parts must be treated as a whole. Each form of transportation—rail, water, highway, pipe line, and air—could and did furnish certain services more cheaply and efficiently than any of the others and should obviously be protected against destructive competition by them. At the same time adequate provision had to be made for easy interchange among them and for the establishment of through and joint rates when such coordination was desirable. Eastman reached the entirely logical conclusion that the system as a whole could not remain permanently half regulated and half unregulated. With his interest in sports, it was not difficult for him to find an analogy: "If the principles of a battle royal are to govern, it is unfair to handcuff the railroads."

After this enunciation of basic theories, Eastman declared that the proper body to undertake unified regulation was unquestionably the Interstate Commerce Commission. He took the precaution of replying in advance to some expected objections: that the Commission was already overloaded; that it was too "railroad-minded"; that it would use railroad rates too much as a base for fixing trucking rates; and that it was in its procedure too bureaucratic, rigid, and cumbersome for the effectual regulation of modern transportation. His defense of the body of which he had been chairman and was still a member was sturdy, but dispassionate. He maintained that some of the complaints about it were the outgrowth of the confusion and instability of conditions caused by the inadequate regulation of railroad competitors. He confessed that the Hoch-Smith Resolution had dumped a tremendous weight of detail on the commission. In conclusion, he repeated one of his deep-rooted convictions—"that the development and technicalization of a bar, both on the railroad and shipper sides, with long training in the complication of rate cases and in aggressive controversy, have prolonged procedure." This last stricture is one which he uttered in private on many occasions. "These confounded lawyers," he would say, "muddle things all up."

In his final paragraph Eastman summarized views which he had already expressed with some fervor to President Roosevelt.

If transportation is to be coordinated, regulation must be coordinated, and the Commission is the natural and appropriate agency for that purpose. It has been in existence for nearly half a century, and few governmental bodies have stood the test of time so well. No other agency has the organization or necessary experience. The regulation proposed will have the best chance of success in its hands.

To his report Eastman appended drafts of specific bills for the regulation of both water and motor carriers. Then, through several carefully prepared talks he undertook to explain to those most concerned what he had in mind—and why. On October 22, in Chicago, speaking before the American Trucking Associations at their first regular convention, he outlined his plans. He was at his best before audiences whom he had to persuade and convert, and in this case he tried to answer every conceivable objection. To these very practical men Joe spoke a language which they could understand.

Sound and well coordinated public regulation of transportation will not stifle the railroads or the trucks or the water lines or the air carriers. In your field it will make it less easy for any Tom, Dick, or Harry to begin commercial operations with a truck on which he has paid down a few dollars and which is likely to be taken away from him and turned over to another victim at the time of the next installment. It will, I hope, curb the activities of certain types of brokers. It will prevent the driving of rates down to a level for which there is no economic justification. It will tend to cause both the railroads and the trucks to abandon operations where the enemy has so great an advantage that they cannot hope to reap the profits. It will, I very much hope, encourage and stimulate cooperation between the two agencies.

Eastman's proposals had their strong supporters, but opposition developed, particularly from persons who were against any government interference with business, and for some months little could be accomplished. In his third Report on Legislation, dated January 21, 1935, the Coordinator renewed his recommendations regarding motor and water carriers. This time a bill covering motor transportation was shortly introduced in both houses and, after extensive hearings and some minor amendments, was passed and signed by the President on August 9. This was the Motor Carrier Act, 1935, known in technical terms as Part II of the "Interstate Commerce Act." The official history of the Interstate Commerce Commission declares that this measure produced the greatest expansion in the commission's duties and powers since the Transportation Act of 1920.

The passage of the Motor Carrier Act was undoubtedly Eastman's most constructive achievement as Coordinator, and its effects are still being felt to this day. Briefly, it extended the regulatory system already administered by the commission to embrace "the transportation of passengers or property by motor carriers engaged in interstate or foreign commerce and to the procurement of and the provision of facilities for such transportation." On October 14, when Eastman again addressed the American Trucking Associations in the same hall in Chicago, he was cheered and applauded. He explained to his listeners that they must be very patient with John L. Rogers, who had been named director of the commission's new Bureau of Motor Carriers. "The new activity on which we are embarking," he said, "is more than a mere experiment. . . . It is an essential part of a plan to give our country a well-ordered and stable system of transportation which will use such means of carriage to the best advantage without all manner of duplication and waste and with a reasonable expectation of fair profit for all." Ten days later, in New Orleans, before the National Association of Motor Truck Operators, he described the Interstate Commerce Commission as "independent, non-partisan, and non-political" and explained for their consolation that it must administer the new law in a spirit of "coldest neutrality."

Temperamentally, Eastman preferred to try for results through persuasion and negotiation rather than dictation. Realizing the undercover hostility of railroad management, but aware also that little could be accomplished while it blocked the way, he regarded the use of his power as only a last resort. The primary object of the Emergency Transportation Act had been to induce the carriers to work together voluntarily; and any attempt at compulsion would have defeated the purpose of the legislation. Furthermore, he knew very well that if he issued orders and his directives were nullified by the Supreme Court, his authority, such as it was, would henceforth be disregarded. For these reasons he moved warily, anxious not to antagonize more than was necessary.

The Coordinator's General Order Number 1, dated July 17, 1933, merely requested some basic employment statistics from the railroads and was in effect until his office closed three years later. On July 26 he issued Special Order Number 1, on a technical matter in connection with the consolidation of the accounting work of the Boston & Maine with that of the Maine Central, involving the transfer of a considerable number of employees. What had started as a mild controversy, however, was quickly adjusted by both parties to the dispute, and then Eastman published Special Order Number 2, canceling the first directive. The incident was trivial, but amusing, like the exploit of the Old Grand Duke of York, who marched his ten thousand soldiers up the hill and then marched them down again.

In October, however, Eastman did issue an order which aroused the wrath of the powerful New York Central. Here, again, the matter in dispute seems to the layman rather technical, but its implications could not be ignored. Two Southern railroads—the Louisville & Nashville and the Nashville, Chattanooga & St. Louis—wished to transfer to Evansville, Illinois, their through passenger cars en route to Florida from one road, the Chicago & Eastern Illinois, to another, the much more affluent and aggressive New York Central. The real question was whether the two interested lines could make this decision "on their own" or whether the public welfare had to be considered. As one of the defending railroads put it, it was to be decided whether "the managerial judgment is to control or whether public authority shall substitute its opinions, not in a matter of public regulation, but in a detail of management." This time Eastman's authority was to be really challenged.

Counseled by his legal adviser, Eastman moved from step to step with the utmost caution and, after an informal hearing, concluded that the effect of the contemplated change would be duplication of service and that, furthermore, the Chicago & Eastern Illinois would suffer financially with unfortunate consequences to its stockholders. The Coordinator forestalled criticism by admitting that he might be exercising governmental power to an extent unknown in peacetime and by adding that he would welcome a full hearing before the Interstate Commerce Commission. The defending roads carried their case to the Federal District Court for Northern Illinois, which sustained the Coordinator. Substantially, the court ruled that the Emergency Railroad Transportation Act was entirely constitutional and gave the Coordinator all the power he wanted or required. Doubtless if Eastman had been willing to take a strong stand in other cases, he would have been backed by the courts.

Eastman was occasionally attacked by "liberals" for not behaving more like a railroad "czar." A young candidate for his university doctorate, Virgil D. Cover, writing in *Public Utilities, Fortnightly*, for February 4, 1937, concluded that Eastman had "preferred to indulge in the gathering of data on the operation of railways and other agencies rather than to embark on a program of direct action." Dr. Cover continued, speaking of the Coordinator: "He is idealistic in his ideas and idealistic in the methods he has conceived for putting them into effect. Action, evidenced by tangible results, has been largely absent." Cover said, furthermore: "At times his unrealistic method assumes an impracticable character and does not readily attract support from men who think in terms of dollars and cents rather than in terms of social welfare." All this had so much of truth that Eastman did not resent the criticism. He did, however, write Cover a letter, dated August 19, 1937—when his work as Coordinator had been terminated—revealing his own attitude toward the job.

I gather the impression that you are not clear that I have been very effectual, but I am not wounded by that. Long ago I reached the conclusion that no man could be certain what effect he was having, and that only time could disclose an approach to the truth. Therefore, time spent in thinking about accomplishment is wasted and a man should be happy if he comes reasonably close to doing the best he knows how to do. If he does that, I have faith that the results will be good. I have no sympathy with the men who withdraw from attempts at public service because they feel that they are accomplishing nothing. They probably are accomplishing more than they think, and at all events it is better to try and keep on trying than to do nothing.

Eastman had plenty of reasons for walking warily; but at one time he was on the verge of what seemed very drastic action. In February, 1936, after giving the subject much thought, he planned the unification of eleven carefully chosen terminal properties and drafted tentative orders which he submitted to the various interested parties. In presenting his proposals, the Coordinator wrote:

Voluntary action on the part of the carriers is much to be preferred, and I have endeavored to encourage such action in every possible way. These efforts, however, have not met with success, and the time has come to use the authority which the act confers. As a first step, I have selected for proposed orders eleven terminal unification projects scattered throughout the country. These are simple projects; they present no operating difficulties; they cannot impair service; and the plans are those which committees of carrier officers have themselves developed. These projects will, I believe, afford a clear cut test of the policy of coordination and of the authority of the government to order it.

Unfortunately, the Coordinator's timing in this campaign was bad. No agreement had yet been reached regarding his proposals for dismissal compensation; consequently, the employees whose jobs were threatened by the terminal unification plan were much disturbed, and in some places, notably Mechanicsville, New York, actually incited riots. The President, who at the moment was having his own difficulties, requested Eastman to hold the orders in abeyance until the negotiations over dismissal compensation were completed. When this matter was settled, on May 21, 1936, it was already apparent that Title I of the Emergency Act would not be renewed by Congress, and the Coordinator therefore refrained from issuing his order. The affair was inextricably connected with the principal purpose of his office, and the outcome proved the futility of his efforts to reduce waste and promote efficiency.

The perennial and complicated matter of railroad consolidation, also on the Coordinator's docket, was assigned for study to Professor Leslie Craven, of the Research Staff. Mr. Craven, with the assistance of William B. Poland, paid especial attention to the so-called "Prince Plan," which had been prepared in 1932 by F. H. Prince, a Boston banker and former president of the Pere Marquette. This proposed the creation of seven distinct railroad systems, two in the East, two in the South, and three west of the Mississippi. The idea was supposed to have the backing of the White House; but again both management and labor joined in opposing the plan, each for different reasons, and Eastman himself saw few advantages in it. He did, however, instigate an intensive analysis of the savings which the sponsors of the Prince Plan estimated would result from its adoption. In his first report (January 20, 1934) the Coordinator announced that "the economics of such a plan would not be nearly so large as claimed, and that in other respects it would not be in the public interest." From time to time he indicated that a bill embodying his own ideas on consolidation was being prepared, but he could never count on the support of the right leaders. He still doubted, as he had done in the 1920's, the desirability of any rigid plan of large-scale consolidation, preferring to consider each suggested unification in the light of current conditions and of the attitude of those chiefly concerned.

Because any discussion of consolidation elicits a pet theory from everybody who participates, unanimity of opinion has so far proved impossible to secure. Purchases and mergers have, of course, taken place from 1920 to the present day, but not in accordance with any discernible comprehensive plan. Consolidations which the victims do not want are not any more likely to be successful than "shot-gun marriages." To the end of his career Eastman maintained that if consolidations were to be made, they would be best brought about on a national scale through government acquisition and operation of the railroad properties.

The Coordinator may have been unnecessarily cautious and even at times uncertain as to the best course to follow; but in his third report (January 25, 1935) he really invited hostility by proposing certain drastic changes in the set-up of the Interstate Commerce Commission. The commission had generously furnished quarters to the Coordinator and his staff and had loaned some of its expert personnel for purposes of special research. While he was Coordinator Eastman still occasionally sat with his colleagues on cases with which he was familiar, and he continued to see them informally and amicably almost every day. The commission, as it was bound to do under the Emergency Act, transmitted the Coordinator's reports to Congress, making whatever comments the chairman saw fit to append. Generally speaking, they were content with perfunctory approval. But when Eastman began to express unconventional views on the organization of the commission, the other members were not altogether pleased.

What Eastman, with the highest of motives, was suggesting was a further extension and centralization of power for the commission. He wished to see legislation passed without delay for the Federal regulation of water carriers and wharfingers, and as soon as possible for the control of air traffic and pipe lines. Hitherto, the chairmanship of the commission had been rotated from year to year, with

the inevitable consequence that sometimes a vigorous presiding officer was followed by a less competent successor. Eastman had reached
the conclusion that the chairman should be permanent, with four
divisions under him: Railroad Division (five members), Motor and
Air Division (three members), Water and Pipe Line Division (three
members), and Finance Division (three members). The chairman
of the commission, with the chairman of the four divisions, would
make up a Control Board—a kind of executive committee of five,
with large authority. In addition, Eastman recommended that a
Coordinator of Transportation be continued, but as part of the commission organization, associated with it in the same manner as was
the Federal Coordinator under the Emergency Act. Eastman's plan
for remodeling the commission was made contingent on the passage
of both the Motor Carrier Act and the Water Carrier Act. It would
have no point, as he said in his third report to Congress, unless such
legislation were adopted.

The proposed arrangement would, of course, abrogate the system
under which all the commissioners were theoretically equal and substitute a plan under which the Control Board would probably
dominate procedure and the other members would have rather less
power. It was expecting too much of frail human nature to suppose
that certain commissioners who had little cause to believe that they
would be selected for the key positions would welcome a delimita-
tion of their authority. In commenting on Eastman's suggestions
the commission, with the single exception of Commissioner Carroll
Miller, maintained that no change was desirable in the set-up even
if new duties were to be imposed upon the members. Everything
was functioning satisfactorily under the existing arrangements, and
it would be premature to contemplate a new scheme until the commission as it was had been condemned as inadequate. The burden of
proof, accordingly, was on Eastman.

In his 1936 report Eastman did his best tactfully to soften this
opposition from men whom he respected; but the "stand-patters"
had a strong case, and the argument that his plan would promote
efficiency did not convince them. He knew, of course, that he was
treading on sensitive toes, but was prepared to accept a calculated
risk. Many of his close friends have noted that he was a poor politi-

cian and believed, as many idealists have done before him, that a well-conceived plan was bound to prevail on its own merits. In this case the situation was especially difficult, because he himself would inevitably be in line for one of the two important posts—chairman or Coordinator. One of Eastman's colleagues is reported to have quoted petulantly the words of Cassius:

> Upon what meat doth this our Caesar feed
> That he is grown so great!

But Eastman was neither overambitious nor "swell-headed," whatever some commissioners might think. Throughout his tenure as Coordinator he was in a delicate situation. There were so many persons to offend. To achieve even minimum success he required at least the neutrality of railway management; yet he was repeatedly placed in a position in which he had to antagonize the executives. Even with his commission associates he had to be careful not to seem to be usurping a leading role; yet he could not escape newspaper publicity and invitations to address large audiences. Between management on the one hand and organized labor on the other, with several of the commissioners not in sympathy with his ideas and the President looking upon him as obstinately independent, his lot was not a happy one. One avowed intent of the Emergency Act was "to administer oxygen to critical patients and to revive those who were suffering from sinking spells." As an economic physician to diagnose and prescribe in the transportation field, no living man was better equipped than Eastman, but what was he to do when he met with stubborn resistance from his patients? Professor Earnshaw has summarized all this by saying:

The Coordinator had the thankless task of trying to reconcile almost irreconcilable points of view, of the users of the railroads with their grievances, of the pessimists with their sinister predictions, the antipathetic, unconcerned public whose interest was really vital, remote though it seemed to them, and finally of the railroads themselves with their apparent inability to face problems as national problems, their increasing tendency as time went on to defend rather than to improve, and their growing impatience with the methods used by the Coordinator in his attempt to spread the gospel of coordination.

On May 4, 1934, the President, by proclamation, had continued Title I of the Emergency Railroad Transportation Act for one year, as he was free to do. During the ensuing months opposition spread, intensified, and became increasingly vocal. In the spring of 1935 the recently formed Association of American Railroads tried to block a joint Congressional Resolution extending the effective period of the Act until June 17, 1936; and President John J. Pelley, of the association, sent a letter to Senator Burton K. Wheeler outlining his objections. He said, in brief, that "no officer of the Government should be given the power now vested in the Coordinator unless at the same time he is clothed with the responsibility for results" and that "the grant of arbitrary and unlimited power is not rendered less objectionable because it is lodged in the hands of a man who uses it sparingly." He added that "without in any way reflecting on the present Coordinator, nothing of substantial value in the way of coordination has been accomplished and we see no promise or prospect of future usefulness in continuing the Act for another year." President Pelley then dismissed the Emergency Act as "a burdensome feature of our regulatory system."

On June 12, 1935, Eastman appeared at a hearing before the House Committee on Interstate and Foreign Commerce to make his rebuttal statement. Although questioned sharply by Congressman Reece, of Tennessee, Congressman Cole, of Maryland, and Congressman Wolverton, of New Jersey, he conducted himself with dignity. R. F. Fulbright, representing the National Industrial Traffic League—an organization of shippers—paid Eastman a tribute by saying that there was no other man in the United States who could have "gone into so many things and turned out such a prodigious amount of study and recommendation as he has done"; but he counteracted this by declaring that the Coordinator's office was unnecessary and involved "an enormous expenditure on the part of the railroads in carrying out the things that they have been required or asked to do by the Coordinator." Fortunately, however, President Roosevelt lent Eastman his powerful support, and Congress passed a Joint Resolution extending Title I of the Emergency Act until June, 1936.

On January 21, 1936, in his *Fourth Report on Transportation Legislation*, Eastman, after repeating his conviction that the railroad and other transportation agencies were either unwilling or unable to bring about greater operating efficiency, asked for a further extension of his office. He also brought up again his recommendation for a complete reorganization of the Interstate Commerce Commission. This time Chairman Mahaffie, in transmitting the report, not only again rejected the reorganization plan but also declined to commit himself and his associates as to the desirability of making the office of Coordinator permanent. He did suggest, however, that if the office were continued, the provision that the Coordinator could call upon the commission's staff should be deleted.

In defending himself and his staff, Eastman asserted that "the Association of American Railroads, while organized for a commendable purpose, cannot be depended upon to achieve the results desired without government help." He added: "The record of that Association since its formation has not been impressive in this respect." Thus, the issue was clearly joined: the railroad executives insisted that they were qualified and entitled to run their own affairs in their own way; Eastman was equally sure that they had failed to meet their public responsibility.

The representatives of labor had just won their battle for dismissal compensation and had their own reasons for being lukewarm about the continuance of any Federal Coordinator. As for the railroad executives, they were now rabid on the subject and were leaving nothing undone to have the office of Coordinator abolished and its incumbent returned summarily to the Interstate Commerce Commission. As early as May 1, Eastman wrote: "I am proceeding on the theory that there will be no extension."

Some letters were sent to the White House asking to have the position of Coordinator continued. On the other hand, nobody in Congress was ready to undertake the active sponsorship of a continuance of the Emergency Act, and a last minute proposal by Senator Wheeler, in response to an appeal from Eastman, to extend it for ninety days failed miserably. Congress having taken no action, Title I of the Act expired automatically at midnight on June 16, 1936, and Joseph B. Eastman, after three years of exciting, but rather sad experience, relinquished what power he had as Coordinator and returned to the Interstate Commerce Commission, wiser than he had been, somewhat bruised and battered, but by no means disheartened. On the day when his job terminated he was in Urbana, Illinois, addressing the American Institute of Cooperatives on "The Future of Transportation in the United States."

Eastman's own explanation of what had happened was well expressed in a letter to Harry Taylor, one of his college classmates, on June 24.

The reason for the discontinuance of the office was that on this one thing the railroad managements and the railroad employees were able to get together. Of course the employees never liked the idea of the elimination of wastes, because that meant the elimination of jobs also. Nor did the railroad executives appreciate having some one comment freely on matters of management, I can understand both their positions, although of course I think they were unwise and did not look sufficiently far ahead.

Eastman delivered his "swan song" as Coordinator at the alumni dinner of the Massachusetts Institute of Technology on June 7, making a strong plea for coordination, as applied to railroads, and for the use of government aid, or force, to bring it about. Even though he had received some warning of what was to be expected, the sudden termination of his authority left everything in confusion. Although reports of considerable importance were in process, no more funds were available. The direct cost of carrying on the Coordinator's work over a period of three years had been about $1,500,000, all of it contributed by the railroads under the terms of the Emergency Act, and this had been supplemented in 1935 by a grant from the CWA for special investigations of the cost of retirement plans and unemployment benefits. Although some money was left over when the office closed, the Comptroller General delayed in handing down a ruling on the use of these funds, and on June 19 Eastman appealed directly to the President, asking that $18,000 be made available to him for winding up the Coordinator's affairs. The carriers at first objected, but finally agreed to waive their rights to the balance remaining from their contributions in order that the unfinished reports might be completed. The actual amount placed at Eastman's disposal was $15,115.36.

Gradually the regular staff found new jobs, often through Eastman's intervention. The field offices in New York and Chicago were closed, and one by one the clerks were discharged. Several reports were carried through to a conclusion, among them *Comparative Labor Standards in Transportation*, which appeared in March, 1937, nine months after the office had formally closed its doors, and *Public Aids to Transportation*, which was published in four volumes between the years 1938 and 1940. This was the last belated product of the Coordinator's staff.

Because Joe had never before been in a position requiring marked administrative ability, his friends watched to see how he would make out. Opinions as to his success varied considerably. Some observers felt that he did not understand how or when to delegate responsibility and kept all the reins too much in his own hands. It has been intimated by a few of his staff that he was too chary of praise, but this judgment is not corroborated by those who were nearest to him. One of his most-trusted examiners writes: "The memories of kind things which he had to say about my work are a constant source of inspiration to me and are the most enduring satisfactions of my professional life." If he appeared reserved to casual visitors, it is because he had to be constantly on guard against exploitation. He complained that even when he spoke at the Psi Upsilon Centennial Banquet in December, 1933, many of the "brothers" hounded him for jobs. The time came when, after some painful experiences, he simply had to be ruthless in dealing with callers who wanted something for themselves. He had his critics, of course, as any executive with positive views is bound to have, but around the Interstate Commerce Building he was generally popular.

The charge that he was a poor judge of men can be justified only if we expect that every office appointee should be satisfactory. He made mistakes, of course, and sometimes defended a weak assistant too long and too vigorously. It was his disposition to trust others, and any evidence of idleness or self-seeking or disloyalty disturbed him greatly. But although he was not "hard-boiled," he knew when he was being deceived. Considering the problems which he had to face, his office was well run.

Both his intelligence and his integrity commanded respect. He grasped facts rapidly, but he was not hasty in his judgments. His mind was discerning, and he had an exceptional gift for weighing and considering evidence and distinguishing the specious from the true. His capacity for absorbing and synthesizing details kept his subordinates in a constant state of amazement and admiration. Sometimes in conferences his attention seemed to wander, and he looked as if he were bored, but he proved later that he had missed nothing essential. Often he seemed dilatory in reaching a decision, but when he had taken a stand, he could not be budged. If his recommendations were ignored, as they were on the matter of the reorganization of the commission, he merely waited and presented them again at the first opportunity. It was by sheer merit that he earned his place as the foremost man on the Interstate Commerce Commission.

Eastman himself felt that his greatest achievement as Coordinator resulted from his exhaustive reports on transportation matters. To those who look back from the perspective of time it would appear that the legislation which he sponsored was even more significant, especially the Motor Carrier Act, 1935. He failed—as perhaps anyone else would have done—to bring about any important consolidations, to eliminate waste and inefficiency, and to win the cooperation of operators and labor unions. But he left behind, even with the Association of American Railroads, the impression of a well-informed, high-minded, and public-spirited government official. Furthermore, he had acquired some experience which was to be of great value when, some years later, he had to face a war emergency. He knew that not too much could be expected. On June 25, 1935, he wrote H. B. Lear:

You may be sure that I shall not be discouraged in trying to bring about improvements, because I know from rather long experience with such matters that results cannot be expected overnight. It takes a long time for the seeds to sprout, although when once they get started they often grow quite rapidly.

Eastman's own best estimate of his accomplishment was expressed in a letter to Judge Anderson, July 27, 1936.

You ask what I think of the general results of my coordination labors. My own feeling is quite strong that the reports which we got out have already had a very good effect and will have still more effect as time goes on. The railroads do not like to admit that they have been influenced by them; nevertheless there is much evidence that they have been so influenced, and also evidence that they are likely to give them increased attention in the future. So while it was somewhat of a disappointment that I was not permitted to carry on this work, I do not feel that our labors were lost. On the contrary, I believe that they were worth while and will bear fruit. Possibly they will be renewed a little later in some form or other. I do not expect much out of voluntary action by the railroads through their Association of American Railroads under their present directors and Mr. Pelley.

The *Railway Age*, June 20, 1936, published some stanzas of doggerel by H. F. Lane, under the title, "Three Long Years." Two stanzas, containing more truth than poetry, are pertinent here.

> Three long years—
> Joe always seemed to wear a smile,
> But it cost the roads $2 a mile,
> And it got their goats in a little while,
> For three long years.

> Three long years—
> He was even-handed with praise and blame,
> And didn't play anybody's game,
> But he got both sides mad just the same,
> For three long years!

The *Traffic World*, on June 20, 1936, when the Federal Coordinator's job was finished, warned the railroads that they had favored the creation of "this excrescence on the transportation regulatory machine" and had then "failed utterly to cooperate with it, in fact and spirit." It admitted frankly that the Association of American Railroads had been a disappointment and offered little hope that it would change its methods. The railroads had "urged foolish excuses and put up weak defenses for their lack of action." This was a verdict from what was presumably a source friendly to the railroads. The marvel is that, under such unfavorable circumstances, Eastman did as well as he did.

XIII

Eastman and the New Deal

THE FACT that Mr. Roosevelt chose Joseph B. Eastman as Federal Coordinator and later reappointed him to the Interstate Commerce Commission indicates that the President had confidence in the latter's ability. But FDR, after the overtures described in a previous chapter, discovered that Joe had plenty of ideas of his own, some of them not easily fitted into the New Deal pattern, and that subservience was not one of his attributes. For some reason—possibly the insistence of aggressive cabinet members—the President indicated that he wished to assert executive control over the independent commissions, including the ICC; and Eastman, who was jealous of its power and prerogatives, was determined not to submit to White House dictation.

Mr. Roosevelt, with all his virtues as a statesman, was a consummate and agile politician. Eastman, on the other hand, detested political strategy and opportunism. Thus, in one very important respect the two men, although superficially friendly in their personal relations, could not find common ground. The President saw in the Interstate Commerce Commission a political instrument, which ought to acknowledge his supremacy and could serve his purposes. Eastman regarded it as autonomous, functioning without interference in its specialized field, and responsible only to the Congress, which had created it, and to the Supreme Court, which under certain circumstances could overrule it. Between two such divergent interpretations a clash was sooner or later inevitable.

Rather early in his administration, Mr. Roosevelt called to the White House a group of leaders of the independent commissions, and in the course of the conference he casually suggested that it would not be a bad idea if they reported direct to him. One by one around the circle heads were nodded in agreement. But when

Eastman's turn came, he said, "I'm sorry, Mr. President, but I can't go along with that. The Interstate Commerce Commission is by law the creature of Congress, and it is our duty to report direct to it." There was a silence, the President's mouth tightened, and it was evident that Eastman's response was both unexpected and unwelcome. The incident was symbolic of a fundamental lack of agreement which was to become more apparent as time went on. The tenacious President and the equally stubborn Eastman, finding themselves wide apart on this issue, did not meet frequently thereafter.

Eastman not only refused to retract, he even neglected no chance to reiterate his convictions. In his report for 1934 as Coordinator he deviated from his narrative in order to clarify his position, saying:

The Interstate Commerce Commission has from the beginning been a bipartisan but nonpolitical body. Its legal status is that of an agency of Congress; the President appoints the members, subject to the approval of the Senate, and may in certain circumstances remove a Commissioner from office; but otherwise he has, in the eyes of the law, no more control over the acts of the Commission than over the deliberations of the Supreme Court.

This was refreshingly plain talk. In his report for 1935 Eastman, in opposing the suggestion that a cabinet minister should cover transportation and communications, declared his fear that "such a position would have too much of a political flavor." He had learned that the Secretary of Commerce, Daniel C. Roper, was very much concerned with political patronage, and naturally he was afraid that the proposed Secretary of Transportation would be selected with party preferment as an important consideration. Not without cause did Eastman dread the interference in transportation matters of some "deserving Democrat."

Joe's straightforward and idealistic mind always rejected expediency as a motive for action. As we have seen, he was not a party follower, and when, in June, 1936, he was requested to serve on a general committee to sponsor Roosevelt Nomination Clubs, he refused, saying, "While I appreciate the honor of this appointment, I do not see how I can properly accept it." He saw no necessity for adding that he had already decided to support the Democratic candidate.

One trivial but diverting incident in the presidential campaign gave Eastman an opening which he could not resist. The Republican National Committee issued a statement for the press as follows: "Joseph B. Eastman, Federal Coordinator of Transportation, has a niece employed by the Federal Housing Administration. Her husband holds an important position with the Home Owners' Loan Corporation."

At the time, of course, Eastman had ceased to be Federal Coordinator and had returned to the Interstate Commerce Commission. He replied, however, in a letter to John D. M. Hamilton, chairman of the Republican National Committee:

> While I am not greatly concerned by this statement, in the interests of accuracy I may say that the pleasure of having a niece has been denied me. The young lady in question is the daughter of my first cousin. My impression is that the technical description of this relation is "first cousin once removed." She is a competent girl and obtained her position in the Federal Housing Administration without recommendation or other help from me. Her husband obtained his position with the Home Owners' Loan Corporation before he married her, and also entirely without help from me.
>
> You failed to discover, apparently, that I have a first cousin, William B. Eastman, who is employed in the Bureau of Accounts of this Commission. He obtained a position in that Bureau as a stenographer and clerk some years ago (in a Republican administration) through the civil service route, and has since had one or two modest promotions. I did not help him to get in and have never made any recommendations with respect to him.
>
> Is it your idea that those who happen to be related to me should be debarred from government employment? Incidentally my last appointment to the position I now hold was by President Hoover.

To this humorous explanation of his alleged nepotism Eastman evidently received no reply. On October 7, 1936, he wrote: "My impression is that Roosevelt is likely to get back without too much difficulty. That seems to be the general impression down here." In November he voted without any misgivings for Roosevelt and even collected a few small bets when the election was over. On the day the result was announced, Eastman wrote the President: "You are probably surfeited with congratulations on the outcome of the election, and I want to add mine. No man in the history of our country has ever had a more wonderful personal victory, and you must be very happy over it. Certainly the country is." He wrote to Clyde Reed, January 5, 1937: "I hope and believe that you are not too downcast over the result of the election. Personally, I think that it would have reflected a little healthier condition if it had been closer, but except for that of course I am very well pleased."

The President was not opposed to making the position of Federal Coordinator permanent, with Eastman as the incumbent. The opposition came from Congress, as a direct consequence of the pressure brought to bear by railroad executives and union leaders. When the office was abolished, Mr. Roosevelt expressed to Eastman in private conversation his regret that the latter's usefulness as Coordinator could not have been continued.

In August, 1936, Joe set off for his usual vacation in Canada, returning after Labor Day to find his desk piled with invitations to address his fellow-countrymen. His major speech of the autumn was before the American Academy of Political Science, on November 12, in New York City, where more than a thousand people cheered him enthusiastically. Thomas W. Lamont presided and referred in pleasant reminiscence to their childhood days in Katonah. Eastman's talk on this occasion was temperate, judicial in its tone, and restrained in its judgments. The New York newspapers gave him a very good press.

Although now only a commissioner, Eastman returned to a busy and engrossing life. As soon as the Motor Carrier Act was signed by the President, on August 9, 1935, the commission had set up a new Bureau of Motor Carriers and had made Eastman chairman of a separate Division, Number 7, created to administer the act. Later, on September 24, the commission reorganized and reduced the number of its divisions, at which time motor transportation was placed under the new Division 5, with Eastman as chairman. On October

1, with Eastman's powerful backing, John L. Rogers was designated Director of the Bureau of Motor Carriers, under the general supervision of Division 5. Thus, during his last months as Coordinator Eastman was doing far more than one man's full-time work.

On July 8, 1936, Eastman wrote his friend John Daniels a long letter, in the course of which he said:

It was disappointing in a way to me to have the Coordinator job wound up, but there are many consolations. I never liked the year-to-year extensions, because they created a great many difficulties, and furthermore the motor carrier work of the Commission is becoming so heavy that I would have had difficulty in carrying on both jobs at the same time. Being in a way the father of the Motor Carrier Act, I felt responsibility for it and thought I ought to help the Commission in connection with this work.

In a similar vein, Joe wrote on July 15: "I have assumed considerable responsibility with the Commission in connection with the regulation of motor carriers, and this work is becoming more burdensome." President Roosevelt had repeatedly expressed his interest in the act, and directly after the election Eastman sent him a six-page letter discussing the whole motor carrier situation which, as he said, was causing him great concern. He declared that the legislation, while desirable, had imposed upon the commission a colossal task, chiefly because of the enormous number of motor carriers and the fact that their operators had no comprehension of what the act required. "Our present trouble," he continued, "is that we need more money." He pointed out that the peak of the work necessarily came at the beginning, but that ultimately, when channels had been established and methods perfected, his bureau could reduce costs. His original request, based on careful estimates, had been for $3,000,000, which had been slashed in the budget to $1,700,000—an amount altogether too small to meet expenses. At this period letters going out from the bureau were averaging 600 per day, and callers were appearing by the hundreds, all of them eager for information. Because of these excessive demands, Eastman asked the President for a deficiency appropriation of $1,300,000 and for an allotment for the next fiscal year of approximately

$3,250,000. He concluded: "If it is thought that we are wasting money or exaggerating our needs, I think we should be told specifically where we are at fault."

In a memorandum commenting at this time on the operation of the Motor Carrier Act, Eastman went into considerable detail regarding his problems.

The Commission is now struggling to bring the administration of the Act into good working order. In many respects it is one of the most difficult tasks that the Commission has ever undertaken, because of the huge number of motor carrier operators and the smallness, in general, of their individual operations. A great many of them operate only a single truck. Under the Act, every common carrier must have a certificate, every contract carrier a permit, and every broker a license, conferring and defining the right to operate. . . . Some idea of the Commission's task may be gathered from the fact that about 80,000 applications have been filed covering existing operations. The Act also requires carriers to file tariffs or schedules stating their rates and charges. Although many such publications have been filed by groups of carriers, over 65,000 separate tariffs or schedules are now on file.

Eastman was very active in motor-carrier regulation, as well as in the other routine business of the Interstate Commerce Commission. In addition, he returned in 1936 to his former position as chairman of the commission's Legislative Committee. By that date he was unquestionably the best-known number of the commission in Congressional circles, and did a great deal to heighten its prestige.

In spite of the differences of opinion that had developed, in the autumn of 1936 Eastman was, so far as he knew, *persona grata* at the White House. His seven-year term as commissioner was to expire on December 31, 1936, and long before that date people were writing to say that they had urged the President to reappoint him. On December 11 Eastman said in a note to a friend: "I do not feel any concern over the matter and personally believe that there is no doubt in regard to the reappointment. There was some talk about my being made Chairman of the new Maritime Commission, but of late that seems to have died down." A week later he confessed, "The fact is that I have no information whatever in regard to the matter, for the President has not discussed it with me and neither has any emissary from him."

The New Year came in, and still there was no word from the President. Under the terms of the Interstate Commerce Act, Joe held over and remained in office until his successor was named; but his friends began to wonder what was happening, and there was comment in the press on the delay of the Chief Executive. The gossip around the Capitol was that Mr. Roosevelt was disciplining Eastman for some of the latter's statements to the effect that the President had no control over the Interstate Commerce Commission. It is true that Eastman had opposed and was opposing the proposal that the commission should be put under the control of a cabinet officer, but that was no valid reason for holding up the appointment of a public servant of Eastman's caliber. Eastman wrote Anderson April 13, 1937: "I do not know why any man of the size of a President of the United States should take exception to an honest difference of opinion." In the same letter, he said: "I have not seen the President for a long time, but so far as I am concerned there has been no break with him, and I have no way of knowing what his attitude towards me may be. I do not know why it should be any different from what it has been in the past."

This period of uncertainty in Eastman's career was made even less tolerable by private grief added to an exceptionally heavy burden of public responsibility. His devoted assistant, Frank Livingstone, on whom he had relied so much, died suddenly in February in a Washington restaurant. In estimating the motives and characters of other men, Livingstone had been invaluable. Always a keen observer, he often warned Joe when others were planning to use him for selfish ends. For example, Eastman simply wouldn't listen to criticism of any member of his staff, and it took clever diplomacy on Livingstone's part to convince his chief that he was being deceived. Furthermore, Livingstone, acting informally and inofficially, could protect Eastman against unnecessary intrusion and thus forestall resentment. A few of Eastman's close friends felt that Livingstone had become a professional "hanger-on" and was in some ways a detriment to his boss, but Eastman certainly never felt so. One of Eastman's associates writes: "I shall always think that Livingstone's death was a major loss to Eastman. He seemed to me to become somewhat more careworn after that. Livingstone knew well how to take him out of himself and take his mind off his cares."

Eastman's normal burden of responsibility was increased during the winter of 1937 by the problems of the Bureau of Motor Carriers. Some idea of their complexity may be drawn from the fact that within a very few months 80,000 applications were received under the so-called "grandfather clause," which authorized the continuance of operations already begun in good faith. These came in from common carriers, contract carriers, brokers, and even private carriers, and of course brought a tremendous routine pressure on the new bureau. Tariff rules had to be passed upon or approved; applications for unification, purchase, transfer, and security issues rolled in like an avalanche; complaints were mounting and hearings had to be held. A series of earlier rulings had speedily been issued, and certain significant test cases had been selected for hearing and decision. All these important arrangements had to be made at a time when the industry itself was expanding with amazing rapidity and when precedents had not yet been set up. Much of this hard work fell on the shoulders of Eastman, who was already under a heavy strain.

As Federal Coordinator Eastman had learned that dictatorial tactics only aroused antagonism and resistance and that it was far easier to secure results by persuading the operators to cooperate with him for the common good. Hence he knew the desirability of conciliating the leaders in the motor transportation business and of gaining the support of such key organizations as the National Safety Council, the Treasury Department, and even the various state commissions. He encouraged the industry to police itself by reporting violations and mistakes. All this meant seeing a great many people. The winter of 1936–37 was for Eastman largely a succession of meetings, which left their aftermath of fatigue.

Meanwhile President Roosevelt, having received a popular endorsement which he regarded as a blank check, was not only in the midst of his Supreme Court fight but also pushing hard his attempts to gain control of the independent regulatory commissions, notably the Interstate Commerce Commission, the Federal Trade Commission, and the Federal Radio Commission,—all of them constituted by Congress and therefore not subject to the domination even of the Chief Executive. These bodies occupied an anomalous position in the governmental structure because they in fact performed functions of all three branches of government—legislative, judicial, and executive. Furthermore, in certain respects an organization like the Interstate Commerce Commission could be affected not only by Congress but also by the President and the Supreme Court. But Eastman always felt that one of the chief values of the Interstate Commerce Commission lay in its independence. When once during the Coolidge administration it was faintly suggested that the independent commission might well be made more dependent upon the executive branch of the government, Eastman asked what purpose this would serve. Answering his own query, he said:

I can conceive of no purpose except to influence in some way the judgment of the Commission or to bring it within the sway of some administrative policy. But plainly, it seems to me, the cold neutrality of the Commission,—to use the expression of the Supreme Court,—ought to be safe-guarded jealously against precisely such extraneous influences.

When the President, in 1935, had removed William E. Humphrey, a conservative Republican member of the Federal Trade Commission who had been outspoken in his opposition to the New Deal policies, the Supreme Court decided that the Chief Executive could take such action only on grounds set forth in the law and not for mere differences of opinion respecting its enforcement. It also implied that this ruling governed members of the Interstate Commerce Commission. The court declared that the Congress intended to "create a body of experts who shall gain experience by length of service,—a body which shall be independent of executive authority, *except in its selection*, and free to exercise its judgment without the leave or hindrance of any other official or any department of the government." With this ruling Eastman was delighted.

But President Roosevelt was not to be blocked thus easily in his designs upon the commissions. In 1936 he appointed a Committee on Administrative Management, headed by Louis Brownlow and therefore often called the "Brownlow Committee"; its ostensible aim was to promote governmental efficiency. In its report to Congress in 1937, this committee recommended that the regulatory commissions be stripped of their administrative functions and left with only purely judicial powers. According to the original plan, which was quickly approved by the President, the Interstate Commerce Commission would become a part of the Department of Commerce. The report itself had many excellent features, but it was, of course, highly controversial. So far as the commission was concerned, the issue was fundamental and raised many doubts about the wisdom of the entire proposal for the centralization of executive authority.

Naturally the idea was not pleasing to the members of the Interstate Commerce Commission, which took vast pride in its traditions and achievements and felt that it had done a commendable job. When the resulting legislation was introduced in the Senate, Eastman, called upon to testify before its Committee on Government Organization, spoke with calmness and sincerity, in the mood of a thoughtful man weighing all the evidence. As a political philosopher with practical experience, he denied that the regulatory commissions were irresponsible. After all, they were accountable not only to Congress, which had created them, but also to the Federal courts and to the Chief Executive himself. As for the Interstate Commerce Commission specifically, it was primarily an arm of Congress, which had deliberately made it nonpartisan and nonpolitical. Moreover, its stability and continuity were guaranteed by the fact that the commissioners had long terms of office so staggered that no administration, even if so minded, could completely transform its personnel. The possibility that any President would or could be elected for four successive terms was not then thought worthy of consideration. Eastman contended that the enormous authority reposed in the commission was carefully guarded against abuse, and he was applauded when he pointed out that no President so far had been able to make it his tool. He expressed the hope that nothing would be done to give the ICC "the slightest political tinge or endanger the characteristics which have distinguished it during the past half-century."

Some of the members of the Brownlow Committee and, indeed,

some students of practical government felt at the time that Eastman was trying to halt an honest effort to promote economy and unity in national administration. He himself admitted that he had read the committee report with much sympathy. He acknowledged that it was endeavoring to bring about greater efficiency in the public administration and added: "I do not think that I have any greater interest in life than that very thing." But after living for many years in the center of official Washington, he had developed a distrust of autocratic management in government as well as in business. He had confidence also in the effectiveness of small committees, free to deliberate with no outside interference and with the assurance which results from guaranteed tenure. Moreover, as he had watched the operations of the New Deal, he had come to dread the tendency toward centralization shown by a political party still boasting of the title "Democratic."

Eastman's testimony, delivered without malice or personal animus, was weighed carefully by the Senate committee. The fact that the Brownlow Report coincided in time with the President's attempt to pack the Supreme Court undoubtedly prejudiced some well-intentioned and thoughtful legislators against it. At any rate, strong opposition developed, and it was clear that any effort to implement the report would be unsuccessful. It was gratifying to have Senator Wheeler say, when the controversy was over: "By and large the Interstate Commerce Commission has gained the confidence and respect of people in this country to an extent that no other Commission which has ever sat here in the City of Washington has enjoyed."

While the status and the future of the commission were thus in doubt, it observed its fiftieth anniversary, with appropriate ceremonies. Commissioner Splawn edited an "appropriate historical statement"—a volume not distinguished by literary charm or dramatic quality, but packed with useful information. The program of speeches, held on April 1, 1937, included some entertaining reminiscences by men familiar with the evolution of the commission; several of the addresses referred directly or indirectly to the current discussion in Congress. Eastman himself presided over the morning session, and he listened with satisfaction to Allan P. Matthew, president of the Association of Practitioners before the Interstate Commerce Commission, as he said:

Speaking finally as an individual and wholly upon my own responsibility, may I express the earnest hope that nothing shall be allowed to transpire which might impair the efficient functioning of a tribunal which has demonstrated its capacity to discharge the duties laid upon it under different but related statutes in a fashion which has commanded general respect. May there be no dissociation of the different units of service which have been welded by time and experience into a homogeneous whole. Above all, may nothing be done which would destroy, or qualify even in the slightest measure, the essential autonomy which has been allowed to the Commission for half a century,—an autonomy which, as we cannot fail to know, is indispensable to the just exercise of the Commission's salutary and far-reaching powers.

This final paragraph in a sense set the theme for the entire meeting. Addresses were delivered by Commissioner Clyde B. Aitchison, former commissioners Patrick J. Farrell and John J. Esch, and two members of the House Committee on Interstate and Foreign Commerce, Clarence F. Lea and Sam Rayburn. Senator Burton K. Wheeler, always a strong supporter of the commission, was unable to be present, but his prepared speech was read by his colleague Senator Sherman Minton. Without mincing any words, Wheeler referred in his address to the current controversy and quoted Senator Pitman as having said: "In creating the Interstate Commerce Commission we made it totally responsible to Congress and not to any department of the Government. We were in hopes that it would be responsible to Congress rather than to a department of the Government or of the Bureau of the Budget." Wheeler's address then continued, in measured language:

I want to say to the Commission that my convictions in this matter have not changed since 1928, and I am unalterably opposed to diminishing the independent, bipartisan character of the Interstate Commerce Commission or of the similar independent agencies by placing them under executive domination, either indirectly as has been the case, or directly as in a pending proposal.

All through the spring of 1937 Joe's friends waited expectantly for the news of his reappointment, but none was forthcoming, and no explanation for the delay was given. Eastman's attitude toward the report of the Brownlow Committee was, of course, understood; and early in 1937 he delivered a speech before the Boston Chamber of Commerce in which he expressed himself as strongly opposed to the plans with regard to the Interstate Commerce Commission. Some observers felt that this angered the President. On the other hand, it was suggested that Mr. Roosevelt was waiting for the passage of the bill for the reorganization of the executive departments in order to give Eastman an important new post. In April the Honorable John F. Fitzgerald telegraphed Senator David I. Walsh, of Massachusetts, asking him to sound out Eastman regarding a position with the Boston Port Authority at a very liberal salary. Joe was flattered, but replied: "I desire to remain on the Interstate Commerce Commission as long as I am permitted to do so, and am not yet looking for any other jobs." Finally, on July 9, without even discussing the subject with Eastman, the President sent in his name to the Senate, and he was duly confirmed on July 26, with virtually no objection. Hundreds of his well-wishers sent in telegrams and letters of congratulation. Almost no criticism appeared in the daily press or in Congress. An editorial in the *Traffic World* tried to explain what had happened.

The long delay by President Roosevelt in reappointing Mr. Eastman a member of the Commission gave rise to the rumor that the President was displeased because Commissioner Eastman had criticised his plan to put the Interstate Commerce Commission under a cabinet officer, and that he might appoint some one else. He finally did reappoint Commissioner Eastman, which led to speculation as to how the breach had been healed. But whether or not there was anything to report,—and there evidently was not,—Commissioner Eastman had thrown another monkey wrench into the presidential machinery by appearing again in firm opposition to the bill and the plan to give the President a "blank check." Such outspokenness on the part of a presidential appointee requires some courage,—which ought to be common, but is not.

Much speculation had arisen as to the real reason for delay in reappointing a public servant of Eastman's acknowledged ability and distinguished reputation. In the retrospect it looks as if the President, piqued by Eastman's independent attitude, had made up his mind to punish him and by procrastination to find out how public opinion would react if he were ignored. If this is so, Mr. Roosevelt soon had his lesson. He was warned by members of the Senate that he would make an irreparable blunder if he turned Eastman down. Furthermore, even the leading railroad executives who once regarded him suspiciously as Federal Coordinator were now on his side. It is possible that the President, with his shrewd political sense, perceived the situation and against his secret desire yielded gracefully to the inevitable. The newspaper reaction proved that he had done wisely. An editorial in the Boston *Herald* summarized popular feeling in saying:

President Roosevelt would have made a grievous mistake of omission if he had failed to reappoint Joseph Bartlett Eastman of the Interstate Commerce Commission. Since President Wilson selected him in 1919, he has become a more and more valuable public servant. He has never allowed whatever prepossessions he may have as to the future of transportation in the United States to interfere in the slightest with his decisions.

Warned by his advisers of the persistent rumor that a rift existed between him and Eastman, the President shortly invited him to Hyde Park, where he was photographed in an automobile sitting between Mr. and Mrs. Roosevelt. In telling his sister about the trip, Joe said that the Roosevelts talked most of the time about farming problems so that he felt at times embarrassingly *de trop*. But at least the visit could be construed as indicating that all was forgiven.

The President, however, was not ready to admit defeat and only awaited a propitious moment for renewing his attack. In the early spring of 1938 the railroads were again reported as being in a parlous state, thirty-seven Class I railways being in the hands of the courts; ten of them in receiverships, and twenty-seven in trusteeships. The net income of Class I steam railways, which had been $896,807,000 in 1929, had fallen by 1937 to $98,527,000. Nor had the decline been arrested. For January, 1938, the freight revenues had fallen off 187 percent from January, 1937; and the total passenger revenue had dropped for February, 1938, almost 5 percent below that of the same month a year before. The New England region and the entire western district did not have enough revenue to cover their operating expenses and taxes in January, 1938, to say nothing of interest charges. For this deplorable condition the marked recession in industrial activity throughout the country was largely accountable, but its effect was greatly aggravated by the increase in competition with other forms of transportation. It looked, indeed, as if railroad transportation were a declining business.

The magazine *Fortune*, in its issue for April, 1938, published a pessimistic article analyzing the railroad situation as it appeared at that critical moment. It estimated the cost of duplicated services as at least $740,000,000 annually and deplored the corporate chauvinism which permitted such a wastage. It declared categorically:

No railroad man of record wants all regulation to cease. . . . For the facts that all their rates must be published and adhered to, and that they can agree on rates in advance without worrying about the antitrust laws, the railroads are grateful to regulation. . . . Beyond that, they resent it, and they particularly resent what they term its intrusion "into the rightful functions of management."

At this critical hour the President brought together at the White House a group of men "for the purpose of considering the serious situation of the railroads of the country and what action, if any, can and should be taken by the Federal Government for the relief or improvement of existing conditions." The persons on the invitation list knew only too well what hazards they were facing. Included were members of the Senate Committee on Interstate Commerce, the House Committee on Interstate and Foreign Commerce, the Department of the Treasury, the Department of Agriculture, the Department of Commerce, the Interstate Commerce Commission, the Reconstruction Finance Corporation, and the Securities and Exchange Commission, together with representatives of the managements, the employees, and the security holders. They met together first on March 15 and continued their deliberations for three days. President Roosevelt then appointed a committee to prepare a report summarizing the conclusions of the gathering.

This committee was headed by Dr. Walter M. W. Splawn, who was chairman of the Interstate Commerce Commission for 1938, and was generally known as the "Splawn Committee." Dr. Splawn, who had held various positions in the field of education, including the presidency of the University of Texas (1924–27), and had served as special counsel for the House Committee on Interstate and Foreign Commerce, had been named to the commission in 1934, by President Roosevelt. The other two members were Eastman and Mahaffie, who were close friends and accustomed to working together.

The Splawn Committee invited and received suggestions from a large number of authorities and finished their report, about fifty pages in length, within a week. Even the indefatigable Eastman confessed that he had never in all his career toiled so continuously without rest. The President had insisted that there was need of immediate action if serious bankruptcies among a large number of railroad companies were to be averted, and the committee, accordingly, felt that it could not argue over trivial or irrelevant matters. At the outset they agreed to disregard political considerations.

The conclusions of the committee included what were called "Means of Immediate Relief" and also a "Long-Term Program." Under the first heading they recommended that government funds to the extent of $3,000,000 be supplied for the purchase of badly needed railroad equipment which would itself be the security for the advances; that the RFC be authorized for twelve months to make loans without certification by the ICC so that certain railroads could meet their fixed charges; that the Government pay the full rate by eliminating so-called "land grant reductions"; that reorganization under the Bankruptcy Act receive the careful attention of Congress; and that the question of reductions in wages be left for the moment in abeyance, even though it would be "a means of very definite and positive financial relief to the carriers." The committee could hardly be blamed for their unwillingness to express an opinion on the subject of wage reduction, which was certainly packed with dynamite.

As a long-term program, it was suggested that a Federal Transportation Authority, made up of three members, be created for a term of two years, for the purpose of "planning, encouraging, and promoting action by railroad companies with a view to eliminating the waste caused by the fact that the railroad system of the nation is owned and operated by a large number of independent companies." This was, of course, merely the revival under another guise of the familiar Coordinator of Transportation, with slightly modified range and powers. It was actually an attempt to secure the advantages of government operation through the device of voluntary monopoly. The committee directed attention to certain financial abuses, including "improper or misleading accounting for the purpose of concealing actual financial condition," as well as "unwise issuance of securities in the interests of those who market such securities." They concluded that it would be altogether desirable to concentrate regulatory activities in a single agency and pointed out that, while this had already been done in the case of railroads, motor carriers, and pipe lines, it should also be accomplished with water and air carriers. Their proposals might have been described as the same old medicine in different bottles and with slightly changed labels.

In forwarding this report to Congress on April 11, the President played further variations on one of his favorite themes. Early in his message he referred to his conviction that the purely executive functions of the commission were "in all probability unconstitutional, in that they create executive authority in a fourth branch of the government instead of in the President." Toward the close, moreover, he improved the opportunity to remark:

From the point of view of business efficiency, such as a private corporation would seek, it would seem to be the part of common sense to place all executive functions relating to all transportation in one Federal Department,—such as the Department of Commerce, the Department of the Interior, or some other old or new department. At the same time all quasi-judicial and quasi-legislative matters relating to all transportation could properly be placed under an independent commission,—a reorganized Interstate Commerce Commission. And such action would be highly constitutional.

I refer to this, not by way of recommendation, but only as one method which should receive Congressional study.

It was obvious that the President had not abandoned his desire to curb the independent commissions and that despite the lack of enthusiasm with which his earlier recommendations had been received he was persisting in his original proposals.

With his covering letter to Congress, Roosevelt included comments by various public officials and government agencies. Secretary Morgenthau, of the Treasury Department, was frankly disappointed and felt that the Splawn Committee's "over-cautious approach" could lead only to more drastic action at a later date. What he wanted was the immediate creation by Congress of a Department of Transportation "with power to move vigorously to properly coordinate our national transportation facilities." This would have suited the President perfectly.

A representative of the labor unions declared that they would "oppose with all the forces at their command an effort to reduce compensation of railroad employees"; and he protested fervently against any contemplated coordinations and consolidations, on the ground that they would result in the elimination of some 200,000 railroad jobs. "What our country needs is more employment,—not less employment" was the verdict of George M. Harrison, of the Grand Lodge, Brotherhood of Railway and Steamship Clerks, Freight Handlers, Express and Station Employees.

The report thus speedily put together by the Splawn Committee was excellent as one more in what has been called "a series of pragmatic adjustments to circumstance." But Congressmen were eager that spring to get home to mend their fences for the fall elections, and nothing could be accomplished in the way of legislation. In September, 1938, the President appointed a new Committee of Six, consisting of three representatives of railroad management and three of railway labor, which made its own comprehensive report on December 23. This group, primarily concerned with the immediate plight of the railroads, were actuated in all their recommendations by a desire to improve their status as against that of competing transportation agencies.

It would be futile to explore the lines of argument here, the complaints and prophecies, the doubts and warnings, which could have been heard at this period in Washington committee rooms. Throughout all the discussion on transportation Eastman was a central and dominant figure, the man to whom the interested parties turned when information was required or advice was sought. Out of all this investigation came what was known as the Omnibus Bill, introduced into the House of Representatives early in 1939 with the strong support of the Association of American Railroads. An exceptionally large number of hearings followed, in both the Senate and the House, for the two bodies could seldom agree. As chairman of the Commission's Legislative Committee, Eastman submitted a comprehensive report on March 20, 1939, and appeared to testify and answer questions whenever he was summoned. The debate lingered along through 1939 and into 1940, without any real crystallization of thought. Finally, in January, 1940, Eastman sent to Senator Wheeler and Congressman Clarence F. Lea, the two committee chairmen, a dynamic letter, criticizing both the Senate and the House bills and suggesting certain modifications, many of which were adopted by the conference committee. This letter, which he drafted by himself without the aid of colleagues or secretaries, has a permanent value as a contribution to the literature of transportation history in the United States. Even then the points of differences were not fully ironed out until late spring. The so-called Transportation Act, 1940, was passed in August, with only a few dissenting votes, and signed by the President. Much of the credit for the measure rightly belongs to Eastman.

This act expanded the power of the commission to cover, with some exemptions, all water carriers engaged in domestic commerce and thus put under its control all modes of transportation except air carriers. These were already operating under the Civil Aeronautics Authority, created by Congress in 1938. To forestall the charge that the commission was prejudiced in favor of the railroads, a three-man board was to be appointed to investigate the relative importance of rail, water, and motor transportation and determine which should be encouraged or discouraged in the intensive competition which existed.

During the debates on the floor of the Senate members frequently referred to Eastman as "the foremost transportation authority in the country" or "our American expert on railroads." Indeed, Senator Walsh, of Massachusetts, took the floor to boast that he had "discovered" Eastman. Meanwhile Eastman was doing his best to educate the general public on the issues involved. Writing in *Barron's Weekly* in September, 1938, he declared that the most important single factor in the tragedy of the railroads was the business depression, for, as he said, "you cannot move traffic unless other industries provide it." Unfortunately, the railroads could not overcome the effect of the depression simply by increasing their charges, for the rates were already higher in many instances than was consistent with financial health. He was sure that the employees, in pressing for and obtaining an increase in wages in 1937, had defeated their own interests, for "payrolls have been kept down by laying men off." He felt that one of the basic evils had been the failure of executives to meet new and different competition.

On April 17, 1939, Eastman spoke at the Town Meeting of the Air, with Senator Wheeler and President Pelley, of the Association of American Railroads, on the broad subject, "How Can We Solve the Railroad Problem?" In commenting on the obvious fact that the railroads were "financially sick," employing about half the men they once did and spending far less for materials, supplies, equipment, and construction, Eastman summed the situation up as he saw it:

What caused this sickness? The chief cause was the general business depression. It greatly decreased the freight and passengers to be hauled. Ranking next was the tremendous increase in competition from other kinds of carriers,—particularly highway motor vehicles, but including steamships and barges, pipelines and airplanes. In the past twenty years or so this country has spent at least as much in developing these other forms of transportation as the entire railroad investment. This competition has not only deprived the railroads of much traffic but has forced wholesale reductions in their rates and fares.

Thus, during Mr. Roosevelt's second term Eastman was busy spreading his economic gospel, speaking before audiences across the country as he had done when he was Coordinator. His disagreement with the Chief Executive on a fundamental question of government reorganization certainly did not damage his reputation, but was regarded as a commendable demonstration of independence. The issue has not even today been decisively settled. The advent of another World War diverted the President's attention from domestic matters to foreign affairs, and during the war itself transportation was so well managed with Eastman in charge that any change would have been deplored and deplorable. So it is that in spite of occasional criticism the Interstate Commerce Commission still exists, unshorn of its powers and retaining the confidence of the public.

The infrequent clashes between Roosevelt and Eastman only revealed and accentuated their temperamental differences. The President wanted around him those who would follow him implicitly on major matters and put his ideas into practical operation. Eastman was not willing to be so docile. Roosevelt saw in politics a convenient machine for achieving his ends. Eastman felt that such tactics were unnecessary, believing like Socrates that if the average man could only be shown the truth, he would instinctively respond. It would probably be unfair to assert that FDR felt that a good end sometimes justified a dubious means; but he certainly used methods which Eastman would have disdained to employ. Eastman was no "starry-eyed" dreamer. He had been through realistic experiences with some unscrupulous people, and the wool was seldom pulled over his eyes. But he never lost his faith in mankind, and for this reason was now and then deceived in this none-too-perfect world.

Having reached a decision, Eastman, like Roosevelt, could be very persistent. In spite of some of his doubts regarding the organization of the Interstate Commerce Commission, he was proud of it and of its accomplishment. He was sure that if left untrammeled it could be wiser and more effective than any cabinet officer. He was convinced that, on the whole, it had been just and impartial. He did not wish to run the risk of having transportation controlled by men with political motives and aspirations. This was at the bottom of his resistance to executive interference. He may have been obstinate, but his was the stubbornness of an honest official who objects to intrusion on his own bailiwick. He seldom lost his temper. He was never noisy or vituperative. But he refused to give ground. To Eastman the commission was an institution worthy, on its record, of preservation.

It must be repeated that Eastman's views on current questions were determined by a philosophy which remained basically the same throughout his adult life. He was working for the good of all the people, and therefore was irritated to the verge of despondency by the sinister maneuvers of pressure groups. The undisguised selfishness of labor leaders drove him in the 1930's into a position which seemed to be a little to the right of center, and at the same time his relationships with railroad executives became noticeably more friendly, especially after he had discovered in them a genuine desire to cooperate. It has been intimated that some shrewd railroad leaders deliberately tried to win his confidence and thus to seduce him for their purposes. But Joe, though he may have seemed easygoing, was no tyro to be taken in by honeyed words or extravagant entertainment. More than most men in high position, he was true to himself and his convictions.

For many years the Interstate Commerce Commission had kept the policy of a rotating chairmanship, under which the members took turns at serving in that capacity for one year. Thus, the position was largely honorary, for necessarily a chairman for such a short period could accomplish little to improve administration. The custom had been widely criticized, and some of the more liberal members decided to try the experiment of a three-year chairmanship. Accordingly, Eastman was elected chairman for a term of three years, beginning July 1, 1939.

The plan at the time was that he would be relieved of much of his casework so that he could devote more hours to planning, but he had so much unfinished business on his desk that he could not free himself immediately. Furthermore, he continued, as chairman of the Legislative Committee, with all the labor which that position entailed. Fortunately, his examiner, Howard Hosmer, volunteered to help on details, and soon an arrangement was made which allowed Eastman more freedom and gave Hosmer more responsibility, to the benefit of both. But it was always difficult to keep Eastman from doing an assigned job all by himself.

Meanwhile the new Interstate Commerce Building, planned as part of President Hoover's $50,000,000 public building program, was completed and was opened on July 9, 1934. For the first time in forty-seven years the commission was housed in a government-owned structure, with all of its activities under its own roof. Seven stories high, it fronted 550 feet on Constitution Avenue and 230 feet on Twelfth Street, and it cost more than $5,000,000. In design, it is a vast complex of corridors and courts, both puzzling and monotonous. The *Traffic World* made plenty of fun of it, saying that it was "a pain to the feet and a strain on the ears" as well as "an irritation to the eyes." It was actually a walk of two city blocks from Secretary McGinty's office to Commissioner Aitchison's. With its vast cafeteria and hundreds of offices, it is a community in itself.

After 1934, then, the commission sat at its formal hearings in a noble room, perhaps eighty feet by fifty feet and about thirty feet high, paneled in English oak, with a large insert map of the United States behind the dais and a built-in bookcase containing the reports of the commission. On one side wall is a beautiful gilded clock, toward which the commissioners, when bored, frequently gaze. The seats for the members are upholstered with red leather and can be turned at a touch into rocking chairs; those for the attorneys and the auditors are exceedingly comfortable, also padded with red leather. The decorations are generally plain, with hangings of crimson velvet and four huge bronze chandeliers. Although the members of the commission wear no robes, they present an appearance of great dignity. The hearings, however, have an atmosphere of pleasant informality, and an attorney making a plea is liable to interruption at any time by a query from a commissioner. An American flag stands at each end of the tribunal platform.

Eastman's new offices, on the fifth floor, were spacious, with plenty of privacy if he desired it and ample room for the clerical staff. Until his death, in 1937, Frank Livingstone was installed in the outer office, where he could greet visitors and act as watchdog, as he had done in the old building. In 1926 Mrs. Edna R. Buchanan came as a stenographer; she was eventually promoted to be Eastman's personal secretary. After Livingstone died, Mrs. Buchanan became indispensable, paying attention to her employer's preferences and dislikes and sparing him in every way within her power.

He had for many years been "Doctor" Eastman, but in 1934 his honorary degree from Amherst was supplemented by similar distinctions from Syracuse University and Temple University. In 1938 he received another LL.D. from Oberlin College. In presenting him for this award to the president of the college, Professor H. A. Wooster said in part:

In 1933, President Roosevelt, in search of a genius for an almost impossible task, called him from the Commission temporarily to serve as Federal Coordinator of Transportation, a newly created emergency office, requiring a degree of technical knowledge, organizing ability, and personal tact rarely found in one man. In this appointment he was given powers seldom, if ever, possessed by an American commissioner in time of peace. The conditions he had to meet were such as to tempt any man with authority to use it to the hilt. Yet he displayed under the most difficult circumstances the fine mettle of the true public servant. With power to compel in his hands, he chose rather to accomplish the purposes of his office by persuasion, recognizing that, in a democracy, projects fostered by compulsion are foredoomed to failure.

On May 6, 1941, Eastman wrote his friend Whitcomb: "Greatly to my surprise, but much to my delight, I am to be given an LL.D. on June 15 by Dartmouth College. My pleasure lies in the fact that my granddad and great-granddad were Dartmouth graduates. The first cousin of my granddad also was a President of that college." The ceremonies at the Dartmouth Commencement moved him very deeply.

Naturally Eastman could take no active part in the presidential campaign of 1940, but he was an admirer of Wendell Willkie and voted for him in the election. He did not like the idea of a third term for any President, no matter how able, and wrote "Jim" Farley a letter praising him for taking a stand against it at the Chicago convention. He also liked Willkie's forthright and uncompromising liberalism and his defiance of the ultra-conservative element in the Republican party.

Roosevelt was reelected in the autumn of 1940, and shortly the United States, although technically a neutral, was moving under his leadership to the aid of Great Britain in her death struggle with Hitler and Mussolini. In his position Eastman continued to face domestic problems and was chary about discussing publicly our international situation, although he welcomed Roosevelt's ringing denunciations of fascism and nazism. He and his associates on the commission were, of course, planning what they should do if or when our country was drawn into the conflict. Nobody needed to tell him that in such a crisis the Federal Government would again call upon his knowledge and experience. The New York *Times*, as early as June 25, 1941, reported that Roosevelt was considering the appointment of Eastman as Emergency Coordinator of Transportation, but that labor was bringing strong pressure for the naming of somebody more openly friendly to it. Eastman himself had recommended Ralph Budd, already the transportation member of the National Defense Advisory Commission. The *Times* said in comment: "Corporate executives recall with some amusement that during the 1920's, when business was in the saddle, Mr. Eastman was outspoken in his criticism of corporate practices, whereas now he is regarded by labor as its foe."

One of Joe's difficulties in contemplating the future was that he had not been feeling well. The strain of long years of overwork had begun to tell, and he found himself slowing up a little, staying at home frequently at night instead of returning to his office, playing squash less frequently, and trying to save himself unnecessary exertion. His physician had warned him that his blood pressure was high and that his heart was not in good shape, and that he should relax and take it easy. But it was only a matter of months before duty was to place another heavy burden upon him and not only keep him from resting but make more insistent demands upon his vitality and endurance.

XIV

The Last Big Job

IN AN ADDRESS delivered in 1943, in St. Louis, Eastman reminded his audience of a statement by Paul Goebbels, Hitler's Minister of Propaganda, shortly after Pearl Harbor, to the effect that transportation, and especially railway transportation, would prove to be the vulnerable Achilles' heel of the American production effort. Goebbels commented particularly on the American shortage of rolling stock, which at a time when the country faced such strange problems as the paralysis of coastwise shipping and the dwindling supply of tires and gasoline would, he predicted, prove an insuperable handicap to our war effort. Our General Staff were well aware that we were facing a "war of movement," and Eastman listened more than once to prophecies from people in responsible circles in Washington that the railroads were certain to break down under the strain. They did not break down, even though they had to handle the biggest traffic load in history.

As a matter of record, conditions had begun to improve months before the United States entered the war. Although railroad cars and locomotives were in 1941 fewer than they had been in 1917, more than $8,000,000 had during the interval been spent on improvement of the properties, and motor truck traffic had effected miracles in short-haul transportation. The number of passenger cars registered in the United States had risen from 2,310,000 in 1915 to about 27,300,000 in 1940. In 1940 alone the automobile industry had produced about 777,000 trucks, and the total number of all types in the country was not far from 5,000,000. While this phenomenal increase in motor transportation was taking place, railway traffic had also improved steadily during 1940 and 1941; it still handled nearly two thirds of the intercity business. So prosperous were the railroads that Eastman wrote to President Roosevelt, October 21, 1941, with reference to "the desirability of utilizing the present favorable earnings of the railroads in the retirement of their indebtedness." He added: "The Commission is thoroughly committed to the principle that so far as it has authority to bring this about, the railroad debt burden will be reduced as rapidly as is practicable." On these recent developments Herr Goebbels was clearly not well informed.

Meanwhile, the Government, under Roosevelt's vigorous leadership, had not neglected the warnings implied in Hitler's aggressive movements on the European continent. With foresight the President, in May, 1940, at a period described by Robert E. Sherwood as one of "bewilderment and frenzied uncertainty," formed a National Defense Advisory Commission. Established as a separate organism reporting direct to the Chief Executive, this commission included such leaders as William S. Knudsen (Industrial Production), Sidney Hillman (Labor), Leon Henderson (Price Stabilization), and others, with Ralph Budd, president of the Chicago, Burlington & Quincy Railroad, representing transportation. Budd was an outstanding leader in his field, with wide connections and high intelligence, in whom Eastman had complete confidence. Frequent conferences in Washington emphasized with cumulative intensity the necessity of getting ready for possible war, and it was early perceived that we must not be handicapped by an inadequate transportation system.

Advanced thinkers were already proposing that, in what resembled an emergency, the Government should plan to take over the railroads as it had done in World War I. Eastman was not now so sure as he once had been that this would be either wise or expedient. In May, 1941, he categorically denied that any plans were in contemplation for Federal operation; but he did stress the paramount importance of transportation to the national defense and warned the railroads that "if any defaults or deficiencies develop, I imagine the government will not long hesitate to assume control if by so doing it can see a way of correcting or averting dangerous conditions." Thus early was the policy outlined of ensuring the good behavior of the railroads by holding over them the threat of government control and operation. It was like saying to a small boy, "You can play any way you wish, but if you get into trouble, look out!"

Nothing in Eastman's correspondence indicates any marked apprehension during those fateful first days of December, 1941. On October 15 he had been appointed a member of the Price Administration Committee of the Office of Price Administration and Civilian Supply and had joked about the length of the title. On the evening of December 4 he attended a dinner in honor of Daniel Willard, president of the Baltimore & Ohio Railroad, whom he much admired. On the next morning he went to Toronto to address the Canadian Motor Freight Carriers' Convention. The news of Pearl Harbor reached him on a week end while he was with a Canadian acquaintance, and he flew immediately back to Washington, where he entered upon a strenuous schedule of conferences with high government officials. To Harold D. Smith, director of the Bureau of the Budget, who wrote at once to inquire about the relationship of the Interstate Commerce Commission to the Defense Program, Eastman answered: "Our work in this respect naturally has to do chiefly with the provision and maintenance of adequate transportation facilities, and it centers chiefly in our Bureau of Service and our Bureau of Motor Carriers."

It would be erroneous, of course, to assume that transportation was caught unawares. Considerably before the attack by Japan had made war inevitable President Roosevelt, with the advice of both Eastman and Budd, had drafted an Executive Order creating an Office of Defense Transportation, authorized to take care of an enormous increase in traffic volume. Meanwhile, Budd, in consultation with the railroads and the motor carriers, had done much to protect the situation. Statistics had been accumulated, charts had been made, and instructions had been prepared for immediate distribution. On December 18, following our Declaration of War on Japan and the counter-declaration of war on the United States by Germany and Italy, the President actually issued the Executive Order. It was, as Eastman later admitted, written out "under stress of the emergency without the benefit of precedent," and it laid down a wholly novel program of governmental activity. The document was ready, and nobody at the moment thought of altering the word "Defense" to its logical conclusion "War."

Eastman himself had repeatedly suggested Budd for the position of Director of Defense Transportation, but the President, although he had had his differences with Joe, knew well that the latter was the only man for an "all out" crisis. Eastman had his own reservations, some of them based on a very modest estimate of his qualifications, some due to the condition of his health. In commenting on the situation to a friend, he wrote: "I do not believe that I have any special qualifications for the job, which seems to me to call for administrative talents rather than for judicial, and I have never considered myself particularly gifted as an administrator. However, the assignment has been given to me, and I'll do the best I can with it."

Once committed, Eastman entered upon his duties with the dogged determination which he had shown in 1933. On the very day of his appointment he told one of his associates that in the previous September his doctor had advised him to undergo an operation. Eastman had replied that the war situation was so serious that he must be ready at any moment to respond to a call, even at the expense of his health. It certainly never occurred to Joe that he might use a physician's diagnosis as an excuse for not accepting an exacting job. "I'm almost sixty, with no wife or family," he said. "It makes very little difference what happens to me!" And so he began to think and to talk of nothing but the conservation of engines and tires, faster movement of freight cars, and the necessity for the American people to accustom themselves to relatively minor deprivations.

The Executive Order creating his new office made it Eastman's primary duty " to assure maximum utilization of the domestic transportation facilities of the nation for the successful prosecution of the war," and he was expected "to develop measures designed to secure maximum use of existing transportation agencies." Calling the conflict a "war of movement," Eastman said to the American Academy of Political Science on November 10, 1942:

The dimensions are global, but my immediate concern is with our domestic transportation system. That system has the duty in the war effort of bringing the raw materials to the war production plants, of moving the semifinished or finished products to points of further fabrication or of use or of embarkation, of moving our millions of troops, of supplying our camps, and of moving the millions of war workers to and from their work.

The director had broad, although somewhat vague, authority not only over railroads but also over other transportation agencies, including automotive highway vehicles, water carriers, pipe lines, and air carriers. He tactfully made it clear at once that the Office of Defense Transportation had been established, "not because the carriers had been in any way delinquent, but to protect the future and centralize the responsibility, which clearly rests upon the Government, of seeing to it that transportation is able to play, and does play effectively and well, its indispensable part in the war effort." He possessed far more potential power than he had been given as Coordinator, and some of the more suspicious operators were wondering how he would use it. But Eastman knew his Shakespeare well enough to remember his *Measure for Measure* and Isabella's words to Angelo:

> O, it is excellent
> To have a giant's strength; but it is tyrannous
> To use it like a giant.

Although Eastman once declared that he had never been formally asked by the President whether he would accept and had learned of his appointment through a communicative newspaper man, it can scarcely be asserted that he was very much astonished by what happened. Within two days headquarters were set aside in the Interstate Commerce Building, and he proceeded to get down to business without any orchids or press conferences or military salutes. On December 31 he referred to "my new work, which has already assumed mountainous proportions." Actually he did not take the oath of office until January 2, 1942, but before that he had built up a skeleton staff from those around him. He was to continue to serve, when necessary, in the deliberations of the Commission, but soon all his energies had to be devoted to his arduous special task.

He did not long delay in explaining the policy which he proposed to follow. The basic principle, as he saw it, was cooperation. Out of his somewhat trying experience as Coordinator, he had learned that you get more out of people by winning their support than by forcing their compliance. Thus, the carriers were not taken over, but remained throughout the war privately owned and managed, and Eastman hardly uttered even a mild threat of government seizure. Occasionally he reminded the operators that the Executive Order creating his office used terms which reflected a program of leadership, coordination, and unselfishness, but always against a background "of ultimate power and authority which can be brought into action, if necessary." He knew perfectly well that he could count on the unreserved backing of the Federal Government and, indeed, of public opinion in whatever compulsive measures he chose to impose. But it was an hour, in his judgment, for trying first the virtues of combined voluntary effort. Hence, from the moment of entering upon his responsibilities he undertook to conciliate and win the confidence of all the contending parties. Promptly he received, as he declared in one of his speeches, "gratifying and unanimous offers of cooperation on the part of both carriers and shippers, including the government agencies."

In January, 1942, the United States was in one of those rare moods, brought about by consciousness of common peril, in which selfish motives are for the moment submerged. If Eastman had been less modest, he might have conceived of himself as an orchestra leader, educing the best from each of those who contribute to the perfection of the symphony—encouragement to the bass viols, stimulus to the woodwinds, guidance to the percussionists—with attention to synchronization, emphasis, and proper subordination of each to the others when the score demanded it. An ignorant or badly balanced leader might, if he lost his head, produce only cacophony.

In his big office on the fifth floor of the Interstate Commerce Commission Building, overlooking the Mall, Eastman faced at once a job of organization even more difficult than that which he had met in 1933. In his first public address as director, delivered on January 27, before the National Council of Motor Truck Owners, he said: "Realizing my own deficiencies, I have tried to select for the key positions in my organization men with extensive practical experience, each in his own line, of marked ability, and possessed of courage, energy, and particularly of initiative, for I want them to be self-starters." Here Eastman's wide acquaintance was invaluable. Over a long period of years he had been thrown into contact with virtually every national leader in the field of transportation. He could summon and even, in an amiable way, coerce them for his needs.

He did not, however, draft many experts from the railroad industry itself, fearing that some of them might, as they had done in the previous war, use their positions to benefit their companies. He did not hesitate to call back to service several of the men who had been under him when he was Federal Coordinator, and this elicited complaints from the railroad executives, one of whom later described Eastman's staff as composed of "has beens and never wases." The Director seems to have been uninfluenced by political or prudential considerations. Indeed after his death *Time* said of him, quite justly, "In politics-ridden Washington he was outstanding as a man who kept his mind on the job." A tremendous number of persons, many of them sponsored by members of Congress, applied with alacrity for positions in his office, and most of them had to be refused with the soft answer that turneth away wrath. In this connection Eastman said in 1943: "I am very thankful to the staff which I was able to assemble around me. All of the keymen of that staff are men of large practical experience in their respective fields of activity. Not one of them sought his job, and they will all be glad when their tours of duty are over."

The logical man for the position of director of the Division of Motor Transport was John L. Rogers, Eastman's fellow commissioner, who had been working in that field ever since the passage of the Motor Carrier Act. He found himself with authority over 28,000,000 passenger cars and 5,000,000 trucks, not to mention several thousand busses. As time passed Rogers was assigned broader duties, and Harold C. Arnot was appointed Roger's chief assistant in charge of motor transport. Eastman, who had been regarded as primarily a railroad specialist and therefore was somewhat suspected by the vast trucking industry, was under the necessity of conciliating its leaders. Within a short period the building of passenger automobiles ceased, and the plants were retooled and used for the construction of military trucks and tanks. Soon the rubber shortage became critical, and it was essential that trucks and tires be watched so as to get the greatest possible mileage with the least possible use. Addressing the American Trucking Association on May 19, 1942, in Chicago, Eastman reminded his audience that "our trucks, busses, and private automobiles, with the tires that are on hand, constitute the most precious stockpile our country possesses, and one that must be protected and preserved at all costs." Most American crude rubber came from sources controlled in 1942 by the Japanese, and the large stock on hand was required for the strictly military needs of the Government, very little, if any, being available for trucks and busses and none for private automobiles. Under the circumstances, Eastman insisted that "truck operators must care for their trucks and their tires as they had never cared for them before." He rather proudly kept on his desk for exhibition a photograph of a tank truck in the Pacific Northwest which had operated 1,223,000 miles. Even the tires had a record of nearly a million miles. They had been recapped or otherwise repaired from time to time, but otherwise they were the same old tires. "See what *can* be done," commented Eastman, as he showed the picture to men in the business.

Eastman never ceased making new plans for the most effective use of motor trucks. A problem nearly as urgent was that of storage —an intrinsically unromantic and little-publicized subject, but one which became increasingly important as our production expanded under the stimulus of the national danger. One of the specified duties of the ODT was "to survey and ascertain present and anticipated storage and warehousing requirements at points of transfer and in terminal areas; and encourage the provision of increased storage, loading, and unloading facilities when necessary." In World War I the Service of Supply had learned that freight cars were designed for movement, not for storage, and that huge stock-pile warehouses must be located at carefully selected points in the interior of the country. Arrangements were shortly made by the Director with the Lend-Lease Administration for the renting of available space, and information was accumulated regarding storage facilities of all kinds throughout the nation, including dry, refrigerator, freezer, liquid, and grain storage. Attempts were made to relieve ports of what was delightfully called "frustrated freight," destined originally for countries which were occupied by the enemy before the movement could be completed. Wars are won by the careful articulation of all varieties of minor activities, each of which is indispensable to the functioning of the fighting machine; if any link in the long chain is weakened or twisted, individual soldiers suffer. Those who have seen Quartermaster depots, with their amazing array of supplies, realize how much material must be accumulated and properly distributed before a division can be put into the field.

This tricky business of storage was assigned by Eastman to Colonel Leo M. Nicholson, of Chicago, who had been trained in World War I under Generals Goethals and Wood. In winning the confidence of the key men he had to display both intelligence and salesmanship, and following the example of his superior he enlisted the services of nineteen consultants from among warehousemen and others experienced in that line. Eventually Federal Emergency Warehouse Associations were formed in thirty-five transport cities, controlling 289 warehouses with 41,000,000 square feet of dry storage space. In February, 1944, addressing the Second Wartime Warehousing Industry Conference, in Chicago, Eastman told the stirring tale of what had been accomplished through farsighted planning combined with sudden improvisation. At the close he referred briefly to some of the many difficulties which he had to face.

No industry can expect to maintain its working force without the utmost degree of resourcefulness and the employment of many men and women who are green and inexperienced and not at all the kind of material that it would like to have. But that is nothing more than those of us who remain in safety at home must expect to do to sustain those who risk their lives on the fighting fronts, and we ought to be happy to be able to do it.

In the job which Eastman had undertaken it was of supreme importance that his associates, the men on whom he depended, should be loyal and efficient. The head of the Division of Traffic Movement was his reliable assistant as Federal Coordinator, John Turney, a sturdy, unconventional personality on whom he relied implicitly. With him in the same division was Henry McCarthy, a young Harvard graduate from St. Louis, familiar with railroad problems. Each morning Turney and McCarthy called for Joe at his house on Cathedral Avenue and motored him to his office, doing a good deal of affable "kidding" as they drove along.

In charge of the Division of Transport Personnel, Eastman placed Otto S. Beyer, who had recently become chairman of the Labor Mediation Board and was shortly to be named as the representative of labor on the War Man Power Commission. As head of the Division of Materials and Equipment, he selected a retired Brigadier-General, Charles D. Young, vice-president of the Pennsylvania Railroad, a tall man with military bearing, two or three years older than his chief. Young was of much assistance to Eastman in setting up the machinery for the Office of Defense Transportation and later, after Eastman's death, he served for a time as acting director. The Division of Local Transport was set up by Guy A. Richardson, of Chicago, who surrounded himself with a body of experts on local transport problems, using them as a flying squad who could be despatched to the centers where their advice and authority were needed.

Very close to Joe during this period of almost overwhelming responsibility was his Amherst classmate, Fayette B. Dow, who had been serving as Consultant for Pipe Lines in the Transportation Division of the Council of National Defense in 1940–41 and was quickly approached by Eastman and named in 1942 as director of the Liquid Transport Department. The two men, as we have seen, had taken vacations together for many years and understood one another's mental processes. It was not merely that Dow was a specialist in oil and therefore very useful when advice was needed in that field; he was also a friend close at hand who had no ulterior motives and could be implicitly trusted. On December 19, 1942, Joe wrote Ernest Whitcomb: "Cap Dow is carrying a heavy load for me, and I am afraid he is beginning to feel it. We neither of us are young, you know. However, I'm holding up better than I expected, and I am not really worrying about Cap."

Not expecting praise from others for accomplishments in the line of duty, Eastman was sparing in his commendation of his staff, and some of them felt that their work was not sufficiently recognized. Once as Turney and McCarthy were driving him into the city, Eastman said, "Henry, you are doing an excellent job." Turney looked at his chief in surprise and remarked: "You know, that's the first time I ever heard you praise anybody." On the other hand, no one could have been quicker to defend his associates against unjust condemnation, and when they were attacked—as sometimes happened—he rushed to their rescue. In the autumn of 1942 Senator Clyde M. Reed, of Kansas, wrote a vitriolic letter questioning the competence and honesty of three of Eastman's subordinates. Joe retaliated with a strong denial of the accusations, ending his letter with this statement: "So far as an investigation by the Senate Committee is concerned, I have never in my life sought to dodge or to discourage such an investigation, and of course I am ready to testify at any time. . . . I should prefer to be heard first in any investigation, because I take full responsibility for what my men have done."

Although some inevitable clashes of opinion and of personalities developed in the organization, it functioned with an ease and effectiveness which soon silenced Eastman's critics. He was himself especially valuable as a conceptual thinker who planted ideas in the minds of those around him. He was a good salesman of his own views and managed to get them adopted without resorting to autocratic methods. He set an inspiring example by working fifteen hours a day, carrying his ever-increasing burden without showing any signs of physical or mental weakness. His staff meetings at first included only major department heads, but before long these were changed to dinners at the Cosmos Club, with more than a hundred present. Whatever the staff members thought of one another, they were loyal to their chief and responsive to his wishes. Keen observers maintained publicly and privately that few government agencies measured, with a minimum of friction, more fully up to the demands made upon them.

Eastman had a peculiar ability to detach himself and his personal bias from his reasoned analyses of people. Although he had dozens of friends who wanted to work with him, he did not invite them to be his administrative associates without considering their effectiveness as well as their charm. Fond as he had been of Fayette B. Dow, he would never have picked him for his staff if he had not assured himself that Dow was not only devoted to him but also the ablest man in his field. Eastman made some mistakes, but he could be completely judicial in appraising candidates for positions under him.

Eastman's self-effacement did not keep him from occasionally revealing pride in the organization which he had built up. On June 9, 1942, speaking to the Cleveland Chamber of Commerce, he said:

My office has in operation a system, dependent upon the use of the most modern teletype and business machinery, which enables us to keep currently informed of the exact traffic situation on every line and every section of railroad in this country and at every important terminal, with especially detailed information in regard to the situation at the ports; and it has men who can follow up and take steps to relieve any impending danger before it becomes acute.

The program which he had originally outlined grew more extensive as the months passed. He told the United States Chamber of Commerce, on April 28, 1943, in New York, how "the short supply of facilities, with expansion drastically curbed, had been enabled so far to carry traffic which has risen high above former peaks." He had done it by keeping equipment moving, by heavier loading, by constant and careful repairing, by relocation of equipment, by a readjustment of transportation peaks, by the utilization of all available facilities, and by the elimination of wasteful service. Outlined in this fashion, the methods of the ODT seem both obvious and simple, but this was far from being the case. The crisis demanded resourcefulness, imagination, complete knowledge of all conceivable situations, prompt decisions, the full exercise of authority when necessary, and constant vigilance. As the results began to show, Eastman himself reported: "The performance has not been perfect, but I think it is an understatement to say it has been creditable."

Like every official in a key position, Eastman was frequently summoned as a witness before Congressional committees and questioned rather sharply. On April 23, 1942, he was asked to appear before the Special Senate Committee—the so-called "Truman Committee"—and was so much disturbed that he asked some of the experts in the Office of Defense Transportation to accompany him, sit by his side, and come to his aid if he needed help. Among those present were Senators Truman, Mead, Herring, Brewster, Burton, and Bell. Following Admiral Emery S. Land, Eastman gave a review of domestic transportation problems. Taking out a small piece of paper on which he had scribbled a few notes, he began an explanation of what his organization was trying to do; he talked for two hours without cessation and with only a few interruptions. Senator Burton at one point asked: "Do you feel that we will be able to meet the emergency of transportation in this war without taking over the governmental operation of our transportation system?" To this Eastman replied: "I hope very much that that will be possible, and I see nothing ahead which would lead me to believe that it will be necessary." When he had finished, something unprecedented happened. Not only the members of the Senate committee but also about fifty citizens who had come in to hear the testimony crowded around to congratulate him, until he was so completely encircled that the photographers were in despair. It was a spontaneous tribute not only to his lucid presentation of a very complicated subject but also to his personal prestige.

When the railroad executives saw that Eastman did not propose to have the government take over their lines, they rallied round him and sang his praises. Furthermore, they developed a gratifying willingness to conform to his suggestions. The harmony which resulted actually contributed much to the ultimate victory. Typical of the operators' reaction was a letter which Eastman received in June, 1942, from Martin Clement, president of the Pennsylvania.

These are days when so much sniping is going on at personalities that I am sure you will not mind a word of admiration for the splendid job you are doing.

If you were not going in the right direction, I would not hesitate to tell you my opinion; consequently I think I ought to tell you when I think you are going in the right direction.

As I review your performance since you have been Director of the Office of Defense Transportation, I feel that you have been doing a most constructive job to the end that the country's transportation necessities shall be met.

Therefore I sincerely hope that none of the carping criticism from publicity and other sources that are not interested in getting the job done bothers you too much. Please don't let it.

Nevertheless, there were moments in the first months of the war when Joe felt discouraged because of the tardy progress which was being made. By the spring of 1942 it was evident that the nation's internal supply lines were showing signs of strain. The War Production Board had to choose between allotting steel for guns, ships, and other war materials and allotting it for freight cars. For example, the railroads estimated that they would require 122,000 new freight cars for 1942, but the prospect in May was that they would get fewer than 60,000. Eastman appealed in March to the WPB to increase the 18,000 limit on the number of new freight cars allowed to be built in the remaining nine months of 1942. He knew better than most people the seriousness of the crisis. More and more traffic was being forced from coastal vessels to the railroads because of the enemy submarines in the waters along the Atlantic seaboard. Requests were tremendously increased for cars to carry raw materials to arms plants, to bring finished weapons to the camps, and to transport troops. Betwen December 7, 1941, and March 15, 1942, the railroads handled troop movements involving almost two million men without interfering detrimentally with civilian activities. The *United States News*, in its issue for May 1, 1942, expressed a general opinion when it said: "Mr. Eastman's office has a tremendous job on its hands if it is to keep transportation from becoming a serious bottleneck to successful prosecution of the war." The whole enterprise was, of course, a careful balance of needs, and Eastman never failed to do his best for his department.

Naturally, Eastman was expected to be the publicity agent for his organization, and he assumed the responsibility for telling the public and the various traffic agencies what was expected of them. He declined to employ "ghost-writers," preferring to compose his own speeches; and his distinctive style, clear, colloquial, and direct, is easily recognizable. The volume entitled *Selected Papers and Addresses of Joseph B. Eastman, 1942–44*, edited in 1948 by Professor G. Lloyd Wilson, of the University of Pennsylvania, includes fifty-one speeches delivered before all sorts of gatherings while he was Director of Defense Transportation; and numerous others were not included because they were inaccurately reported or were mere repetitions or were not regarded by him as important. Naturally he repeated himself and used the same basic material many times. But even under the excitement of war, Eastman simply could not overstress or exaggerate. He talked as he always had done, deliberately, with the Yankee drawl in his voice and an occasional touch of humor as he recalled a funny incident. Although he seldom had the leisure to polish the phraseology of his formal addresses, he was so full of his subject and had discussed it so often that he found no difficulty in saying what he meant. His audiences felt that they were listening to a plain blunt man, talking extemporaneously and from the heart.

On January 27, 1942, he was speaking to the National Council of Motor Truck Owners, in Washington, on "What ODT Is and Is Not." His final address of this nature was delivered on February 14, 1944, in Chicago, on the topic, "Storage,—Partner of Transportation," before the Second Warehousing Industry Conference. During the intervening months he was flying here and there about the country, urging American citizens to "Keep 'Em Rolling!" He spoke to encourage, to warn, to placate, and, if necessary, to threaten, but always with even temper and disarming frankness. Of course he made enemies, but they were those whom he was proud to make.

He complained mildly that he seemed to be always on a platform. But much of his best work was unpublished, even unrecognized, as is that of the unseen genius who pulls the puppet strings while the tiny figures strut about on a miniature stage. He adjusted conflicting needs, scribbled a few lines of commendation where he thought they might do good, and was sparing but scathing in admonition. Often he became disheartened, but his optimistic temperament carried him through many a Valley of Tribulation. At one decisive moment in the spring of 1943, when troop movements were at their height, he published an article in *The Rotarian* headed, "Don't Travel Now!" In it he said that there were two ways of curing the current situation: one was a rigid system of travel controls; the other was voluntary renunciation of travel on the part of the public. He requested everybody to keep his automobile in repair and to use it only when absolutely necessary. Then he made six specific suggestions, urging people to take their vacations at home, to avoid overnight trips, to carry as little baggage as possible, to plan their vacations for winter instead of July and August, and to take all their vacation at one time. He ended with the words: "Let's pull together,—hard! Let's not travel now!"

He appealed especially to American citizens to postpone conventions and urged schools and colleges to reduce travel by eliminating their usual spring vacations. But he never resorted to absolute prohibition. In the early winter of 1943 he specifically requested educational institutions to abandon their customary Easter recess. Some of the headmasters involved refused to comply with the appeal, on the ground that it would seriously disrupt their programs. When he learned that these schools declined to help except under a direct order, Joe said sadly: "My God, I just can't force them. But if they only knew what is going on at the front, they might be more cooperative." He had to deal constantly with selfishness, inertia, and ignorance, but he never swerved from his initial purpose —to keep troops and materials moving at any sacrifice.

Every possible device was utilized for informing American citizens of their duty. The director induced the American Trucking Association, in July, 1943, to reprint a statement which he had made as a little booklet entitled "Trucks Must Roll to Victory." The central theme, in Eastman's own words, was as follows: "Any general breakdown in motor transportation, or even a breakdown in one or more areas, would have consequences, in its impact upon our transportation service, so serious that they would react gravely upon our whole war effort."

This was widely distributed and quoted in editorials by many newspapers.

From time to time, as the situation presented new aspects, Eastman took the public into his confidence, so to speak, so that their ardor would not wane. On June 22, 1942, he told the Advertising Federation of America:

It is a commonplace that the wars of to-day are wars, not only of armies and navies, but of entire populations and the sum totals of national resources. The one thing that ties all these multitudinous activities together is transportation. We cannot fight without it, and we cannot fight our

best unless transportation is on the job and functioning somewhere near
100 per cent every minute.

Then he continued, with justifiable satisfaction: "I can say without boasting that our domestic transportation has come reasonably
close to such a performance ever since the beginning of the emergency in 1939." Some brief quotations from his speeches will indicate the course of his thought. On October 5, 1942, when our resources were feeling the strain more acutely than in the spring, he
warned that "the country has not yet reached the peak of wartime
production or the peak of traffic movement." On the following
day, before the Traffic Club of New York, he outlined the four
great dangers which faced transportation: the increase in the volume
of traffic; the rubber shortage; the limited supply of other critical
materials; and the limitations of man power. On November 10, in
a widely quoted address before the Academy of Political Science
in New York City, he lauded the existing cooperative arrangement
between the Federal Government and the carriers, emphasizing
particularly the fact that people were beginning to realize that the
war could not be won without an "all-out effort." Later in the
month, before the National Industrial Conference Board, also in
New York City, he quoted some significant figures: "In 1941, the
railroads set a new all-time record of ton-miles of revenue freight
carrier. This year they are surpassing that record by nearly 30 per
cent, and they are doing this with about 30 per cent less freight
cars than they had in 1929, with considerably less locomotives, and
with less aggregate tractive power."

On October 6, 1943, before the New England Shippers' Advisory Board, in Boston, he declared that the performance of the
carriers, under very difficult conditions, had been superlative, but
also added that the next six months would be the critical period
for domestic transportation. A week later, in St. Louis, he mentioned some of the alarming conditions ahead—the coming winter
season, the manpower shortage, the special shortages which threatened gasoline transportation, the increasing pressure on the western
railroads, the growth of traffic in farm products and foods, and the
certainty that the passenger traffic demand would continue to exceed the capacity to transport. So he continued ceaselessly to explain

and to exhort. Even in the last major speech before his death, in February, 1944, he prophesied: "I hope I am wrong, but I greatly fear that there is a long, hard road ahead of us to travel before we reach the end of this war." Fortunately the victory was to come sooner than he had thought it would.

It cannot be denied that some of Eastman's most painful experiences were with organized labor. He had early been a strong supporter of unions and had been happy over the higher wages and improved working conditions which they had brought their members. As Federal Coordinator, however, he had seen them in another aspect, and his enthusiasm for them somewhat cooled. Some prominent labor leaders tried secretly to block his appointment as director in 1941, but desisted when they learned that the alternative was Ralph Budd. On December 24, 1941, within a few days after he took charge of the ODT, he was disturbed by a quite unnecessary strike of employees of the Greyhound Bus Lines and immediately sent off a telegram to William D. Mahon, president of the Amalgamated Association of Street Railway and Motor Coach Employees of America, as follows:

The national emergency can tolerate no interference with or stoppage of our transportation facilities. I call on each of you to end present strike on Greyhound Lines and adjust your differences by mutual agreement or arbitration. Please wire if you will agree for men to return to work immediately and submit all disputes for arbitration.

Eastman's position on the general problem had been expressed clearly in a letter to Wilbur LaRoe, dated June 5, 1940, in which he said: "I do not rate myself as 'anti-labor' at all, but I do think that labor needs some good advice now and then from men in public office, which it seldom gets." Such sound advice he administered more than once as persistent strikes weakened the national war effort. On March 5, 1943, at a meeting in Philadelphia, he spoke out courageously on a subject which was troubling all loyal Americans.

I fear that labor unions are in some danger. They are new to power. Here and there it has gone to their heads somewhat, and in some cases they have allowed abuses to creep in. They are for liberty and democracy, they are against tyranny and despotism, but have they always carried these precepts into practice in their own affairs? The pendulum always swings from one extreme to the other. There is danger of a public reaction against labor unions, and already I see signs that it is setting in. If their houses are not in order, I suggest that they clean these houses themselves.

There is no better breeding time for such reaction than wartime. Practices which the public will overlook in normal times, they will not overlook in days of war. They will resent it bitterly, if they come to the opinion that the unions are placing their own special welfare ahead of their country's welfare. In times of widespread unemployment, they will tolerate make-work devices, absenteeism, and the cutting of hours to the bone. But they will not excuse these things in days of manpower shortage when the country is in dire need of the greatest possible production. Nor will they fail to resent strikes at such a time when the Government has set up all manner of machinery for the fair settlement of labor disputes, nor demands for extra-ordinary wages at a time when inflation is one of the greatest dangers and the boys in the Army and Navy are risking their lives for a pittance.

In the critical autumn of 1943 "feather-bedding" by railroad unions seemed to Eastman so much of a menace that he insisted on the abandonment of various "make-work" practices which were responsible for what he called "an inexcusable wastage of railway manpower." He added his belief "that substantial numbers of train and engine service men are not yet working the number of hours which can reasonably be considered to be full time under present conditions." As a direct response to these charges, the railroads and the shippers agreed to undertake an intensive campaign to raise operating efficiency, if possible, by as much as 10 percent. On October 28, 1943, in a statement before the Special Emergency Board, National Mediation Panel, he urged a quick settlement of a current wage controversy, pointing out that the failure to reach an adjustment was causing "disturbance of the morale of the railroad employees."

It has often been alleged that Eastman became more conservative as he grew older and that he showed himself more sympathetic with railroad management. Undoubtedly bitter experiences did bring about changes in his attitude. On January 21, 1944, he told the American Economic Association and the American Political

JOSEPH B. EASTMAN, AS DIRECTOR OF WAR TRANSPORTATION
RIDING IN HORSE DRAWN BUGGY IN 1943

EASTMAN ON HIS LAST FISHING TRIP

Science Association, in Washington, that the consistently better record of the railroads in World War II over that in World War I was due "to the circumstance that management and operation had been left in private hands." But the decision against government operation, as far as he was concerned, was one of expediency. In commenting on his own views, he said:

This does not mean that I am a dogmatic opponent of public operation of railroads or other public utilities. There are conditions where such operation is wise, and even where it may be the only recourse, as many countries have found, and as we found in the last World War. The choice is one which should be made after a cold-blooded appraisal of conditions, as free as possible from prejudice one way or another.

When asked whether he had moved to the right in his economic philosophy, Eastman always maintained that conditions, not he, had altered. When the railroad operators were behaving without regard to the public interest, he opposed them. When the employees took the same selfish stand, he became critical of them also. As Director of Defense Transportation he was shocked to discover that even labor unions had, as he wrote in a private letter in 1943, "their racketeers, their would-be Hitlers, and their tricksters." He felt, in a sense, as if his trust had been betrayed. Toward the end of his career the name of John L. Lewis was sure to evoke from him a brand of profanity which was expressive of tumultuous feelings.

The chief trouble in the autumn of 1943 arose from the so-called "nonops"—the nonoperating employees. A fact-finding board selected under the provisions of the Railway Labor Act had recommended a raise of 8 cents an hour, with time and one-half pay for all hours of work over forty a week. Unfortunately this decision— which had seemed to Eastman very fair—was held up by the Office of Economic Stabilization, with disastrous results to working morale. Eastman at that time wrote to James F. Byrnes, Director of the Office of War Mobilization, offering himself as a "burnt sacrifice." "The President," he said, "could, if he so desired, ask me to sit down with the parties and see whether I could bring them into agreement." If Eastman had been so requested, he would have approved the original conclusions of the fact-finding board. But the President did not want him in that capacity. Speaking on the subject before the National Association of Manufacturers, East-man remarked: "The railroads are now faced by a wage crisis. I shall be bitterly disappointed if the employees, because of any such controversy, cripple their country in time of war by stopping rail-road transportation. I hold them in such high esteem that I will not believe they can do that."

In some moods and in certain phases of the war, the Director felt it essential to give everybody a pat on the back. In one of his last public utterances he bestowed credit in all directions.

The private managers have been put on their mettle, not only to do their part in the war effort, but also to show that private enterprise is capable of rising fully to the needs of a grave emergency, and they have responded wonderfully well. A similar spirit has imbued the shippers of the country, and their cooperation has been of a value which it is difficult to over-estimate. The same has been true, except for the wage controversies, of the employees, and to a very considerable extent it has been true of the general public.

This was a tactful, although perhaps a little too-cheerful estimate of the contributions made by the various elements of our economy to the war effort. Eastman was gratified by the unexpectedly friendly attitude of the operators; he was equally disappointed at times by the uncooperative resistance of some of the railroad unions. But he never lost hope. He was convinced that "through the close contacts of present war experience, government, business, and labor leaders have learned more about and from each other than they ever knew before." In amplifying this idea he said:

One thing that these leaders must surely have learned is the great degree of similarity in broad groups of men, of the varying motives, intelligence, and emotions which control human action. Another is that the best men in these groups must find a way of working together for the common good, if we are to make real progress in solving our problem. It is far more sensible for all of the sheep to work together against all of the goats than for the composite groups of sheep and goats to war against each other.

Eastman's problems as Director were very different from those which he had encountered as Federal Coordinator. There was now

little time for research. The emphasis was on action. In comparing
the situation he wrote in 1942:

In 1933, the railroads had a great surplus of facilities, a minimum of
traffic, and were drifting into bankruptcy one by one. The problem
was to find ways of saving expense and also of attracting traffic. My
recommendations, which met with very little success, were directed
towards those ends. At present the railroads have no surplus facilities, at
least of equipment; their traffic has risen to record heights and is steadily
increasing; and the problem is to move it promptly and effectively, regardless of cost.

Proceeding on this theory, Eastman undertook without delay to
persuade the shippers to load and unload with the greatest possible
speed so that freight cars could circulate freely. His General Order
Number 1, aimed to increase the loading of railroad less-than-
carload freight from an average of about 4½ tons per car to about
12 tons. His General Order Number 18 required the loading of
all cars to capacity and eliminated what is called "cross-hauling"
or other excessive hauling of commodities. Speaking on November
19, 1942, before the National Industrial Traffic League, Eastman
declared himself disappointed with the attitude of the industries.
He did not wish to issue drastic transportation orders, but he declared that if his office could not secure the help and advice of the
industries, it would have to try to get along without their assistance.
By this date Eastman's manner, while never truculent or offensive,
had become so firm that the shippers knew he meant business. Fortunately the situation improved markedly, and without any intervention from him, within a few months.

Widespread complaint greeted his General Order Number 21,
which caused Eastman more distress than any other directive which
he issued. On September 19, 1942, in a radio address, he announced
that after November 15 no truck or bus or other commercial vehicle
could be operated without a Certificate of War Necessity. Gasoline
rationing was to go into effect throughout the nation on November
22. Meanwhile it was essential to determine for each commercial
operator how much fuel he should be allowed so that the way could
be paved for a reduction in the aggregate mileage of commercial

vehicles of 40 percent as compared with 1941. Said the Director: "It was not a theory but a condition which made General Order Number 21, necessary. It has only one objective, and that is to keep all the trucks rolling by the elimination of all waste in operation." Soon 142 separate field offices were set up, and Eastman's organization had more employees working on this order than on all other phases of its program put together. Thus, reluctantly Eastman was forced into something resembling regimentation. "The sooner we can get rid of it we shall all be pleased," he said, "and no one will be more pleased than I."

In the numerous speches and public appeals made by the Director to his countrymen in a time of doubt and apprehension it was natural that he should deal largely with facts and should resort to repetition. He knew that certain ideas had to be reiterated if they were to make an impression. On special occasions, however, and under the stress of emotion he rose to spiritual heights. On July 14, 1942, in Cincinnati, before the Transportation Department of the Y.M.C.A., he devoted himself to national morale, addressing himself particularly to the traveling public and calling upon Mr. Average Citizen to sacrifice many luxuries, and even comforts, which he had normally been able to enjoy. He ended with an eloquence unusual for him:

One further comment on the public frame of mind. Everyone is familiar with the teachings of the "Sermon on the Mount." They breathe a wonderful idealism which I have never been sure is practical in this erring world of ours, and certainly it has never been put into practice in any appreciable degree. Not for a moment would I now urge that it be tried out on the battle front, but I do believe that we could try a slight modicum with advantage on the "home front." It is a time for the utmost solidarity and for the submergence of peacetime quarrels. It is no time for the pressing of contentious and self-seeking claims, and I do not believe that the great majority of people want them to be pressed. Some of our politicians, labor leaders, farm spokesmen, and other purported representatives of special groups are likely to find this out in due course. They would be wiser to realize it now.

The war went on. Throughout the first half of 1942 came disaster after disaster, while the United States bent all its resources toward the herculean task of preparation. Then in the autumn came the swing in what Mr. Churchill has called the Hinge of Fate. In late October arrived the news of the victory at El Alamein. In early November followed Operation "Torch," the landing in North Africa, which began as Leon Fraser said, "over the American railroads." Eastman's labors to keep traffic and men moving were beginning to fructify as American soldiers and sailors fought in strange foreign places around the globe. On December 2 the Director of Defense Transportation spoke in Los Angeles, before the California Chamber of Commerce. Once again he attempted to explain why controls of some sort were necessary.

There seems to be some feeling throughout the country that Washington is full of overzealous bureaucrats who delight in the exercise of their authority, are devotees of regimentation, and are keen to place the populace in the bondage of various and sundry regulations, regardless of whether there is any need therefore. I shudder to be placed in such a class, because it runs counter to my lifelong tendencies, hopes, and beliefs. Nor do I think that my fellow officials can fairly be so regarded and I am a rather impartial witness, because I am a member of no political party and I have been appointed to office by presidents of both the leading parties. Of course we all make mistakes. That is always so, and it would be a miracle if it did not happen more often than normally in a time when new problems are arising on all sides, quick decisions are necessary, and new administrative organizations must be created over night.

But bear in mind that we are in war and a terrible war. Several millions of our young men cannot be taken out of production and devoted to fighting, and our productive capacity cannot be used, to the extent that it is being used, wholly for purposes of warfare, without severe dislocations in our life and economy which create the need for extraordinary precautionary measures and restrictions. . . . I hope the people of the country will be forbearing and keep these things in mind. May we all, without bickering or scolding, pull together and with our last ounce of strength in the common cause of victory.

Eastman was called "The Nation's Backseat Driver," because he seemed to be watching by proxy every mile covered by a private automobile or truck. Throughout 1943, as American forces fought their way through Sicily into Italy and the long-deferred Second

Front was being planned and the conferences were held at Quebec and Teheran, the military situation improved, and the director could actually chart the results of his unceasing labors. His own share in it, although he did not know it, was almost over. There had been disappointments, of course, but on January 21, 1944, before a brilliant audience in Washington, he allowed himself modestly to comment on some of the achievements. He confessed that the efforts of the Office of Defense Transportation had met "with whole-hearted cooperation and, to date, with a high degree of success, all things considered." As compared with record of public operation in 1917–18, the earnings of the railroads had been "extraordinarily good." Railroad rates had been increased in 1942— 6 percent or less in the case of freight and 10 percent in the case of passengers, to compensate for an increase in wages in 1941; but in 1943 the freight increases had been removed. The greatest contributing factor to this excellent performance, he continued, was "the circumstance that management and operation have been left in private hands."

Toward the end of this impressive speech, which, coming almost at the close of his life, seemed to sound "the trumpet of a prophecy," Eastman ventured a glimpse into the future.

The role of the Government, while it will shrink after the war is over, will continue, I believe, to be considerably greater than it was before the war, and problems of tremendous scope and difficulty will be involved. The Government will, of course, deal imperfectly with these problems, for everything human is imperfect, but I sometimes fear that it will not deal with them well. No doubt that is merely the pessimism of age. For what it may be worth, however, my judgment is that to deal with them well, we must have a better-informed and disciplined citizenry and public officials with a higher average of sound and strong character. Even when their aims are good, they must show less inclination to regard the end as justification for the means and more readiness to endanger their personal careers in the defense of principles. They must not regard Gallup polls and like tests of public opinion of the moment as controlling guides, for often these only prove the need for more general enlightenment. It may be that what we need most is a renaissance of religion in some form. Certainly we all stand in great need of prayer, not only while this war endures but thereafter.

More than most bureau heads in the capital, Eastman kept almost exclusively to his special job; indeed, it might almost be said that he thought of nothing else. He was invited to several White House conferences, but seldom to those which discussed broad war strategy, and he knew only those military secrets which concerned the ODT. His acquaintance with such master minds as Stimson and Marshall and Harry Hopkins was only slight. Nevertheless, he felt that the contribution made by his staff was important—and it was. Those who conceived the plans for the major war movements never doubted that he could be relied upon to ensure that transportation would not fail; and because of his arrangements, regiments moved safely from camp to port of embarkation, destined for strange places like Iceland or Tunis or Guadalcanal. To this one task he devoted himself with single aim and unsparing energy. The Secretary of War once remarked: "Eastman is one of the most completely reliable men in Washington." Once during the winter of 1942 a friend with whom I was walking in the late evening along the Mall looked up and, pointing to the lights still burning on the fifth floor of the Interstate Commerce Building, said, "There's Old Joe Eastman, slogging away! He never knows what it is to rest."

So much absorbed was Eastman in his duties as Director that he had no leisure to worry over his reappointment. He was sure that he could not live out another seven years. Furthermore he remembered very well the embarrassing delay in 1937. But this time it was different. As early as October 18, 1943, Mr. Roosevelt wrote him: "It goes without saying that whether you like it or not you will be reappointed when your term expires." To this cordial assurance Eastman replied: "On February 19, 1944, I will have served 25 years. Sometimes I wonder whether I ought not to turn my hand to something else and let new blood take my place. However, I know of no one whom I would rather serve than Uncle Sam, and certainly I am very grateful to you for the indication of confidence in my service which you gave in your letter."

On December 2, 1943, the President, carrying out his promise, nominated both Eastman and Rogers to succeed themselves on the commission. Confirmation was not as prompt as in the past, for Senator Wheeler's committee summoned both nominees to appear before it, and Eastman was rather sharply questioned about one of his associates who at the moment was not popular. Eastman defended this particular department head, and indeed all of his staff, with much vigor, but the affair was not pleasant. After it was over Eastman remarked to Mrs. Buchanan: "That hearing took a lot out of me"; and at least one of his friends believes that the incident actually shortened his life. However, Eastman and Rogers were both confirmed on the Senate floor without debate on January 24, 1944.

By this date the results of Eastman's careful planning and thoroughness were apparent. The organization was complete, the machinery was in motion, and the appeals of the Director had won the support of the public. On August 23, 1942, when he was less sure of his ground, he had written Whitcomb:

So far I have been fairly lucky in my work and have had a pretty good public reception. But I don't kid myself. A wartime job is a perilous one, and I expect to be thrown out on my ear before I get through. It won't be, however, because I haven't done my damndest, so my conscience will be clear. The fact is that I fear this is going to be a long war, and this country will feel it much more severely than it does before we get through. The people in general don't yet realize what war is or may be.

When 1944 opened, however, most Americans were fully aware of what war means and were in a confident mood. The Russians had turned back the German hordes. The Japanese were retreating slowly from island to island. Production in the United States had broken every record in history. With our bombers turning German cities into rubble, it seemed clear that victory was just a matter of months. Meanwhile the Office of Defense Transportation was functioning with less and less friction. Eastman could be proud of the part which it and he had played in making America strong.

XV

The End of the Road

ALTHOUGH he often overtaxed his strength, Eastman's health had been reasonably good for many years, and he had tried to maintain his physical fitness by frequent exercise, short afternoon naps, and regular habits. In the autumn of 1940, however, he had a severe attack of jaundice and after his convalescence discovered that he was having difficulty with his breathing. For the first time in his life he consulted a specialist, who reported that he had a rather serious heart ailment, accompanied by high blood pressure, and advised him to slow down his activities, get more rest and sleep, and avoid worry. This was not an easy prescription for a man as active as Joe to follow; but he did rather regretfully abandon his squash games. It was suggested that he might spend his evenings at home instead of in his office, but this he was never able to do. The doctor prescribed the customary nitroglycerine pills, which he swallowed when he suffered from the oppressive symptoms of angina pectoris. He still occasionally walked the three miles from Cathedral Avenue to Twelfth Street, but his companions noticed that he often paused to catch his breath and that sometimes he would surreptitiously gulp a pill to secure relief.

Thus, when he accepted the post of Director of Defense Transportation, Joe was well aware of his disabilities, but he never thought of using them as an excuse for refusing to serve. Naturally the demands of the position were great and could not be escaped even by a less conscientious patriot than Eastman. The mere preliminary business of creating an organization would have been tough for a young and healthy man—and he was unfortunately neither young nor healthy. He took the wise step of visiting his physician each month for a routine check-up. He even stole a few days off during the summer to seek refuge and relief in the deep woods. As late as September, 1943, he took "Cap" Dow with him to the St. Maurice Fish and Game Club, near LaTuque, in Canada, for one precious week. The weather was cold, but he landed one two-pound "square tail" and came back refreshed.

But somehow the moment for carefree relaxation never seemed to arrive. More and more demands were made upon him for speeches, and his engagement calendar was filled with names and places. His friends noticed that, although he rarely complained, he was less resilient than he had been. In his correspondence he often reverted to the past. He wrote "Freddy" Bale of his "happy recollections of Christmas Eve bridge games with old Frank Riley and Frank Livingstone and you, on Beacon Hill." He sent to the Gamma Chapter of Psi Upsilon, at their request, one of his photographs, saying that some of his pleasantest memories centered around the old red chapter house facing on the Amherst Common. He tried to go back to the meetings of the Amherst Trustees whenever possible, largely because they took him for a few hours away from the atmosphere of tension. It was almost at times as if he were in the mood of Marvell's lover, who cried:

> But at my back I always hear
> Time's winged chariot hurrying near;
> And yonder all before us lie
> Deserts of vast eternity.

Death comes to all men, but it was Eastman's good fortune that his life closed at an hour of climax. He had just taken the oath of office as a member of the Interstate Commerce Commission for the fourth full term of seven years. As the quarter century of his service was finishing a group of his friends and admirers made the arrangements for a Silver Anniversary Dinner in his honor. It was planned under the auspices of the District of Columbia Chapter of the Association of Interstate Commerce Practitioners; and because the ODT was discouraging passenger travel a genuine effort was made to confine the guests to a relatively few men in Washington and vicinity. But when the word spread around the demand for seats became almost overwhelming. Eventually more than seven hundred people gathered in the ballroom and two adjacent auditoriums of the Hotel Statler, on the evening of February 17, 1944. The toastmaster was Joseph C. Colquitt, chairman of the local Chapter, and the speakers were all in some way connected with transportation: J. Carter Fort, general counsel of the Association of American Railroads; Senator Burton K. Wheeler and Representative Clarence F. Lea, chairmen of the committees of the Legislative Branch of the Government before whom Eastman had appeared so many times; Clyde B. Aitchison, the only older member of the Interstate Commerce Commission; and Warren H. Wagner, president of the Association of Interstate Commerce Commission Practitioners. Eastman's speech concluding the program was his last and his best.

This Silver Anniversary Dinner, although it had its serious undertone, was enlivened by pleasant reminiscences and amusing stories, with plenty of good-natured "kidding." Mr. Fort's speech was declared by one listener to be the most glowing eulogy he had ever heard on any living public official. He told his audience that he had recently conversed with two gentlemen, neither of whom entirely approved of Eastman. The first one remarked: "I think Mr. Eastman is a very fine man, but in my opinion he is a little to the left." This evoked a snort of derision from the second man, who answered: "Yes, he is a little to the left,—just a little to the left of Mark Hanna!" A broad grin appeared on Joe's face, and shouts of laughter came from a group thoroughly familiar with Eastman's controversial battles with operators and employees. Mr. Fort alluded entertainingly and discriminately to Eastman's outstanding qualities—his superb professional skill, his mastery of the tools of his trade, his vision, his sagacity, his unfaltering courage before "the onslaughts of pressure groups of special interests or of others seeking unfair advantages." Then he concluded:

I like to think too of his sincerity and his integrity, bright and unshadowed through the years. He has never done a shabby thing, he has never thought a shabby thought. He has never sold the truth to serve the hour.

Most of all, I like to think of his kindliness, his warmheartedness, his sympathetic and compassionate understanding of other men and their trials, their triumphs, and their disappointments.

Mr. Eastman is a spiritual leader in the mold of the finest American tradition. His hands are given to unceasing toil, and his eyes are ever turned towards those things high and shining.

It must have given the modest Joe Eastman immense inner satisfaction to hear the sincere praise heaped upon him that evening by people who had known him so well. Senator Wheeler described him as "an ideal public officer"; Congressman Lea emphasized the unity of purpose and morale that Eastman had "instilled into the different and competing transportation agencies of the United States"; Commissioner Aitchison, his associate throughout his entire quarter century, nominated him for the Distinguished Service Medal; and Wagner handed him two years' pay as Director of the Office of Defense Transportation—one bright new silver dollar and one greenback dollar bill. Representing the Association of Interstate Commerce Commissioners, he also presented him with a plaque in recognition of his long and devoted service to the commission.

When Eastman was finally introduced, he was received with an ovation such as even the most sophisticated guests had seldom seen or heard. His sister had wondered whether he could get through such an ordeal of congratulation. He was obviously very much moved and began in a faltering voice; but he soon straightened himself up and replied gracefully and appreciatively to all that had been said about him. He told his audience that once at a meeting of the Senate Committee on Interstate Commerce, Huey Long burst into the room. Senator Wheeler, who was presiding, stopped the proceedings and asked, "Huey, do you know Mr. Eastman?" "Yes," sneered Long, "I have known him just as long as I have known you,—and just as unfavorably!" Joe also recalled that when he was a young man and attended a hearing before the full commission in Washington, he noticed that Commissioner Daniels rose, stood for a minute or two, and then leaned for a short period on the back of his chair. "Is that allowed?" whispered Eastman. "Yes, if the Commissioner wants to do it." "What's the idea?" "Probably because he wishes to keep awake." "That," continued Eastman, "was a little trick that I afterwards employed myself!"

After some other impromptu reminiscences, especially of some of his associates, he proceeded to read what he called "a sort of twelve-point primer," with which he had taken much pains and which, as events turned out, was his formal valedictory, or credo. At the time it made a profound impression, and it has often since been quoted, for it was and is an accurate and complete reflection of the character and mature philosophy of the man. His first point, which he developed most impressively, was that tribunals like the Interstate Commerce Commission must not be "under the domination or influence of either the President or Congress or of anything else than their own independent judgment of the facts and the law." He added: "Political domination will ruin such a tribunal. I have seen this happen many times, particularly in the States." This was his carefully considered and final verdict on the long controversy between himself and President Roosevelt as to the administrative freedom of the commission.

In his second major point, Eastman alluded to another delicate subject by expressing the view that the courts, which had once been "much too prone to substitute their own judgment on the facts for the judgment of administrative tribunals"—as the Supreme Court had done in the O'Fallon Case—were now in danger of going too far in the other direction. He defended the broad thesis that "it is an error of law to render a decision not supported by substantial evidence."

Eastman then dealt, as an "Elder Statesman" had a right to do, with the responsibilities of his own commission as an administrative body. It should be always ready to institute proceedings on its own motion, whenever constructive enforcement of the law demanded it; it should take all the time necessary for "full hearing and argument of the issues"; it should in its decisions state clearly the reasons for its conclusions. The personnel of the commission was to him far more important than the wording of any statute, for "good men can produce better results with a poor law than poor men can produce with a good law." It was not essential, however, for the commissioners to be technical experts. Here he dwelt briefly on the equipment which they should possess.

The important qualifications are ability to grasp and comprehend facts quickly, and to consider them in their relation to the law logically and with an open mind. Zealots, evangelists, and crusaders have their value *before* an administrative body, but not on it. Other important qualifications are patience, courtesy, and a desire to be helpful to the extent that the law permits.

In his eighth point Eastman reverted to one of his favorite themes —the perils involved in an abuse of power and the need of restraint in those who possess it. In words distilling the essence of his long experience, he said:

Power is not a permanent but a shifting thing. I can well remember the time when it was a dangerous thing to incur the displeasure of bankers, but there has been no danger in this since 1932. It became a greater danger to incur the displeasure of army or labor organizations. There is nothing more important than to curb abuse of power, wherever it may reside, and power is always subject to abuse.

Eastman had often felt the displeasure of pressure groups and knew the insidious influence, direct and indirect, that they can exert. This makes the need for moral courage in public officials even more desirable. They must have the strength to resist selfish importunity and the subtle threats which often accompany it.

The members of an administrative tribunal must guard against becoming special pleaders for their respective sections. Furthermore, they must not permit themselves to be corrupted by a little brief authority.

Sitting in dignity and looking down on the suppliants from the elevation of a judicial bench has its dangers. A reversal of the position now and then is good for the soul. It has for many years been my good fortune to appear rather frequently before legislative or Congressional committees. They are a better safeguard against inflation than the O.P.A.

Again speaking out of experience, Eastman urged that full recognition and reward be given to those individual members of the commission staff by whom such a vast amount of routine "spade work" had necessarily to be done.

Finally, Eastman declared, while the importance of sound regulation should not be minimized or neglected, it is tremendously vital to the country that business should be encouraged whenever it shows resourcefulness or initiative in management. This statement recalls a comment made by Eastman in 1937, when it seemed likely that President Roosevelt might not reappoint him. "When the Old Deal was riding high in the 1920's," he said, "I did not approve of that,—and now when its opponents are in the saddle and also riding high, I discover that I do not find that altogether to my liking either." It is significant that in his "twelve-point primer" the man who had so often been denounced as a "radical" should in almost his last public words speak favorably of private enterprise. But Joe had never been a man to take and hold an extreme position. He had learned that no matter how much regulation might be necessary, there is a place for inventiveness, imagination, and even for legitimate competition, which regulation should not suppress and with which it ought not to interfere.

Eastman's former fellow-commissioner Thomas F. Woodlock called this "twelve-point primer" a "Magna Charta of principles governing administrative law":

Coming from a man the greater part of whose life has been spent in administrative office, and who was generally regarded as an outstanding example of the qualities required in such positions, the speech is a veritable landmark in a territory which badly needs a thorough surveying. It is of permanent value and importance,—literally a classic in its field,—and should be so treated.

It was often reprinted, especially in trade journals, and I have seen selections from it framed on the desks of railroad magnates and their junior executives. It seemed to express in small compass and colloquial language what many people were thinking and were glad to have so convenient as a guide and creed.

Having reached this brilliant climax of his prepared address, Eastman threw down his typed pages and said a few extemporaneous words in appreciation of the help which his colleagues had given him. In conclusion he prophesied that the Office of Defense Transportation, as a "war baby," would ultimately pass out of existence and be forgotten.

But the Interstate Commerce Commission, if it abides by its traditions, like Old Man River, will just keep rolling along. It has rolled along for fifty-five years, and I expect to see it go rolling on for a long time in the future. I shall be proud and happy to carry on with it, and I want to thank each and every one of you for what you have done in my case tonight.

Unfortunately he could not carry on with it any longer. As the hundreds of guests passed by to shake his hand and congratulate him, he sometimes felt faint, but he bore up until the last one had departed. Then he went home with his sister to rest.

Joe never again returned to his office in the Interstate Commerce Building. Two days later his exhausted heart gave way, and his physician sent him to the Emergency Hospital in Washington. A thorough examination proved that his condition was critical and that he must have a complete rest for at least two months. He at once notified the President's Secretary, Stephen Early, offering his resignation. On the following morning the President sent him a note by special messenger:

Dear Joe,—

I am so sorry to hear that you are feeling somewhat below par. Your health is of primary concern and must receive every consideration.

Follow strictly the doctor's orders and take that much needed rest. Do not for a moment think of resigning. Get yourself back in good form, for the job needs you and the country needs you.

With every good wish,

Very sincerely yours,
Franklin Delano Roosevelt

While he was lying in his hospital bed on New York Avenue, becoming gradually reconciled to his unaccustomed semi-invalidism, Joe missed a meeting which he had particularly wished to attend —the luncheon of the Associated Traffic Clubs of America, on February 24, in Cleveland. He had promised to be the honor guest for the occasion, and everybody was sorrowful when he had to cancel his acceptance. General Charles D. Young, the deputy director, was present to represent him, but he was sadly missed. An audience of more than eight hundred people, the ablest leaders in the transportation field, applauded tumultuously while speakers from the various carrier groups praised the absent Director. Lachlan Macleay, president of the Mississippi River System Carriers' Asso-

BUST OF JOSEPH B. EASTMAN BY OSCAR MUNDHENK
In the lobby of the Interstate Commerce Committee Building

ciation, after confessing that he had not agreed with Eastman's views regarding the regulation of inland water carriers under the Interstate Commerce Commission, admitted that the Waterway Section of the ODT had done so many things helpful to the waterway services that it would be impossible to recount them all. He ended: "The work of the ODT is a war emergency task. As such, it has been exceptionally well done."

Next John B. Keeler, president of the National Industrial Traffic League, representing the shippers, declared, "ODT has applied controls in a spirit of leadership without the use of arbitrary methods; it has been fundamentally fair and has sought and relied upon and received the cooperation of shippers, receivers, and carriers."

Then Chester G. Moore, chairman of the Central Motor Freight Association, asserted that while Eastman had never lacked the dignity essential in his position, he had not degenerated into a "stuffed shirt." Recently on a visit to Texas, Eastman had burned a hole in his trousers and had to send them out to be mended. While he was waiting in his bedroom clad only in a shirt and shorts, a delegation of truckers was admitted. He talked to them until his trousers arrived and then put on the garment "without dropping a syllable or a comma."

"What I think we all like best about Mr. Eastman," Moore continued, "is his undiminished confidence in voluntary cooperation and his pronounced distaste for a multiplicity of orders and regulations." He then paid him a generous tribute by concluding:

It is hardly necessary to say, although I am sure it is not inappropriate, that not everything Mr. Eastman has done has met with the unqualified approval of our industry. Nor has it always taken the type of action which he had advocated. That, of course, was to be expected, and no doubt has contributed to that aspect of Mr. Eastman's official life which keeps it from becoming monotonous. Whatever his decision in such situations, we have always found it motivated by sincerity and courage.

Finally W. M. Jeffers, president of the Union Pacific Railroad, expressed his opinion that Eastman's success as a public servant was due largely to his humility and simplicity. He always remembered that he was "an employee of the American taxpayer." Summing up the unanimous judgment of the miscellaneous assembly, he said: "Mr. Eastman approaches his problems with an open mind. He thinks a thing through. He still believes in common sense,—and if there is any one thing we need most in this country it is still common sense,—more Main Street thinking."

The projectors of this affair compiled for him a richly bound volume of testimonial letters from several hundred friends—childhood companions, college and fraternity mates, railroad presidents and former office boys, representatives of both operators and labor unions, employees of the Interstate Commerce Commission, people who at various times had been drawn within his range. The list of contributors began with Clyde B. Aitchison, Eastman's oldest colleague on the commission, and closed with Charles D. Young, the deputy director. On the title page, in gold, was the inscription, "A Token of Friendship and Esteem to Joseph B. Eastman." The tributes were naturally of many different kinds and emphasized different matters. One of the best came from John S. Fineil, who wrote:

Perhaps you will not take it amiss if I say that you, more than anyone I know, are best entitled to the claim of having proved the truth of the adage, "He laughs best who laughs last." In twenty-five years I have seen at various times attempts to undermine you by big shippers, by various railroads, and by the powers that be. That all of these now unite, and for a long time have united, in recognizing that your services are indispensable and irreplaceable, and your rendition of them wholly impartial, must constitute not the least of your compensations for the heavy burdens that have been imposed upon you.

With this beautiful volume was sent a large plaque, silver on wood, presented to Eastman "With Sincere Appreciation of Your Outstanding Record of Public Service, Dedicated to Honesty, Efficiency, Faithfulness, and Unselfishness." The book and the plaque, together with a certificate of honorary membership in the Associated Traffic Clubs of America, were brought to him in the hospital and placed by his bedside, where he could contemplate these tangible recognitions of his achievement.

Joe's condition was at once diagnosed as very serious, but he was permitted to read, and he passed the time with his favorite detective and adventure stories. On March 12 he dictated a letter to Ernest Whitcomb describing his condition:

No one, to look at me, would think I was ill, and I feel O.K. It is all due to modern medicine. For two years I have had angina in a mild form. I went to the doctor periodically. This winter the strain has been bad, and since I went to the doctor on February 19, my description of events led him to have a cardiogram taken at once. What it showed convinced him, and the heart specialist, that I had a slight occlusion. My doctor, Matthew Perry, is Hull's doctor and went to Moscow with him. The heart specialist, Leonard, is said to be one of the best. I like them both. A slight occlusion can, they say, easily develop into a bad one. So the modern idea is to put the patient to bed at once and give him complete rest for a month, so that the heart can heal. My progress is good, except for an increase (for the time being) of some digestive trouble. They may keep me in *status quo* for a little longer, but I expect to be up and about before long now, and then I hope I can go to Don Symington's place for a week or so in the country before I go back to work. All along I have felt quite capable of getting up and doing my bit as usual, but the docs are playing safe.

Although at first the physicians did not allow Joe to see visitors, except his sister, he was permitted as he seemed to improve to receive two members of his staff, Fayette B. Dow and Joseph White. They spent fifteen minutes with him, told him the news of the office, and gave him some relief from his hospital routine. To the very end he remained calm and hopeful, reading with keen interest each day the news of the war with the progress of which he had had so much to do. It was not a cheerful period in American affairs. Winston Churchill was recovering from an attack of pneumonia. Madame Chiang Kai-shek had delivered a moving speech before Congress, pleading for the cause of China; and the military leaders had some fear that she might bring about a changed attitude in our basic strategy. American troops had suffered a mauling from the Germans at Faid and Kasserine passes and had been forced to give ground. Anthony Eden had arrived at the White House and on March 14 dined with Roosevelt and Hopkins to discuss the postwar geographical problems of Europe.

On that same day Eastman was making plans for a trip to Puerto

Rico when he became convalescent. He also wrote a short note to W. J. Bailey, of the West Virginia Pulp & Paper Company, thanking him for a thrilling "Whodunit" which he had sent him. The concluding sentence of this letter—the last line he ever composed—was: "I am glad to say that I seem to be making good progress, and from all prognostications I shall be back in circulation again before too long."

Unfortunately Joe was too optimistic. On the following morning, March 15, about six o'clock he awoke feeling very ill and rang for a nurse, who brought him some medication. He seemed to rally, and she left to get some breakfast. When she returned, he was gone. No one was with him when he died.

That afternoon Miss Elizabeth Eastman received a note from Mr. Roosevelt: "May I send you this message in the retirement of your grief to record my own sorrow in the sorrow which has been laid so heavily upon you in the loss of a loved and loving brother. My heart goes out to you in deepest sympathy."

Although Joe had not been the communicant of any religious denomination, the funeral was held from All Souls' Memorial Episcopal Church, on March 17, with a vast throng of friends present to honor his memory. The services were conducted by the Reverend H. H. D. Sterrett. The honorary pallbearers were Chief Justice Harlan F. Stone, Interstate Commerce Commissioners Mahaffie and Caskie, J. Carter Fort, John B. Keeler, Frank C. Wright, Frederic A. Delano, and John R. Turney. The six active pallbearers were Stanley King, Ernest M. Whitcomb, the two Symington brothers—Donald and Charles—Joe's cousin Charles Judson Smith, and Fayette B. Dow. At the hour of the funeral the Office of Defense Transportation shut down for a five-minute silence. His body was cremated, and the ashes were interred in the family lot in Binghamton, New York.

In June, 1944, just after the Allied invasion of Normandy, the Maritime Commission named a Liberty Ship in Eastman's honor. At the launching Miss Eastman broke the traditional bottle of champagne over the prow, and the Bethlehem Shipbuilding Company gave a dinner to commemorate the event. The company presented to Miss Eastman a beautiful silver piece, which she graciously acknowledged, and Fayette B. Dow, called upon to speak for the guests, talked in a happy vein, telling some of Joe's favorite stories. It was an occasion which Eastman would himself have enjoyed.

Still other signal honors followed. In March, 1945, the Association of Interstate Commerce Commission Practitioners of Washington presented to the commission a bronze portrait bust of Eastman, modeled by Oscar Mundhenk, Frank Livingstone's brother-in-law, ten years earlier from a life mask. This was unveiled where it is now placed in the rotunda on the ground floor of the Interstate Commerce Commission Building. At the dedicatory ceremonies Judge R. P. Fletcher, of the Association of American Railroads, spoke eloquently of Eastman and his work. In June, General C. P. Gross, Chief of Army Transportation, made to Miss Elizabeth Eastman the posthumous award to her brother of the Medal of Merit, saying in his citation that Eastman's "broad experience and wisdom were given unstintedly to the armed forces." He added: "The value of his contribution to the war is incalculable." Eastman's portrait, painted by Harold Abbott Green, was presented in November to the Trustees of Amherst College. He was also awarded posthumously the Boston City Club Medal for 1943, particularly because of the importance of his work in relation to Boston as a transportation center.

The most appropriate memorial of all was to come a little later and was designed to be an instrument for training young men through many generations in the traditions of public service which Eastman had exemplified. After a sleepless night following the news of Joe's death, Fayette B. Dow conceived the idea of a Joseph B. Eastman Foundation. The story of the inception and development of the project has already been told by Stanley King, and need not be repeated or amplified here. Dow secured the cooperation of some of Joe's friends, including Frank P. Wright and Gilbert Montague, and then drafted a proposal which was eventually accepted by the Trustees of Amherst College, who agreed to use the fund for three primary purposes: the establishment of graduate fellowships for advanced study; research and publication in the field of political economy; and basic courses of instruction at Amherst College. The raising of the fund was largely Dow's personal enterprise, and his solicitation met with a generous response. One of the substantial gifts was made by the National Industrial Traffic League, an important association of shippers, and was an act without precedent in the long history of that group. It was announced on October 27, 1945, that donations had already been received to the amount of almost $160,000, from more than a thousand contributors, in forty-one states and one foreign country. Since then the fund has been considerably increased, and gifts are still being made to it. It now amounts to a capital sum of more than $400,000.

Under the direction of the foundation a volume entitled *Selected Papers and Addresses of Joseph B. Eastman, 1942–44* was edited, in 1948, by Professor G. Lloyd Wilson, of the University of Pennsylvania. At the same time Earl Latham was appointed professor of government at Amherst College on the Joseph B. Eastman Foundation. Other projects of a similar nature have been planned. The foundation represents an attempt to keep vital for many years to come the spirit, character, and accomplishments of the man in whose honor it was established.

Many of the problems which Eastman had to face are still living issues. He did his best, especially as Director of Civilian Defense, to convince the labor unions that any action which strengthened the hard-pressed railroads would in the long run be beneficial to the workers, even though it might for the time being reduce the number of jobs. Recent efforts, however, to retain two firemen on a Diesel locomotive when but one is needed prove that Eastman never converted his hearers. The possibility of executive interference with the commission is still a menace; indeed, as late as 1950, when under the veil of economy attacks were being made on the commission, one of the staff adapted Wordsworth to cry: "Eastman, thou shouldst be living at this hour!" The South still complains at intervals of discrimination in railroad rates. The question as to whether the carriers are subject to the anti-trust laws has never been settled. No one has yet persuaded the railroads to cooperate in peacetime as they did under the impact of war.

It is Eastman's attitude and spirit rather than any legacy of opinion which have preserved his reputation. After his death, the *Practitioners' Journal* reprinted literally hundreds of newspaper editorials from the New York *Times* and the Chicago *Tribune* and lesser journals in smaller cities across the country, all emphasizing this point. Their conclusions can be summed up in one sentence from the *Railway Age,* "Mr. Eastman was the nation's best-known and, with justice, its most-honored public servant—without any near runners-up to dispute the position."

Why did he deserve this distinction? The answer is not difficult to find. Disputes flare up and die down; perennial topics for debate arouse discussion and are then temporarily obscured; the same old questions reappear from decade to decade. Operators and union leaders can never agree on many matters; the viewpoint of the locomotive engineer will not be that of the executive at his desk in a city terminal; carriers and shippers will necessarily have antagonistic interests to further. What is important is that all men directly involved, whatever their status, should receive sympathy, fair treatment, and a full hearing, but that the rights of the general public should be paramount. All this Eastman knew, and he practiced what he preached.

With the Interstate Commerce Commission Eastman is still a proud tradition. He died at the apex of his career, with no "slow gradation of decay," and he is remembered as a fighting figure. Even in his last public appearance he was an advocate of principles which other men, even when they cannot follow them, instinctively admire. One day he was there in the building, meeting all his responsibilities without a sign of weakness and inspiring others with his leadership. The next day he was gone. But he has become a legend, and, like John Brown, "his soul is marching on."

XVI

The Measure of a Man

UNSPECTACULAR PUBLIC SERVANTS such as Joseph B. Eastman are too often taken for granted and seldom receive the popular acclaim accorded to leaders in other branches of government. Dominant chief executives, such as Andrew Jackson and Abraham Lincoln and Theodore Roosevelt, are inevitably in the public eye and catch the imagination. Generals and admirals, as a matter of course, get rewarded with medals and statues. Has not London reserved two of its most conspicuous centers for the victors at Trafalgar and Waterloo? Strong policy-makers in cabinet and diplomatic positions, such as Elihu Root and Henry L. Stimson, may be ranked as heroic figures. But bureau heads, who coin no startling phrases and are denied the opportunity for soul-stirring speeches, may, even when their work has been productive, be relegated by the historian to the limbo of forgotten men.

It is all the more remarkable, then, that Eastman should have received such widespread recognition. The matters with which he dealt, although vital to the welfare of the country, had few dramatic elements. He himself did no unconventional things and offered no spice to sensation-loving columnists. He was picturesque neither in dress nor in conduct and, although far from being a shrinking soul, did shun publicity. Not through self-advertisement did Eastman build up his reputation as one of the most trustworthy men in Washington. It was because he had been tried and not found wanting, because his character and personality commanded respect, that he was understood and admired by the average American in Albany or Omaha or Dallas.

Of the many estimates of Eastman published after his death, the most thoughtful was written by Mr. Justice Frankfurter and printed in the New York *Times* for March 17, 1944. It reads in part as follows:

The main issues confronting our society,—the mastery of unemployment, involving the wise direction of the processes of production and distribution, the well-being of agriculture, the conduct of public utilities, the control of disease and crime,—are deeply enmeshed in intricate facts. Merely to analyze these issues requires a vast body of technical knowledge. Such analysis is only a preliminary to exploration of possible remedies. In a world more or less dominated by technological forces, government must have at its disposal the resources of training and character,—men equipped to understand and to deal wisely with the complicated issues to which these technological forces give rise. We are more than a century removed from Jacksonian days of versatile improvisation.

Without a permanent and professional public service, highly trained, imaginative and courageously disinterested, the democratic aims of our society cannot be solved. Such a body of public servants is indispensable, no matter what social and economic policies may express the popular will, in the executive and legislative branches of the government. Of this need, Joseph B. Eastman symbolized the best fulfillment. He not only furnished striking proof of the extraordinary gifts which the government attracts. His reappointments to the Interstate Commerce Commission, by Presidents of varying outlook, prove that disinterested capacity will find effective support even from those who suffered adverse rulings. For Eastman's reappointment to the Commission was strongly urged by railroads whose views on vital issues he rejected.

One of the most genial Presidents remarked that "government after all is a very simple thing." The truth is, of course, that no enterprise is more complicated than modern government. No enterprise is more in need of skilled and devoted service and a large measure of continuity in that service. That can only come if men of high talents and character and disinterestedness are attracted to government.

Eastman's public service is a just cause for pride. It ought also to make us ponder on the needs of our public service and the conditions for its adequate fulfillment.

This discerning analysis by one outstanding public servant of another's contribution to effective governmental administration shows the impression which Eastman made on those around him. It may be worth while to describe some of his distinctive qualities and habits. But caution must be exercised, for different friends emphasize different traits, and there is also not a little disagreement among those who knew him best. What follows is an attempt at balanced judgment, based on evidence from many sources.

Eastman was clearly no genius, in the generally accepted interpretation of that term. He had no rare and precious gifts, like those possessed by Edgar Allan Poe or Herman Melville or Daniel Webster. He did have talent, and he developed some of the finest attributes of the ordinary man to an extraordinary degree.

Furthermore, Eastman's imagination did not range beyond his ability, and he wisely kept his activities within definite limits, aware that there was enough for him to do. As Federal Coordinator, for example, he did not express opinions on the broad problems of our national economy except as they concerned his office. Seeing in his own field an almost unbounded scope for improvement, he did not presume to encroach on the prerogatives of other branches of administration. As Director of Defense Transportation, he did not concern himself with the tactics of our generals in North Africa or Italy. His job was to carry our soldiers to their locations as safely and expeditiously as possible. He once remarked that a transportation expert should no more try to devise a new form of taxation than a brain surgeon should meddle with urology.

That he was our chief transportation expert was everywhere conceded. In his own specialty he was supreme, as much of an authority as Einstein was on atomic energy or General Eisenhower on military maneuvers. After he had reached professional maturity, no conference on transportation could have been held without him, and no Congressional hearing relating to that subject was complete without his advice. Not Colonel Stimson or General Marshall or even the President would have tried to solve a transportation difficulty without consulting him. He made no claims outside of his own circumscribed area, but within it he was the "Old Maestro," familiar with all the history, statistics, theories, and personalities. "My views are the product of twenty-seven years' experience in the public regulation of railroads," he once told a Congressional committee; and he added, with mild irony, "They may not be any the more valuable on that account!"

Eastman's sense of duty, always with him an impelling motive, would have kept him from neglecting any assignment even if he had detested it; but he was actually very happy in his routine work. To his cousin Margaret he wrote in 1919: "Having few gifts except the ability to work hard, it is difficult for me to keep my nose off the grindstone, but I am going to try hard to break away before I grind it off." He seldom did break away, however, except for his annual month's vacation, and in emergencies he gave up even that. Setting for his subordinates an example of almost unmitigated activity, he would allow nothing to interfere with his stated obligations. It is easy for a bureau official to relapse into a placid, comfortable existence, and more than one has done so. Furthermore, social life in the capital is tempting and engrossing, and a government employee can always decide that the pursuit of pleasure is an obligation. Not so Joe Eastman! Without being a "kill-joy" or a recluse, he could always find an excuse for declining invitations to cocktail parties or formal dinners, except at the homes of intimate friends.

When he had a baffling problem to settle, he allowed himself to think of little else. The night watchmen at the Interstate Commerce Building grew accustomed to his return at eight in the evening, and he often remained until after midnight. In 1935 and 1936, when he was Federal Coordinator, he was frequently driven home at eleven o'clock by Dr. Charles S. Morgan, the Director of Research; and on the way out Eastman would still be absorbed in a matter which required concentration of thought. He was criticized occasionally for staying too much in his office and thus cutting himself off from important personal contacts and also for being unwilling to delegate authority in minor matters. His conduct in both instances can be explained by his extreme conscientiousness. He felt that he was more efficient as a researcher and judge than as an "outside man" and that he did not want to sign a report, no matter how trivial, unless he knew all the details involved.

Although Joe was no born mathematician, he acquired a taste for statistics when he was probing into the finances of the New Haven Railroad, and later, as commissioner, succumbed to their strange fascination. For hours in his office he would sit deep in a cushioned armchair, a drawing board across his knees, scribbling additions and subtractions on sheets of yellow paper. In his comprehensive memory he retained the rate scales between different cities and could quote them as fluently and accurately as if he were reading from a printed schedule. From a sheet of published rates he could select with unerring perspicacity those which had any relevance to a dispute. He was not infallible, but he was so seldom mistaken that lawyers pleading before him quickly learned to avoid exaggeration and vagueness.

Eastman had a disconcerting propensity for going directly to the heart of any subject under consideration. Often after a petitioner had presented his cause with unnecessary rhetoric and circumlocution Joe would snap out a single question which would rip the carefully prepared thesis into tiny bits. One admirer described him as "America's greatest master of the Socratic method." Several people have recalled the occasion when, lifting one corner of his mouth into a whimsical grin, he inquired of the president of the Prudential Insurance Company whether any class of investments besides railroads were causing him concern "at the present time." The "present time" was in the midst of the stock market collapse of 1929.

Eastman's questions, though often troubling to their victims, were devoid of personal animus. As he twiddled the famous eraser between his fingers, gazed thoughtfully at the ceiling, and propounded an unexpected and searching inquiry, he was not the prosecuting attorney, but the seeker after truth. His examination was aimed, not at the witness, but at the problem under consideration, and he was trying to elicit the facts, not to discomfit anybody.

More than most men Eastman could view problems objectively, like an observer from another planet, without condescension, but with an attempt to understand human motives and passions. Donald Richberg has said: "Joe was one of the most amazing persons I have ever known in his ability to maintain his neutrality." Leslie Craven, who knew him equally well, remarked, "Eastman's independence made him something of a lone wolf, for though he was friendly with every one, no one had an inside corner with him." His feeling about some notorious labor leaders was expressed in one sentence: "It is hard to be sympathetic with people who take a wholly selfish role"; but he made substantially the same comment about a few uncooperative railroad executives. Their limited outlook he could not comprehend. Labor men have told me that they thought his approach to their controversies with the operators was cold, unsympathetic, and academic. George Harrison, a well-known union officer, once asked Eastman why he did not consult with labor before issuing his car-loading order, as he had talked the matter over with management. Eastman replied: "Your opinion would be so extremely partisan that there would have been no point in getting it." On the other hand, as Coordinator or Director he seldom reached a decision without consulting Otto S. Beyer, to find out what labor would think about it.

It was as natural as breathing for Eastman to approach disputed issues with an unbiased mind and an effort to weigh the evidence. He judged questions on their merits alone, without being swayed by his own predilections. Thus, his mood was usually judicial rather than argumentative. He did not, of course, lack positive and well-defined convictions supported by a basic philosophy, especially on moral issues. The pattern of his thinking had been clarified and fixed by the date he arrived in Washington, but he was intellectually flexible enough to adjust himself to the shifting emphases of our economic life. A member of a Congressional committee in the 1930's challenged him on a statement which he had made in a hearing, saying that it conflicted with one which he had made some years earlier. Not at all embarrassed, Eastman replied: "All that I can say is that I have grown wiser as I have grown older." Opposition never made him faint-hearted, and he stanchly defended his ideas against all-comers. However, he could see the other fellow's viewpoint and respected it. Once he wrote to James H. Hustis, president of the Boston & Maine:

It is extraordinary what an amount of misunderstanding there is because men are not acquainted with each other. At present I have many acquaintances and some friends among radicals, labor unionists, conservatives, and capitalists, and I am often impressed with the part that prejudice and bitterness play in their opinions of each other. It is a great step forward when one is able to differ from a man without hating him and a still greater step forward when one is able to differ from him and at the same time appreciate his good qualities. As a matter of fact, the ideas of most men are controlled quite largely by their environment, and if that environment could be changed their ideas would be considerably modified.

Eastman never lost sight of the fact that on the commission he had certain assigned duties to perform. Far better than generalizing, he liked to face specific situations which could be settled through conclusions based on evidence. His private interpretation of his responsibility is well expressed in a letter in 1932 to Morris L. Cooke.

A Commissioner is not a judge, but in some respects he resembles one. There are general statements in regard to the regulatory system and the principles which should control it which he could properly sign. . . . He must be careful, however, not to prejudge issues which may come before him and on which he has not yet passed officially. The time for him to speak out on those is when all the evidence is in and all the arguments have been made. Then he can speak appropriately and officially and much more forcefully and effectively than in any abstract statement. As a matter of fact, I doubt very much whether any such general statements accomplish much. Discussion is good, and also exchange of ideas. But the most effective discussion, both by Commissioners and by those who represent the public side unofficially, is in concrete cases where official decisions must be rendered.

A theory closely related to this and exhibiting the same pragmatic philosophy appears in a letter to Marshall H. Dana, dated December 5, 1934: "Personally I have no great sympathy with an attempt to plan the future very far ahead because I think none of us know enough or are wise enough to do this successfully. We must feel our way along from point to point."

Some intruders who sought interviews with Eastman went away convinced that he was unresponsive, even cold. He could be reserved, in the sense that he did not confide in every casual visitor. Like everybody in such a position, he was beset by acquaintances seeking jobs for which they were not qualified. Henry Adams, after observing official Washington, wrote cynically: "Every friend in power is a friend lost." It is equally true that any man in power is sure to be hounded by mendicants in the guise of well-wishers. Eastman listened patiently to tales of misfortune and was made the victim of occasional "touches" by indigent fellow-collegians. To one such who requested a modest loan of $1,000, he replied: "If I should lend you $1,000, I should have to go out and borrow it myself." Eastman can hardly be blamed for stiffening his back against shameless importunity. He saw too much of it. On the other hand, he also performed many

> Little, nameless, unremembered acts
> Of kindness and of love.

It has been hinted in some quarters that Eastman was niggardly in his recognition of those who did well for him. If this is true, it is partly because he himself did not expect praise for what he was supposed to do as a matter of course. Some of those who worked under him felt that he did not concern himself about them sufficiently to get their salaries raised or to urge their promotion. Doubtless in such cases he had his own good reasons for not pressing the matter harder. His letters show, however, that in several instances he went out of his way to recommend reappointment for his colleagues on the commission and to secure advancement for his subordinates—often without their knowing about it.

Once, in the shadow of World War II, when Eastman was far from well, he brought to Howard Hosmer, his chief examiner, a request from the Boy Scouts for a message to be read at one of their national gatherings, and asked him to draft it. Touched by this unusual manifestation of confidence, Hosmer tried hard to put himself in the place of his chief and was, of course, anxious to learn how he liked the result. There was no immediate indication. Late in the afternoon, however, Eastman said to Hosmer, "I took your Boy Scout letter up to the conference and read it to the Commission." That was all—but Hosmer still thinks that this was the highest compliment he ever received.

To those whom he rated as intimates Joe was gracious, understanding, and uniformly considerate. In some moods he had a boyish manner, even an exuberance, which completed his charm. When an article was published after Eastman's death saying that he was not warm-hearted, John Daniels, who had known him since his South End House days, wrote Miss Elizabeth Eastman:

How the Johns Hopkins man could have got so far astray as regards Joe's qualities as to think him cool and aloof is beyond my comprehension,—unless he reasoned in the abstract that one so wholly free of injustice or favoritism, so personally disinterested, so true to honesty and justice, simply must have been detached and impersonal. But Joe was a rare blend,—too rare for easy understanding.

Eastman was at heart a very simple person, who based his conduct on elementary principles, all of them included in the moral law. Unlike some bureau heads, he was never corrupted by authority; and while he possessed an unmistakable native dignity which did not encourage liberties from strangers, he was no "stuffed shirt." He disliked people who tried to attract attention. He was disgusted with the typical fanatic—the prohibitionist or the single taxer or the self-appointed censor of harmless pleasure. He did not relish subtleties, and although he could express himself with clarity and vigor, he did not strain for epigrams. His prose style, therefore, was unpretentious, with no tricks of phrasing or ventures into rhetoric. He dressed in excellent taste, but inconspicuously. He moved through the corridors of the Interstate Commerce Building without a trace of arrogance or aloofness. His democratic spirit permeated all that he said or did.

Mere integrity is too often taken for granted, but there are degrees in honesty and shadowy areas between all black and all white. Washington departments are full of good fellows who do not like to say "No," and the significance of the *quid pro quo* is something which an old hand like Eastman could hardly miss, especially since it was brought so often to his notice. He complained somewhat in private conversations of the unsavory "deals," the undercover agreements, the minor "graft" among legislators and lobbyists. That he was personally incorruptible has already been stressed. If there had been any stain upon his record, his enemies would have exposed it and used it for that furtive blackmail which pressure groups never hesitate to employ. But even though tempted, Eastman refused to purchase support by even a wink or gesture of acquiescence.

It would be wrong, however, to picture Eastman as a helpless lamb among wolves. Judge Thomas L. Anderson, of St. Louis, in a letter written in 1933, described Joe as having "about as much political sense as a half-witted Hottentot," and former Commissioner Caskie has said that a little practical sagacity would have aided him immensely. Furthermore, Joe himself once remarked: "I am probably the worst salesman on the government payroll," and he was correct in the sense that he was not a "one time salesman." On the other hand, he knew how to take care of himself. He was rarely led astray by the methods and motives of the politicians who called on him, and, possibly because he was so open and frank, he got along with them astonishingly well. He had a native common sense which kept him from playing the role of Simple Simon. He might have been deceived temporarily by the luster of a gold brick, but nobody could have persuaded him to buy one. He was no Don Quixote, engaged in unreal battles with an imaginary foe and therefore easily victimized by unscrupulous worldlings; nor was he so irrevocably unromantic that he could not indulge in dreams. Perhaps his best defense was the fact that he wanted nothing for himself.

Eastman cared little for money or honors, and even less for the flesh-pots. Again and again he refused to accept fees for articles or addresses, maintaining that his salary was supposed to cover any recompense for such special performances. When in 1943 he was sent a large check by the New York *Times* for an essay which he had written for the magazine section, he gave it as a contribution to the American Red Cross. It has truthfully been said of him that he had "an entire disinterestedness in his own personal fortunes."

At the time when Eastman was appointed Director of National Defense, he had never owned an automobile. Queried on this point by newspaper men, he replied:

In the first place, I have never had any particular need for a car. My travel is principally between my home and my office, and for years I got my principal exercise, except for an occasional handball game, by walking to and from work. If I needed public transportation locally, —which was seldom,—I always found plenty of taxicabs and street cars available. As you know, I am a bachelor and live with my unmarried sister, so we have no large demands for a family car. Whenever she has need for a car, she just calls a public rental station and has a car and chauffeur sent for her. If I had a car and chauffeur, they would merely involve needless expense.

So it was that perhaps the only high government official who did not possess an automobile was the man in control of all motor traffic throughout the nation. Eastman did not despise, but was indifferent to, the recognized appurtenances of success. Compared with those who headed other bureaus of equal importance to his he seemed self-denying, but it never occurred to him that he might be losing something.

Joe was never offensively virtuous, nor did he begrudge others their cakes and ale. Indeed, he enjoyed as well as the next man a stein of beer or a highball; he was a mighty smoker of the pipe, with a collection of briars which was the envy of his friends; he was, in the proper mood, not unappreciative of those stories which are told in the smoking compartment with no ladies present; and he could, under provocation, burst out in a resonant and very sincere "Damn!" He enjoyed immensely both prize fights and musical comedies, as well as the vaudeville performances at Keith's theater. In describing Eastman's habits, Herbert Corey wrote:

He wears loose clothes, smokes crusty pipes, and likes cats. He is addicted to airplanes, facts, and notions which are presented so reasonably that hostile audiences cheer him. . . . He believes in the average man but does not cry over him. He would not abolish cash registers, and he thinks the world is better than most of us believe.

To sum up all this, Joe was a "good fellow," who did his share of the chores and was tolerant of the idiosyncrasies of others.

John Hay, after serving as Abraham Lincoln's private secretary, once remarked: "No great man is ever really humble." It is undeniably true that most leaders, however well they may conceal their feelings, are fully aware of their own importance and that many of them have their odd little vanities, including a desire for applause. But in all Eastman's correspondence and speeches I have discovered no boastful sentence or evidence of self-conceit. It would have been very easy for a small-minded man in his position to become dictatorial, to turn his back on old friends and cater to those in supreme authority, to "scorn the base degrees by which he did ascend," to forget the relationship of his own job to those of countless others in the same department—indeed, to yield to all the temptations which beset the bureaucrat. But Eastman, to the close of his career, was the same unpretentious, unspoiled person that he had been as an Amherst undergraduate. One of the severest critics of his policies has said: "Joe Eastman never had a shabby thought or committed a shabby act."

Something of Eastman's modest, whimsical spirit comes out in a letter which he wrote in 1931 to his Amherst class secretary, Fred E. Sturgis, in response to some personal queries.

How do I look? As a disinterested observer, pretty well, thank you. Hair a little moth-eaten in spots, and some other signs of wear and tear, but not so bad. How do I feel? A man in public office develops such a thick skin that this particular sense becomes atrophied. My feelings and emotions are not much to brag of. How am I? About the same as usual. What am I doing? Working for the Government, and fairly hard too. Sometimes I wonder how it would get along without me. Maybe it would rock along somehow, but it does seem doubtful. What are my interests? I am interested in everything that I get a chance to be interested in, which isn't so much outside of my work. How about my family? Why, Fred, what a question! Ask me that ten years from now, I still have hopes. Am I coming back to our 30th Grand-(father's) reunion? You bet, if I am still on deck.

In some respects Eastman's interests had a limited range, natural enough in a man whose days and nights had been devoted to one type of work. In his childhood he learned to play the piano in fumbling fashion, and in Boston he attended an occasional symphony concert, but in later life he was too busy for this form of diversion. I cannot find that he paid much attention to painting, classical or modern, or visited galleries when he had a few hours to spare in New York or Chicago. Within the walls of the Interstate Commerce Building, Picasso and Sibelius, Dali and Gershwin, seemed very far off. He did, however, admire the enthusiasm of his colleague Aitchison in organizing and conducting the Interstate Male Chorus, composed of approximately fifty employees of the commission; and Joe whimsically lamented his inability to lead them in "Lord Jeffrey Amherst."

In his reading Eastman shunned metaphysics and speculative philosophy and had little leisure to enjoy poetry. In 1941 he wrote Woodlock: "One of the things that I deeply regret is that I am so occupied in reading the things that I must read to do my work on the Commission that I have very little opportunity to keep in touch with current literature in regard to more important matters. Hence I am rapidly getting into the non-educated class." This is doubtless an exaggeration, for his home library was well filled, and he subscribed to most of the better magazines. Felix Frankfurter once wrote him: "It made a great hit in Boston when I brought back the highbrow intelligence that the *New England Quarterly* was part of the reading matter to be found on the table of an Interstate Commerce Commissioner." When he was tired, he followed the example of other distinguished men, including Woodrow Wilson, and read detective or adventure stories to get relaxation. His friends could always please him by sending him a volume of Dorothy Sayers or Margery Allingham.

More than once he was asked to write a volume on his own specialty, but he declared that his literary monument would have to be found in the countless reports which he had sponsored. When Alfred A. Knopf wrote him in 1940 to suggest that he prepare "a good comprehensive book written for the general public and dealing with the whole present problem of railroads," Eastman refused, saying: "Quite apart from the question of whether I could with propriety write such a book so long as I remain on the Commission, the fact is that I have absolutely no time available for that purpose."

No characterization of Eastman would be complete without some reference to his quiet but unfailing sense of humor. The *Railway Age*, on March 18, 1944, said of him: "He rarely made a speech, rendered a decision, handed down a comment from the bench, or engaged in a conversation when he did not provoke chuckles from his auditors by a sly and kindly wit which pleased his hearers even when, as usual, they themselves were the targets of it." When in a sportive mood he loved to "kid" others, and was at his best in the give-and-take of affectionate banter at a family dinner party or at the table in an office conference. It was noticeable, however, that he did not allow himself to arouse a laugh at the expense of a friend's feelings. His speeches as reported and printed show few traces of humor, but this is because the amusing sections were interpolated in the text, brought in as asides or used extemporaneously to illustrate a point. He once remarked: "One of my difficulties is that I see the funny side of everything, even when I am sitting on the Commission, and this sometimes gets me into trouble with serious-minded people."

Joe had many stories in his repertoire, one of which was repeated so often that it became known as "Eastman's chestnut." It concerned a salesman who was trying to sell a bill of goods to a country storekeeper who was obviously hard of hearing. The conversation went as follows: "I'm sorry you're deaf. How long have you been that way?" "About thirty years." "Ever do anything about it?" "Yep—saw a doctor and he said to quit drinkin' so much." "Didn't you follow his advice?" "Yep—I cut out the booze and got where I could hear everything that was goin' on." "How come, then, you can't hear now?" "Wal, I liked what I was drinkin' so much better than what I was hearin', I made up my mind I'd ruther be deaf."

Joe always enjoyed greatly a joke on himself. Once an article appeared in the New York *Herald-Tribune* in which he was mentioned as "the former railroad conductor"—a misprint for "Coordinator." The assistant editor responsible sent Eastman a contrite letter, to which he replied: "Don't worry about that,—if that were the worst thing people called me, I'd consider myself lucky."

On another occasion, after lunching with his friend Mrs. Ernesta Barlow, he escorted her to the Washington Union Station so that she might take her train back to New York. He stepped with her into the Pullman, and while they were talking the train started off for Baltimore. When the conductor came along, Eastman, who was then Director of Defense Transportation, attempted to explain that he had no ticket, but the official would not listen and berated him, saying: "You're just another of those 'dead-beats' who think you can get away without paying!" Joe said nothing, but quietly reached in his pocket and handed him the fare. As the conductor started to move away, Mrs. Barlow couldn't resist saying to him, "I guess you don't know that your 'dead-beat' is Joe Eastman." The man, much ashamed, returned and made his abject apologies, to which Eastman answered: "Don't worry, you were just doing your duty, and I knew it."

Although Eastman was not averse to office gossip out of hours, he seldom participated in it, and he made few critical remarks about his associates. He was too good-natured and tolerant to be severe on others. Furthermore, he kept himself under careful control and rarely gave way to outbursts of temper. His occasional outbursts of anger could, however, be withering. In 1922, when Joe was being considered for reappointment to the commission, "Cap" Dow discovered that a scurrilous anti-Eastman pamphlet was being covertly circulated in Washington, apparently distributed by agents of the New York Central. Dow promptly went to New York, saw Dwight W. Morrow, but could get no information that would help him. Finally Morrow ascertained that the offensive booklet had been prepared in the Cleveland office of the railroad, and had it immediately suppressed. When Eastman heard about the incident, he was much annoyed at Dow for interfering and declared in picturesque language that he could get along all right by himself.

Eastman seldom became really angry except over cases of what he thought to be injustice. Henry McCarthy, his capable young assistant while he was Director of Defense Transportation, was once driving with him and another colleague from Eastman's home to the Interstate Commerce Building. On the way the third member of the trio started to comment on the alleged weaknesses of another man on the staff. Joe was obviously disturbed over the turn which the talk had taken; finally, as they stopped at a red light, he turned to his companion and said: "For God's sake, shut up!" That, for Eastman, was a torrential outburst, which neither of the other two ever forgot.

At Amherst, Joe had a reputation as a confirmed and incorrigible misogynist. Once in a fraternity debate he upheld enthusiastically and successfully the affirmative of the question "Resolved, that the proximity of Smith and Mount Holyoke Colleges is a detriment to Amherst." Later, although he could refer humorously to his "single blessedness" and joke about his celibate loneliness, he never took the preliminary steps to relieve it. But he was by no means allergic to the opposite sex, and his attitude might be described as one of cautious admiration from a distance. He was shy in the presence of women, conscious that he had no small talk and did not understand the superficial give-and-take of polite society. Yet without being aware of it, he did appeal to discerning women, and we hear of several who deliberately sought him out, realizing that he was not one likely to make advances. One of his close friends writes: "I remember his telling me of one instance in which, under the combined influence of charm and moonlight, he suddenly found that he had unwittingly said something which could conceivably be taken as a proposal of marriage. He was staggered, but managed somehow to beat a quick strategic retreat." On other occasions when he felt that he was perilously near romance, he backed away.

His cousin Mrs. Smith, who enjoyed his confidence, writes:

Joe dedicated his life to his work. He felt that if he married a young woman, she would expect, and have the right to expect, that he devote some of his time to her and to social affairs. This he saw he could not do, but I know that he hoped the time would come when he would be more free. . . . He was very happy and contented in his home. Everything there was planned for his comfort and happiness, and he and Elizabeth were most devoted and congenial.

In the fall of 1941 Joe spent a week end at the farm of his old friends the Donald Symingtons, near Baltimore. The first afternoon he was sent out by his hostess to walk over the rolling pastures he loved and knew so well. His companion was another guest at the house party, Mrs. Ernesta Drinker Barlow, of New York, a stranger to Joe. The oblique approach to human beings was not in this lady's nature. With Joe Eastman she dealt as directly as he would have dealt with an unexplored situation in railroad management. They had covered several miles of autumn countryside when she said without further preamble, "Mr. Eastman, have you ever corresponded with some one you didn't know?" "No," Joe answered. "Why?"

"I have always thought," the lady replied, "that it would be a great luxury to write to a perfect stranger. One could say almost anything to a person one didn't know,—it wouldn't matter much what he thought of you. Why don't you write to me,—write a lot, whatever comes into your head?" She had guessed at once the fundamental loneliness of this man with whom work was an obsession and shyness an insulation from normal companionship. He had no response to her suggestion of an exchange of letters, and she let it pass; but when she returned to New York she found a letter in Joe's even, legible hand. The note told her in his simple, modest way what he had been doing and what he planned to do. From that time until his death he wrote her every week, always in longhand. His last letter was mailed from the hospital three days before he died.

It was a new experience to Joe, to be treated with the breezy informality of an old friend. Right after Pearl Harbor, when he had seen her only a few times, she called him on the telephone. "Joe," she said, "I'm here in the Union Station, and I'm in a jamb for a typewriter or a stenographer. Can you tell the railroads to get along on their own for a while or stop running and let me use your office for a few minutes?" "Come right up," he said. He put his big desk and secretary at her disposal, gave her advice when she asked for it, and then suggested lunch. "I hope we can get a taxi," he said. "I thought," she replied, "you were an expert in transportation." She looked about his commodious office. The whole building was of monumental proportions. "Joe, aren't you a big enough man to be allowed your own car?" she chided. "Every tuppeny, ha'-penny public relations man in Washington has one, and you are one of the most important men down here." "They would give me a car, I suppose," he admitted, "but I never really need one, and so I don't care."

From that time on whenever she was in Washington or he in New York they met for lunch or dinner. Occasionally he took her to a play. "You never do anything but work," Ernesta reproached him. "No, not enough else," he agreed. "I'm not particularly bright. I have to work harder than other people. Whatever I've done has been through hard work. There's nothing exceptional about my brains." "There is something very exceptional about your common sense," she answered promptly. "It amounts to brilliance." "That never occurred to me," he said, obviously much pleased.

In this correspondence Joe reveals more of his inner self than in any documents which I have been able to find. It was clear that

Mrs. Barlow supplied something that he needed—a feminine companionship which he could trust. On January 2, 1944, he made a confession very rare with him:

I have been unfortunate, so far as women are concerned. They have always attracted me greatly, but I was afraid of them, and more than that I was always waiting for some overpowering passion for a particular one, which never came. Many times I have thought myself in love, but it was never overpowering enough nor lasting enough to meet the test. The trouble probably lay in my being too self-centered. Now it is too late.

Mrs. Barlow, sympathetic, charming, and exceptionally intelligent, brought out the best in Joe. She was soon speaking frequently over the radio, and he helped her by introducing her to some influential people. He also tried, wherever he was, to take time out to hear her weekly broadcast and give her his candid opinion of it. On August 16, 1942, he wrote:

Herewith my weekly report. I don't want to be just a chorus of approval, because I know the value of criticism. But really I thought you extraordinarily good to-day. . . . It was all very interesting to me, and it went over in fine shape. If you write your own script, as I am sure you do in large part, you can qualify in the literary class.

When he, in his turn, was beginning to give radio talks, in the summer of 1943, he wrote:

Please forgive me for not letting you know about my broadcast last Sunday, when I functioned with "Wings over Jordan" for five minutes. I meant to send you advance word, but preoccupation with one of those damnable crises was what interfered. To-day I spent three minutes on the air with Billy Burke in "Fashions in Rations." Unfortunately she was in Hollywood. They say she is 63, but she sounds like a kitten, and is very silly and cute. I couldn't compete. Fact is, I am a little downhearted by my broadcasting. Last Saturday I made a record with an Omaha broadcaster,—local affair. When they played it back, he said, "You remind me of some one." He thought hard and then came out with this, "I know who it is,—Herbert Hoover!" Wouldn't that make you feel good?

From these letters dashed off from Chicago and Denver and Dallas in the midst of wartime stress and confusion it is possible to discover what Eastman was really thinking. On July 3, 1943, he wrote:

Things are generally in a stew down here, but fortunately I have been able to keep out of the hurlyburly. Others are welcome to my share of the limelight. Probably it is timidity rather than virtue, but I have no craving for the headlines. Senator Pepper referred to me the other day as "the mild-mannered Eastman." But the Bible says, "The meek shall inherit the earth." The trouble is that it doesn't say when. Before this war is over, also, I am afraid the earth won't be worth much!

In June, 1943, he told Mrs. Barlow that he was suffering from the gout and had not had a walk through the park in a "dog's age." In early September, he added:

I have survived down here, but the going has been tough enough. All work and no play, with plenty of heat on the side. My health has stood up, but I certainly can see old age creeping up, which of course it has a way of doing. I cheer every victory for the Allies, not only for the cause, but for purely personal reasons.

On the day after Christmas he sat down to write her a long letter about his problems.

We are having plenty of excitement now over the railroad strike. I still do not believe that it will actually come off, but emotions are running high, and you never can tell. Whether or not, if the President takes over the railroads, I shall have the job of running them, I do not know. He hasn't said anything to me about it, but with him that doesn't necessarily mean anything. I got my present job without one word from him in advance. It was just dropped in my lap. If I don't get this one, there won't be any mourning from me, for I have enough mental stress as it is. Of course I shall do my damndest, if I get the job. However, I really expect no job from any one.

A week later, on January 2, 1944, he made a report to bring her up to date.

You were wrong about the railroads. They were, as you know, turned over to the army and not to me. There was logic in that, for the Government was taking the railroads over, not because their management had failed, but because there was danger of interruption of service. . . . I do not think it was necessary, for I am sure the men would not have quit. However it was spectacular and had the guise of a good brave deed. From what I hear, those whom Hugh Johnson used to call the "palace guards" had much to do with it, including one Anna Rosenberg, of New York City. Do you know her? Some compare her to Cleopatra. I was not consulted in any way.

Joe had known for many months that he was not a good physical risk and had talked to Mrs. Barlow more than once about his weakness. When he was taken to the hospital, Mrs. Barlow wrote him immediately: "Take a brace, Joe, they need you." It was almost the last letter that he read before he died.

Even as a college undergraduate Eastman was skeptical of orthodox religion, as expressed in creeds and rituals. In 1925 he wrote to William S. Culbertson, who wanted him to serve as a member of the local committee to have charge of the National Council for Religion in Higher Education:

I fear that I would not be an appropriate member of this committee, for I am not now and never have been a member of any church. Although I am sympathetic with Dr. Kent and what he is trying to accomplish, such religion as I have is of so unconventional a character that I do not feel I ought to serve on the committee.

Only a few months before his death he wrote Mrs. Louise Trask Conn with reference to a project of hers for spreading religious ideas through motion pictures.

I was brought up as a child in exceptionally religious surroundings, since my father was a minister of religion and a man of deepest sincerity in thought and conduct combined with a very lovable personality. That the training I thus received was of the best I have always been persuaded. Yet I have never been able, intellectually, to accept many of my father's premises, and have never been a church member. That humanity needs religion is very clear to me, but my conception of religion is very broad and quite different, for example, from that of my friend, Tom Woodlock, or even of my dad. I would have difficulty in defining it at all clearly. About all I can say is that while I cannot accept any of their beliefs, I have the utmost sympathy with our religious institutions and feel that their efforts are of great value and ought to be supported.

In November, 1943, he thanked George R. Farnum for sending him an article entitled "The Bible in the Lives of Great Americans," adding, "I particularly liked the statement of Lincoln which you quote to the effect that he thought he might claim the benefit of the beatitude that 'pronounces a blessing upon those who hunger and thirst after righteousness.'" A few days later, just before he entered the hospital, he wrote to Henry A. Scandrett:

I am much interested in your conviction about the need for a renaissance of religion. While I was brought up in a minister's family, I have never been an active churchman, and my religious beliefs take a very broad form. Fundamentally, however, I am sure that religion in some form is something that humanity greatly needs, and that this need has not been adequately met in recent years.

Here, perhaps, the subject should be left, with a reminder that however unorthodox he may have been, his whole life was guided by moral and ethical standards. For example, he had a very active sympathy for the "under-dog," wherever located, and would spend hours of his valuable time trying to rectify a case of alleged injustice. In his letters I have learned that he helped a secretary who was having domestic troubles, a railroad passenger penalized by a foolish regulation, a taxicab driver who had been in an accident, and a group of railroad employees who had been dismissed without adequate cause.

As an earnest advocate of the doctrine "nothing in excess," Eastman sometimes questioned the methods of fanatical reformers. In January, 1943, when a friend implored him to do something about the employment of more negroes on railroads, Joe made it clear that to him as Director of Defense Transportation this was a manpower problem, not "a question of social reform." He added that in his judgment, the Fair Employment Practices Committee would accomplish more if it "chose to speak softly." "I feel," he continued, "that we can reduce the heat and increase the light in regard to this very explosive issue by foregoing inflammatory publicity, mass meetings, et cetera, and by adopting quieter, less emotion-rousing tactics, even though an approach of this kind requires at times a certain tolerance even of intolerance." This brief quotation illustrates perfectly Eastman's cool-headedness, his unwillingness to ally himself with extremist movements, and his perception of all the possible consequences of untimely action, even when well motivated. It is not difficult to see why he was opposed to the passage of the Eighteenth Amendment to the Constitution and welcomed its repeal in 1933.

Eastman's insistence on absolute fairness, no matter who or what was involved, was well shown in an incident related by Stanley King. At a meeting of the Amherst trustees during the war, President King was explaining with some justifiable satisfaction that the college had been accumulating a large reserve of coal in case of a shortage. Joe squirmed around in his chair for some time without saying anything, but finally muttered: "Why, Stanley, you just can't do that!" Later he sent his friend the president a note, and no more coal was added to the college bins, even though the action had been within the law. Joe's conscience would not allow him to be silent, even when the welfare of his *alma mater* was concerned.

Joe once told Howard Hosmer that he would have liked to be an explorer; and he was probably at his happiest on the many trips which he took to the Canadian forest, usually in August, on fishing expeditions. Although several different persons at various times went with him, his most frequent companion was Fayette B. Dow. Over a period of more than twenty years Eastman covered a considerable area of Canadian territory, often in sections remote and seldom trodden. For three summers in succession, from 1924 to 1926, he went to the Lake Claire Preserve, north of the St. John River, hunting new and less accessible streams each season. In 1932 he canoed more than three hundred miles in the wilderness north of Lake Nipigon, meeting nobody along the route but a few Indians. In 1936, when he was exhausted after his labors as Federal Coordinator, he set out with Dow for Sioux Lookout, where they took a plane to the Fort Hope Post of the Hudson's Bay Company— a very isolated spot. From there they proceeded into a rough country along the Wabassi River, then up the Albany, and finally to Ombabika, a little station on the railroad. The fishing on this particular trip was poor, but Eastman and Dow had the satisfaction of penetrating an area which white men had rarely seen. Indeed, it was the first time their guides had been in those waters.

Commenting on Eastman's traits as a woodsman, Dow has written:

If a camper is one who can set up a tent and stay a week at one camp site, if a fisherman is one who can fish a stream all day, then Joe is neither a camper nor a fisherman. He is an incessant *voyageur* by canoe and on foot. One night at any camp site is the rule. Two are the limit, and these occasions are rare. He is not restless, but he wants to move on. He reminds one of Kipling's Explorer. There is something "hid behind the ranges," and he wants to find it. Whether paddling in the middle of the river or poling foot by foot along the shore against a swift-flowing current, he is never a passenger. He does his share with paddle or pole. Over a portage short or long he carries a heavy pack and frequently goes back with the guide for another load. After supper he lights his pipe and is ready for a quiet talk. His mind has been freed for the time being of the problems of Washington and does not willingly return to them. Alway travelling in a country new to him,—frequently new to the guides themselves,—he looks over maps, studies the contours of the country and the courses of the rivers, and looks forward to the adventures of the rapids that lie ahead. His vacations and his work are entirely different and yet entirely alike. Both are characterized by intense effort and a zest for exploration.

Eastman was an eager angler, who liked to make his preliminary arrangements as early as June in each year to be sure that nothing went wrong. Like every good sportsman, he was fussy about his tackle; and in 1925, when he sent in an order to Iver Johnson for himself and Dow, he was insistent that they should have the finest possible equipment, including rods, reels, casting lines, flies (mostly wet), landing nets, and fly books. He himself, after some experimentation, pinned his faith to a light Leonard rod. Not until relatively late in life did he venture to use dry flies, and even then he did not like them, maintaining that his casting was done in waters so turbulent that dry flies were not deceptive. When he was consulted in 1940 about the best flies to take to Canada, he replied,

I have always thought that the ability of trout to distinguish between different kinds of flies is much over-estimated. When they are biting well, they will take one kind as well as another, and when they are not biting well they will not take any. . . . In Canada I have always had good luck with the Montreal, and also with the Parmachenee Belle, which is so gay that one would expect it to scare trout away, but apparently it doesn't. I had my best luck on that fly this summer.

We have an excellent detailed diary account by John Daniels of a trip which he took with Eastman and Dow in August, 1928. After spending a day in Montreal to replenish their equipment, they boarded the night train for St. Felicien, in Quebec, where they were met and driven eighty-five miles by automobile to McLeod's Falls. There they embarked with three canoes and a guide apiece for a trip covering three weeks on the Peribonka and Manouan rivers, a total distance of more than two hundred miles. The three of them really roughed it, sleeping on the bare ground under a tent, poling, paddling, and portaging, running rapids, eating "catch-as-catch-can," contending constantly with black flies and mosquitoes, gradually limbering up their stiffened muscles, and enjoying the delight which comes to civilized man when he returns to his primitive state. The fishing was certainly miscellaneous, including fly casting, trolling, and just plain bait on a hook. Only two ouananiche (landlocked salmon) were killed, the larger one weighing four pounds. There were plenty of lake trout, including one taken by Dow weighing ten pounds, the largest catch of the trip and heavier than any landed by him or Eastman on any of their previous expeditions. And there were always pike, Joe capturing one that weighed almost ten pounds—"his biggest ever." Some small brook trout were caught on flies in the little streams flowing into the main river.

In commenting on this experience—the first canoeing and fishing trip that he had ever taken—Daniels summed up his pleasures in the following order: the good fellowship ("that is the best of it all"); the relaxation, refreshment, and recreation which come from getting away from one's work and routine; the close contact with and enjoyment of nature; the muscular play, rhythm, and exhilaration of paddling a canoe, roughing it in general; and finally the fishing ("no doubt an angler would rank this higher, but I don't"). Perhaps the trio were happiest when after supper they sat down with their pipes in front of the log fire, even after it had died down to little but ashes, talking on the infinite variety of topics which suggest themselves to men freed from their conventional environment. For Eastman, so much of whose time during the remainder of the year was spent indoors, these trips were life-savers, and he always returned in high spirits. In his khaki shirt and his trousers tucked into his woodsman's boots, he seemed to be completely at home in the wilds. The chief excuse for dwelling at such length on these outdoor excursions is because of the influence which they had on his development. He was a more reasonable human being as a result of his sojourns with nature.

To his friends, at least, he seemed a completely "reasonable" man. Although frequently branded as "socialistic"—almost as damning an adjective in the 1920's as "communistic" has become in the 1950's—Eastman was really a philosophic liberal, such as Thomas Jefferson and Woodrow Wilson, in the sense that his mind was free and open to new ideas. Only by contrast with political and social reactionaries did he seem radical. In the Coolidge Era he was disturbed, even shocked, by the illiberalism of the Republican party, and against that background he stood out as a more advanced thinker than he actually was. Later, in the 1930's, he was just as strongly opposed to some of the aberrations of the New Deal, and was therefore in some quarters thought to have become conservative. He was never an agitator, as was William Lloyd Garrison, ready to accept any so-called "reform" merely because it was novel. Furthermore, he had a full appreciation of the value of tradition. Consequently, falling between two extremes, he remained a "Mugwump," or Independent, preferring to pursue a policy of enlightened opportunism, supporting the candidate or the party best suited in his opinion for the needs of the moment. It was the mood of the country that shifted—not he! This is not to say that he was static. Rather, he kept his poise as the trends around him veered or increased in intensity. He seldom went "all out" without reservations for any faction or leader.

Whatever "radical" inclinations Eastman may have had were undoubtedly stimulated and sustained by Frank Livingstone, an avowed iconoclast and rebel. Joe had numerous conservative friends, like Ernest Whitcomb, who cautioned him against rash decisions; but Livingstone, although ostensibly a personal secretary, was also a trusted companion with whom Eastman discussed matters as some husbands do with their wives. Even in the commissioner's office Livingstone was under no restraint, and occasionally a sensitive visitor would complain that he was too assertive in his *obiter dicta* on government affairs, as he grumbled about bankers and capitalists and "stand-patters." When the routine hours were over, however, then Livingstone became indeed the "devil's advocate," tossing off unconventional theories without having the responsibility of putting them into practice. Eastman called Livingstone his "hair shirt," and missed him and his provocative conversation after he died. No doubt his influence was salutary, and to some extent corrective. But Eastman, although he listened attentively to others, was under nobody's domination and formed his own opinions. He judged ideas on their merits, after carefully weighing the available evidence. Strong in his mind as a determining factor were the interests of all the American people, whose servant he was.

The fairest estimate of any man should be based on his own considered words, and much may be learned from Eastman's comments on his contemporaries. His comments on Calvin Coolidge, for example, reveal much about himself. Writing to his friend Charles E. Elmquist, under date of October 28, 1924, Eastman said:

I have your letter of October 24, and cannot forbear certain further comments with respect to the President. I do not think that I look at him through glasses colored by my knowledge of his history in Massachusetts. It is true that in his political career in that state he was never distinguished by his advocacy of progressive measures. He may have voted for some, but he certainly was never an active aggressive figure in their behalf. However, notwithstanding his history, I was quite prepared to give him the benefit of the doubt and ready to applaud him if he did well in the presidential office. I am sorry to say that his record since he became President has not commended itself to me. You say that "his economy program has been forcefully and consistently maintained and it is one which appeals to the rank and file." Economy, to my mind, is one of the least of the virtues, and as a matter of fact, I believe that his program of economy, as it has been applied, is injuring the public service. You say also "that no President has ever exercised greater courage than he did in vetoing the bonus bill." I am also unable to agree with that statement. A man in political life shows courage when he runs counter to the views of his friends and supporters. It would have required courage for Coolidge to sign the bonus bill. He was sure of warm approval from the men who have always been his supporters and backers when he vetoed it. In fact, his record as President strongly emphasizes the point which I made in my last letter to you, namely, that he has never taken a position which has been offensive to men of wealth. I have seen no indication of any strong, intellectual grasp of public questions. I have seen many occasions since he became President when he exhibited, to my mind, a lack of courage and decisiveness. However, I shall not undertake to argue the matter further, for I do not expect to change your vote. I think that he will be elected, and I hope that he will make a good President for the coming term. I shall applaud him if he does.

Still with President Coolidge on his mind, Eastman wrote on November 9, 1925, to James J. Storrow, in part as follows:

President Coolidge appears to be a firm believer in the virtues of private enterprise motivated by a desire for personal pecuniary gain, and Government is to him a necessary evil to be deprecated and minimized as much as possible. He lives up to his lights. My own point of view is quite different. I am not a Communist nor even a Socialist, and I have no desire to eliminate private enterprise or personal gain, but I do very firmly believe that such gain is not the only impelling force in human beings which can produce desirable results. Indeed, I would go so far as to say that the most important services to mankind have been the products of higher motives. But however that may be, I am persuaded that there are many most important things that a Government can do which private enterprise cannot do one-half so well. Naturally I should like to see some one at the head of the Government with such a point of view and with a passion for finding out the things that the Government ought to do and an equal passion for seeing to it that it does them well.

Still another letter, written on November 10, 1928, to Elmquist, after the results of the presidential election of that year had been announced, indicates his growing dissatisfaction with existing conditions.

I am glad that you were so much pleased with the results of the election. It did not please me so well, as you can no doubt imagine, although I had very little expectation that Smith would be elected. I hope very much that you are correct in believing that Hoover will make a fine President. If he does, it will be a great relief after the administrations of the past eight years, which have been profoundly depressing for many cogent reasons. Before the campaign began, I would have shared at least some of your anticipations as to the quality of our next President, but I feel considerably less confident now. Hoover fell in my estimation throughout the campaign, and Al Smith continually rose. This is contrary to the impressions which you received, but it simply goes to show that great minds differ.

In this instance I am not in so much of a minority as I often find to be the case. Although he will have very few votes in the electoral college, Smith was really given a very handsome popular vote. I believe that it was larger than that received by Coolidge in 1924. When you consider the extraordinary handicaps under which Smith labored, including the opposition of the drys, the bigots, and the snobs, and also those who feared his Tammany associations or were unable to penetrate below the surface of his East Side twang, the vote which he received was quite remarkable. I wish he could have had an opportunity to demonstrate his worth to the country in the presidential office, but that is not to be. It would, I believe, have been like a breath of clean, fresh air in a room which has been closed for eight years.

If Eastman could have seen a clearer alignment of political parties along natural lines of cleavage between voters of conservative and progressive tendencies, he would doubtless have joined the latter group, if only to demonstrate that he was opposed to special privileges and eager for a more equitable distribution of opportunities and blessings. As events turned out, he was dissatisfied with Franklin D. Roosevelt, although not for the same reasons or to the same extent as he had been with Calvin Coolidge. The Presidents in his lifetime that he rated the highest were Theodore Roosevelt and Woodrow Wilson.

From Eastman's immense correspondence several passages have been cited illustrating his personal philosophy and beliefs. Especially significant is a letter written on February 8, 1941, to President Martin W. Clement, of the Pennsylvania Railroad—whom he addressed as "Dear Clem"—thanking him for a copy of an address which the latter had recently delivered in Pittsburgh. At one point Eastman remarked:

Your discussion of the three groups of Government, Business, and Labor is very good indeed. I have had an opportunity for rather close observation of many people in all three of these groups, with the net result that I feel that they are inherently very much alike. The percentage of intelligence, sincerity, honesty, and other qualities is, I think, about the same. Certainly I would be unable to set one group above another in these respects.

In the last part of your address in the discussion of regulation, you were not any too complimentary to the personnel of the regulatory bodies, but I would not quarrel with you especially in regard to that. Possibly my characterizations of railroad managements in general would not be any more complimentary.

Upon the subject of the encroachment of regulation upon management, I think that our differences of opinion are not fundamental, although you may not agree as to that. Any disagreement that you may think exists arises, I believe, out of some misunderstanding of my point of view in regard to this matter.

This quoted passage illustrates well Eastman's direct way of replying to those with whom he was not fully in accord. It was difficult indeed to start a quarrel with a man who could be so disarmingly frank on controversial issues. This happy combination of candor and tact accounts, of course, for the popularity which Eastman enjoyed even among those who thought him mistaken and was shown so widely at the time of his death. Chester G. Moore, speaking at the Cleveland meeting dedicated to Eastman and his achievement, said:

It seemed to me significant, when those who are regulated sometimes against their will and often, perhaps, to their disadvantage, gather to express their appreciation of the honesty, ability, and personality of the man who has done the regulating. A career which has won such endorsement has literally emerged unmarred from an acid bath. Our associated industries, those who ship and those who carry, are noted for their vigor and drive,—yes, even for excessive vitality and at times some little turbulence. Sometimes, indeed, we are regulated with considerable difficulty. But he has done the job, and done it so well and fairly, that we are here to-day to pay him tribute.

When it was necessary, however, Eastman could administer a well-deserved rebuke. A letter sent on August 12, 1933, to Pierre S. Dupont on the advisability of limiting the salaries of railroad executives is a fine example of how effectively a man of high standards can dismiss an argument based on materialism.

You say elsewhere in your letter that in the "affairs of railroads the proper reward of the executive must be measured by salary alone." With all due respect, this impresses me as being a most narrow, not to say ignoble, view of the matter. The best reward that any man can have is the joy of creative work well done, and my observation is that it is a far more potent incentive in human affairs than is commonly supposed. Another reward which ranks lower in the scale but nevertheless has much force is that which comes from the possession of power and rank. As Napoleon well knew, titles, insignia, and even mere ribbons have a powerful appeal. All these rewards rank higher than money. A man whose desire is concentrated on money reward alone is a dangerous man. The world has suffered more from such men than it has ever benefited.

The respect which official Washington paid to Eastman as Director of Defense Transportation is a fine example of what character in a public figure can accomplish. His sturdy and impregnable independence, his forthright thinking, his indifference to pressure groups, his avoidance of political intrigues, his dislike of publicity —all these gave him a standing which inspired confidence. To the average American he was, perhaps, less well known than the White House satellites, but he did far more than most of them to prepare for war and carry it through to victory. His personal qualities would have brought him distinction on any governmental level, including the highest. Probably he could never have been chosen to an elective office, but he would have adorned any cabinet position, and he would have made, as Chief Justice Stone once said, a first-rate judge. He was a good routine official, but he was at his best in a crisis, when his moral strength made him a reliable leader.

Out of all his many addresses the one which best summarizes his mature philosophy was delivered to the Senior Class of Amherst College at Commencement in 1934. Speaking of the past, but aiming toward the future, he said:

For twenty years I have been in the public service. Personally I would rather be there than anywhere else, but that is probably an eccentricity. The point I want to make is that from now on the public service will be more pervasive and far-reaching than ever before. That is inevitable. It behooves every good citizen, therefore, to keep an eye on that service and do what he can to improve it.

In the past it has been the habit in this country, at least among the business and professional classes, to regard public service askance or even with contempt. It has not had the place in public esteem which it has had, for instance, in England. It has been looked upon as a necessary evil, and the habitat of rather low-minded politicians and like gentry. This always was a superficial point of view, but for the future it clearly will not do. The Government will have far too important and intimate a relation to the lives of all the people to permit of any such attitude towards the forces which administer the Government. The college-trained citizens can play a very important part in changing that attitude, or at least they should be able to if education amounts to anything. They are no longer a negligible factor in the community, in view of the many thousands who every year receive diplomas at Commencement exercises like these all over the country.

I have seen enough of public service in Washington and in the Commonwealth of Massachusetts so that I am not at all discouraged as to its possibilities. There is much to criticise, of course, but I believe there has been quite as much and more to criticise in our businesses and professions, and much more work of fine quality has been done in the public service than most people suppose. I do hope that you boys who are commencing your life in the world of affairs will realize the vital importance of every form of government, from the little local town governments up to the national administration, to say nothing of organizations for dealing with international efficiency and the general esteem in which they are held. I urge this, not as a mere matter of broad and vague public spirit, but as a matter of very immediate self-interest. You can help yourselves by helping the government.

And before I close let me suggest one further thought. It is a common thing for men of character and education to get steamed up on the subject of good government. They work feverishly for a time, and then become discouraged and quit because they feel that they are accomplishing nothing. The fact is that no one can be at all sure that he is accomplishing nothing by such efforts, because it is quite impossible to say what the situation might have been if the efforts had not been made. Personally I have no doubt whatever that our governmental affairs would now be in much worse shape if it had not been for the activities of reformers, even though they may in their day have seemed to be mere voices crying in the wilderness. More important, however, is the fact that such efforts bring their own reward, for it is far more satisfying to have made a gallant attempt than never to have tried at all.

I wish you all a good hard fight in a fascinating period of the world's history, and your fair share of triumphs.

If, as Eastman thought, we are destined in these United States to have more and more government by bureaucracy—and this seems inevitable in the present organization of our complicated affairs—it is of vital importance to each individual citizen that the permanent commissions be administered by men of strict probity, political neutrality, wide experience, and unceasing interest in the public welfare. Government in any form, whether despotic, oligarchic, or democratic, derives its strength from personalities. History has shown that even an autocracy like that of the Antonines may be benevolent under a wise emperor. So in a country where representative government prevails, it cannot long be maintained unless the elected legislators command the respect not only of their own constituencies but also of the entire nation. It is also evident that republics set up like ours are peculiar in that such bodies as the Supreme Court, the Interstate Commerce Commission, and the permanent staffs in the various government departments possess a stability and continuity not enjoyed by the Executive and Legislative branches. Because of this permanence, they can exercise a decisive influence on our economic and social policies. If, then, we are to build wisely and well, the men and women in charge of these departments must have honesty, vision, and fixity of purpose. In his own field of transportation Eastman set a fine example for every bureau in Washington.

Eastman's specific accomplishments, concerned though they were with what he himself called a "declining industry," were certainly far from negligible. He formulated principles and established procedures which will long be associated with his name. But his attitude of mind, his conception of human values, will outlast his decisions and dissenting opinions. What was enduring about him was the spirit in which he approached his duties and his problems. A government in which all bureaus were administered by men with his intelligence, motives, and ideals might make mistakes, but it could scarcely avoid being trusted. As a transportation expert, Eastman had a knowledge and experience upon which the Chief Executive and the people could rely. But his influence was broader than his immediate environment. Indeed, it was said that a hundred "bureaucrats" of his type could make our government a model government if the politicians would only leave them alone.

Eastman's conception of public service is admirable and desirable in a democracy at any period. But it is especially needed in a period when government bureaus, major and minor, have multiplied beyond anything dreamed of by the Founding Fathers. Thus, like other able men throughout the ages, Eastman was more important for what he was than for what he did. But being what he was, he could have done no other than he did.

Index

p140